THE LEVANT EXPRESS

MICHELINE R. ISHAY

The Levant
Express

THE ARAB UPRISINGS, HUMAN RIGHTS,

AND THE FUTURE OF THE MIDDLE EAST

Yale UNIVERSITY PRESS   NEW HAVEN AND LONDON

Published with assistance from the Mary Cady Tew Memorial Fund.

Yale University Press books may be purchased in quantity for educational, business, or promotional use. For information, please e-mail sales.press@yale.edu (U.S. office) or sales@yaleup.co.uk (U.K. office).

Set in Scala type by IDS Infotech, Ltd., Chandigarh, India.
Printed in the United States of America.

Library of Congress Control Number: 2019931362

ISBN 978-0-300-21569-4 (hardcover : alk. paper)

A catalogue record for this book is available from the British Library.

This paper meets the requirements of ANSI/NISO Z39.48-1992 (Permanence of Paper).

10 9 8 7 6 5 4 3 2 1

To my father, the late Edmond Ishay, my mother, Rachel Bazini, and the many other wanderers, expelled, and refugees.

For Stephen Bronner, who lit a path, and my students, who carry the torch.

For Adam and Elise, who remain my steadfast compass on earth.

CONTENTS

Farewell to Abu Dhabi

Mixed emotions, deep fatigue.
In eerie harmony with the fogged sky
The plane just lifted off from Abu Dhabi.

The desert disappears into dust,
From the dust a soft line reappears,
Blurring earth and heaven.

I leave vast sands dotted with modern skyscrapers,
Architectural bravado built in rushed disharmony,
Refugees from the merciless sun.

I leave the winds of the Arab Gulf,
Molding majestic dunes
And whistling between the walls of fashionable malls.

I leave Arab Springs and Arab Winters
In convulsion and remission.
And I dream about fall and peach cherry colored leaves.

I leave a country torn between wisdom and wealth,
Between a legendary past and insatiable envy
Uncertain of its yesterdays and its tomorrows.

I leave many who are finding their way, and others blinded by the sun.
Like a Bedouin shepherd, a wandering Jew, an invisible woman,
Unveiling what has been too long hidden, eclipsed, and stifled.

I am back to Ithaca, with cyclops, princesses, maids,
Court jesters, prophets-in-the-making, messengers of turbulence,
Companions in my travels through tempestuous seasons.

I will bring you along to my new refuge,
An ambassador for dreams yet to bloom.

Micheline Ishay
July 2, 2013

Introduction

I SPENT THREE YEARS in the United Arab Emirates, from June 2010 to July 2013, as a visiting professor at Khalifa University. During that time, I traveled through much of the Middle East and North Africa (MENA) region. I had studied the history of revolutions and human rights, and for a scholar in my discipline, having the chance to witness unfolding events in the Arab world was a remarkable opportunity. This book is the result of the long journey that began when I first arrived in Abu Dhabi with my family during a hot month of Ramadan. Traveling to the United Arab Emirates (UAE) felt like an improbable dream. I had a sense that I was breaking historical barriers, both as a woman and as a Jew, hoping to reconcile hostile worlds. My academic hosts knew my background and made special arrangements to make me feel welcome. I was both eager and apprehensive to learn more from this part of the world and to understand how people had built a new mecca of capitalism in the desert. As I climbed into a waiting black limousine at the airport, my glasses were so foggy due to the late night's mugginess that I had no choice but to blindly follow my escort to my new life.

My partner and I were invited as senior faculty members to help develop a new academic institution, Khalifa University, which had recently been built under the patronage of the royal family, al-Nahayan. Khalifa was the first Emirati university to accommodate both women and men in the same classroom. I was thrilled to be part of an effort to help change the gender dynamics of a Gulf country, and part of a political dialogue that could have lasting social effects in the region. I initially expected to stay in the UAE for two years, but the uprisings that shook the Arab world in December 2010 and throughout 2011 persuaded me to stay longer. During my time at Khalifa University, I helped develop the curriculum for the humanities and social sciences, organized and hosted a distinguished speakers' series, and taught a course called Introduction to the History of Human Rights, all before I became aware of the revolutionary contagion on the horizon.

While I was working on the social science curriculum at Khalifa University, I invited the participation of two Arab scholars who had been teaching Islamic studies and Arab culture. Already accustomed to warm Arab hospitality, it was difficult for me to hide my surprise when these two religiously conservative gentlemen greeted me coldly and avoided my gaze, as if I were carrying the plague. They were Islamists, and the older of the two, perceiving my discomfort, told me it would be inappropriate for him to sit near me or even to shake a woman's hand. He picked a chair far away from me, "out of respect," he said. His younger colleague, bearded and thin, wondered aloud why I had been put in charge of a senior administrative task when I had just arrived. More to the point, they were not used to women in an authoritative role.

My sense of displacement was further heightened one day when my then-seven-year-old daughter came home upset from the French Lycée Matignon of Abu Dhabi. Each of the children had been asked to draw five national flags of their choice. One of the flags she chose was that of Israel. The teacher admonished her for not drawing correctly (though her work was perfectly accurate, I found out later) and cut the Israeli flag from my daughter's notebook with a pair of scissors. Was the teacher trying to protect her or punishing her for recognizing Israel as a state? This question remained unanswered, but the incident made me keenly aware of our tenuous place in the Gulf. My son was in a safer environment at the American Community School of Abu Dhabi. His school was a foreign microcosm, where children of expatriate diplomats, architects, financiers, petroleum engineers, and war moguls mixed happily. Abu Dhabi seemed a quiet place, but during the Arab uprisings it was the eye of the storm. Wealthy people fled the turmoil to find safety there or launder their money; international political figures came to strategize or conspire;

soldiers of fortune came seeking adventure and profit. Abu Dhabi then was a bit like Casablanca during World War II.

For the three years I remained in Abu Dhabi, I did my best not to draw attention to my background, not wanting to invite trouble for myself or my family. I am a French speaker who was raised in Luxembourg and Brussels, and no one had a problem with that. But Arabic translations of the *Protocols of the Elders of Zion*, a nineteenth-century Russian pamphlet that falsely accused Jews of organizing in secret societies to take over the world, could be found in the windows of many bookstores in the UAE. There was no shortage of tales about Israeli and American conspiracies, blaming Israel or the United States for the September 11 attacks and many other international evils, and even many educated Emiratis subscribed to these preposterous theories. But the UAE is a bundle of contradictions; I also found one of my own books, *The Human Rights Reader*, in a bookstore at the Dubai Mall.

My undergraduate course on human rights, approved by Khalifa University's new American president, was the first such course in the Gulf countries, and perhaps even the first human rights course offered in the Arab Middle East. When it was first authorized by the university administration, we had no way of knowing that calls for human rights were about to transform the region. On December 17, 2010, shortly before the class began, a street vendor named Mohamed Bouazizi set himself on fire in Sidi Bouzid, Tunisia. Popular rebellions would soon challenge one regime after another across the Middle East.

By January 2011, when my course began, the UAE was abuzz with news of the uprisings. Television screens, tuned to Al Jazeera around the clock, showed mass demonstrations in Tunisia and then Egypt. I adjusted my course syllabus, creating more space for class discussion of those events. The rulers of the Gulf countries were on high alert; the UAE would soon join Saudi Arabia in crushing mass protests at the Pearl Roundabout in Bahrain. The atmosphere was tense, and class discussions were electric. I taught the students how to research and analyze the causes of unfolding events, focusing on socioeconomic and political factors as they gathered information from newspapers, television, and websites. The world was changing in front of us.

Yet despite the bursting energy of my classroom, my course was downsized, the result of a campaign by my Islamist colleagues. Their complaints caused concern at the top academic level and even among some members of the political echelon. Gradually, in the UAE and else-where in the region, freedom of speech in the classroom would be further limited in response to the unfolding events of the Arab Spring, as freedom of opinion could also imply rebellion. The university leadership had asked me never to criticize the Emirati government, and I always complied. To enforce this request, I understood later, my classes were taped and class-room conversations monitored by an Emirati student who audited the course. But, I felt I had nothing to hide, and I made sure that my lectures remained evenhanded and academically rigorous. My students often asked my views about their country, but I stuck to my promise and did not permit the politics of the UAE to be discussed. Yet I did address women's issues, revolutions, separation between state and religion, polygamy, gay rights, genocide, the Holocaust, self-determination, dictatorship, and democracy, because I saw these subjects as crucial for my students' understanding of their changing culture. These themes produced varying degrees of discomfort among some Emirati administrators; when one student complained about a reading on gay rights, I was asked to take that subject off the syllabus. The volatility of the time was very much felt at the university.

Once the Arab uprising was under way, my expertise in political philosophy was solicited at the royal palace for an ongoing series of conversations. These afforded me a remarkable vantage point from which to view the changes sweeping the Middle East and North Africa—with a select group of the Emirati political elite. In those powerful circles, the events of Tahrir Square and rights-based demands had spurred strong interest in the meaning of human rights. I was able to draw on concepts I had developed in my History of Human Rights course to explain the causes and pitfalls of revolutionary contagions. My host was curious and highly intelligent and always displayed an open mind. The guests he gath-ered came from the worlds of journalism, finance, education, and engi-neering. They were energetic and serious but could also fall into spirited bantering. My distinguished host often reminded them that the times were grim and that our attention to deeper questions was necessary to understand what was taking place in the Gulf and beyond.

After three years in the eye of the hurricane, I returned home. Once back in Denver, I resolved to carry on the tradition of progressive

Orient Express Railway Poster, 1891.
By Rafael Ochoa y Madrazo
(1858–1935).

realists—a category that includes people as diverse as Franklin Roosevelt
and Antonio Gramsci—who have tried to untie the Gordian knots that
prevent a regional peace predicated on economic development and the
advance of human rights. In this book, I consider how the pendulum,
which has moved since 2013 from Enlightenment to counter-Enlightenment, can swing back toward a sustainable Enlightenment pole. These
days, few academic analyses anticipate progress in the Middle East. I
explore grounds for optimism, focusing on the current reality and its
subterranean contradictions while drawing from past historical lessons to
help guide future social transformations. No one can offer a blueprint for
the future, but I sketch alternatives that are today obscured by sectarian
conflict, religious extremism, and authoritarian repression. I invite others
to enter into this conversation by adding, altering, or proposing different
paths. In short, this book is an effort toward restoring a human rights
engine for a better future in the Middle East—what I am calling the
"Levant Express."

Like a train hurtling across the Levant, the Arab uprisings raced
across the Middle East, signaling the long-awaited arrival of the

Enlightenment in a region long ruled by monarchs, theocrats, and dictators. While that Levant Express was derailed, its challenge to counter-Enlightenment ideologies and sectarian wars signaled a historical shift. In this book, I assess the Arab Spring in the context of past struggles to advance the Enlightenment against powerful countervailing forces. Drawing lessons from the reconstruction of post–World War II Europe, I argue for a Rooseveltian approach in which pragmatic Middle East policies—linking human rights, equitable economic development, and security—can be drawn from FDR's Enlightenment vision based on the four freedoms he identified as the rights of all people.

I have divided my argument into three parts. Part I focuses on the advance of human rights, or the initial surge of apparent progress toward a new Enlightenment. Most revolutionary contagions initially fail, as the conditions that lead to uprisings persist after the toppling of authoritarian regimes. I argue that five factors, external and domestic, explain the conditions that lead to revolution, consolidation, and democratization. Further, lessons drawn from past contagious revolutions illuminate the factors that impeded, then helped trigger the Arab uprisings, and finally explain why the Arab Spring turned out differently in various countries. These lessons also suggest particular paths forward within different subregions within the Middle East. In a sense, the standard for current policy approaches is the extent to which they establish preconditions corresponding to the 1989 "velvet revolutions," which—unlike other revolutionary contagions—enabled Eastern Europe to experience economic development, regional integration, and peaceful democratic transitions.

In Part II, I maintain that the same conditions leading to revolutionary contagions can create fertile ground for counter-Enlightenment ideologies. Here I argue that in today's Middle East, as in the European interwar period, economic distress, power vacuums, fragmentation of civil society, and the lack of a coherent progressive ideology create the space for Bonapartism (that is, the rise of charismatic and strong leaders), who in these fractured contexts champion ultranationalism or a belligerent religious radicalism.

In Part III, I strive to address these problems, arguing that Roosevelt's four inalienable and indivisible freedoms—freedom of speech, freedom of worship, freedom from want, and freedom from fear—which were applied to post–World War II reconstruction efforts, provide guidance for progress toward a new Enlightenment. While these four freedoms are critical, they are not complete. Therefore, I introduce a fifth freedom, freedom from sexual discrimination, widely invoked during and after the Arab uprising. Far from utopian, these principles are grounded in ongoing efforts, common interests, and historical lessons.

In today's Middle East, where freedom of speech is often seen as a threat to governments, the spread of existing public and virtual spaces for open discussion will strengthen civil society and human rights. Religious tolerance (or freedom of worship), scientific discovery, and critical thinking, important elements of Islamic civilization, were once fostered by a network of commerce that made Islam's Golden Age possible. Likewise, burgeoning investment based on freedom from want, as with Roosevelt's New Deal and the integrated economic development that followed World War II, can help reignite a new Arab Enlightenment. Because freedom from fear is essential to protecting all other freedoms, different subregional security architectures—shaped by current geopolitical and economic realities— should be devised or deepened to move the Middle East to a more stable future. Further, women's demands for freedom during the Arab uprising continue to demonstrate that human rights are sustainable only if they thrive in both the home and the public space. The Palestinian question remains a lightning rod for the region. A similar application of Roosevelt's freedoms, I contend, could guide the development of a confederate alternative to this seemingly intractable problem. Finally, I conclude that there is a strong affinity between the crisis of the Middle East, the need to resolve it, and the contemporary revival of populism and fascism.

Overall, the dominant metaphor in the book is an imagined railroad, the Levant Express, which provides a convenient, easily graspable, and historically resonant (if perhaps nostalgic) way of talking about the MENA region's progress toward an equitable human rights regime. It is also appropriate that railroads and the Enlightenment are of the same vintage, both being products of eighteenth-century intellectual developments and nineteenth-century modernization. I ultimately argue that the relation of human rights and railroad infrastructure, as a particular technology of commerce, communication, and travel is not only metaphorical. A concrete plan for a regional railway system, which I describe in this book among other proposals, could spur economic progress and contribute significantly to regional peace.

PART ONE DEPARTURE: HUMAN RIGHTS UPRISINGS

"HEGEL REMARKS SOMEWHERE that all great world-historic facts and personages appear . . . twice," Karl Marx said, "the first time as tragedy, the second time as farce."[1] In recent years, it was sometimes hard to tell which version was being acted out in the Middle East. When millions of hopeful people marched in 2011 to topple their governments, they did not anticipate the tragedies that would ensue. To the Egyptians who supported a military coup to overthrow an illiberal government, hoping to halt the derailing of their revolution, the imposition of an even more authoritarian regime must have felt like a farce. Today the question many ask about the region is: Can we prevent the recurrence of tragedy?

The uprisings that swept across the Arab world in 2011 raced like a high-speed train, which I call "The Levant Express." These revolutions were, of course, not the first such events in modern history. Similar waves of revolution took place in 1848, 1947, 1968, 1970, and 1989. An inquiry into those revolutionary contagions reveals recurring patterns that can illuminate the prospects for advancing human rights in the Middle East. These circumstances include a synergy of destabilizing forces that spill across borders. Overall, the ingredients for revolutionary contagions are present when a hegemonic international order is vulnerable, a regional economic crisis is rampant, the local elite fails to undertake reform in the face of a disenchanted citizenry, civil society is mobilized, and human rights ideals are disseminated.

RAILROAD AND REVOLUTIONS

The poster "Railroad and Revolutions" depicts six revolutionary figures, waving to the crowd as they stand in small open wagons towed by an old locomotive. Marianne, symbolizing the revolutions of 1848, raises the French tricolor with her right hand and grips a bayonet with her left; Mahatma Gandhi, epitomizing the anticolonial struggle, which began in 1947, lifts a handful of salt (from his famous march to the sea) with his right hand and leans on a walking stick with his left; John Lennon, in hippie garb, exemplifying the 1968 youth rebellion, waves an album cover reading "Revolution" with his right hand and carries a bouquet of flowers in his left; an Argentine woman from the Playa de Mayo, representing 1970s defiance against

For the most part, however, revolutionary contagions are generally unsuccessful, at least in the short term. And even if revolutionaries succeed in consolidating a new regime, the transition to democracy and a flourishing human rights regime takes a long time. Asked in 1968 whether the French Revolution had been a success, Chinese premier Zhou Enlai is reported to have said it was too early to tell. Suffice it to say that when international order vanishes, economic benefactors are absent, and civil society is fragmented, chaos tends to prevail, and new regimes may discover they lack the ability to consolidate the kinds of institutions needed for progress in human rights. Most contagious revolutions eventually derail. In that phase, the elixirs of nationalism, religious radicalism, and cooptation pervade the political discourse, leaving universal human rights ideals as an empty chimera, incompatible with reality and distant from popular needs.

Enlightenment will ultimately prevail. Even when the restoration of authoritarianism crushes all dissent, the spirit of human rights is not extinguished. Instead, it tends to rise again, more forcefully, under more propitious circumstances. The 1968 revolutions, for example, threatened to spread throughout the Eastern bloc but were crushed by Russian tanks rolling through the streets of Prague. In 1989, however, as grassroots activism dismantled the Communist bloc, the human rights spirit of Prague, East Berlin, and beyond was rekindled. Unfolding events in the Middle East and North Africa need to be understood within that broader context, which encompasses centuries of global struggles over human rights.

Latin dictators, waves a white scarf in her right hand and passes pictures of missing children in her left; Lech Walesa, the union leader identified with the 1989 Polish uprising against communist rule, brandishes with his right hand the *Solidarność* flag and clasps a plumber's wrench in his left; finally, a Tunisian woman, wearing blue jeans and a long-sleeve T-shirt, typifying Arab revolutionaries in 2011, raises a cell phone in her right hand and holds a travel mug in her left. Each protester looks back to the past, as one rebellion learns from earlier ones. The historical train, the Levant Express, now moves faster, forward in time on an aqueduct, through rubble and smoke, toward an uncertain destiny. Created by Brooke VanDevelder, 2017 (© 2017 Micheline Ishay).

CHAPTER ONE

Railroads and Revolutions

IN 2011, THE TUNIS GARE CENTRALE was torched as protests against the dictatorship of Mohamed Ben Ali swelled into the revolutionary contagion that would soon engulf North Africa and the Middle East. The station, built in 1872 during the age of the steam locomotive, was a classic symbol of technological progress and industrialization, when relentless friction between the engines of modernity and lagging poverty often yielded social unrest and sometimes revolutions. Railroads accelerated economic development in the industrializing world, enabling imperialist powers to extend their influence to the interiors of far-flung lands, as freight cars carried new products vast distances and extended the reach of new ways of thinking. For the peoples being colonized, however, this technological revolution often drove them off their land and into poverty. Popular discontent and social revolutions were the predictable result. The metaphor of the train conveys the power and speed of technological progress, the mounting disenchantment that accompanied it, and ultimately the advance toward human freedom.[1]

Regional and worldwide revolutionary shocks occur when a range of domestic and international forces—international instability, economic crises, domestic political impasses, social activism, and human rights ideals—are activated simultaneously. While most revolutions fail, bringing nothing more than hypernationalism or sectarianism, each setback informs the direction of future revolutionary endeavors. From 1848 to 1989, each revolutionary contagion had a slow simmering impact in the Arab world. But the rise and regression of the Arab Spring, which follows the patterns of other historical contagions, have more in common with the revolution of 1848 than with that of 1989.

In 1848, the Ottoman Empire was late to industrialize and internally corrupt and fragmented. The fragile Caliphate would not survive World War I, after which the imperial powers of Britain and France would dissect it into new spheres of influence. After World War II, as the British and French Empires were collapsing in turn, Arab calls for national independence led to the rise of Arab nationalist leaders like Gamal Abdel Nasser in Egypt and the Ba'athists in Iraq. These men had the virtue of being anticolonialist, but over the decades their authoritarian patriotism calcified into despotism. Popular aspirations were continually distracted by other concerns. In 1968, when Eastern and Western youth under both capitalist and communist regimes were rising against their leaders, their Arab contemporaries were preoccupied with the humiliating impact of their defeat by Israel in the 1967 Six-Day War. While social activism continued to spread elsewhere, especially against Latin American dictatorships in the 1970s, many Arab youth found themselves embroiled in yet another war with Israel, the October War of 1973, then divided by conflicts between the major Arab powers and Iran. The democratic uprisings of 1989 had a greater impact on the Middle East–North Africa (MENA) region, but not a hopeful one. In the West and among Arab dictators, the Soviet threat was replaced by new concerns: a belligerent and rising Islamist menace, a preoccupation with stable oil production as the region's only significant source of wealth, and a new security order that came at the expense of people's yearning for freedom. The suppression of these hopes would last until 2011.

The Arab Spring is thus the latest extension of a largely frustrated revolutionary tradition that goes back to 1848 Europe. If the Arab uprisings unfolded with the speed of an express train throughout the Levant, we can imagine each revolutionary contagion before 2011 as a train speeding through a large swath of territory: the Trans-Europe Express (1848), the Cape-Cairo Express (1947), the Prague Express (1968), the Panama Express (1970), and the Berlin Express (1989).

Gare Saint-Lazare, by Claude Monet, 1877. Courtesy of the National Gallery, London.

THE TRANS-EUROPE EXPRESS, 1848

The Gare Saint-Lazare was the main train station in the burgeoning city of Paris. Built in 1840, it was a bustling hub, its smoke-shrouded platforms and tracks painted repeatedly by Claude Monet in powerful evocations of urban industrialization. A poster from the time, showing priests blessing a new steam locomotive in Calais, symbolized the alliance between the church and the new industrial and financial elite. On the other end of the social spectrum, in *Les Misérables* Victor Hugo described the barricade symbolizing popular despair and resistance in the revolution of June 1848: "The spirit of revolution covered with its cloud this summit, where that voice of the people which resembles the voice of God was growling, and a strange majesty was disengaged from this titanic mass of stones. It was a dungheap, and it was Sinai. . . . It, this barricade, an accident, a disorder, a misunderstanding, an unknown thing, had, facing it, the constituent assembly, the sovereignty of the people, universal suffrage, the nation, the republic."[2]

By the 1840s, rivalries within the Concert of Europe—the order created by Austria, Prussia, the Russian Empire, and the United Kingdom following the defeat of Napoleon I in 1815—had contributed to the spread of human misery throughout Europe. The Concert attempted to maintain a balance that contained the ambitions of each great power while preserving autocratic rule. It was not intended to address the needs of a growing population. England would soon emerge as the major arbiter of that balance of power, as its expanding economy and dominant navy propelled a rising world empire. The Concert gradually fell victim to growing feuds among the members, which diminished their abilities to cope with their citizens' demands. Borders were not redrawn based on national identity but rather on deals struck between autocrats. As protests morphed into insurrections, the increasing weakness of the Concert enabled the Parisian revolution to spread from state to state.

The economic fluctuations that had roiled Europe for decades were particularly significant in France, where the widespread prosperity of the 1830s was followed by a major depression. Economic expansion, encouraged by industrialization and the railroads, was increasingly hobbled by social inequity, exploitation of industrial workers, and rising unemployment. In 1848 Paris, more than 50 percent of the working-age population could not find work. A crisis in food production driven by crop failures of potatoes and cereals made things worse, as did urban population growth. The population of Paris had almost doubled between 1801 and 1848, and as a bulging generation of youth faced unemployment and hopelessness, crime rates soared. The chasm between the swelling ranks of the marginalized and a small privileged elite grew wider. Karl Marx, then a young revolutionary about to write *The Communist Manifesto* with his colleague Friedrich Engels, later commented, "Initially, it was not the French bourgeoisie that ruled under Louis Philippe, but one faction of it: bankers, stock-exchange kings, railway kings, owners of coal and iron mines and forests, a part of the landed proprietors associated with them—the so-called financial aristocracy. It sat on the throne, it dictated laws in the Chambers, [and] it distributed public offices, from cabinet portfolios to tobacco bureau posts."3

The French state also faced a dire political crisis and popular mounting discontent. King Louis-Philippe, regarded initially as a benevolent, reform-minded monarch, was forced to abdicate. The Parisian revolution of 1848 took place in two main movements. First, in February, an alliance of the middle and working classes toppled the king. Following the overthrow of the Orléans monarchy, a Second Republic began ruling France, inaugurating previously repressed freedoms of speech and association, along with social welfare projects. Over the course of a few months, however, the Second Republic took a conservative turn, ousting socialists from the Constituent Assembly and closing the National Workshops. The second movement occurred in June, when tens of thousands of Parisian workers rose up against the government in an insurrection that became known as the June Days uprising. They were met with brutal repression by the troops of General de Cavaignac, whose cannons roared in the streets of Paris. As Friedrich Engels reported, "Cavaignac was appointed dictator by a frightened National Assembly. . . . The insurgents were either driven out or massacred and among the bloodstained ruins 'order' triumphed."[4]

This setback did not prevent social agitation from spreading as a contagion to Rome, Vienna, Prague, and urban centers in the German confederation of states and across Europe. The 1848 revolutions were, in that sense, a watershed. While the triggers were often similar, the rebellions followed diverse trajectories in different countries. In the most industrialized countries, such as France, social upheavals challenged monarchical absolutism and contributed to progressive human rights perspectives that would persist into the twentieth century. In autarkic and industrially backward societies, such as those in eastern Europe or in nationally fragmented countries like Italy or Germany, imperial dynasties were opposed primarily by liberal nationalists, who called for self-determination or national unity.[5] Regardless, 1848 was aptly characterized by the British historian Eric Hobsbawm as the first international revolution.[6]

Modern industry, its power accelerated by rail transport and the telegraph, increasing population density, and advances in printing and papermaking, contributed to unity among workers and the establishment of trade unions. "It was just this contact [between workers]," Marx observed, "that was needed to centralize the numerous local struggles, all of the same character, into one national struggle between classes. But every class struggle is a political struggle. And that union, to attain which the burghers of the Middle Ages, with their miserable highways, required centuries, the modern proletarians, thanks to railways, achieved in a few years."[7]

The spread of human rights discourse was unprecedented. While liberals retained their preoccupation with civil and political liberty, Chartists and socialists focused on the troubling possibility that economic inequity could make liberty a hollow concept—a belief that resonated powerfully with the burgeoning class of urban working men and women. In this sense, socialists became legitimate heirs of the Enlightenment, applying the universal promises of *"liberté, égalité, fraternité"* to the political reality of the nineteenth century. At that point, the socialist movement moved to the forefront of the struggle for civil, political, and economic rights, which included the rights to trade unions, child welfare, universal suffrage, a restricted workday, and education, as well as other social welfare rights.[8]

The great powers of the Concert of Europe succeeded in crushing the 1848 revolutions. In France, the short-lived Second Republic was soon superseded by the Second Empire under Napoleon III. As the first and only president of the Second Republic, Louis-Napoleon staged a coup in December 1851, dissolved the National Assembly, and ordered the military occupation of Paris, arresting thousands of protesters. A year later, he became Emperor Napoleon III, censoring the press and repressing other basic freedoms. In the Austrian Empire, the army progressively reasserted control over pockets of resistance in different urban centers. It recaptured Prague and established martial law in June 1848. The imperial army briefly lost control of Vienna in the October Revolution, then laid siege to the city, reclaimed it after four days, and executed the insurgents. Austria's Habsburg rule was reimposed in Milan and Venice in early 1849. In August 1849, with the help of Czar Nicholas I of Russia, Austria brought an end to the Hungarian Revolution. In the words of the British historian G. M. Trevelyan, 1848 was "the turning point of history at which history failed to turn. . . . The military despotisms of Central Europe were nearly but not quite transformed by a timely and natural action of domestic force. It was the appointed hour, but the despotisms just succeeded in surviving it, and modernised their methods without altering their essential characters. The misfortune of European civilisation in our own day sprang in no small degree from those far-off events."[9]

Throughout the nineteenth century, the idea of universal reason acclaimed during the French Revolution and later in the 1848 revolutions would be attacked by counter-Enlightenment forces elevating instead cultural traditions and nationalism. This occurred during the unification of Italy and Germany and under the banners of competing empires throughout the nineteenth century and into the world wars. The yearning for the Enlightenment spirit, rational discourse, and human rights, however, kept returning. Despite its international breadth, the revolutionary contagion of 1848 did not reach the vast Ottoman Empire. The Ottomans, entrapped in feudal structures that blinded them to the

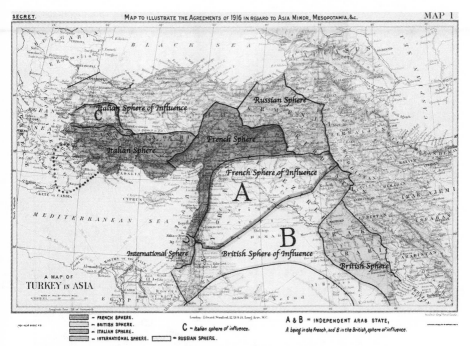

Apportionment of Territories as established by the Sykes-Picot Agreement, 1916.
Courtesy of Institute for Curriculum Services, San Francisco, CA.

productive explosion of industrialization, would not build their first
railway until 1860, decades after trains had been running in Western
Europe. The Ottomans' growing relative weakness left them vulnerable to
ethnic uprisings and, more immediately, to the rising power of expan-
sionist European powers. The threat of European conquest, the lack of
technological innovation and industrialization, and the fragmentation of
minority groups meant that the revolutionary human rights ideas
sweeping Europe would remain dormant in the Arab world.

The collapse of the Ottoman Empire after World War I left that region
largely in the hands of the British and French, who used the Sykes-Picot
Agreement of 1916 and the Versailles peace talks in 1919 to carve out new
states with arbitrary borders. That effort to transfer control of the region
from one empire to two others engendered local resistance against all
forms of imperial and arbitrary power. After World War II gravely weakened the colonial powers of Britain and France, the stage was set for active
anticolonial struggles in Asia, Africa, and the Middle East.

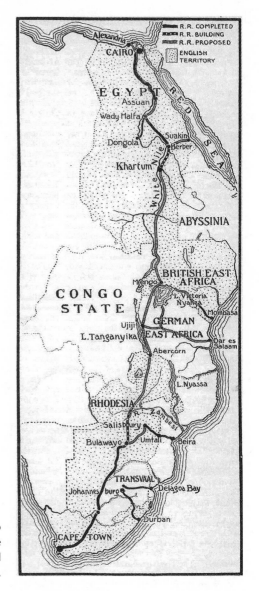

Route of the proposed Cape to Cairo
Railway, 1899. Courtesy of Sir George
Grey Special Collections, Auckland
Libraries, AWNS-18991110-8-4.

"THE CAPE-CAIRO EXPRESS," 1947

In the late nineteenth century, hoping to connect British-held Egypt to the
British-held southern states of the African continent, the business tycoon
and South African politician Cecil Rhodes built the Cape to Cairo Railway. A
cartoon from the late nineteenth century depicts Rhodes as a giant, his legs
straddling Africa like the Colossus of Rhodes. Just as in 1848 Europe, trains

The Rhodes Colossus, by Edward Linley
Sambourne, 1892.

in colonial India, Asia, and Africa symbolized accelerating modernization as
well as the growing inequities between possessors and dispossessed. The
means of transportation and communication associated with timekeeping,
punctuality, and predictability produced "counter-tempo" backlashes against
European standards of efficiency, which were seen as dehumanizing and
disruptive of traditional social rhythms.[10] Yet trains were also a means to
convey human rights messages from South Africa to Egypt.

Gandhi was a scathing critic of trains and of modernity in general,
which he believed placed technology above individuals. "Railways,
lawyers, and doctors have impoverished the country so much," he wrote,
"that if we do not wake up in time, we shall be ruined."[11] Later, he added,
"machinery helps a few to ride on the back of millions. The impetus
behind it all is not the philanthropy to save labor, but greed. It is against
this constitution of things that I am fighting with all my might. . . . [The]
supreme consideration is man."[12] Despite Gandhi's sentiments, the train
provided an important impetus to human rights. In 1893, as a young
Indian lawyer working in South Africa, he refused to comply with racial
segregation laws on a South African train and was forcibly ejected at the
Pietermaritzburg station. Years later, as the widely admired leader of the
Indian National Independence Movement, he would often describe that

incident as the moment that launched his lifetime of activism, a commitment that ultimately, in 1947, forced England to liberate its most prized
colony. Starting in 1924, Gandhi traveled mostly by train across the vast
Indian territory, reaching an ever-growing portion of the Indian masses
and ultimately drawing them into his call for national sovereignty.

Likewise, the charismatic Egyptian president Gamal Abdel Nasser
enjoyed traveling Egypt by train along the tracks built by Cecil Rhodes.
Old film footage shows him using that foundation of colonial expansion
to galvanize anticolonial nationalism throughout the Arab Middle East
and North Africa. Nasser, who led the coup that toppled the Egyptian
monarchy in 1952, traveled from town to town, condemning imperialism
and calling for a pan-Arab government animated by a socialist vision of
rights. He was hailed as a champion of self-determination, Arab unity,
anti-imperialism, social justice and modernity in the service of human
welfare.

Just as in 1848, the cascade of anticolonial struggles that began in
1947 resulted from a declining international hegemonic order. During
World War II, the dramatic weakening of European governmental control
in colonized territories created venues for human rights activities. This
was particularly true in Asia, where independence movements that had
been brewing for decades exploded as the war drew to a close. The
supplanting of European dominance by Japanese imperialism during
the 1930s accelerated nationalist aspirations throughout the region; the
early Japanese victories over European forces signaled to Indonesians,
Vietnamese, Burmese, and Middle Easterners that the Europeans were
not as invincible as they imagined. Africa, which was less industrialized
and more divided by ethnic tensions, experienced a similar awakening of
national awareness, but later.[13]

The devastating economic crisis that plagued post–World War II
Europe put an end to colonial endeavors that just decades before seemed
destined to last forever. During the war, some four million workers were
engaged in munitions production, but the war turned Britain from the
world's greatest creditor nation into the world's greatest debtor. By some
estimates, Britain expended a quarter of its wealth in the war, and by 1945
a substantial portion of its labor force was tied up in the occupation of
defeated Germany.[14] When the United States ended the Lend-Lease
program in 1945, Britain was forced to request an American loan. A

rejection, warned John Maynard Keynes, would have resulted in "a large-scale withdrawal on [Britain's] part from international responsibilities."[15]

That loss of global influence and prestige was not readily accepted by British leaders, but the decline would prove irreversible. As the colonial powers went bankrupt, the leaders who emerged from fledgling civil societies throughout the colonial world increasingly demanded independence. In the end, European governments had little choice but to grant it. While Europeans had long suppressed any form of rebellion, they were ultimately responsible for developing a civil society, however embryonic, in their African and Middle Eastern colonies.[16] Industry's search for cheap labor had created a working class in the colonies, just as the need for local management had created educational and economic opportunities for indigenous elites. The most privileged benefited from overseas Western education, from which they absorbed the principles of democracy and human rights. With the weakening of empires after the war, colonized people, under the leadership of that educated elite, toppled colonial rule in one country after another. From Ho Chi Minh in Vietnam to Léopold Senghor in Senegal to Nasser in Egypt, a cohort of leaders demanded the right of self-determination, challenging old imperial structures along the railroad lines built by European imperialists.

The new frontiers of the Middle East had been drawn on the ruins of the Ottoman Empire, but it took the collapse of British and French rule to give those young states a chance to become republics under their own sovereign rulers. For a short time, from 1958 to 1961, Syria (which had been independent since 1936) joined Egypt in the United Arab Republic. Tunisia and Morocco declared independence from France in 1956, and Britain removed its forces from Palestine in 1948, from Jordan in 1957, from Iraq in 1958, from Kuwait in 1961, from Yemen in 1962, and from Bahrain, Qatar, and the newly formed United Arab Emirates in 1971. As happened with most anticolonial struggles, however, the eventual outcome would largely disappoint supporters of democracy and human rights.

As the 1960s progressed, voices from these newly independent countries grew more prominent in the international arena. The composition of the United Nations began to change as the freshly minted nations became member states, contributing to the adoption in 1966 of two major international agreements on human rights: the International

Covenant on Civil and Political Rights and the International Covenant on Economic, Social and Cultural Rights. Each recognized the right to self-determination in its first article. The struggle for self-determination had achieved international legal legitimation, but it had done so at the expense of other dimensions of rights.

It is fair to say that the spirit of the Enlightenment had been abused in the colonized world. Ho Chi Minh reminded Western audiences of these abuses in the Declaration of Independence of the Democratic Republic of Vietnam, which emphasized that "Life, Liberty and the pursuit of Happiness," as written in the US Declaration of Independence, and the idea that "all men are free and have equal rights," as stated in the French Declaration of the Rights of Man and Citizen, had been violated by imperialists who acted "contrary to the ideals of humanity and justice."[17]

Despite Ho Chi Minh's rhetorical appeals to individual liberty, the rulers who consolidated power in the postcolonial world soon became dictators or monarchs, and the newly independent states quickly aligned with the geopolitical and economic interests of the two rising super-powers, the United States and the Soviet Union. Development slowed and even regressed in many former colonies. The language of rights and sovereignty was superseded by a counter-Enlightenment wave of illiber-alism, authoritarianism, nationalism, and exclusionary policies. The president of Uganda, Idi Amin Dada, blending authoritarianism with anti-Semitism, embraced the darkest of these doctrines, claiming that the death of Jews in the gas chamber was justified.[18] In far too many places, the Enlightenment vision seemed to be fading.

Like Europe's revolutionary train in 1848, the once promising Cape to Cairo Railway was delayed over and over by mismanagement and regional crises. The train was sidelined, awaiting the promise of economic and moral progress. In *Blood River*, his 2008 account of retracing H. M. Stanley's famous 1874 expedition to map the Congo River, Tim Butcher describes finding a train, still on its tracks, completely overgrown by jungle. "It was," he writes, "a complete reversal of the normal pattern of human development. A place where a railway track had once carried trainloads of goods and people had been reclaimed by virgin forest, where the noisy huffing of steam engines had long since lost out to the jungle's looming silence. It was one of the defining moments of my journey through the Congo."[19] As young postcolonial economies ground to a halt, any chance for a robust civil society was choked out by the repressive autocrats who replaced the foreign colonizers. The foundations of resistance would lie dormant for decades to come.

Meanwhile, as bids for independence overwhelmed and exhausted the British and French colonizers, rising independence movements also had to contend with the United States and the Soviet Union. While these two superpowers characterized their enmity in terms of competing visions of human rights, they both, at least within the former colonial world, proved ready to back brutal dictators willing to support their side in the Cold War. As the postcolonial world emerged, the post–World War II generation in the United States, Western Europe, and behind the Iron Curtain began to pose human rights challenges directed at one or the other superpower, culminating in a wave of social unrest that spread throughout the West in 1968.

THE PRAGUE EXPRESS, 1968

In 1968, the United States and Russia both faced problems that spilled over from their geopolitical competition. Revulsion against the nuclear arms race was a worldwide phenomenon. Many young Westerners saw the brutal Vietnam War as the result of capitalist "neo-imperialism." Both the USSR and the United States had pursued the worldwide competition for allies, resources, and the dissemination of their rival ideologies at the expense of addressing domestic problems. Prior to the Prague Spring, the Russians had been distracted by their split with China, marked by the Chinese Cultural Revolution, the Red Guards' attack on the Soviet Embassy in Beijing, and territorial disputes over Mongolia, Tibet, and especially Xinjiang.[20] In the Middle East, Russian influence quickly crumbled after Israel's victory in the 1967 Six-Day War, which revealed the uselessness of Soviet military aid to the Arab states. Meanwhile, America was sinking into an intractable stalemate in Vietnam while waging proxy wars in Africa and Asia to counter Soviet-backed factions. Elite preoccupation with these global struggles contributed to mounting domestic challenges for both countries.[21]

By the mid-1960s, communist regimes faced mounting economic problems. The Soviet government could sustain employment and welfare programs only with heavy domestic subsidies, yet it was also striving to keep afloat the feeble economies of its satellite countries. After Josef

Stalin's death in 1953, Nikita Khrushchev's "thaw" inaugurated nearly a decade of relaxation, easing censorship and repression, releasing Soviet political prisoners from Gulag labor camps, and promoting harmonious coexistence with other nations. This openness was limited, however, as the Soviet army ultimately crushed a large number of protesters in East Germany in 1953 and Hungary in 1956. With the appointment of Alexander Dubček as first secretary of the Communist Party of Czechoslovakia in January 1968, marking the beginning of the eight-month period known as "the Prague Spring," popular calls for democratization, or "socialism with a human face," spread throughout Poland and other communist dictatorships. The Soviets once again feared losing control over Eastern Europe.

In the West, the economic recession of 1966–1969 had a significant social impact, resulting in a general strike of ten million French workers in May 1968 that brought the government of General Charles de Gaulle to its knees. Similar strikes took place in Germany, and Italy experienced a "hot autumn" of industrial confrontations. At the same time, American political institutions were under growing strain. The civil rights movement descended into rioting in major American cities, and a massive antiwar movement spawned a violent revolutionary fringe that aimed to "bring the war home." Mass demonstrations, whether anti-Soviet, antiracist, anti-US, antiwar, or antinuclear, filled urban spaces from Prague to Paris and from Washington to Tokyo. It was in 1968 that John Lennon and Paul McCartney composed "Revolution 1," endorsing the widespread aspiration to "change the world" while informing violent leftist factions that "you can count me out."

By 1968, the postwar baby boomers were becoming young adults. Distressed by poverty, economic inequity, and lack of freedom, they were ready to agitate for change across the globe. Their sources of outrage included the nuclear balance of terror, political repression, environmental hazards, consumerism, patriarchy, and racism, and the boomers envisioned a third path beyond communism and capitalism. Their association of political possibility with generational change was captured by the slogan made popular by the leftist antiwar social activist Jack Weinberg: "Don't trust anyone over thirty."[22] Amid the violent protests that marred the Democratic National Convention in 1968, the Youth International Party (Yippies) held an alternative presidential nomination convention with their own candidate, Pigasus (an actual pig), drawing enormous media attention.

In Eastern Europe, resentment against Soviet rule merged with the spirit of resistance sweeping the West, causing rebellions to flare in Prague, Belgrade, and beyond. Students protested high unemployment, demanding political rights and freedom of movement. Vaclav Havel, then a Czechoslovakian dissident, wrote that "a specter is haunting Eastern Europe: the specter of what in the West is called 'dissent.' This specter does not appear out of thin air." It is a product of "the unadulterated, brutal, and arbitrary application of power, eliminating all expressions of nonconformity."[23] Czech intellectuals, activists, and politicians were galvanized by reformist writer Ludvík Vaculík's "Two Thousand Words That Belong to Workers, Farmers, Officials, Scientists, Artists, and Everybody," a document that welcomed a socialist program but deplored the way it had fallen into the hands of the wrong people.[24] Inspired by the Prague Spring, mass demonstrations occurred in March 1968 in Warsaw. Later that summer, students and faculty in Belgrade demanded that Yugoslavia's dictator, Josip Broz Tito, recognize their right to political assembly and free speech.

The revolutionary contagion of 1968 offered considerable evidence that the vision of the UN's Universal Declaration of Human Rights had been brought back to life. Parisian demonstrators chanted "*liberté, égalité, sexualité*"; the American civil rights movement struggled against institutionalized racism; and the International Convention on the Elimination of All Forms of Racial Discrimination entered into force in 1969. Such progress faced continuing opposition, however, and violence, too, was in the air. In the United States, hope turned to mourning with the assassinations of Martin Luther King Jr. and Robert F. Kennedy, and women's rights, as always, lagged behind. It would be another eleven years before the UN Convention on the Elimination of All Forms of Discrimination against Women (CEDAW) entered into force, in 1981, and it has not yet been ratified by the US.

The anticolonial contagion of 1968 represented the most widespread resistance to established power since World War II. Support for human rights spread in part due to advances in transportation and communication. Assisted by new technological instruments of globalization, students read the same books, now often published internationally at the same time, crossed borders on cheap trains, and used newly reduced airfares to fly from Paris to Havana and Saõ Paolo; they dressed in the same hippie style, sang the same songs, lived the same lifestyles, and challenged the postwar consumer society in similar ways whether in Prague, Paris, or Berkeley. With the Prague Express, political ideas were broadcast on both sides of the Atlantic in a movement that resisted both American capitalism and Soviet oppression.

The 1968 contagion achieved notable, yet unfinished, human rights success in the West, particularly through the civil rights movement. The Paris Accords brought an end to US involvement in the Vietnam War in 1973, and Western European students and workers won academic reforms and improved union representation. The sexual revolution promoted the emancipation of Western women, and the environmental movement assumed center stage in progressive politics. On the other side of the Iron Curtain, however, the Polish and Yugoslavian uprisings were defeated by their communist governments, and the Soviet invasion of Czechoslovakia in August 1968 silenced dissent, at least for a time.[25] A new wave of illiberalism spread with a vengeance throughout Eastern Europe. The Brezhnev doctrine held that Moscow could intervene in any country where a communist government was under threat, turning the communist claim of Enlightenment values into a self-serving nationalist rationale for Soviet imperial power. The revolutionary contagion was checked; there would be no change of regime, let alone a move toward democratization and human rights.

The revolutionary events of 1968 caused barely a ripple in the Arab world. The Levant had undergone its own version of anticolonial struggle and was now caught up in a different conflict. The Israeli victory over Egypt, Jordan, and Syria in the 1967 Six-Day War was seen as a humiliation across the region. When the war ended, Arab students, unlike their European and American peers, did not direct their energies toward promoting greater freedom but instead organized conferences and political forums to discuss how they might promote solidarity on the Palestinian question. In Lebanon, students raised funds for Palestinian students affected by Israel's occupation of the West Bank and Gaza. These young people did not define a new political role for themselves based on broader political and human rights aspirations. The Arab defeat by young, tiny Israel helped reenergize an Islamist group, the Muslim Brotherhood (al-Ikhwan al-Muslimin), in Egypt, where the army's battlefield collapse

An illustration of the Panama Canal Railway by F. N. Otis for his book *Isthmus of Panama: History of the Panama Railroad*, 1867.

validated the accusation that Nasser's secular regime was weak and corrupt. For the Arab world, it was 1967, not 1968, that came to represent the rise of new political dynamics. Arabs would remember the late 1960s not as a harbinger of new advances in human rights but for the ascension of political Islam. Latin America, however, echoed the protests of 1968 into the next decade. Marchers in Bolivia, Ecuador, Venezuela, Chile, Brazil, Argentina, and Uruguay denounced the military, decried cuts in welfare spending, demanded university reforms, and paved the way for yet more waves of revolutionary unrest.

THE PANAMA EXPRESS, THE 1970s

The construction of the Panama Railroad in 1850, initially called the Interoceanic Railroad, was vitally important for the creation of the Panama Canal. The California Gold Rush of 1849 had increased the traffic through the isthmus, and tracks would soon be laid between Panama and other parts of Central and South America. While that project was made possible by the steam locomotive, construction through infested swamps caused thousands of workers to die of cholera, yellow fever, and malaria.

Theodore Roosevelt and His Big Stick in the Caribbean, by William Allen Rogers, 1904. Courtesy of the Granger Collection.

With the arrival of long-distance railways, along with a canal that transformed the movement of goods by water, modernity roared into Latin America. Greed and concentrated wealth choked the lives of indigenous people, fostering widespread popular discontent.

A popular caricature from that early stage of modernization depicts a giant Theodore Roosevelt wading through the Caribbean, with his trademark "big stick" resting on his shoulder, pulling a chain of naval ships as a child might drag a toy. The first ship is called "The Receiver," another "The Sheriff," and the last is "The Debt Collector." While the US was a nonoccupying force, as opposed to the European imperial powers, the poster depicted the onset of US "police power" in Latin America, a story of US-backed authoritarian elites extracting wealth from impoverished masses, provoking a revolution in Mexico (1920), significant popular mobilizations in the 1930s, successful revolutions in the 1950s (Bolivia 1954, Cuba 1959) and then a contagion of social upheavals against authoritarian regimes in the 1960s and 1970s.

International instability once again aided these later contagious uprisings. After the Cold War divided Europe, Latin American nations, historically considered part of America's "backyard," were not permitted to remain neutral. The US required its southern neighbors to remain faithful allies against Soviet efforts to penetrate America's sphere of influence. The USSR achieved its main success with Fidel Castro's takeover of

Cuba in 1959. With a policy goal of "no more Cubas," Washington provided assistance to encourage modernization, economic development, and military readiness for countries that would secure US objectives. Having offered minimal economic aid during the 1950s, the US, under the Kennedy and Johnson administrations, collaborated with multinational companies to pump billions of dollars into Latin American economies. The Alliance for Progress contributed to the region's economic growth during the 1960s, but social and agrarian reforms—seen as threatening by economic and political elites—made no headway toward a more equitable distribution of wealth.

With infant industries and an underdeveloped middle class, Latin American countries were unable to compete in the world market. The rapid rise in oil prices starting in 1973 and again in 1979 further hampered economic development, and rising interest rates during this period greatly compounded the problem. The import substitution strategies of Latin American countries had not been able to make up for their dependence on expensive foreign goods. As the value and volume of exports lagged even further behind with the increasing costs of oil and debt repayment, they found themselves trapped not just in trade deficits, but in a debt crisis. The crisis hit Jamaica and Peru first, and it soon spread to other countries in the region, prompting an expanded role for the International Monetary Fund (IMF). As debts rapidly rose, the IMF began lending more money and prescribing austerity measures to debtor countries to stabilize their economies.[26]

From the 1970s through the 1980s, the prolonged economic crisis tended to strengthen bureaucratic authoritarianism regimes—that is, repressive governments typified by military rule and a centralized, technocratic approach to policy making.[27] As wealth flowed overseas, increasingly violent means were used to suppress the opposition. Chile's General Augusto Pinochet is perhaps the most notorious example of this pattern. Following his coup against Chile's democratically elected president, Salvadore Allende, Pinochet spearheaded an experiment with trade liberalization and export promotion that would later be adopted by other countries. Guided by advisors trained at the University of Chicago, Chilean dictator Pinochet imposed antiunion, free-trade economic policies in order to attract investment from multinational corporations, while conducting a violent campaign against dissidents. More than forty thousand of Pinochet's political opponents were imprisoned and tortured during his seventeen-year rule, and over three thousand were killed or forcibly "disappeared."[28] The other dictators, who continued to embrace import substitution strategies, pursued similar crackdowns against political opponents. In Argentina, military dictator Jorge Rafael Videla waged a "Dirty War" in which more than thirty thousand socialists and other opponents of his regime were hunted down and killed between 1974 and 1983.[29] Brazil's dictatorship, which had doubled down on import substitution, reached the height of its popularity in the 1970s thanks to the so-called Brazilian miracle, even as the regime censored all media, while torturing and banishing dissidents.

From the mid-1970s through the mid-1980s, waves of protest rose across much of Latin America, further fueled by unprecedented population growth yielding increasing numbers of unemployed youth and a more educated middle class drawn to social activism.[30] The train of modernization had left too many aspiring passengers without tickets, and they abandoned the railroad platforms for urban barricades or guerrilla warfare. Nations where economic hardship is combined with a societal capacity for mass mobilization are obviously at risk of unrest. The Catholic Church, which until the early 1970s had generally provided legitimacy to the state, became to some degree part of the protest movement with a new social agenda after Vatican II. Marked by the 1969 conference of bishops in Medellín, many priests, particularly in Peru, Brazil, Nicaragua, and El Salvador, began to merge Catholicism with Marxist ideology, a hybrid known as liberation theology. During that same period, political trade unions in Chile, Argentina, Peru, and Uruguay played a major role in grassroots mobilization, advocating various forms of socialism (from social democracy to communism) and organizing resistance to repression by police, national guards, and armed forces. In Brazil, Nicaragua, Colombia, Mexico, Paraguay, and Venezuela, indigenous movements fought in defense of land rights, traditional systems of law and self-government, and bilingual education. After multiple reports of torture, arbitrary execution, and disappearances of political dissidents, international NGOs like Amnesty International devoted resources to documenting these abuses. In Argentina, the Madres of the Plaza de Mayo, covered with white scarves, drew international attention beginning in 1977 by demanding information about their "disappeared" children and other loved ones.

With the waning of the Cold War, US disengagement from supporting right-wing military dictators opened opportunities for these protest movements to progress to democratization. Diverse coalitions, including a growing middle class and facilitated by the ascension of moderates over extremists on both right and left, now united in opposition to military rule. Human rights progress spread across the region. Most of the nineteen Latin American countries moved toward democratic elections, a trend famously labeled by Samuel Huntington as a "third wave" of democratization. The trajectory was not smooth, and it was punctured by illiberal setbacks. Compared to the Arab world, "the Panama Express" would witness greater accomplishments, as in the 2000s, when the Pink Tide of leftist governments were elected, instituting social reforms in the context of the prevailing post–Cold War climate of neoliberalism. While Latin American efforts to reduce inequality and poverty face continuing challenges, the economic environment of the region has been significantly bolstered.

During the same period in the Middle East, power politics was on the front burner. With the exception of the Kurds and the Palestinians, every Arab people that once lived under imperial rule had gained independence by the end of the 1970s. Taking advantage of a period of détente between the United States and the Soviet Union, many Arab states looked for ways to expand their power and influence in the region. Egypt and Syria, still feeling the humiliation of the Six-Day War, launched a surprise attack against Israel in October 1973. They were driven less by a hope of victory than by the need to recover their lost prestige. Egypt briefly regained control over territory it had lost in 1967 beyond the Suez Canal, but Syria's attempt to reclaim the Golan Heights from Israel failed. While a ceasefire restored the prewar status quo, the Saudi-led oil embargo imposed on the countries that had supported Israel revealed, for the first time, the enormous leverage the Gulf oil states had over the capitalist world economy. Despite US threats of war to halt the embargo, Iran and the Saudis engineered a fourfold increase in the price of oil. In 1979, the fall of Iran's Shah, followed by the Ayatollah Khomeini's establishment of a Shi'a Iranian theocracy, steered the region in a new direction. Iran ascended as the champion of Islamist Shi'a power in the Islamic world, and Saudi Arabia redirected much of its economic power to boost supporters of radical Sunni ideology. Iran became a theocracy in which the secular government was clearly subordinate to the ayatollahs; in Saudi Arabia,

Leonid Brezhnev and Erich Honecker kissing, on the east side
of the Berlin Wall. Vlasta Juricek, www.flickr.com/photos/
vlastula/.

the royal family retained nominal control but was tightly constrained by
the power of Wahhabi religious leaders. The two countries' "Cold War," in
which both sides have incorporated a mixture of geopolitics, insurgencies, and terrorism, continues to shape Middle Eastern politics.

Ever since World War II, interest in preventing Soviet control over
vital oil supplies had led the US to ally itself with the Saudi monarchy and
other authoritarian Gulf regimes, which feared both domestic communists and their Soviet backers. US-supported regimes suppressed not only
leftists but all opponents, a policy that helps explain why the waves of
revolutionary protest washing over other regions were so delayed in the
Arab world. Once the Soviet threat dissipated, the United States would
become much more tolerant of Arab mass politics. When the revolutionary hope of 1968 resurfaced in 1989, it met little resistance.

THE BERLIN EXPRESS, 1989

One important period of revolutionary contagion began when V. I. Lenin,
joined by twenty-nine Russian refugees, traveled by train from Zurich to
Saint Petersburg in April 1917, marking with his arrival the onset of the
Bolshevik Revolution. Once in power, the Bolsheviks used trains and ships
to carry agitators armed with leaflets, posters, and other forms of propaganda throughout the world. Equipped with radios and printing presses,

the trains brought Moscow reports on the political pulse throughout the collapsing Russian Empire, and they delivered instructions for stirring up revolutionary unrest.[31] After World War II, an expanding rail system integrated the different parts of Russia and also tightened the Soviet grip on the Eastern bloc. The train had become not only an instrument for the acceleration of modernity but a symbol of Soviet power and the popular appeal of communist ideology.

At the end of World War II, four different armies occupied parts of the defeated German territory. The American, British, and French zones reunited on May 9, 1949, to form the Federal Republic of Germany, or West Germany; five months later, the German Republic (GDR), or East Germany, was created from the Soviet zone as a client state to the USSR. The former German capital of Berlin lay wholly within the GDR, but it was divided between the two new countries. From 1945 until 1961, Germans freely crossed the east-west border in Berlin to work, shop, or go to the theater. But growing numbers of East Germans chose not to return home, prompting communist leaders in 1961 to construct a barrier wall with only three checkpoints for passage between East and West. At each of the checkpoints, East German soldiers screened diplomats and other officials before they were allowed to enter or leave, and few others could get through. In 1989, as Soviet exhaustion followed years of failed efforts at reform, the travel restrictions placed on East Germans were suddenly lifted. Tens of thousands of East Berliners heard the statement live on television and flooded the checkpoints, demanding entry into West Berlin. Two days later, all border controls disappeared.[32]

A number of factors allowed the protest movement of 1989 to expand into "velvet revolutions" throughout Eastern Europe. First, after four decades of superpower rivalry, the Soviet aspiration to world hegemony had stalled. The capitalist world's ever-expanding market economy, new forms of production, and revolutionary innovations in information technology had left the stagnant Soviet economy hopelessly unable to compete. Starting in 1981, the United States had increased support for insurgencies against Soviet allies in the developing world. The prospect of a renewed arms race, highlighted by President Ronald Reagan's call to develop the "Star Wars" missile defense system, further convinced the Soviet leaders to exchange Cold War objectives for political and economic reforms. Both superpowers had found their hegemonic ambitions challenged in 1968, but by the 1980s, only the Soviet regime faced serious threats to its legitimacy.

Without the resources to counter mounting US pressure, Mikhail Gorbachev, the last leader of the Soviet Union, famously called for *glasnost* (political openness) and *perestroika* (political and economic restructuring). This action was directly opposite to what Leonid Brezhnev had done in 1968, and it created spaces for a remarkable outbreak of open dissent and political mobilization in Eastern and Central Europe.[33] Facing a crippling economic crisis, the USSR proved incapable of significant political reorganization. As Giovanni Arrighi wrote, "The cleavage between a rapidly changing productive apparatus and a comparatively immobile institutional apparatus grew . . . until it became intolerable, not just for the subjects of Communist rule, but for the most enlightened members of the ruling elite itself."[34] While the structural causes of communism's collapse were similar throughout the Soviet empire, the orientation of the revolutions that swept the Eastern bloc depended a great deal on local political contexts. In Poland and Hungary, for example, the revolutions were gradual and peaceful, and radical changes resulted from negotiations between reform-minded ruling elites and moderate representatives of the opposition. In Czechoslovakia and the GDR, Gorbachev's refusal to use force against mass expressions of civil disobedience led to disarray at the top and the crumbling of the entire party and government machinery.[35] Unlike their counterparts in 1968, the Soviet leaders two decades later had lost the will, and perhaps the ability, to crush the revolutionary contagion. The Soviet Union itself broke up into fifteen successor states.

With rapid changes occurring in the international order and political crises throughout the Eastern bloc, civil societies in 1989 were in turmoil. The late 1980s witnessed an explosion of transnational nongovernmental organizations in the developing world, and the fortieth anniversary of the Universal Declaration of Human Rights, in 1988, coincided with a wave of international protests against the nearly complete global hegemony of the United States and its powerful entourage. This movement would soon take to the streets of Seattle and Genoa. Activism within civil society received an additional boost with the arrival of the digital age.

Overall, the ease of travel and communication resulting from technological improvement brought societies closer together. Yet it also drew attention to cultural and socioeconomic differences, heightening tensions and fragmentation in both the developed and developing worlds and creating ever more specific, and ever more conflicting, human rights demands. The year 1989 witnessed a heartening advance in human rights activism within the noncommunist world, but it brought increasing disagreement over which rights, and whose rights, should take precedence. For example, trade unions and labor activists sought to make labor rights central to the debate, yet organized labor was still divided on two fronts: internationally, between workers from rich countries and those from poor countries, and domestically, between the interests of union members and unrepresented workers. Moreover, environmental threats spurred the activism of a global ecological movement; at the same time its agenda reflected the divergent interests between the developed and developing countries. The Western nations had been able to emit as much carbon as they wanted to build their industrial bases; this privilege was now to be denied the developing nations. Certain nations faced catastrophic consequences from global warming—even complete inundation from sea-level rise—whereas other nations felt little urgency to act. Finally, while progressives after the Cold War placed their hopes on the development of a global civil society and citizenship, the backlash in the West against poor foreigners (especially immigrants and guest workers) after the events of September 11, 2001, increased rivalries and distrust between cultures. Ever since the fall of communism, the human rights debate continues to be split along political, socioeconomic, and cultural lines.

The Berlin Express sped with fierce intent throughout the Soviet bloc, toppling one communist regime after the other and creating new spaces for democratization and vibrant civil societies. The Eastern European countries' subsequent integration into the European Union (EU) led, for most, to economic growth and stability. More recently, however, the success of 1989 has been complicated by a multitude of challenges. These include the Greek debt crisis and lingering concerns about the Eurozone; the continuing influx of migrants and refugees; the resurgence of Islamist terrorism; Russia's 2014 invasion of Ukraine and its annexation of Crimea; the rise of right-wing populist parties; and the June 2016 vote in the United Kingdom in favor of leaving the EU. Despite these challenges, European integration was a decisive factor in the stability of postrevolutionary Eastern European states, creating conditions more favorable for human rights after 1989 than during any previous revolutionary contagion, and establishing integrative economic and institutional foundations that successfully emulated the post–World War II reconstruction efforts.

In the MENA region, however, the fall of the Berlin Wall had an unfavorable impact. With no more need to contain the Soviet Union, former US allies like Iran and former Soviet allies like Saddam Hussein's Iraq felt empowered to assert their interests more forcefully. The region was shaped by a new "Cold War," regulated by the sole superpower and three regional powers—Iran, Saudi Arabia, and Iraq—each pursuing often conflicting ambitions. With a history of backing friendly Gulf monarchs against Arab nationalist regimes allied with the USSR, the United States had based its Middle East policy on geopolitical stability and oil interests. The US policy was slow to recognize the danger of violent Islamist extremism, failing to anticipate the 1979 Khomeini revolution in Iran and supporting radical Sunni groups in their insurgency (from 1979 until 1989) against the Soviet-backed government.[36] Overall, these policies shrank any space for political reform and grassroots resistance against authoritarianism, particularly after the United States led one of the widest international coalitions ever assembled into Kuwait in 1990 to expel Iraq's occupying army. A decade later, President George W. Bush embraced a policy of regional transformation, beginning with the 2003 invasion of Iraq.[37] For a time, that new form of external pressure allowed greater space for local pro-democracy activism throughout the region. Bush's vision backfired, culminating in a withdrawal from Iraq under President Barack Obama in 2010, but it helped convey the possibility of democratic change; its connection to the Arab uprisings of 2011 cannot be entirely discounted.

In short, while the revolutionary contagion of 1989 was more promising than other contagions, it produced drastically different political and economic outcomes for Middle Easterners than for Eastern Europeans. Arab states did not follow the trend toward economic liberalization, so the end of the Cold War left highly centralized states like Egypt and Saudi Arabia unable or unwilling to diversify and privatize key sectors of their economies. While the Washington Consensus for economic liberalization predominated elsewhere, security concerns prevailed in the Middle East.[38] The global recession of 2008 greatly increased the hardship experienced in already stressed Arab economies, feeding the pressures that would unleash revolutionary contagion two years later.

Although the struggle for national independence after World War II represented a major milestone in the Arab political awakening, it would be another fifty years before social and economic forces ripened into mass demands for human rights. When we consider the historical sequence of five periods of revolutionary contagion, we see that these revolutions were all provoked by similar conditions, growing out of contradictions rooted in modernization. Yet there were also notable differences among these contagions. Which revolutionary contagion most resembles the Arab uprisings of 2011? Is it the 1848 Spring of Nations, crushed by Europe's monarchic powers? Is it perhaps the "velvet revolutions" and collapse of communism in 1989, which revived the promise of 1968? The 1989 revolution saw the lives of Eastern Europeans greatly improved, based on their integration into an enlarged and stable European Union, whereas 1968 was another turning point in history where history failed to turn. Other revolutionary contagions fall between 1848 and 1989. Unlike 1848, the anticolonial struggles following World War II were not directly thwarted by imperial powers, which reluctantly relinquished their colonial possessions. Rather, once freed, some former colonized states became sites of proxy wars, fueled by superpower rivalry. In either case, true political sovereignty, political rights, and economic viability proved elusive. The 1968 revolutions had a mixed result with respect to political and social freedoms. Western Europe witnessed human rights accomplishments for students, workers, women, blacks, and gays. In the Eastern bloc, however, activists were defeated, leaving them with dashed hopes that only subsequent history could fulfill. In Latin America, revolutions stretched beyond the 1970s as human rights advocates struggled to overturn years of US-backed oppression, often under military dictatorships. Over time, free enterprise, a strong middle class, and grassroots social activism gradually helped build important human rights pillars and strong economic foundations. That the US was looking the other way at the end of the of the twentieth century, after years of anticommunist authoritarian regimes, no doubt favored the free expression of human rights. Obstacles remain, but the region is very different than it was in the late 1970s.

Sadly, at this juncture, the Arab Spring resembles most the failed revolutions of 1848. It is important, however, to remember that even in places where revolutions failed, the progressive spirit of those revolutions seeped into the political culture, ready to reemerge when conditions allowed. We can only hope that, as in post-1848 Europe, the aspirations that launched the Arab Spring will eventually be realized. The causes of the Arab Spring, and the reasons for its failures (the subject of the next chapter), remain a great source of debate. The pessimists in that debate should be reminded of Thomas Jefferson's long-term optimism about rebellion: "I hold it that a little rebellion is a good thing, and as necessary in the political world as storm in the physical."[39]

CHAPTER TWO

The Levant Express and the Arab Spring of Nations

FROM THE 1880S UNTIL WORLD WAR I, France continued to expand its holdings in Tunisia and extracted more of the country's resources through an expanding rail system, the construction of a naval base at Bizerte, and improved port facilities in Tunis, Sousse, and Sfax. Tunisians generally lacked the means to invest in these ventures, nor did they profit from them as workers. "The railroads and the companies developing the ports," writes the historian Kenneth Perkins, "hired French and Italian laborers and even in the mines migrants from Tripolitania, Algeria, and Morocco were given preference over Tunisians, whom European foremen often characterized as unreliable and incompetent."[1] To the colonists, the railroad promised modernity and social welfare, but it left the majority of Tunisians disadvantaged and resentful. Over time, opposition spread among the rural population and occasionally became violent.

In 1881, infuriated by the French capture of Sfax and the subsequent destruction of olive plantations and farms, Tunisians attacked the Oued Zergha railway station, set it afire, and massacred a French stationmaster and ten employees.[2] When the main train station in Tunis was burned to the ground and shops looted in January 2011, during the riots and mass protests that forced President Ben Ali to step down, many heard an echo of that earlier rebellion.[3] This time, Tunisia's protests sparked revolution across North Africa and beyond. Like previous revolutionary uprisings, the

Domino Effect, © Zapiro, originally published in *Mail and Guardian*, © 2011. Republished with permission—for more Zapiro cartoons visit www.zapiro.com.

unfolding of the Arab Spring came in three stages. Stage 1 focused on the toppling of the old regime; stage 2 dealt with the challenges of consolidation; and stage 3 addressed the human rights challenges in revolutionary transition.[4]

THE SOURCES OF REVOLUTIONARY CONTAGION

In December 2010, Mohamed Bouazizi, a Tunisian vegetable seller, immolated himself in protest after unfair treatment by the police; in January 2011, four Algerians in a span of five days doused themselves in gasoline and set themselves on fire.[5] In Cairo, Ahmed el-Sayed followed the same tragic path. Isolated suicides morphed into mass protests, mass protests into revolutions, and regimes that had seemed securely in place for decades suddenly started to crumble. The Arab Spring had begun. With the fall of Ben Ali on January 14, 2011, in Tunisia, the bittersweet fragrance of the Jasmine Revolution awoke the Middle East. As one dictatorship after another was shaken by the force of popular uprisings, the freedom train accelerated through the unsettling seasons of 2011 and 2012, propelled in part by digital messages flying through cyberspace. Human rights protests spread with startling celerity from Tunisia to Egypt, Palestine, Algeria, Bahrain, Libya, Morocco, Syria, Yemen, and Saudi Arabia. Beneath the surface, one could detect the same underlying conditions that contributed to earlier cases of revolutionary contagion.

Arab Uprisings 2011

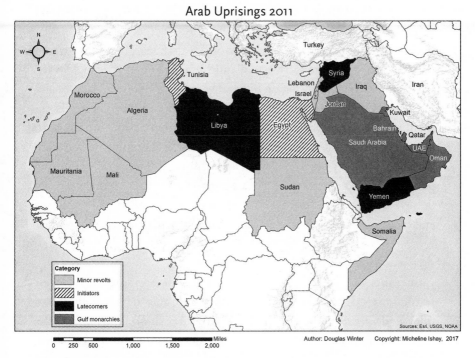

Timing and location of the Arab uprisings, 2011. Map by Douglas Winter and Micheline Ishay (© 2017 Micheline Ishay).

Five factors that contributed to previous revolutionary contagions also played a role in 2011. First, the great powers had retreated from their roles as custodians of the regional order; second, an economic crisis was exacerbated by the 2008 global recession, contributing to unprecedented unemployment of young people despite their rising levels of education; third, promises of political reform had gone unfulfilled; fourth, new media outlets created a platform for a growing culture of resistance; and fifth, human rights activism and civil society actively galvanized disenchantment. No one cause in isolation can explain how the revolutions began.

Great Power Withdrawal

In 1848, the powers comprising the Concert of Europe, which had orchestrated a new world order after the defeat of Napoleon, became preoccupied with internal disputes, leaving working- and middle-class Europeans free to confront their repressive leaders without outside great powers defending the established conservative order. In the same vein, when imperialist countries, devastated by World War II, loosened their grip on their colonial possessions, a wave of anticolonial struggles began. In 2011, US power in the MENA region had waned, as it withdrew from Iraq, and Russia was still rebuilding from its post-Soviet free fall. The retrenchment of these great powers weakened their authoritarian Arab allies. In particular, with America's patronage of local dictatorships in question, the people of the Levant sensed an opportunity. If the retreat of external powers removed one prop sustaining regional stability, what followed can only be understood in terms of localized economic and social pressures and the response of regional elites to the changing dynamics of power.

Economic Stress

Latin American societies experienced economic pressure during their revolutionary period in the 1970s, but they were able to open their economies and secure paths toward democratic transition. In contrast, the MENA economy had been sclerotic for decades. In *The People Want*, Gilbert Achcar insightfully described how Arab leaders inhibited the development of productive forces.[6] Economic changes took the form of a halting neoliberalism, or *infitah* (opening), which benefited only a thin upper crust of the population. In retrospect, many members of Egypt's financial elite recognize their failures. Wael Ziada, the former executive chair of the investment bank Hermes Financial Group, told me in a private conversation in July 2017 that globalization and privatization had made a very late start in the region due to the high degree of patrimony, nepotism, crony capitalism, and corrupt bureaucracies. Hopes for economic development stalled, overtaken by revolutions and subsequent sectarian conflicts.

Many regional experts failed to anticipate the powerful impact of surging numbers of unemployed young people—a factor that also fueled the revolutions of 1848 and 1968. By 2011, close to 30 percent of young people aged fifteen to twenty-four in the Middle East were unemployed.[7] This rate was among the highest in the world, compared to 18 percent in Sub-Saharan Africa, 17 percent in Latin America, 16 percent in Southeast Asia, 10 percent in South Asia, and 8 percent in East Asia.[8] A burgeoning educated class, with little opportunity to achieve the wealth and freedom for which they had prepared, was growing ever more frustrated with authoritarian leaders' empty promises of reform.

Although overall education levels had risen substantially in the region for several decades, academic training did not translate into new jobs. Gains in educational attainment were uneven; Egypt, Iraq, and Yemen combined to account for about three-quarters of the almost ten million illiterate people in the region. Meanwhile, the education gap between boys and girls narrowed in Tunisia, Syria, Algeria, and Libya, prompting more women to compete for scarce jobs, a problem magnified by the 2008 economic crisis. In contrast, the much wealthier Gulf states (Bahrain, Kuwait, Oman, Qatar, Saudi Arabia, and the United Arab Emirates) did not suffer the same predicament. Further, they invested far more in education infrastructure than anywhere else in the region and did not suffer from similar high unemployment rates. Reducing the education gap between nationals and non-nationals, Gulf countries were striving to become less dependent on foreign expertise.[9]

Failure of Political Reforms
The elite's broken promises of political reform made the prerevolutionary picture markedly worse. Modest reforms or concessions in developing and transitional societies often follow social pressure for change, but when reforms prove inconclusive, disappointment leads to more radical protest. In France, before the 1848 revolutions, Louis Philippe II raised popular expectations by pledging political reforms but then abandoned these programs. This reversal caused popular rage and set the stage for the uprising. A similar relation between spikes in social activism and unfulfilled governmental promises was particularly evident in the states that initiated the Arab Spring.

In Tunisia, structural economic impediments to social mobility were reinforced by regime policies that continued to block real reforms. Elections were held in 1989, 1994, 2004, and 2009, but the majority of seats in the Tunisian parliament, the Rassemblement constitutionnel démocratique, were reserved for the ruling party of Ben Ali. Only a small quota of seats was available for other parties. Even when other candidates were allowed to run against him for the presidency, Ben Ali remained the guaranteed winner—an inevitability further entrenched by constitutional "reforms" that allowed him to run for additional terms. By 2010, he had

been in power for twenty-two years. Declining major power interest in the
MENA region, the 2008 global economic crisis, a high youth unemployment, and an eroding middle class made the ruling party's entrenchment
not just infuriating but intolerable.[10]

Young people in Hosni Mubarak's Egypt experienced similar pressures. Deregulatory economic reforms, which started in the 1990s and
accelerated in 2004, led to major layoffs while benefiting the economic
and military elite, causing a number of opposition organizations,
including the Kefaya (Enough) movement, Hizb al-Ghad (the Tomorrow
Party), Nadi al-Quda (the Judges Club), and al-Ikhwan al-Muslimin (the
Muslim Brotherhood), to mount popular protests. Mubarak answered
with some window-dressing reforms, carving space for dissenting political expression, but his dominant Egyptian National Democratic Party also
placed unfair electoral restrictions on opposition parties.[11] The Egyptian
rapper Ahmed Rock captured the rising anger of Egyptian youth when he
sang: "Whoever gets a taste of freedom, even if it's an illusion / Never lets
it go . . . / Try to imprison our voices! Try throwing us behind bars! / Truth
shall prevail, even when there are a million jailers guarding it!"[12]

Tunisia and Egypt, the two pioneering revolutionary states, had relatively homogenous populations, which favored united action (at least
initially) against their authoritarian regimes. In Libya, Syria, Bahrain, and
Yemen, however, social inequities intersected with tribal or sectarian privileges and helped turn the uprisings into bloody civil wars. Libya at the
time had the highest human development index in Africa, with its citizens receiving free education, free health care, and financial assistance
for housing and fresh water. Yet its youth unemployment had soared
to 43 percent.[13] Despite a comprehensive social welfare system, many
Libyans saw their regime as a kleptocracy whose major beneficiaries were
Gaddafi's family and tribe. As the world was convulsed by a global
economic recession, Gaddafi planned a more inclusive redistribution of
oil revenue. The Libyan political system, however, was primarily designed
to ensure the Gaddafi family's continued dominance amid tribal feuds.
Political frustration mounted, especially among the youth. On February
17, Libyan protesters announced a Day of Rage in four cities. Many in the
surging crowds sang the words of Libyan hip-hop artist Ibn Thabit:
"Muammar, you have never served your people. / Muammar . . . / Our
revenge is coming for you / Like a train through the wall."[14]

Just like Libya, Syria had near-universal primary school enrollment and had closed the educational gap between boys and girls in secondary education. Adult literacy in Syria in 2011 was 84 percent and youth literacy was 95 percent, much higher rates than those of other countries experiencing the uprisings.[15] Syria produced little oil, however, and its youth unemployment, then at 33.7 percent, was concentrated within the Sunni majority.[16] It suffered the highest gap between the level of education and available job opportunities in Arab countries outside the Gulf region.

The political picture in Syria changed dramatically after Bashar al-Assad became president in 2000. His inauguration sparked new optimism for economic and political reforms, and his "Damascus Spring" consisted of a package of promises, including the emergence of seventy "dialogue clubs" for promoting discussion between Syria's civil society and its political elite. Opposition parties were allowed to play an active role, and two independent magazines were permitted: *Ad Dumari* and *Al Eqtisadiah*.[17] In a 2000 speech, Assad proclaimed that "democracy is our duty toward others before it becomes a right for us . . . administrative reform is a pressing need for all of us today."[18] These reforms, however, continued to favor Alawites (Assad's religious group) and the Shi'a minority at the expense of the Sunni majority. In 2011, as ordinary Syrians were immersed in the news of the revolutions sweeping the region, Assad's refusal to make additional reforms in a time of economic crisis led to growing political frustration. On March 23, peaceful demonstrations escalated into a violent uprising after the Syrian government massacred protesters in Daara. In June, Syrian rapper Ibrahim Qashoush led a chorus of a thousand demonstrators to the old main square of Hama, singing: "Bashar depart from here; you lost all your legitimacy; . . . Freedom is near."[19] The government responded by having the singer's throat cut, propelling Syria's descent into an unending sectarian bloodbath.

As in Libya and Syria, the economic disparities in Bahrain were magnified by sectarian tensions. The Shi'a majority rose in protest against a hierarchy of wealth and power that favored the Sunni minority.[20] A small island country in the Persian Gulf with less oil wealth than its neighbors of the Gulf Cooperation Council (GCC), Bahrain did not have the kind of petrodollar-funded, cradle-to-grave welfare program seen in Qatar, Kuwait, Oman, Saudi Arabia, and the United Arab Emirates, and the Shi'a experienced higher unemployment and fewer opportunities than the country's official statistics indicated.[21] Still, the Bahraini monarchy had embarked on a program of political reforms well before the uprising: a parliament (albeit weak) was elected, political exiles were pardoned, and there were reforms of prisons and police. The first nongovernmental organization (NGO) was licensed, and many stateless people were granted citizenship rights. Those reforms, however, stopped short of limiting the ruling family's power or bringing equality to the Shi'a majority. Freedom of the press was still restricted, in spite of governmental assurances to the contrary.[22] In the context of growing frustration with the parliament, the torture of activists, the suppression of websites and political publications, and rising unemployment, hopes for real and sustained economic and political reforms had dissipated by the end of 2010. As revolts swept from west to east in the Arab world, the Bahrainis declared a Day of Rage, beginning a series of large demonstrations at the Pearl Roundabout in the capital of Manama.

The Yemeni uprising represented a unique case, as that country was already plagued by domestic conflicts. By 2011, Yemen was the second most populous nation in the Arab world. With 42 percent of youth between the age of fifteen and twenty-five unemployed, social mobility was nonexistent. Fifty percent of the population was illiterate; life expectancy was low; only 3 percent of the land remained arable; and oil reserves were nearly depleted.[23] Like other Arab dictatorships, Yemen had embarked on limited reform, directed toward a system best described as tribalized authoritarianism. Following the 2003 parliamentary elections, political reforms aimed to strengthen political parties and develop civil society, but the country continued to be plagued by tribal feuds. The reforms turned out to be meaningless given President Ali Abdullah Saleh's determination to hold power despite uninterrupted waves of protesters. "Leave Ali, leave!" shouted growing crowds throughout the country. Intensified by ethnic strife, the Yemeni uprising soon descended into an ever more intractable civil war.

New Media and the Culture of Resistance
Economic crises and frustrated political factors may produce a revolutionary powder keg, but human rights ideals can be best disseminated by an independent media and galvanized by a widening cultural space for resistance. The arrival of the Internet and the privatization of television

initially offered new paths forward beyond the reach of censorship. With the rise of semi-independent newspapers and ubiquitous satellite dishes streaming Al Jazeera and other new media outlets, governments lost their monopoly over political coverage. Simultaneously, the penetration of the Internet into the Arab world provided a forum for activists and bloggers and a political platform for educated and idealistic youth. All these mechanisms had the capacity to create a sense of unity among disadvantaged groups, hastening the revolutionary contagion.

The introduction of satellite television in 2005 provided an uncensored alternative to government-owned and -regulated media; it represented an important shift to much more diverse sources of information and gave ordinary Arabs wider exposure to new cultural and political influences.[24] The satellite dish exposed people to new tastes, from Islamist programming to art and pornography. It shaped social participation and a sense of possibility, creating a new Arab cosmopolitanism. At least in the sense of mass communication, the Arab dream of unity, invoked in politicians' speeches for fifty years, was becoming a reality.[25] Al Jazeera connected popular discontent across the region into a unified narrative, highlighting simultaneous protests on split screens and employing identical language to describe the aspirations of protagonists in different contexts.

With the publication of three Egyptian semi-official dailies, *Al Ahram, Al Akhbar,* and *Al Gomhoria,* the media scene saw the birth of small opposition newspapers. Egypt is one of many nations where the shift from state ownership and complete governmental control to private ownership and individual or party control brought an increase in media diversity. Some of the new opposition newspapers were very critical of the government, and some even broke widely held taboos by criticizing senior government officials by name, including the president.[26]

The potential impact of new media coverage and communication technologies in the region had first gained attention during the mass demonstrations in Iran that followed the 2009 elections there. *New York Times* columnist Thomas Friedman observed in June of that year that "secular forces of moderation have used technologies like Facebook, Flickr, Twitter, blogging and text-messaging as their virtual mosque, as the place they can now gather, mobilize, plan, inform and energize their supporters, outside the grip of the state."[27] Unfortunately, Friedman's assumption that new forms of communication would remain "outside the

grip of the state" overlooked the familiar race, common to all power struggles, between measures and countermeasures. As soon as the leaders of
regimes in Iran, Egypt, Libya, and Yemen recognized the danger in the
uprisings, they rushed to shut down the flow of information. Despite this
obstruction, however, the revolution continued to surge forward. While
Internet technology helped galvanize the revolution on the streets, one
should not conclude, as the media often imply when they refer to the
uprisings as the "Facebook revolution," that the revolution was caused or
enabled by social media.

Social media nonetheless provided new channels for popular and
artistic rebellions, such as rap music. Throughout the Middle East, rap
provided the rhythm of resistance. Tunisian rapper Hamada Ben Amor
(aka El General) posted a song called "Rais-LeBled" ("Head of State"),
which became an anthem for the uprisings. With easy access to YouTube,
resistance rap spread swiftly through the streets and alleys, real and
virtual. No one had dared to publicly blame a president for unemployment
and injustice, but El General sang fearlessly; his courage and words were
contagious. Throughout the Middle East, rap became the revolutionary
music of young artists.

This alternative music defied both the dictators and their jihadist
enemies. In Marrakesh, the Moroccan group Fnair sang a counter-jihadist
tune ("Maktish Bladi," meaning "Hands Off My Country") that was
embraced throughout the Levant:

> Hands off my country, land of my ancestors
> People dear to my heart, land of mine and my grandchildren
> I refuse terrorism in my country, and I cry it out loud
> Hands off my country, land of my ancestors.[28]

At the same time, Muslim rappers reclaimed a peaceful Islam in music.
The Moroccan woman Soultana rapped:

> They said we are terrorists because we are Muslims
> Because one criminal did it wrong in the name of Islam
> Our Islam is peace, love, respect
> We are the generation calling for peace.[29]

The Internet had become a venue for infectious new forms of popular
expression that nurtured a cultural language of resistance and human

rights that both helped to set the stage for the 2011 Arab uprisings and hastened the contagion. Calls for revolutions and news about uprisings, however, had circulated long before the Internet, from Bastille Day in 1789 to the bloody July Revolution of 1848. Pamphlets and newspapers had spread from cities to the countryside and between cities and nations. Even when printing presses were not available, such as in Haiti at the end of the eighteenth century, colonial slave rebellions spread with the sound of the drum, echoing across mountains and valleys. Such free expression in the public sphere was backed by an activated civil society, yielding a broader movement toward human rights.

Human Rights and Civil Society

Ultimately, key actors in civil society sit in the driver's seat of revolutions. As events unfold, diverse members of the population (some from the "silent majority" and others from NGOs, unions, women's groups, the Muslim Brotherhood, and other social entities) join the revolutionary leadership. In general, emancipation requires a sturdy civil society,[30] but during the Arab uprisings the condition of the public square varied from one country to another. In Tunisia and Egypt, where the uprisings began, civil society was already vibrant and relatively homogenous, whereas the state had been greatly weakened by its incapacity to enact political and economic reforms. In the highly divided authoritarian societies of Libya, Syria, and Yemen, civil society was still too fractured by tribal and sectarian divisions to confront the state effectively, and the revolutions stalled. In the Gulf monarchies of Saudi Arabia, United Arab Emirates, Kuwait, and Oman, civil society was far weaker than the state and proved unable to spark much revolutionary fervor.[31]

Unions in Tunisia, Egypt, and Bahrain already provided an outlet for workers to express their economic discontent. More independent than some of its counterparts, the Tunisian Union Genéral du Travail (UGTT) capitalized on the economic plight of Tunisians, forever symbolized by the self-immolation of Mohamed Bouazizi, to demand political change. It galvanized popular protests across the country, from Kasserine and Gafsa in the hinterland to Sfax and Sousse on the northeast coast. The Egyptian Trade Union Federation (EFTU), less autonomous and more marginalized than its Tunisian counterpart, had a more modest human rights goal: to advance economic rights demands rather than regime change.[32]

It contributed to a series of factory strikes, but most were mobilized by other social groups, like the April 6 Youth Movement. The General Federation of Bahrain Trade Unions was more like its Tunisian counterpart, demanding not only economic rights but greater political freedom, including the creation of a fully elected parliament.[33] Its efforts failed when Saudi Arabia and the UAE sent thousands of soldiers and police to crack down on protesters in Manama.

The activism of labor unions intersected with local activism. In Egypt, there were several local groups. The grassroots organization Kefaya emerged in 2004 in solidarity with the Palestinian Intifada of 2000–2005, directing its anger against Mubarak's presidency and permanent emergency laws. The April 6 Youth Movement was formed in 2008 to support the workers' strike in the industrial town of El-Mahalla, located in the middle of the Nile delta.[34] One year earlier, the National Association for Change, led by Mohamed ElBaradei, launched its own pro-democracy activities. These groups formed the core of the premobilization stage of the uprising, providing the organizational foundation beneath what looked like a spontaneous gathering of youth.

Since the mid-1990s, both the US and the Europeans had provided substantial funding to human rights organizations in the MENA region. Even though the Arab awakening was homegrown, these external organizations offered critical practical assistance. While the ruling elites in Egypt and elsewhere indulged these NGOs through the early phase of the revolutionary turmoil, their tolerance did not last as the uprising intensified. Numerous NGOs were shut down throughout the Middle East, newspapers were censored, and journalists imprisoned. With the exception of Tunisia and possibly Morocco, governmental censorship returned to at least the status quo ante and occasionally to greater repression.

The sanctuary of the mosques, often left uncontrolled by the state, was another important space of resistance. Some mosques openly recruited young activists and served as hubs for demonstrations following Friday prayers. The role of Islamist groups, invisible to world cameras during the heyday of the 2011 protests, gradually became more apparent. Islamists were initially able to bridge class differences and connect the professional and middle classes with workers and poor citizens.[35] While many Islamists sought to gain new converts, others took a more inclusive approach, seeking an interface between Islam and human rights. The

Muslim Brotherhood remained carefully hidden during the revolutionary phase; it would later use the space provided by mosques for a highly disciplined mass mobilization campaign, achieving victory in the first elections held in Tunisia and Egypt.

If digital information opened the space for human rights activism, strengthening NGOs, unions, women's and Muslim groups, it also became a space for surveillance—an Orwellian use of information technology by authoritarian regimes to suppress freedom. China had led the way in denying freedom of access to politically sensitive websites and tracking email to identify and arrest dissidents, and Arab leaders began to follow China's example. Even in the absence of such repressive measures, the revolutionaries discovered that social media can as easily fragment a cause as unify it. Women, Internet organizers, bloggers, and mosque-goers, unified in public squares, were quick to rediscover their differences in cyberspace once the dictators of Tunisia and Egypt were toppled.

These political revolutionary divisions repeated a historical pattern. After the arrest of the French king Louis XVI in August 1792, fierce fighting broke out between economic classes, with the conservative and constitutional monarchists, the Club des Feuillants, on one pole and the radical Jacobins, the Montagnards, on the other. Continuing social struggles led to the expedient centralism of the Committee of Public Safety, a political body that gained control over France during chaotic years between 1793 and 1794, and finally to the Thermidorian reaction—a counterrevolution coup d'état organized by moderates and royalists who overthrew that committee. Similarly, as discussion about the meaning of democracy unfolded in Tunisia and Egypt, the marriage of convenience between the Muslim Brotherhood and the secular opposition yielded to deepening contention. Unified in their opposition to a dictator, people with different agendas ultimately clashed over the revolution's basic goals, creating social chaos and, at least in Egypt, an analogous Thermidorian reaction, manifested in al-Sisi's coup d'état.

The Tunisian and Egyptian revolutions were not organized overnight. It took years for organizers to marshal their resources and prepare their campaigns. With the help of outsiders and beneath traditional local political radars, they were able to disseminate their strategies in virtual space. Even if Google had not yet attained the far-reaching impact it would gain throughout the Arab Middle East in the wake of the uprisings, the Internet

Postcard of Ramses Central Railway Station, Cairo c. 1892.
From the collection of Dr. Paula Sanders, Rice University.

and satellite TV were able to disseminate unprecedented amounts of
information during the 2011 revolutionary wave. Nevertheless, as the
region entered a second stage of the revolution, divergent political goals,
coupled with different social and economic trajectories, yielded distinct
revolutionary paths and new opportunities for regime consolidation.

REVOLUTIONS ON DIFFERENT PATHS

In the second stage of the revolution, the Levant Express made numerous
stops, staying longer at Cairo's Ramses Central Railway Station (also
called Masr Station) and allowing passengers to observe the historic selec-
tion of Egypt's first democratically elected government. Many remained
on the train, peering nervously out the windows, fearful that a victorious
Muslim Brotherhood would stifle the optimism surrounding the revolution. Everyone, realizing they had arrived at a new phase of the revolution,
wondered with trepidation whether the Muslim Brothers, who were
winning elections in Egypt and Tunisia, would realize the promises of the
uprising, and whether the postrevolutionary phase would be similar in
Syria, Libya, Bahrain, and beyond.

The condition of the Egyptian railroad itself might have made some
passengers skeptical. In operation since the line from Cairo to Alexandria
opened in 1854, Egypt's once impressive rail system has recently been
marred by tragic accidents. In 2002, a fire spread from car to car on an
overcrowded train as it traveled from Cairo to Aswan. With the driver and

first-class passengers unaware of the conflagration engulfing the rear of the train, where third-class cars were jammed far beyond their capacity, the blazing train continued to fly down the tracks as more than 370 passengers died. The tragedy revealed the lack of safety for low-income travelers, often sequestered in suffocating carriages.[36] Egypt's prime minister defended the beleaguered railway: "All trains are in good shape and at the highest degree of efficiency, and they are reviewed completely and regularly."[37]

The tragedy did not cause conditions to improve. In December 2012, there were 130 accidents, rooted in worsening financial and administrative corruption, a declining commitment to worker training, and increasingly irregular maintenance.[38] Not all railroads manage to move passengers safely from one destination to another, nor do most revolutionary movements. They may begin with celebration and promise but end in tragedy. Most revolutionary movements encounter great obstacles when trying to address the problems of the old regime in a time of political and economic volatility.

In 1848, 1947, 1968, 1970, and 1989, the conditions underlying a successful transition from one stage to another depended on political, social, and cultural dynamics that differed from one country to another. In this vein, it is useful to cluster Arab revolutionary states into three types. The first, the initiators, are states like Egypt and Tunisia that trigger revolutionary contagions. The second type, the latecomers to revolutionary contagion (Libya, Syria, Bahrain, and Yemen), often experience more prolonged violence. As we have already seen, unlike the initiators, whose societies are at least somewhat homogenous, the latecomers are all deeply divided along tribal, religious, and ethnic lines. A third category consists of the resilient regimes, found in the wealthy oil monarchies of the Gulf, that are able to forestall revolution or avoid it entirely.

The factors that facilitate the toppling of regimes do not necessarily lead to the consolidation of a new government. Consolidation comes when a revolutionary movement has the capacity: (1) to solicit the sympathy and assistance of relevant international actors, (2) to draw on civil society's human and economic capital for sustainable economic growth, increased employment, and greater economic equity, (3) to include different segments of the population in the new political process, (4) to partner with the forces of order, and (5) to carry forward the promise of universal inclusion, leading people to prefer human rights over authoritarian nationalism.

The international community was somewhat disengaged when the revolutions started in Tunisia and Egypt. Because the initiators were relatively homogeneous (with Egypt's 15–20 percent Copt population the most notable dimension of diversity), they were able to galvanize a common front against their country's dictatorial regimes. In each case, the state became a shell, allowing what Antonio Gramsci calls a "war of movement," that is, the rapid assembling of overwhelming social force to overthrow the authoritarian elite. Once that was accomplished, however, consolidation did not come easily. Both postrevolutionary regimes lacked either the political capacity or the human and economic capital to sustain governments. After the Muslim Brotherhood took control of the Egyptian government following the fall of Hosni Mubarak, the International Monetary Fund resisted providing loans and foreign investments dried up. Tunisia, with a better-educated population than Egypt's, had greater opportunities for postrevolutionary economic growth and, in that dimension at least, better prospects for consolidating the revolution. Moreover, because the military apparatus was less organized and entrenched in Tunisian society than in Egypt, competing interests in civil society may have had a greater opportunity to reach political consensus along human rights principles and avert a descent into anarchy or civil war. Conversely, one could maintain that the strong Egyptian military offered the prospect of a more stable—yet less flexible— transition toward democratic political pluralism, or else a return to the authoritarianism that preceded the revolution. In 2017, soon after the fourth anniversary of the June 30 coup that removed the Muslim Brotherhood from power, a former Muslim Brother told me that even the famous Egyptian sense of humor has disappeared, and a Cairene investor explained to me that the "Egyptians have moved from a police state to a military one." In short, while similar conditions in the two initiating states led to popular readiness to revolt and to the rapid collapse of the dictatorial regimes, the revolutionary consolidation stage brought different concerns to the fore, leading to different strategies and potentially different outcomes.

The societies of the latecomer states (Libya, Syria, and Yemen) were deeply divided, making them slower to launch their uprisings and more vulnerable as they encountered resistance. In Libya, the international community's initial engagement backfired. The uprising lasted eight months, and Gaddafi might still be in power had NATO not intervened. As soon as the regime was gone, however, the resulting vacuum triggered prolonged and ideologically motivated tribal warfare. The new transitory Libyan government was not able to solicit reliable support from the international community. The uprising in Syria, fed by Russia and Iran on one side and the West and the Gulf states on the other, also turned into a civil war. In Yemen, eleven months of fierce protests led to a US- and GCC-backed transfer of power from President Saleh. His successor, Mansur Hadi, was not able to stop the slide into civil war, which was animated by deep divisions along sectarian and tribal lines, overlapping with entrenched economic divides and opposing regional power interests. These civil wars, intensified by international actors, greatly impeded the consolidation phase for the latecomer states. Postrevolutionary consolidation must draw on a variety of factors, including human capital, economic resources, the effectiveness of state bureaucracy, and the views of influential outside actors. While Syria had a more educated population than others, Libya's domestic wealth, generated by its oil-based economy, seemed to provide greater postrevolutionary prospects. Yet state-promoted tribalism and sectarianism in both countries perpetuated a divide-and-rule authoritarianism that increased the duration and severity of the internal conflict.

The divided societies of Algeria, Morocco, and Lebanon failed to join the revolutionary contagion, in part because of their long histories of civil war and preventive political reforms. This is not to suggest that these countries were stable and well governed. In 2011, Algeria had more than 40 percent youth unemployment, and there were multiple protests in 2012 against housing shortages, food prices, police corruption, and other problems. Memories of their civil war during the 1990s, in which brutal military repression finally defeated a terrorist Islamist insurgency, may be the only reason Algerians have not turned to revolution.[39] In Morocco, a series of protests forced the king to institute political and constitutional reforms, but he retained ultimate control. Parliament was given more authority; Amazigh (Berber) became the second official language after Arabic; the king is no longer seen as "sacred" (though he remains "inviolable"); and international human rights conventions take primacy over national law.[40] Like Algeria and Morocco, Lebanon did not follow other Arab countries into revolution. Lebanese democratic institutions are better entrenched in civil society, the economy is overall in better shape, and as in Algeria, memories of civil war make the Lebanese averse to renewed domestic violence.

Despite a loosened alliance with the West, the GCC's enormous oil wealth enabled its members to preserve their regimes in the face of revolutionary uprisings and internal social division. Independent civil society hardly exists in these states, and old tribal loyalties combine with tight monarchical control over politics, society, and much of the economy. While the Arab hereditary monarchies have proven more stable than regimes that base their legitimacy on a nominal republican ideology (such as socialism or pan-Arab nationalism), they are not necessarily impervious to regime change. These countries can be compared to nineteenth-century Britain, whose elite warded off the continent's revolutionary contagion in 1848 by gradually adopting democratic reforms. England, however, was endowed with a far more vibrant civil society than the Gulf states.

The combination of wealth and weak civil society enabled the Gulf monarchs to buy stability by offering generous welfare programs and coopting disenchanted groups. In *Democracy in America*, Alexis de Tocqueville deplored revolutions that yielded to the tyranny of the majority, but he also blamed the French monarchists for failing to avoid the revolution, which he thought they could have done by undertaking substantive political reforms. Tocqueville's insight has not been sufficiently appreciated by the Gulf monarchs, whose repression of political dissent has increased since the Arab uprisings, their resistance to reform intensified by the rise of the Muslim Brotherhood, their growing fear of Iran, and the rise of the Islamic State at the gates of the Arabian Peninsula.[41]

HUMAN RIGHTS AND ITS CHALLENGES

In January 2011, the Levant Express was accelerating with blinding speed, spreading the message of human rights and freedom, but in 2012 it was derailed by the rise of Islamist parties. Then Egypt's military deposed the elected Muslim Brotherhood government in a 2013 coup, introducing yet more uncertainty into the prospects for democracy and human rights in the Middle East. The liberal impulse that had drawn passengers aboard the Levant Express was under challenge—both by the election of an Islamist party whose commitment to democracy was in doubt, and then by a coup that restored a measure of stability but crushed any short-term hopes for democracy.

Many revolutions never progress from the second to the third stage—from consolidation to democratization. John Locke reminds us in his *Second Treatise of Government* that removing dictators is far from easy, as people endure abuses for a long time before they demand radical change. Even if they succeed in consolidating the new regime, democratizing a society in accordance with human rights is harder to accomplish. Revolutions always create social vacuums, and leaders trying to build institutional stepping stones toward democratization must be aware that in unstable times, major reforms with unclear consequences could cause the state to collapse. Many counterrevolutions have rationalized their retreat to authoritarianism as rescuing society from the abyss of anarchy. This is not to suggest that the yearning for freedom and human rights that inspired the 2011 revolutions will be buried forever. When the call of human rights seems to have gone silent, it often continues—even intensifies—in less conspicuous venues, only to reemerge when the time proves again more propitious.

The recurrent human rights demands in the Arab world since World War I were driven by particular contexts, articulated selectively rather than comprehensively. They provided, however, a tradition of human rights discourse that was revived during the Arab uprisings and can still be reclaimed. The right to self-determination was championed during World War I and again during the struggle against imperialism after World War II; the call for economic rights emanated from underdeveloped postcolonial states during the Cold War; cultural rights were advocated against globalization, widely perceived as another form of Western intrusion; and civil and political rights moved to center stage when Arabs rose against their tyrannical governments. When we review these quests for rights from World War I to the present, we can see that each wave pushed human rights forward—even when wars and economic crises caused dire historical regressions—and that with each new wave, the discourse of human rights has become more comprehensive in the Arab world.

The Arab revolt of 1916–1918, led by Sharif Hussein bin Ali, sought a unified, independent state stretching from Aleppo in Syria to Aden in Yemen. However, with the Ottoman Empire collapsing, Britain and France were already making deals, particularly the 1916 Sykes-Picot Agreement, to divide the region based on imperial influence. In the 1919 Treaty of Versailles, imperial powers continued to infantilize the Arab world, informing Arab leaders that they were not ready to exercise their right to state sovereignty and that they needed to reach political maturity before claiming full control over their territories. A few decades earlier, Rudyard Kipling justified colonialism as the civilized man's moral responsibility to rule over people who were "half devil and half child" and who needed discipline and oversight in order to become fully civilized.[42] Kipling's famous poem "The White Man's Burden" reflected the mind-set of the imperial leaders who would continue to dominate the Middle East after World War I, when most Arabs were given only partial independence at best.

After the devastation of a second world war in Europe and worldwide anticolonial struggles, the 1948 Universal Declaration of Human Rights (UDHR) created new opportunities in the Middle East. Most Muslim countries were not yet members of the UN, although several of those that were independent—including Egypt, Iran, and Pakistan—signed the UDHR. Charles Malik, Lebanon's ambassador to the UN, was a member of the first Commission of Human Rights and a contributing drafter of the UDHR. "What interests me most concerning this question of the Bill of Rights," he said, "is the whole problem of personal liberty. . . . [I]f we fail in the formulation of our International Bill of Rights, it is not going to be on the grounds of failing to state explicitly the rights of the individual for food, housing, work, migration. . . . Rather, it will be on the grounds of failing to allow sufficiently for the all-fundamental problem of personal liberty."[43] Not all Arab leaders agreed. Saudi Arabia and Yemen did not vote in favor of the UDHR, and Saudi King Abdul Aziz reasserted his adherence to Shari'a law and the Qur'an. The declaration, he claimed, was drafted in violation of Islamic law and failed to take into account the cultural values and religious beliefs of non-Western countries.[44] The conflict between religious and individual liberties would reemerge later as a core human rights debate in the Middle East.

During the Cold War, an imperialist and paternalistic version of human rights, with its vestigial intimations of the "white man's burden," was rejected with growing disdain in what became known as the "Third World." Those who fought for self-determination would not allow a repeat of Versailles. On the other hand, the UDHR provided a powerful weapon in the arsenal of human rights activists against efforts by European powers to retain their colonies. It would similarly strengthen the fight against apartheid in South Africa and would be invoked by numerous groups seeking self-determination. Although few Arab states were independent immediately after World War II, the anticolonial struggle filled the regional map with sovereign states. In 1966, when the right to self-determination was stated in the first common article of the International Covenant on Civil and Political Rights (ICCPR) and the International Covenant on Economic, Social and Cultural Rights (ICESCR), there were thirteen Arab states; nine more came into existence within the next few years. With the exception of the Palestinians and the Kurds, the right to self-determination seemed to be secured across the Middle East.

With more Arab states becoming members of the United Nations, a new wave of human rights claims shifted toward economic rights. Developing countries upheld the ICESCR as a critical document, to be contrasted with the notions of individual rights, often associated with the ICCPR and widely praised in the West. Arab elites insisted that, only after the successful modernization of a newly independent state, individual rights (viewed as secondary) could be implemented. Despots everywhere have asserted that national development justified the suppression of individual rights. In the Middle East, the charismatic Egyptian president Gamal Abdel Nasser offered that line of argument: "The first essence of the Revolution was to tear down the social barriers between classes and the redistribution of the countries [sic] wealth more fairly. It also aimed to restore the basic freedoms to the regular Egyptian citizen, such as the freedom to work, the freedom of sustenance, the freedom of owning the land he toils, the freedom to protect himself and his family, and the right to a share of the national wealth and to superintend it. These are all rights and freedoms, which helped the citizen to restore his sense of honor and personal dignity, both of which are a natural human right."[45]

With the waning of the Cold War, chronic economic crises, and state failures to implement equitable economic reforms, authoritarian leaders continued to regard pressure for civil and political rights as a threat to their regimes. Concessions to Islamists were not new but now à l'ordre du jour; it was useful to counter liberal demands by invoking adherence to a 1,400-year-old religious order. Sayyid Abu al-Ala Mawdudi, an influential Muslim theologian, claimed that human rights originated in Islam and had been distorted by the West. In his view, the rights given by the Prophet outweighed competing conceptions of social justice. "It refreshes and strengthens our faith in Islam," he wrote, "when we realize that even in

this modern age which makes such loud claims of progress and enlightenment, the world has not been able to produce juster [sic] and more equitable laws than those given 1400 years ago."[46]

In 1989, the fall of the Berlin Wall sent a shockwave through the
world. With the collapse of the Communist bloc, the maestros of globalization announced the universal triumph of Western liberalism over the
parochial notions of cultural rights championed by religious leaders in
the Middle East, Asia, and Africa. Islamist defenders of cultural rights
replied defensively to the spread of Western culture by promulgating the
1990 Cairo Declaration of Human Rights, which offered both an Islamic
view of human rights and a reaffirmation of Islamic Shari'a as a guide for
Arab states. Article 1 affirmed that true faith is the only guarantee for
enhancing dignity along the path to human perfection and that Islam is
"the religion of unspoiled nature." In its reliance on Shari'a law, however,
the Cairo Declaration failed to protect the equal rights of women and non-
Muslim minorities, putting it in direct conflict with the idea of universal
rights. These chasms between Islam and Western values were captured
by Samuel Huntington as "a clash of civilizations."

Among the things Huntington did not anticipate was that clashes
over the meaning of human rights could erupt *within* the Arab world. The
Cairo Declaration's challenge to women's rights, combined with the rise
of Islamism and civil war in Algeria, contributed to a sudden rise in
women's rights organizations in the Middle East. In Algeria, Tunisia,
Egypt, Morocco, and the Palestinian territories, women devised new strategies to gain influence in the public sphere. Many women's organizations
were sponsored by the UN Economic and Social Commission for Western
Asia (ESCWA), based permanently in Beirut. In preparation for and
subsequent to the 1995 Fourth World Conference on Women in Beijing,
ESCWA publications addressed women's lack of employment rights in
the workforce, the absence of civil rights, and the inequality between
women and men in positions of authority. The organization also called for
an end to domestic violence and honor killing.[47]

Such demands encroached upon the Islamist worldview, which was
also making political inroads in the 1990s. Secular authorities found it
convenient to side with the Islamists against increased demands for
universal human rights, and rights violations intensified in the MENA
region as the new millennium approached. Guardians of the international

order continued to ally with the dictatorships of Ben Ali, Hosni Mubarak, Bashar al-Assad, and other dictators to secure their geopolitical and economic interests. Military repression, police brutality, and torture (often in cooperation with Western intelligence agencies) increased after the September 11 attacks further justified emergency laws in the name of "national security." A revolutionary situation, intensified by the 2008 global economic recession, continued to brew beneath the radar of dictators despite many forewarnings.

The Arab scholars and former senior level policy makers who drafted the UN Development Program's Arab Human Development Report in 2009 wanted to shift the world's attention from national to human security, and to the persistent obstacles to human development in the MENA. Their analysis drew attention to the fragility of the region's political, social, and economic structures, its lack of people-centered development policies, and its vulnerability to outside intervention. "In the Arab region," the report states, "human insecurity—pervasive, often intense and with consequences affecting large numbers of people—inhibits human development. It is revealed in the impacts of military occupation and armed conflict in Iraq, Sudan, Somalia and Occupied Palestinian Territory. It is found in countries that enjoy relative stability where the authoritarian state, buttressed by flawed constitutions and unjust laws, often denies citizens their rights."[48] The report, widely read in the fields of development and human rights, fell on deaf ears in both Arab and Western policy-making circles. The absence of political reforms, compounded by the economic crisis that followed the 2008 global recession, as unemployment rose despite improved levels of literacy and education, turned the Levant into a fertile site for popular revolts. Demands for human rights ascended again, thanks to the renewed activism of NGOs, unions, bloggers, and women.

After the 2011 uprisings, constitutional reforms moved some nations toward democracy. Tunisia took critical steps in that direction. Unlike their Egyptian counterparts, Tunisia's revolutionary leaders were able to institutionalize a pluralist society thanks to a constitution based on human rights, without fear of retaliation by Tunisia's relatively weak military. While Tunisians negotiated differences in a parliamentary setting, the Egyptian army reestablished its power to prevent consolidation by an Islamist regime. Unlike Egyptian civil society, Tunisia's, with a longer tradition of human rights activism, was sturdier and in a better position to supplant the old regime. Nonetheless, democratization is still far from complete. Many Tunisian intellectuals rightly believe that to consolidate a democratic civil and political revolution, the nation still needs a social revolution, and that the future of their country may yet be imperiled by a weak economy and the continuing threat of Islamist terrorism.

As I write this, we have witnessed across the Arab Middle East both the first stage of revolution—the toppling of some authoritarian regimes— and to some degree the second: consolidation with the formation of new governments. Everywhere except Tunisia, however, human rights have encountered tragic obstacles. That does not negate the historical mile-stones that marked progress from the Arab rebellion in 1916, to the anti-colonial struggle after World War II, to the 2011 uprisings. Recent reversals may not be dissimilar from what was experienced in Europe, which required more than a hundred years of human rights benchmarks to foster an environment amenable to sustainable human rights regimes.

Sadly, the counter-Enlightenment has now taken center stage, as radical Islamists have expanded their reach in Tunisia, Syria, Iraq, Libya, and beyond, authoritarian regimes have intensified their repression, and sectarian violence persists in much of the region. Capturing the transition from the Age of Reason to Romanticism (which announced the era of nationalism), the German philosopher G. W. Hegel evoked the image of the "owl of Minerva spreading its wings only with the falling of the dusk."[49] History can be understood only as a series of contradictory stages. The furious return of religious radicalism has shifted our Levant Express into reverse.

PART TWO   DERAILMENT: HUMAN RIGHTS IN RETREAT

WITH THE END OF THE FRENCH REVOLUTION, the Age of Reason came to a halt. With the end of the Arab revolutions, the Enlightenment faded into a blur. In its place, "faith and patriotism [became] the greatest thaumaturges of this world. The one and the other are divine: all their actions are prodigies. Do not talk to them about the examination of choice, of discussion: they will tell you that you are blaspheming, they only know two words: submission and faith."[1] The French aristocrat and advocate of the counter-Enlightenment, Joseph de Maistre, offered these insights in the first decades of the nineteenth century; they seem all too applicable today.

Antiliberal reactions, such as the extreme version experienced after the Arab uprisings, often follow unsuccessful human rights struggles. The Concert of Europe, comprising the major regional powers, crushed the democratic revolutions of 1848. Similarly, during the period following World War I, Italian Fascists and German Nazis crushed the human rights spirit of the League of Nations, mocking Woodrow Wilson's claim that US intervention in World War I would make the world "safe for democracy." When the human rights struggle against colonialism finally ended after World War II, dictators of the Left and the Right in the newly independent states repressed democratic socialist movements throughout Asia and Africa. Today, on the heels of the 2011 Arab uprising that promised the promotion of human rights, reactionary Islamists—and in one small corner of the region, Jewish organizations—have joined the ranks of history's anti-Enlightenment movements.

RAILROADS AND REFUGEES

The poster "Railroads and Refugees" depicts two trains, each crammed with refugees. One, on the left side, is exiting Berlin. The other, on the right, is arriving. The first train is filled with Jewish refugees fleeing after Kristallnacht, the first Nazi mass murder of Jews, in November 1938. The second overflows with Syrian refugees, escaping sectarian warfare in the Middle East almost eighty years later. In the middle of the poster, the majestic columns of the Konzerthaus are completely wrapped in 14,000 orange life vests, discarded by Syrian refugees as they arrived at the Greek island of Lesbos. Transported to Berlin and assembled here by the dissident Chinese artist Ai Weiwei, the life vests give a visual testimony to an unfolding human tragedy. Created by Brooke VanDevelder, 2017 (© 2017 Micheline Ishay).

How can past counter-Enlightenment episodes help us understand the Islamist reaction to the Arab uprising? When great powers loosen their control over a region and when the absence of external support leaves a revolutionary state unable to deliver sufficient social and economic goods to its population, a political vacuum is created. In the absence of a viable liberal alternative, nationalist or religious ideological fervor can fill these political voids, sinking their roots into the fissures of civil societies. Popular appeals to cultural pride, the myth of the nation, or religious identity can transcend selfish instrumental and material interests, inspiring a broader sense of national or supranational unity (for example, ISIS's vision of a caliphate). As demagogues summon lost sheep to return to the safety of the fold, illiberal and regressive agendas reshape the political terrain, their ideology scorching the land through various media. Widespread revolutions trigger chaos, unleashing civilizational crises and greater hostility toward the dispossessed. For the inhabitants of postrevolutionary states and beyond, the only anchors remain the clan, the tribe, the nation, or the religious community. In those circumstances, charismatic leaders assuage the fear produced by social tumults and wars by offering visions of solidarity, enticing anxious citizens to enter a lost paradise.

The dark side of modernization, already exposed during the Cold War, had grown increasingly evident under the reign of globalist conquistadors. Politicized religious leaders challenged the dictates of neoliberalism, thriving in places where political legitimacy was eroded by chronic crises. The regionwide appeal of political Islam and the growing political influence within Israel of Orthodox Judaism are partially attributable to vast and deepening inequalities in wealth and income within the MENA region. Religious movements stepped in to galvanize the poor and the disenfranchised, fought to resurrect traditional communities, and restructured politics according to divine interpretations. In its extreme form, belligerent Islamism bears striking ideological, social, and economic similarities to historical fascism from the interwar period. If all these anti-Enlightenment movements emphasized equity for the disenfranchised, they simultaneously conveyed a more sinister message that the persecution or exclusion of minorities is essential to cleanse one's nation—or one's caliphate—from alleged spoilers.

CHAPTER THREE

Arab Winters

NONE OF THE ARAB REBELLIONS has arrived at a happy end. Libya, Syria, and Yemen are torn by civil war; Egypt and Bahrain are more repressively authoritarian than they were before the 2011 protests. Many Middle Eastern cities have fallen into ruin, and millions of refugees have fled their homes. Tunisia, the one beacon of hope during the uprisings, suffered alarming setbacks in 2015 when a terrorist attack at the Bardo Museum in Carthage killed twenty-two people, and another thirty-eight were massacred at a seaside resort in the coastal city of Sousse. The Arab Spring of Nations turned into an Arab Winter with the rise of the Muslim Brotherhood in 2012 and the spread of jihadism from the Arabian Peninsula across the Maghreb.

On the other side of the Mediterranean, yet connected to the drama in the Levant, Berlin stands at the center of a historical irony. In 1941, hundreds of thousands of German Jews were deported by train to concentration camps. Today, from the vestige of Hitler's bunker to the Museum of Terror, many relics of Berlin's dark history remain evident throughout the city. Yet the city now styles itself a sort of German Ellis Island, a clearing site for hundreds of thousands of Syrians seeking asylum in Europe. If, in the wreckage of World War II, Berlin was seen as a city of despair, today it is the destination of desperate families displaced by the Syrian civil war that began in 2011.[1] At least sixty million people lost their

#SafePassage, by Ai Weiwei, 2016. Image courtesy of Oliver Lang, © Oliver Lang, 2016.

lives in World War II; the casualties from Syria, Iraq, and Yemen remain small in comparison. Yet despite the vast differences between those two times and places, the powerful anti-Enlightenment movements represented by European fascism and Middle Eastern religious radicalism have much in common.

Some may argue that this is nothing new, that radical religious violence has been a feature of Islam since its origins. Many Westerners insist that the chronic tensions within the Muslim world leave little hope for change; they regard the conflict in the Middle East as insoluble, both internally between Sunni and Shi'a and externally between Islam and the West. These views falsely reduce Islamic societies to monolithic entities dominated by predetermined and fixed characteristics.[2]

History validates a different set of propositions. First, counter-Enlightenment ideologies have often thrived after failed human rights promises, finding a sympathetic audience among people in dire socioeconomic circumstances and fractured civil societies. Second, extreme counter-Enlightenment worldviews—such as historical fascism and the ideology of the Islamic State of Iraq and Syria (ISIS, also commonly known as Daesh)—harness social despair and popular fears through the ideological appeal of a charismatic leader championing a higher national or religious cause. Third, to achieve greater unity, these ideologies target domestic scapegoats and allegedly evil outsiders, ultimately propelling refugees to seek safety in exile.

WAVES OF COUNTER-ENLIGHTENMENT

The transformative and often socially disruptive global capitalist economy has imposed shifting pressures on modernizing societies. During the interwar period in Europe, from 1918 to 1939, depression and economic protectionism curtailed the economic growth necessary for postwar recovery and domestic stability, setting the stage for the rise of extremist movements. In the Gulf countries, the oil boom of the 1970s brought great wealth to Iran and Saudi Arabia, but it created social inequities that enabled a radical version of political Islam to reach commanding heights.

European fascism and extremist Islamism both reacted against international orders perceived to be unjust, and both grew from popular frustration with the government's inability or unwillingness to redress those grievances. In Italy, the fascists believed that the country's more powerful allies in World War I failed to give Italy a sufficient share of victory's spoils. In Germany, they railed against the punitive peace imposed by the Treaty of Versailles and the liberal international order orchestrated by the League of Nations. Yet neither moderate liberalism nor democratic socialism could gain traction in either nation. A combination of weak state structures and divided civil society created fertile ground for what the Italian communist leader Antonio Gramsci called "Bonapartism" or "Caesarism"—the appearance of a strongman who promises to transcend the conflicts tearing society apart.[3] Exploiting popular fears of both Bolshevism and concentrated capitalist wealth, Benito Mussolini advanced an anti-Enlightenment ideology based on a single organic community united by a similar creed, forging an alliance between the church, the military, and, as historian Eric Hobsbawm put it, the "little men, in a society that crushed them between the rock of big business on one side and the hard place of rising mass labor movements on the other."[4]

Islamic fundamentalism thrived decades later in a world that in many ways resembled 1920s Europe. People in the Middle East felt deep grievances over externally imposed arrangements, including humiliation at the hands of outside powers and a destabilizing encounter with globalizing capitalism. The region was beset by an unstable international order, nonhegemonic civil societies, weak state structures, and Bonapartist bids for power in the name of a transcendent, extreme nationalism. These socioeconomic and structural dynamics helped propel five Islamist waves.

The First Islamist Wave: The 1967 Six-Day War and the
Rise of Political Islam

The conclusion of the June 1967 war between Israel and the alliance of Egypt, Jordan, and Syria was seen in the Arab world as a catastrophic event. The dream of secular pan-Arabist unity, heralded by Sati' al-Husri and Gamal Abdel Nasser after Arab decolonization, was gravely weakened. The young Israeli state had humiliated its neighbors, particularly the armed forces of Nasser, the iconic figure of Arab nationalism. Egypt's military defeat coincided with growing social tension and a national economic crisis. Centralized state socialism was not delivering on its promise. Peasants, workers, and students, following in the footsteps of the 1965 Qamish peasant uprisings, challenged the social compact based on Arab nationalism. Elsewhere, rising social and economic tensions, exacerbated by the Arab defeat in the Six-Day War, yielded military coups in Iraq (1968), Sudan (1969), and Libya (1969). Humiliation, rage, and instability swept the region like a prairie fire.[5]

In Egypt and other leading Arab states, the situation might be summarized as the "crisis of the petty bourgeois regimes."[6] The crisis did not lead to radicalization from the Left but rather toward conservative alternatives. In Egypt, as Nasser's nationalism nursed its wounds, the Muslim Brotherhood—an Islamist religious and political organization founded in 1928 by Hassan al-Banna—took advantage of social inequity and a fragmented civil society to gain political influence. While the Brothers suffered a series of governmental crackdowns, imprisonments, and executions, Nasser's followers intermittently appeased them to stem popular unrest. Egypt's policies had to accommodate both the middle class and the Brotherhood at home, as well as conservative Arab regimes such as Saudi Arabia and Kuwait.

The Brothers eventually exported their ideology to establish branches throughout the Middle East. In each country, they presented themselves as a political alternative, drawing on Egyptian theologian Sayyid Qutb's lamentation that the world had lapsed into a new *jahiliyya*—a state of ignorance and false belief similar to what had prevailed before the arrival of the Prophet Muhammad. Faithful Muslims, Qutb wrote in *Milestones*, needed to purge the political system of corruption and reclaim ideal Islamic communities (*salfiyya*). This conservative religious influence would be further radicalized and popularized during the mid-1970s

Sayyid Qutb in prison, Nasser's Egypt, 1966.

as a vast infusion of oil wealth wreaked havoc on traditional societies, creating the preconditions for the triumph of theocracy in Iran and for Islamism's tightening grip on the Saudi monarchy.

The Second Islamist Wave: The Oil Crisis, the Iranian Revolution,
and the Rise of Saudi Arabia
In Iran, the association of the prevailing power structure with humiliating external control was sealed by the US-backed coup that installed Shah Mohamed Reza Pahlavi in 1953. The shah's "white revolution" included significant reforms: he extended suffrage to women, improved the education system, began a free government program to nourish school children, and stewarded important infrastructural, technological, and cultural projects. In a 1974 interview, he promised: "In twenty-five years, Iran will be one of the world's five flourishing and prosperous nations."[7] Despite the shah's oath to protect the constitution and promote social justice, inequality and popular disenchantment grew.[8] The quadrupling of oil prices led by Iran and Saudi Arabia in 1973 should have lifted most Iranians from poverty, but the shah and his entourage spent most of the new cash on strengthening the military and paid little attention to the middle and lower classes. The coercive state apparatus, vast arms purchases, and mismanaged modernization programs challenged landowners, outlawed independent trade unions, weakened both traditional

merchants and the fledgling middle class, and utterly impoverished the peasantry, stimulating massive migration to urban shantytowns.

In Iran's weak and fragmented civil society, a broad segment of the population proved receptive to Ayatollah Khomeini's condemnation of modernity and secularization, adopting his vision of an Islamic state. As thousands of demonstrators called for the death of their secular ruler, the shah fled his country on January 16, 1979. A few days later, Khomeini, surrounded by his revolutionary guards, emerged as the new Bonaparte to fill the political vacuum. Forging and then discarding tactical alliances with other opposition groups, Khomeini's Islamist revolutionary commit-tees and tribunals began murdering thousands of leftist and liberal opponents, consolidating radical fundamentalism in the new theocratic state.

Saudi Arabia, which had scarcely pursued economic growth and modernity since the state was founded in 1923, found its economy growing explosively in the 1970s due to vast oil wealth, and by the end of the decade it had become the primary Sunni counterforce to the Iranian Shi'a theocracy. Sudden affluence brought increased Western influence and almost instantaneous modernization, including women appearing on television and wearing bikinis at hotel swimming pools. In *Inside the Kingdom*, Robert Lacey depicted the new hopes of traditional Saudi people, as well as their sudden estrangement: "The money came. Everybody bought cars, drove out of town and built themselves villas behind high walls . . . and suddenly we found we were separate. We felt somehow empty inside."9 Not surprisingly, Sunni religious radicals denounced the embrace of modernization.

When an ultraconservative Islamic group calling itself al-Ikhwan briefly took over the Grand Mosque at Mecca in an attempt to overthrow the Saudi monarchy in November 1979, the rulers feared the spread of insurrection. Mindful of Khomeini's claim of religious authority over all of Islam, they worried about their vulnerability to radicals within the kingdom and calculated that they could best avert both internal and external Islamist threats by embracing their own brand of Salafism. After reaching a political modus vivendi with the conservative Wahhabists, the regime continued its cautious modernization while counterbalancing Iranian expansionism in the region. The rise of Islamist theocracies in the Gulf's two most powerful states, each committed to a hegemonic

Shi'as and Sunnis in the Middle East

Author: Douglas Winter   Copyright Micheline Ishay   2017

Shi'as and Sunnis in the Middle East. Map by Douglas Winter and Micheline Ishay
(© 2017 Micheline Ishay).

vision based on its particular understanding of Islam, set the stage for extensions of radical Islam—not to mention conflict between the major factions—far beyond their borders. If the embrace of radical Islamist aspirations by the two leading Gulf states represented a second Islamist wave, the regional expansion of their rivalry initiated a third wave that continues today.

The Third Islamist Wave: Iranian and Saudi Regional Imperialisms

For Khomeini, Islam's scope was universal, and Shi'a revivalism demanded that the revolution be exported. Competing with Saudi Arabia for geopolitical influence and Islamist legitimacy, Iran, starting in the 1980s, sent hundreds of *pasdaran* (revolutionary guards) to train the emerging Hezbollah organization in South Lebanon, helping the Shi'a in their struggle against Israeli occupation. The Saudis, meanwhile, set out to spread Wahhabism throughout the region. They backed Zia ul Haq, the Islamist ruler of Pakistan, and financed Islamist insurgents against the Soviet occupation of Afghanistan. For years, the competition between Saudi Arabia and Iran unfolded through proxies. Later, the end of the Cold War and the loss of US interest in the region enabled al-Qaeda— whose interpretation of Wahhabism repudiated the legitimacy of the Saudi ruling family—to expand with little notice.

The US invasion of Iraq in 2003 created a major new battleground for Sunni-Shi'a sectarianism. The removal of Saddam Hussein empowered Iraq's Shi'a majority and drove many Sunnis into the hands of al-Qaeda, whose barbaric attacks on Shi'a civilians provoked intervention by Iran and various extremist Shi'a militias. This virulent Islamist sectarianism resurfaced with a vengeance after the US withdrew from Iraq in 2010, even as the Arab Spring's rage against the region's secular Arab nationalist dictators created still more power vacuums to be exploited by Islamist political movements.

The Fourth Islamist Wave: The Muslim Brotherhood Wins Elections

The rise of jihadist nonstate actors gained new momentum with the fall of Arab secular nationalist leaders during the 2011 uprisings. For over a year, hopes for human rights were raised throughout the Arab world, but enduring economic and institutional problems soon punctured those dreams. Foreign investments, stimulated by an early liberalization policy in the 1990s, enriched Arab nationalist leaders and their kleptocratic entourages but failed to meet basic popular needs. The proclaimed benefits of global economic integration never reached Tunisia, Egypt, Libya, or Iraq. Sclerotic local economies, made worse by the 2008 global recession, left a third of young adults unemployed and created fertile soil for revolution. After the departure of Ben Ali and Hosni Mubarak, the Muslim Brotherhood—by far the best-organized opposition party—attempted to fill the political and ideological vacuum by installing Mohamed Morsi in Egypt and the Ennahdha government in Tunisia. This revival of political Islam, coupled with the US withdrawal from Iraq, dashed liberals' hopes for an enduring Arab Spring.

The political victory of the Muslim Brotherhood in 2012 surprised the world, as they and the Salafists had remained largely in the shadows throughout 2011. While the Brothers were sufficiently well organized to take power, however, their first effort at governing proved to be a disaster. It is not uncommon to see tactical alliances among revolutionary groups disintegrate after an old regime is toppled. In 1848 France, the working class joined with liberals in a democratic revolt against the aristocracy. Once successful, the liberals balked at extending voting rights to their less privileged allies, and the revolution collapsed. In 2012 Egypt, it was the liberals who felt betrayed by the more powerful Muslim Brotherhood. Not only had the liberals led the revolution while the Brotherhood held back, but many voted for Morsi based on the Brotherhood's promise to build an inclusive democracy. After their victory, however, Morsi and the Muslim Brothers imposed a constitution that enshrined Islamic Shari'a law as a basis for legislation, directly challenging the rights of women and rejecting universal human rights as the foundation of governance. Combined with Morsi's failure to address Egypt's economic free fall, this set the stage for social protests and instability throughout 2012.

In Tunisia, with a relatively better educated and more literate public than in Egypt, there was a better chance that Ennahdha (the Tunisian Muslim Brotherhood party) would accommodate liberal parties and successfully consolidate the revolution. The World Bank approved a $500-million loan, and the United States, the European Union, and Qatar offered loans of $300 million, $400 million, and $500 million, respectively.[10] But the country's precarious economic situation, worsened by political instability, challenged the Muslim Brotherhood's hold on power. In late 2012, with Tunisia still at a political and economic crossroad and the government still not meeting most Tunisians' basic expectations, there were new waves of social unrest and widespread demands for a more progressive constitution. Since that constitution was not yet written, however, elections were postponed until the following year.

While newly enfranchised Tunisians and Egyptians were working arduously to consolidate their electoral victories in the second act of their revolutions, Gulf monarchs were working equally hard to ward off the contagion of popular revolt. Following the Bahraini crackdown of 2011, the Gulf Cooperation Council moved toward a policy of zero tolerance for any group challenging monarchic rule. In Saudi Arabia, even a mild appeal for political reform could bring arrest or deportation. After briefly tolerating a degree of public discussion of democratic reform, the UAE muzzled freedom of expression in academia, the press, and on the Internet. At the same time, recognizing the role of economic discontent in igniting the Arab Spring, Saudi Arabia and the UAE channeled tens of billions of dollars into their most impoverished areas. In less wealthy Oman, stirrings of labor unrest promptly resulted in higher wages, even as protests were repressed. The rulers of Kuwait suspended their nation's parliament, then dominated by elected Islamist representatives, in May 2012. With the notable exception of Qatar, the Gulf monarchies began to treat the Muslim Brotherhood as an increasingly serious threat and to take decisive steps in defense of authoritarian rule. In 2012, ninety-four Emiratis were jailed for allegedly plotting to overthrow the ruling dynasty. The UAE rulers concluded that the Egyptian Muslim Brotherhood was responsible for the plot and had several Egyptians arrested as well. Islah, the Emirati branch of the Muslim Brotherhood, went underground, and Saudi and UAE monarchs joined Egypt's secular liberals in supporting a military coup in Egypt. They believed a government in Egypt led by the Muslim Brotherhood posed an intolerable threat to their own regimes, although an even more radical wave of Islamism was looming.

The Fifth Islamist Wave: The Spread of Jihadism and ISIS

Al-Husri's prophecy of secular Arab unity was now a distant dream, and political Islam promised to be the purifying movement capable of unifying Arab people against corrupt secular regimes. If the Muslim Brotherhood's 2012 triumph in Egypt had sent a chill through liberal circles, however, the growing power of more radical fundamentalists in Syria, Iraq, and Libya in 2014 was even more shocking. Libya, a weak state incapable of unifying after the toppling of the Gaddafi regime, increasingly became a hotbed of Islamist radicalism. Elections for a General National Congress took place in July 2011, but the impotent interim government was challenged by numerous well-armed militias that refused to disband. Libya was soon overcome by escalating violence in the form of tribal clashes, deadly attacks on foreign diplomatic missions and international organizations, destruction of religious sites, kidnappings, and targeted killings.

These disquieting developments can be traced to the initial months of the Arab uprising, particularly in Libya, where the post-Gaddafi era offered fertile ground for jihadist organizations. Before the 2011 uprising, Libya's most organized fundamentalist movement, the Libyan Islamic Fighting Group, had de-radicalized and largely disbanded. As the dust of the revolution settled and tensions grew between the eastern and western parts of the country, new groups emerged, including Ansar al-Shari'a in Benghazi. In 2012 and 2013, two events marked Libya's further destabilization: American Ambassador Christopher Stevens was killed by a jihadist attack on the American Embassy in Benghazi, and Libyan Prime Minister Ali Zidan was briefly kidnapped by an Islamist militia. With gang members disguised as revolutionaries and revolutionaries turning into jihadists, the increasingly lawless country became a gathering place for al-Qaeda-allied groups from around the world. When it had the chance, the state had failed to create legitimacy, build consensus between tribal divisions, equitably distribute the nation's oil wealth, or form a competent national army representing all tribal factions; now the nation was paying the price.

Several hundred miles to the northeast, the Syrian revolution would fail to achieve even its initial aim. Unlike in Libya, where Western military intervention shifted the balance in favor of the uprising, the Syrian opposition faced a formidable army heavily assisted by external Shi'a forces. The effort to topple the Syrian dictator Bashar al-Assad quickly spiraled into a humanitarian disaster. State-led violence against peaceful mass protests spawned civil war. Sharp internal divisions, intensified by the wider Sunni-Shi'a conflict, turned the civil war into a sectarian struggle. The Syrian Alawite Assad family, supported by Iran and the Iran-financed Hezbollah Party, was opposed by the region's Sunni-dominated states, led by the wealthiest members of the GCC. Amid escalating violence on both sides, Islamist extremists in Syria became far stronger than the jihadist insurgency in Libya, drawing some moderate opposition factions into tactical alliances, and mercilessly attacking those who resisted.

Yemen became another hotbed of jihadism. Despite diplomatic efforts by the US and the Saudis to restore some form of stability, the Yemeni uprising did not end after the 2012 departure of President Ali

Abdullah Saleh. Instead, civil war intensified, with two opposing factions claiming to represent the Yemeni government. The Shi'a Houthis, still in control of the capital of Sana'a and the northwest region of the country, remained affiliated with Saleh. They clashed with rival forces supporting the new president, Abd Rabbuh Mansur Hadi, whom they captured and kept under virtual house arrest before forcing him to relocate to Aden. The fragmented Yemeni society became fertile terrain for two rival extremist Sunni groups: al-Qaeda in the Arabian Peninsula (AQAP), which controlled a strip of territories in the hinterland and sections of the coasts, and the even more radical ISIS, which siphoned members from AQAP.[11] Just as in Syria, outsiders helped fuel the conflict. Saudi Arabia went to war in support of Mansur Hadi's forces, and Iran sided with the Houthis, locking the two regional powers into a proxy war as the Yemeni population descended into another humanitarian disaster.

These enclaves of jihadism mushroomed with the United States' withdrawal from Iraq and the political marginalization of Iraq's Sunni population by Prime Minister Nuri al-Maliki. Many disenfranchised Sunnis now joined ISIS. That movement, which had originated as an Iraqi branch of al-Qaeda following the 2003 US invasion, grew rapidly under the charismatic leadership of Abu Bakr al-Baghdadi, recognized for his strict Salafist interpretation of Islam and his merciless brutality, particularly toward Shi'a Muslims. Even his former allies in al-Qaeda disavowed his cruelty. Al-Baghdadi and his followers aspired to establish a unified Islamist hegemony in the Levant under a new caliphate, first absorbing the current states of Iraq, Syria, Libya, and Yemen and then targeting Jordan, Israel and Palestine, Lebanon, Kuwait, Cyprus, and Hatay in southern Turkey.

After gaining control over major cities, such as Raqqa in Syria and Mosul in Iraq, ISIS offered a demonstration of how life would be organized in its caliphate. "Rome will be conquered next," al-Baghdadi announced, as he vowed to protect Muslims from China to Burma and from India to Palestine.[12] His rapid conquest of large parts of Syria and Iraq and the carnage he inflicted on non-Sunni civilians vastly escalated the region's sectarian conflict, increasing the terrorist threat within and beyond the region. It seemed possible that the sectarian war would draw the region's entire population, from North Africa to Iran, into a fundamentalist Armageddon, as each sect became dominated by its most radical elements. Was this, one might wonder, the beginning of an Arab War of Reformation similar to the Thirty Years' War from 1618 to 1648 between Catholics and Protestants—a conflict that killed off a third of the population in what is now Germany?

Since 2011, hundreds of thousands of people have died in Syria, Iraq, Libya, Yemen, Bahrain, Egypt, and Gaza, making this one of the bloodiest periods of Middle East history. Innocents have been killed by Assad's barrel bombs, massacred by ISIS, struck by Saudi airstrikes in Yemen, caught in the crossfire of countless ground battles, or blown up in suicide bombings from Benghazi to Baghdad, often in the name of God. Christian and Yazidi women were raped and sold as slaves, and unknown numbers of ISIS victims were beheaded, crucified, or set on fire. Feeling compelled to react, but without clear direction, the West forged coalitions with "enemies of enemies" in a world of obscure alignments and ambivalent partners.

Building on al-Qaeda while expanding its aims, ISIS developed a two-pronged strategy to achieve power: guerrilla warfare based on attrition and a state-building strategy. The first, which ISIS strategists called a "war of vexation," was intended both to distract enemies' attention and gain local support in troubled areas such as Yemen and Nigeria, while the second focused on centralizing ISIS operations in Syria and Iraq. In each of these contexts, ISIS devised ways to "manage savagery" in pursuit of its ultimate aim: the consolidation of a caliphate whose influence would stretch into the future *ummah*, the worldwide Muslim community. With Iraqi Sunnis marginalized under the US-backed Maliki government, ISIS was able to recruit highly skilled Iraqis to operate its oil refineries and administer the bureaucracy of its proclaimed caliphate.[13]

During the summer of 2014, as ISIS forces reached within an hour's drive of Baghdad, the United States forced the resignation of Iraqi Prime Minister Maliki; hastily assembled a coalition that included England, France, and most of the Sunni Arab states; and returned to war in the Middle East. As of this writing, Iraqi-led ground forces backed by US-dominated airstrikes have killed tens of thousands of ISIS fighters and have liberated Mosul, the last Iraqi city under al-Baghdadi's control. In Syria, US-led airstrikes and a coalition of Arab and Kurdish ground forces that surrounded Raqqa have brought the caliphate to a bloody end. Yet many regional analysts agree that unless the West has a corresponding diplomatic strategy for redressing the roots of sectarian strife, ISIS will likely return to the guerrilla and terrorist tactics it initially employed in Iraq—tactics that it has consistently employed outside of its now-dissolved caliphate, in Egypt, Libya, Pakistan, Afghanistan, Somalia, Nigeria, Paris, and Brussels, and through the use of "lone wolves" recruited online in the United States and elsewhere. With Russia and Turkey drawn into combat on opposite sides of the sectarian divide, only history will judge whether and how the destruction of the purported caliphate will affect the overall level of violence in the MENA region. In its initial phase of rapid conquest, ISIS's goals were reminiscent of Nazism's lebensraum policy. The similarity is particularly striking when we compare the ideologies of these two movements.

HISTORICAL FASCISM AND ISLAMIC BELLIGERENCE[14]

The word "fascism," as Zeev Sternhell observed, is often invoked "as *the* term of abuse par excellence, conclusive and unanswerable."[15] George W. Bush's critics felt his use of the term "Islamofascists"[16] fell into this category—an epithet used to dramatize the adversaries' evil nature, but not a meaningful characterization of their goals or ideology. Here, my use of the term "fascism" refers to the movements that emerged after World War I, characterized by Walter Laqueur as "headed by a leader who had virtually unlimited power, was adulated by his followers, and was the focus of a quasi-religious cult. The party's doctrine became an obligatory act of faith."[17] While the state was the centerpiece of that doctrine, some European fascist movements also combined nationalism, to varying degrees, with affirmations of Christian belief.[18] Laqueur describes belligerent movements stressing religious fundamentalism as "clerical fascism,"[19] and others use the phrase "fascistized clericalism."[20] Other scholars maintain that an essential characteristic of fascism is its rejection of religion in favor of a secular ideology predicated on faith in the state. From that perspective, fascism is similar to the other totalitarian ideology that emerged during the same period: Soviet Communism under the leadership of Stalin. The essential point is that the extreme Left and the extreme Right embraced similar tools of coercive control.[21]

Political leaders bent on total control may certainly adopt similar methods, whether their ideology stems from the Left or the Right and whether it is secular or religious. It is important, however, to recognize that the ideological roots of fascism and communism are very different. Communism, for all the horrific excesses and distortions that occurred in the Soviet Union and elsewhere, is rooted in the Enlightenment. Communist theory accepted the Enlightenment commitment to universal human rights, with the crucial reservation that liberal affirmations of unlimited property rights would leave ordinary people with no rights at all.[22] The communists also shared the Enlightenment endorsement of secularism, holding that reason rather than faith must be the standard for determining truth and shaping political institutions. In that sense, the socialist roots of communism had much in common with the liberal beliefs that communists later challenged. Although some socialist movements abandoned those values in practice, even the most murderous communist regime felt compelled to rationalize its ideology in terms of a commitment to genuine democracy and universal rights.

The opposite was the case with the fascist movements, which attacked liberalism and socialism with equal anger, and for the same reasons. Common to those movements was a total rejection of the Enlightenment's values. Democracy and human rights were despised as pathological elevations of the individual over the organic community, and faith, not reason, was affirmed as the standard of truth and the basis for political action. From this perspective, whether the leader of a particular fascist movement emphasizes faith in the state or in God is less significant than complete acceptance of the leader's ideology and zealous rejection of the values of the Enlightenment. That split illuminates the challenge fascism posed to European civilization from the 1920s until its defeat in World War II, and it can shed similar light on violent Islamist movements today.

Although we may be persuaded by the body of scholarship that affirms the compatibility (under certain circumstances) of fascism and religious faith, it does not follow that Islam has any special vulnerability to such distortion. Judaism, Christianity, and Hinduism have also produced anti-Enlightenment fundamentalist movements whose members bitterly condemn moderate voices within their own religions, endorse violence, and join the assault on secular thought.[23] Islamism is one of many anti-Enlightenment ideologies, and a comparison to these other movements—fascism in particular—can help us understand it.

Anti-Enlightenment ideologies require individuals to submit to an organic community claiming superiority over all others. Leaders of these

movements contend that their community's dominance has been temporarily lost, perhaps due to humiliating treatment by a historic enemy or
corrupt current leaders' slavish submission to foreign dictates. Ordinary
people have forgotten their true identities; they have been seduced by
modernity, consumerism, and immorality, justifying the leader's calls for
a return to past glory and a transcendent communal faith. In this sense,
fascist or belligerent fundamentalist movements are neither liberal nor
conservative but contemptuous of anyone who seeks compromise with
other factions across the political spectrum. The liberal democratic idea of
a viable "center" is regarded as contemptible, its adoption a sign that
society is ripe for destruction.

The sense of common identity and purpose produced by such attitudes can be intensely elevating and gratifying, marked by passionate
devotion and an unlimited willingness to sacrifice. The leader mobilizes
this devotion, calling for shared struggle and cleansing violence that will
be directed internally against rivals for power and externally in merciless
wars against all foreign enemies. Violence for these purposes, even if it
results in one's own death, is considered a supremely spiritual and
rewarding experience. Death is not a means to an end but an end in itself,
a purifying process.

"War alone," pronounced Mussolini, "keys up all human energies to
their maximum tension and sets the seal of nobility to those peoples who
have the courage to face it. . . . Fascism carries the anti-pacifist attitude
into the life of the individual."[24] As men prepare for battle, women are to
raise as many children as possible, adding to future ranks of fighters. For
Mussolini, "War is to the man what maternity is to the woman."[25] The cult
of the leader, expressed in self-sacrifice and martyrdom, recurs powerfully in Islamist militancy. A typical example comes from an influential
Islamist theologian Abu Bakr Naji, who stated in his 2006 treatise *The
Management of Savagery* that "the leader . . . must be the object of complete
reliance within the movement, and entrusted with its actions and its
secrets."[26] Such a leader is needed to counter violently the Western world
and infidels.[27] Al-Baghdadi would later add: "Islam was never a religion of
peace. Islam is the religion of fighting. No-one should believe that the war
that we are waging is the war of the Islamic State. It is the war of all
Muslims, but the Islamic State is spearheading it. It is the war of Muslims
against infidels."[28]

Such a perspective despises democracy. It wants to subsume the will of individuals to a higher communal purpose comprehended only by the leader. As Mussolini argued, "Democracy is a kingless regime, infested by many kings who are sometimes more exclusive, tyrannical, and destructive than one, even if he be a tyrant."[29] Abu Musab al-Zarqawi, the late leader of al-Qaeda in Mesopotamia, expressed a similar contempt for democracy: "Government of the people [and] by the people . . . is the religion of democracy which is being praised and glorified with much fanfare. . . . That is the very essence of heresy and error, as it contradicts the bases of the faith . . . because it makes the weak, ignorant man Allah's partner in His most central divine prerogative—namely, ruling and legislating."[30] Al-Baghdadi reiterated that view: "[We] will cause the world to hear and understand the meaning of terrorism, and boots that will trample the idol of nationalism, destroy the idol of democracy and uncover its deviant nature."[31]

Fascists reject socialist appeals to the interests of the working class and the poor as divisive attacks on the spiritual unity of society, and they condemn capitalism as a system devoted to personal profit, crass materialism, and unlimited self-interest. "Fascism," wrote Mussolini, "believes now and always in sanctity and heroism, that is to say in acts in which no economic motive, remote or immediate—is at work."[32] Fascism thus transcends both communism and capitalism. Islamists offer a similar worldview. As Laurence Wright summarized the perspective of Sayyid Qutb, the leading Islamist intellectual of the post–World War II period: "The real struggle . . . was not a battle between capitalism and communism: it was between Islam and materialism. And inevitably Islam would prevail."[33] Naji later conveyed the same view, writing that "whatever fuels the actions of the West are material interests and desire to survive," motives he derides as "Western eternal interests."[34]

For the Islamist, the evils of materialism are attributable in large measure to Jews, who they believe must, at a minimum, be stripped of their enormous power. From the 1988 Hamas Covenant: "[Zionists] were behind the French Revolution, the communist revolution. . . . They were behind World War I, when they were able to destroy the Islamic caliphate. . . . They were behind World War II, through which they made huge financial gains. . . . There is no war going on anywhere, without [them] being behind it."[35] Bin Laden's successor as leader of al-Qaeda, Ayman al-Zawahiri, also subscribes to Jewish conspiracy theories, often found in fascist circles, that allege Jewish control over world politics and finance.[36] In December 2002 he stated: "Let the Muslim youth not await anyone's permission, for *jihad* against the Americans, Jews, and their alliance of hypocrites and apostates is an individual obligation."[37]

There are, of course, differences between Islamist fundamentalists and the European fascists, two of which are particularly worth noting. First, while the fascist leaders promoted their doctrines almost as a religious faith, they did not draw directly from religious texts. Second, European fascists relied on the nation-state as a fighting machine to extend their reach; Islamists focus on the organic unity of the *ummah*. During the ascendance of ISIS, many Sunni jihadists moved closer to an ideology like that of Mussolini's Italy, declaring a new state with imperial ambitions.

This distinction between the nationalism of the European fascists and the exclusive theology of Islamist radicals goes beyond differences over transnational strategies. In contrast with the notion of Aryan supremacy (and, less intensely, Mussolini's notion of a superior Roman civilization), Islam represents not a particular people but a faith, which can, in principle, be embraced by anyone. In the words of Hassan Nasrallah: "Islam is a religion designed for a society that can revolt and build a state."[38] Religions affirm moral arguments that cannot simply be swept aside; even violent extremists refer to arguments, however convoluted, that rationalize their plans and actions in moral terms. The fascists of Europe faced no such constraints. Moreover, moral arguments enable Islamist fascist movements to proselytize even without violence in their pursuit of domination. What totalitarian and theocratic regimes share is a sense of unity demanding the exclusion of perceived outsiders.

OUTSIDERS AND STATELESS PEOPLES

In times of economic crisis and social inequality, the polis is easily fractured. Nationalism, whether couched in secular or religious terms, unites aggrieved individuals while excluding perceived outsiders. The social contract, or what is left of it, applies only to privileged members. The demarcation between "us" and a hostile "them" is reconfigured in sharp terms, lending itself to the language of social purification. Cohesion is achieved only at the expense of society's allegedly disposable elements.

Defenders of human rights, liberals, and leftist intellectuals are labeled immoral and unpatriotic, and castigated for favoring foreigners and marginalized people at the expense of their compatriots. Meanwhile, thanks to the new propaganda, bigots, racists, and xenophobes become the "moral" guardians of the polis, elevated to the status of heroes.[39] Regarding the masses as erratic and impatient, radical nationalist and religious leaders deflect domestic rage by turning attention toward outsiders. In these highly volatile situations, war can easily erupt, creating refugees and newly stateless people who may then serve as scapegoats for social crises.

The politics of extreme exclusion is not uniquely associated with fascism or with jihadist ideologies. Ethnic cleansing and genocide also took place under alleged Enlightenment ideologies, including Soviet Stalinism and Pol Pot's Khmer Rouge. In counter-Enlightenment ideologies, absolute truth and political action is neither right nor left; instead, it is an uncompromising elevation of the community purified from the alleged evil of "the other," both from within and without. More than with Mussolini's fascism, it was the Nazism of Adolf Hitler that took xenophobia and racism to their ultimate extreme. The Islamic State brought belligerent Islam a major step closer to the racial policy of the Nazis. In close alignment with Nazi ideology, ISIS members were committed to *takfiri*, the purification of the Islamic world by killing vast numbers of undesired people. Most totalitarian movements, based on the purification of corrupted elements of society, are determined to purge minority groups from their midst. Like the Nazis, ISIS became merciless in its cleansing. Based on the idea that miscegenation with inferior types would lower the purity of the nation, or in ISIS's case the *ummah*, the process begins by degrading people allegedly spoiling the human race, parading them in cages, making them wear distinctive markings, forcing them into trains as if they were cattle, and finally sacrificing them on the altar to the god of war before they are buried in mass graves.

Roughly two hundred million Shi'as were condemned by ISIS as apostates who must be extinguished if Islam is to be purified. The two main branches of Islam diverge in their beliefs over who is the true heir of the mantle of the Prophet Muhammad. While the Shi'as believe that Islam was transmitted through the household of the Prophet Muhammad's son-in-law Ali and his sons Hussein and Hassan, Sunnis contend that the elected leader comes from the followers of the Prophet

Muhammad, who, they claim, are his chosen people. There is no way physically to distinguish a Shi'a from a Sunni, but members of ISIS identified their victims by their typically Shi'a names or by noting their different methods of prayer. The ethnic cleansing of Shi'a after ISIS's takeover of Mosul in 2014 amounted, in the words of the then US secretary of state John Kerry, to genocide.[40]

The Jews of interwar Germany, like the Shi'as in much of the Islamic world, were well integrated in their communities and not easily discernible from others. Policies of demarcation were artificially engineered. German Jews were distinguished by common surnames, the practice of male circumcision, or the extent to which their physical appearance differed from the idealized blond, blue-eyed Übermensch. Not only Jews but Roma, gays, and various "others" were dehumanized as unredeemable, blamed for Germany's defeat in World War I and its subsequent humiliation and economic misery. In *Mein Kampf*, Hitler promised that the non-Aryan race would be deported and exterminated: "Blood mixture, with the lowering of the racial level which accompanies it, is the one and only reason that old civilizations disappear. It is not lost wars which ruin mankind, but loss of the powers of resistance, which belong to pure blood alone."[41] The Aryan race, he claimed, needed to be purified of the Jews, who were never truly nomads but parasites in the bodies of other nations.[42] Nazi views about subaltern races were immune to the most obvious contradictory evidence. One memorable example was the African American runner Jesse Owens, who repeatedly defeated his allegedly superior "Aryan" rivals at the 1936 Olympics in Berlin while Hitler watched.

In ISIS-controlled territory, members of other faiths, notably Shi'as, Christians, and Yazidis, faced the same fate as Jews under the Nazis. With Jews in the Arab Middle East largely beyond their reach, they commissioned foreign terrorists in Europe to target them in their home countries. Despite calls for interfaith tolerance by other Muslim leaders, who see the spirit of the *ummah* as favoring interfaith harmony, ISIS and other Islamist zealots perceived the *ummah* as under attack. They called for a jihadist war to purify it from unsavory people. For Baghdadi, there was no possible reconciliation with other faiths. In a recorded message in which he entreated Muslims, without exception, to join the jihad against "the Jews, Crusaders, apostates, [and] their devils," the ISIS leader closed with a prayer: "O Allah, there is no god but You. . . . O Allah, all the armies of *kufr* [denial of the truth] from amongst the Jews, Crusaders, atheists, and apostates gathered against us. They did so in opposition to Your religion. . . . Therefore, O Allah, support Your soldiers and bring Your religion triumph. . . . Defeat them with the worst of defeats they will ever suffer. Divide their gatherings, split their body, dismember them completely, and make us raid them and not them raid us."[43]

In Baghdadi's caliphate, the privilege of membership extended only to those who adhere strictly to a Salafist, or fundamentalist, interpretation of Islam. When the Islamic State conquered Mosul in June 2014, the militants labeled Christian homes with the letter *n*—the first letter of *nasrani,* an Arabic term for Christians that is often used as an insult. ISIS delivered an ultimatum: "All Christians in the city must either convert to Islam, pay a tax, the *jizya,* or face execution." Most of the three thousand Christians left in the city fled their homes, marking what could be the end of Mosul's centuries-old Christian community.[44] Many who refused to convert to Islam were slaughtered and crucified.

In theocratic and totalitarian regimes, exclusion and liquidation typically enforce a patriarchal social hierarchy that privileges mythical notions of virility. Women are compelled to docile submission, and all forms of sexual expression that threaten this narrow concept of manhood (such as homosexuality or other forms of perceived sexual deviance) are crushed. The girls and the mothers of "outsiders" or "infidels" may be kept alive only to be subjected to sex slavery. Like the Nazis' victims before them, Yazidi women were displayed as property and referred to as *sabaya* (slave), a word that was added before their given names.[45] They were captured and enslaved in large numbers and subjected to repeated rape, each violation ritualized as a religious act. "I kept telling him it hurts—please stop," said a Yazidi girl who later escaped. "He told me that according to Islam he is allowed to rape an unbeliever."[46] Sex slavery was also highly bureaucratized and legalized through contracts notarized by the ISIS-run Islamic Court. Religious license for sexual assault became an ISIS recruiting tool.[47]

Forced prostitution or sex slavery also prevailed in Nazi Germany. Women in existing brothels were forced into house arrest to cater to the German clientele, and Jewish women—who were forbidden by strict racial law to have sexual contact with German men—were thrown into compulsory prostitution. Resistance meant deportation to concentration camps. Nazi men, like their jihadist counterparts, were encouraged to develop a warrior mind-set by sexually dominating women of inferior faiths and races, who were therefore reducible to objects of enjoyment for others. While rape has always been an instrument of dominance during war, it is worth noting that rape in Nazi Germany, as in ISIS-held territories, was highly regulated with the common objective of preventing venereal disease or pregnancy in order to use their victims' bodies as many times as possible. Beyond rape, women from these dehumanized "minorities" are often the object of other forms of barbarism, well chronicled by eyewitnesses in documentaries such as *Nuit et Brouillard* (*Night and Fog*, 1955).

Gays, too, are regarded as impure and dehumanized, often summarily executed for softening male potency in a "revitalized" society seeking to be cleansed of heresy and perceived social ailments. The leaders of ISIS regularly mocked the Arab Gulf countries not only for their rulers' materialism and corruption but for the "feminization" of their societies. One of ISIS's recruitment messages to disaffected young Saudi men associated the adoption of their strict Muslim ideology with the attainment of manliness. Public executions of gay men warned the gathered crowds to maintain ideological purity. The Qur'an states that men having sex with each other should be punished, though it does not describe how and leaves space for gays to repent. But the Hadith (second to the authority of the Qur'an) sentences gays to death based on various alleged sayings of the Prophet Muhammad. Accounts differ on the method of killing, and some prescribe lesser penalties depending on the circumstances. The Islamic State's murder of gays was based on an account in which Muhammad reports that homosexuals "should be thrown from tremendous heights and then stoned."[48]

The Nazi regime was no less merciless toward gays, and many died in concentration camps. Both the Nazi and fascist ideologies were built on the association of virility with violence. Jews were depicted as effeminate, and in 1930, Wilhelm Frick, representing the Nazi Party, described homosexuality as a typical Jewish vice.[49] Nazi propaganda portrayed gays as soft, cowardly, cringing, and untrustworthy.[50] Like Jews forced to wear the yellow star, gays had to wear a pink triangle in concentration camps. Between 1933 and 1945, 100,000 men were arrested as homosexuals; around 10 percent were incarcerated in concentration camps or sentenced to death.[51]

Also on the long list of social "parasites," the disabled were persecuted by fascist regimes, particularly in Nazi Germany. ISIS may also have targeted the disabled: there were unconfirmed reports from within Mosul indicating that Islamic Shari'a judges issued an unwritten "oral fatwa" to kill children with congenital deformities or Down syndrome. Nothing, however, compares to the eugenic policy of the Nazis, who murdered over a quarter million people with disabilities in the name of improving the Aryan race.

Among the undesirable, only the lucky succeed in escaping oppression or extermination. But as refugees they face new calamities. Their suffering is perpetuated by a double standard contained in international human rights law and norms, which offer allegiance both to the sovereignty of the state (the 1947 UN Charter) and to universal human rights that transcend the jurisdiction of states. The international system, based on the Westphalian principle, continues to rely on the state as the guardian of human rights, but the state is also the entity against which people's rights need to be defended. If a state fails to make a minimal effort to defend basic rights, and people are forced to flee, as Hannah Arendt reminds us, "No law exists for them, not that they are oppressed but . . . nobody wants even to oppress them." Their tragic situation, she maintains, "is not that they are deprived of life, freedom, law and freedom of opinion, but that they no longer belong to any community whatsoever." When people are denied a right to a residence "which jailed criminals would enjoy as a matter of course, they have been reduced to the wretched of the earth, with no legal recourse to secure minimal rights and their right to life."[52]

The obligation to secure the rights of refugees falls on the international community. Yet that community consists of individual states, within which refugees often encounter either indifference or xenophobia. As millions of Syrians flee mass atrocities inflicted by the Assad regime or their jihadist enemies, those who would welcome them are increasingly overwhelmed by popular fear and paranoia, based on beliefs that jihadists mingle in the refugees' ranks or, more insidiously, that their Islamic heritage marks them as enemies. The Europeans and Americans, historical champions of universal human rights, are increasingly inclined to turn these war victims away. The end of this tragedy is not yet in sight. The Levant Express, launched as an engine of hope and then derailed, now evokes the far darker image of trains filled with the oppressed, headed toward an ominous fate.

CHAPTER FOUR

Frost in Jerusalem

THE HEAVIEST SNOWFALL IN FIFTY YEARS fell in Jerusalem on December 13, 2013. While trains into the holy city were still running, the mantle of snow left many people stranded. Throughout the region, the Arab Winter set in with a vengeance, bringing a hard frost to the Israeli and Palestinian hopes that had blossomed in the now distant Spring. Each peace initiative had been stalled by intifadas; each Palestinian rebellion or attack was followed by Israeli retaliatory incursions. Frustrations fed radical religious and nationalist sentiments on both sides.

In July 2015, two young Jewish men, twenty-one-year-old Amiram Ben-Uliel and a minor whose name the authorities did not release, firebombed a Palestinian home in the West Bank village of Duma, killing an eighteen-month-old toddler and his parents.[1] A few months later, a Palestinian from East Jerusalem rammed his car into a crowd of Israeli civilians at a bus stop, then began stabbing them with a meat cleaver— one of a string of random attacks against Israelis that led some to believe the Palestinians were on the brink of a third intifada.[2] Any hope of peace seemed buried by cycles of violence in the name of a vengeful god. The Levant Express was off its tracks.

A stroll through the Israel Railway Museum in Haifa reveals old railroad maps from a bygone era when Mandatory Palestine was not isolated from its neighbors and rails connected Arab cities throughout the region.

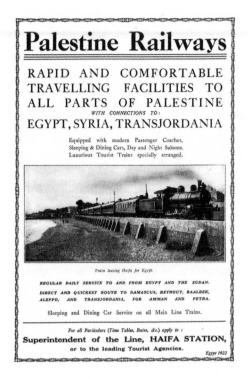

Palestine Railways poster, 1922.
Source: Palestinian Railways,
Khoury House, Haifa.

A French company, Société du Chemin de Fer Ottoman, opened the first line between Jaffa and Jerusalem in 1892. Later, from 1920 until 1948, Palestine Railways ran all public railways in the British Mandate of Palestine. Its many lines included one linking El Kantara in Egypt with Haifa, branching to Jaffa, Jerusalem, Acre, and the Jezreel Valley. Muslim passengers took the Hejaz Railway to make the Hajj pilgrimage to the holy cities of Medina and Mecca, traveling by narrow-gauge steam trains from Haifa, Damascus, and Amman. In those days, people circulated freely between neighboring cities and countries.

But those times are gone. The region is fragmented and disconnected, oppressed by an anti-Enlightenment climate. For a long time, Israel has been viewed as a Western sword implanted in the heart of Islam; a sword that needs to be dislodged at all costs. Likewise, many Israelis, convinced that Palestinian organizations intend the destruction of the Jewish state, embrace security-based policies (including the expansion of Jewish settlements in the West Bank) that further strengthen the ideological appeal of the Islamists. The Arab Winter increased these tensions, creating a favorable environment for extremist animosities on both sides. Unresolved, the Israeli-Palestinian question remains one of the fundamental problems in the region, a seemingly insurmountable obstacle to progressive forces in their broader effort to promote stability and human rights in the Arab world.

What accounts for the divisive rise of religious radicalism and nationalism in Israel and Palestine? Like the Arab world's serial failures to entrench human rights during the Arab Spring, Israeli-Palestinian peace efforts are repeatedly derailed. The short-lived Allon Plan of 1967, the 1978 Camp David Accords, the 1993 Oslo Accords, and the 2000 Camp David Summit all failed to bring comprehensive peace, feeding, on both sides, the rise of a fearful and angry worldview consistent with exclusionary counter-Enlightenment ideologies. Nationalism and religious radicalism have grown as privatization and liberalization widen the social and economic gaps within and between Israeli and Palestinian territories. The fracturing of civil society on each side has yielded a chronic political paralysis, providing fertile terrain for social agitation to erupt again and again, from "Occupy Rothschild" to the "Palestinian Arab Spring."[3] With progressive parties weakened and in disarray, religious radical and extreme nationalist ideologies have gained the upper hand, carving a unifying space amid parliamentary crises. These movements draw on social despair and popular fear, congealing their societies by vilifying the other side. Their new religious and nationalist base becomes the pulse of political life.

THE ZIGZAG TRACKS OF PEACE AND WAR

When peace efforts fail and economic opportunities disappear, popular frustration fans the flame of anger, increasing rivalries between groups and discrimination by the strong against the weak. In such a climate, the rule of law and separation of powers are seen as impediments to an impatient executive elite striving to implement order amid chaos. Walls, both real and psychological, are built to secure neighborhoods, cities, and regions. Regardless of the actual level of threat, there is always a sense of urgency. Alleged barbarians must constantly be repelled from the gates before they destroy "life as we know it." The train of peace is thus derailed, surrounded by a dense fog of war, which has appeared in recurrent waves since 1967.

The First Wave: The Six-Day War

The June 1967 war contributed greatly to the rise of the religious right in Israel and the upsurge of Palestinian nationalism, just as it strengthened the Muslim Brotherhood in the Arab world. In 1966, Palestinian guerrilla groups based in Syria, Lebanon, and Jordan launched attacks against Israel, leading to a strong Israeli retaliation. Nasser rushed to the defense of the Palestinians, instituting a blockade of Israeli shipping in the port of Eilat and signing a defense agreement with Jordan and an alliance pact with Iraq. Tensions heightened along Israel's borders. On June 5, 1967, in response to apparent war preparations by its Arab neighbors, Israel launched a preemptive air assault that destroyed more than 90 percent of Egypt's air force.

Days before, a prominent leader of the religious Zionism movement, Zvi Yehuda Kook, gave a speech that would shape the vision of the national religious camp: "Nineteen years ago, on the night when news of the United Nations decision in favor of the re-establishment of the state of Israel reached us, when the people streamed into the streets to celebrate and rejoice, I could not go out and join in the jubilation. I sat alone and silent; a burden lay upon me. During those first hours, I could not resign myself to what had been done. I could not accept the fact that indeed 'they have . . . divided My land'! Yes, where is our Hebron—have we forgotten her?! Where is our Shehem, our Jericho—where?! Have we forgotten them?"[4] The ensuing war with a pan-Arab force led by Egypt, Jordan, and Syria lasted just six days before the UN brokered a ceasefire, by which time Israel had taken control of the Gaza Strip, East Jerusalem, the West Bank, the Golan Heights, and the Sinai.

As soon as the war ended, Israeli minister Yigal Allon proposed a plan to restore most of the West Bank territory to Jordan, retain military settlements along the Jordan River, create a Druze state in the Golan Heights, and return the Sinai to Egypt.[5] Except for the return of the Sinai, the Allon Plan was never implemented. Israeli settlements in the Occupied Territories grew in subsequent decades, hardening the positions of Israeli and Palestinian hawks. King Hussein's Jordan would relinquish its claim on the West Bank in 1988, facilitating further Israeli expansion. The 1967 war, followed by the failure to implement Allon's or any other peace plan, set the stage for rising extremism on both sides.

As the Muslim Brotherhood strengthened in Egypt and elsewhere in the Arab world, the first political expressions of anti-Enlightenment worldviews in Israel and Palestinian territories germinated. Pan-Arabism collapsed, compelling Egypt and other Arab nations to retreat within their own borders. Palestinian political hopes now centered on the surging influence of the Palestinian Liberation Organization (PLO), a secular organization that had formed in 1964. In 1968, the PLO amended its charter to formally endorse armed struggle against Israel and recommit itself to the "total liberation of Palestine." The world took notice of militant Palestinians' violence against civilians when Black September, a Palestinian organization, assassinated Jordanian Prime Minister Wasfi al-Tal in 1971, murdered Israeli athletes at the 1972 Olympic Games, and hijacked civilian airplanes throughout the 1970s.

On the Israeli side, with the expansion into the West Bank, the Land of Israel Movement (LIM) brought together strange bedfellows: religious fundamentalists, ultranationalists, and leftist zealots. Other extreme religious fundamentalist groups, such as the Gush Emunim (the Bloc of the Faithful) and Kach, would join LIM in the 1970s. Gush Emunim members were young and driven by a messianic ideology that encouraged Jewish settlements in the occupied West Bank and Gaza, which, following the Hebrew scriptures, they called Judea and Samaria. Meir Kahane, an American-Israeli Orthodox rabbi and ultranationalist, endorsed by Rabbi Kook, appeared on the Israeli political scene in 1971 and called for the deportation of the Arab population. Many religious radicals had grown impatient with decades of Labor governments that had not improved their economic and social lot. They would later see Likud's Menachem Begin as the grand champion of a true and undivided Israel, as he reassured settlers after his 1977 electoral victory that there will be "many more Elon Morehs," namely, many more Jewish settlements in the West Bank.[6]

On October 6, 1973, Egypt and Syria simultaneously attacked Israel on two fronts. Hostilities continued until October 26, at which point Israel rebounded from early losses to advance well beyond the Suez Canal, reaching within about 61 miles (99 kilometers) of Cairo. Under a ceasefire ratified in January, Israel withdrew back into the Sinai and Egypt agreed to reduce the size of its force on the east bank of the canal. Six months later, the 1974 Disengagement Agreement between Israel and Syria established a UN buffer zone and left Israel with a substantial portion of the Golan Heights. The 1973 war had proven costly for Egypt,

Syria, and Israel alike, but it created a propitious environment for a more lasting agreement and brought about a new round of peace negotiations at Camp David.

The Second Wave: Camp David Accords (1978) and the First Intifada (1987)

Islamist fundamentalists were well on their way to seizing power in Iran, and extreme Wahhabists were strengthening their position in Saudi Arabia, when Egyptian President Anwar el-Sadat and Israeli Prime Minister Menachem Begin signed the Camp David Accords in 1978, bringing peace between Egypt and Israel. With President Jimmy Carter leading the negotiations, the two parties stopped short of a comprehensive peace that solved the Palestinian problem; instead they forged a bilateral agreement that averted a descent into renewed war.

Extremists on both sides saw the agreement as an act of treason. Begin lost the support of the religious right when he made peace with Egypt and initiated an autonomy plan for Palestinians in the West Bank. Many of his constituents were stunned when he ordered the Israeli evacuation of the Sinai desert and the Jewish settlement of Yamit. The ultra-right-wing bloc saw it as the ultimate betrayal. B'nai B'rith Ne'emanei Eretz Israel (the Covenant of Eretz Israel Loyalists) was created on November 1, 1978, in reaction to the Camp David Accords.[7] The ultranationalist political party, Kach, catapulted into a new sphere of radical right activism, and some members of Gush Emunim began operating covertly, forming in 1984 what became known as the Jewish underground.

Right-wing Israelis were not the only ones taking matters into their own hands. Radicalism had been rising on the Palestinian side for some time, reflected in the acts of Black September, the 1978 Palestinian coastal road massacre of Israeli civilians, and the relentless attacks by Palestinian guerrilla forces, the feddayeen, against Israel's agricultural collective cooperatives, the kibbutzim and moshavim.

It has often been argued that the failure to involve Palestinian representatives in the Camp David Accords contributed to Palestinian radicalization.[8] However, the PLO was not then positioning itself to negotiate for peace, and there was a real inconsistency between its violent operations and the relatively more quiet and integrated lives of Palestinians in the Occupied Territories of the West Bank and Gaza. In 1979, US Secretary of

State Cyrus Vance asked Edward Said, then a member of the Palestinian National Council, to deliver a message to PLO Chairman Yasser Arafat, promising to recognize the PLO if it would accept UN Resolution 242, which called on Israel to return to its pre-1967 borders and for all states in the region to respect one another's sovereignty, territorial integrity, and political independence without threat of violence. After Said relayed the American offer, Arafat replied: "Edward, I want you to tell Vance that we're not interested. . . . We don't want the Americans. The Americans have stabbed us in the back. This is a lousy deal. We want Palestine. We don't want to negotiate with the Israelis. We're going to fight." Years later, Said observed, "There were many such deals that went on later through the 1980s as he [Arafat] got weaker and weaker. He had no troops to command. It was clear to me, at any rate, in the 1970s, that we had no military option against Israel, any more than they had against us, but he turned it down."[9] Ultimately, the PLO's hard-line policy was broken only by campaigns of passive resistance by Palestinians in the West Bank and Gaza.

With the PLO exiled in Tunis after the war in Lebanon in 1982, Palestinians from Gaza and the West Bank felt left alone to face their own destiny. In 1987, they launched the First Intifada—a rebellion expressed mostly through nonviolent civil disobedience against Israeli rule, the current economic crisis, and their lack of social mobility. They refused to pay taxes, boycotted Israeli products, drew political graffiti, and threw stones at Israeli soldiers. This new form of resistance led the international community to soften its position toward the Palestinians and recognize the need for a lasting resolution of the Israeli-Palestinian conflict. This new attitude paved the road to Oslo.

The Third Wave: The Oslo Accords of 1993 and the New Cycle of Nationalist and Religious Activism
While Iran and Saudi Arabia confronted each other in proxy wars in Pakistan, Afghanistan, Iraq, Syria, Lebanon, and elsewhere, the Palestinians' struggle in the West Bank and Gaza helped prepare the way for the Oslo agreement in 1993, with President Bill Clinton assuming Carter's role as Janus overseeing the sacred rituals of peace. An effort to find a permanent resolution to the Israeli-Palestinian impasse, the Oslo framework bestowed a limited form of self-governance in the West Bank and the Gaza Strip by creating the Palestinian Authority (PA), recognized

by the Israelis and the international community as the legitimate representative of the Palestinian people. For its part, the PLO renounced
terrorism and recognized Israel's right to exist in peace. Soon after, in
1994, the Hashemite Kingdom of Jordan signed a peace agreement with
Israel. A short-lived wind of hope swept through the region.

The promises of peace were celebrated again in Oslo when the 1994
Nobel Peace Prize was awarded to three people: PLO Chairman Yasser
Arafat, Israeli Prime Minister Yitzhak Rabin, and Israeli Minister of
Foreign Affairs Shimon Peres. In his acceptance speech, Arafat said that
peace "enables the Arab spirit to reflect through unrestrained human
expression its profound understanding of the Jewish-European tragedy";
it also, he said, allows the Jewish spirit to express its empathy for the
suffering endured by the Palestinian people over their ruptured history.[10]
Some Israelis saw the agreement as an act of treason. An Israeli religious
radical assassinated Rabin on November 4, 1995, as the Israeli prime
minister was leaving a national celebration of the accord. Within a decade,
many on both sides were denouncing the agreement as a fiasco. In the
words of Edward Said, Oslo was nothing more than a "Palestinian
Versailles" that would ultimately create a backlash.[11] His view proved
prophetic, as the prospect of a Palestinian state has all but vanished, and
many Israelis have relinquished all hope for harmonious coexistence
with their Palestinian neighbors. Oslo may have represented a historical
milestone, but it did not live up to its promise, and in the end, it was a
setback for aspirations toward universal human rights. A Palestinian
state was not established, and Palestinian socioeconomic distress deepened after a failed peace negotiation in Camp David, sowing the seeds for
the next intifada.

The Fourth Wave: Camp David 2000 and the Second Intifada
(2000–2005)
The 2000 Camp David Summit brought together Israeli Prime Minister
Ehud Barak and Yasser Arafat, chairman of the new Palestinian Authority,
in an effort to resurrect the Oslo agreement. Once again, President
Clinton involved himself in minute details of the peace process, the
spatial transition, the intricacy of maps, and boundaries of the city gates.
His efforts proved unsuccessful. The collapsed peace process stoked the
fires of resistance in the West Bank and Gaza, contributing to a growing

sense of despair that burst into violence in the Second Intifada and strengthened the Muslim Brotherhood. Hezbollah, the Shi'a fundamentalist militia supported by Iran in southern Lebanon, assisted Palestinian resistance. The peace train was winding backward.

The Muslim Brotherhood had been operating across the Palestinian territories since 1967 and stepped up its social service activities after 1973. Salafism, a fundamentalist form of Islam, also took root there in the early 1970s,[12] as Saudi Arabia extended its influence beyond the Arabian Peninsula. These and other Islamist movements, such as the Palestinian Islamic Jihad, increasingly challenged the secular nationalist PLO and other leftist pan-Arabist Palestinian groups. Though largely nonviolent, the secular groups sometimes resorted to violence against their Muslim rivals as they vied for power in the region.

Hamas, created as a Palestinian offshoot of the Muslim Brotherhood during the First Intifada, opposed the PLO's newly adopted strategy of nonviolence and began carrying out scattered attacks against Israeli forces. Excluded from the Oslo negotiations in 1993 and the Camp David Summit in 2000—the PLO was the only internationally recognized Palestinian entity—Hamas tried to gain legitimacy by boosting its confrontational stance toward both Israel and the PA. The failure of the Camp David Summit, coupled with growing popular frustration, led the more violent Salafist groups (such as al-Aqsa Martyr's Brigades) to join forces and wage a ruthless struggle against Israeli occupation that included attacks on civilians. Sari Nusseibeh, a Palestinian scholar and an important figure of the First Intifada, deplored the strategy and ideology of Hamas. "With this latter explosion of violence," he said in 2007, "I refuse to call this an intifada, because it had neither a leadership, nor a vision, nor a plan. It was simply—in my opinion—a crazy expression of frustration and anger, totally useless, chaotic and certainly counterproductive, involving acts of violence and of terrorism that only brought ruin to the Palestinian people and to our achievements."[13]

This more brutal Palestinian confrontation with the Israeli military and civilians fed an Israeli perception that Palestinian leaders could not be legitimate partners in a peace process. During the Second Intifada, suicide bombers attacked within major Israeli cities, initiating unprecedented terror. "Kahane was right!" shouted angry crowds. Kahane's radical religious party, Kach, had been marginalized and outlawed in previous elections, but in 2003, thanks to the impact of the Second Intifada on the Israeli public, the party was re-legitimized. The Israeli political climate again favored the popularization of a right-wing conservative and insular worldview.[14]

For Israel, the cost of the Second Intifada had been too high, and after General Ariel Sharon became prime minister in 2001, he decided to withdraw unilaterally from the occupied Gaza Strip. Israel's disengagement, in 2005, included the evacuation of twenty Jewish settlements, most notably Gush Katif, whose abandonment was seen as another strike at the heart of the settlement movement. From the perspective of the radical religious right, the time was ripe to unite the opponents of Sharon's policy. The religious and the secular right often disagreed on economic, social, and ethnic issues. Avigdor Lieberman's secular Jewish Home, for instance, favored social services for Russian immigrants and a deregulated economy. Arie Derie's Shas was religious, championing underprivileged Mizrahim (Arab or Sephardic Jews) and greater economic subsidies for the Orthodox Jews and the poor. Despite drawing on different rationales, these parties converged tactically into a radical right bloc eager to preserve religious settlements and expand beyond the 1967 security borders from the Mediterranean Sea to the Jordan Valley.[15] The settlers slowly began to infiltrate the secular Likud leadership, hardening its conservative ideology. This process reinforced the Jewish state's national identity and legitimized the occupation and settlement expansion in the occupied Palestinian territories. These actions further strengthened Palestinian resistance and weakened the PA, the only Palestinian party with which Israel had been willing to negotiate.

In a study of the dynamics of anticolonial struggle in Africa, the French psychiatrist and scholar Frantz Fanon explained how nationalist liberation movements tend to keep their "distance with regard to violence," offering to be liaisons between "throat slitters" and colonial powers.[16] In this sense, the PA benefited from the violent Islamist groups, which allowed it to present itself as the only moderate entity capable of negotiating peace with increasingly nervous Israelis. This apparent leverage placed the PA's ruling party, Fatah, in a precarious position, as it was ultimately trusted by neither grassroots Palestinians nor Israelis, a position further challenged by Fatah's inability to meet economic needs amidst the advance of neoliberal economic policies in Israel and the West.

Palestinian Loss of Land 1947 to Present

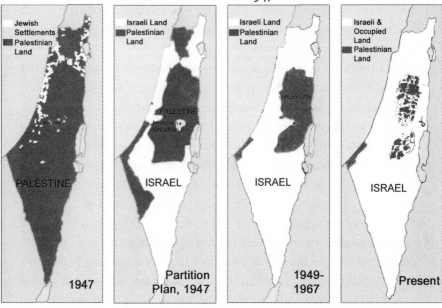

Map showing Palestinian loss of land, 1947–2017. Courtesy of Friends of Sabeel North America.

NEOLIBERALISM AND ITS DISCONTENTS

A Greek myth tells us that Plutus, the god of wealth, had clear sight, bestowing wealth only on the good and the just. Then Zeus blinded him, and he began to distribute wealth without regard to whether the recipients deserved it. A more socialist version of that myth, applied to the history of Israel and the Palestinian territories, might argue that the Labor Party—based on social justice and economic equity since the founding of Israel in 1948—lost its vision during the 1980s, when it rushed to embrace neoliberalism after the oil crisis of the 1970s. A culture of greed took root, with rising inequality of wealth and a weakened social contract that drove the society's most vulnerable members into despair. The subsequent Israeli recruitment of foreign workers, the collapse of remittances from Gulf countries, and the corruption of the PLO after Oslo drove the Palestinians into further poverty, prompting cycles of violence. Radical religious forces, strengthened by globalization's failures, gained increased leverage across the whole Middle East.

Although they lagged behind other industrialized countries, Israelis and Palestinians were not immune to the global trend toward privatization and a greater flexibility of labor production induced by new technologies, or post-Fordism, that began in the mid-1970s and intensified after the Cold War.[17] Fundamentalist movements sank deeper roots in places where secular legitimacy had been eroded by economic crises. The liberalization of a previously state-managed economy had an important impact on both Israeli and Palestinian civil society. Against the backdrop of the oil and other economic crises in the 1970s and 1980s, the end of the Labor Party's dominance and the rise of the right-wing Likud Party paved the way for Israel's Economic Stabilization Plan in 1985. This plan, a response to an inflation rate that reached nearly 400 percent in 1984, included measures to reduce government subsidies, devalue the currency, restrict wage growth, and open the economy to foreign capital and privatization. But it also marked a turning point toward liberalization and the emergence of a privileged class independent from the state.[18]

The people who devised this policy were initially members of the Labor Party, not neoliberals from Likud. Shimon Peres, then the prime minister and the driving force, later seemed to be the architect of the New Middle East.[19] He asked about the region, "What is its place in the changing world—facing winds of glory and ghosts of the past, or facing winds of change bearing hope for a new era?"[20] He was convinced that entering the global economy and creating bonds of economic interdependence would lead to regional prosperity, which in turn would strengthen peace efforts. Plutus's indiscriminate distribution of wealth, Adam Smith's "invisible hand," and Kant's democratic peace based on economic interdependence were united in hopes of reinvigorating both the fragile social contract and the declining Labor Party. If Labor Party doves advocated privatization and deregulation as a way to promote peace, the Likud of Benjamin Netanyahu embraced the same policies as a way to enhance Israel's power. The Israeli economy moved quickly to embrace high technology and attracted increasing foreign direct investment.[21] The economy grew markedly in the 1990s as Microsoft, IBM, Cisco, Intel, Motorola and other multinational corporations opened local branches for production and research.

In the wake of inflation, the weakening of the state-owned sector, and the flood of foreign capital into Israel in the late 1980s and 1990s, a

dominant class, previously linked to the Labor Party, emerged in control
of new entrepreneurial activities. By the 1990s, Israel's ten wealthiest
families, long linked to the political establishment, accounted for more
than 20 percent of the nation's GDP. The sociologist Daniel Maman estimates that just eleven Israeli companies control two-thirds of its GDP.[22]
This consolidation of power attests to the traditional ruling elite's capacity
to reacquire, in Gramsci's phrase, "the control that was slipping from its
grasp."[23] Concentrated wealth did not trickle down to the masses. After
the Second Intifada, Israel entered one of the worst recessions in its
history, with unemployment reaching 7.3 percent in 2007 and 1.65
million people falling under the poverty line.[24] Thirty percent of the
impoverished were Arab Israelis, 30 percent were Haredim (religious
orthodox), and a significant number were Mizrahim.[25]

From 1967 through the early 1980s, the Palestinian economy had
grown in conjunction with Israel's. This relative prosperity was initially
driven by its partial integration into the Israeli economy, along with
opportunities resulting from the Gulf oil boom. The opening of the Israeli
market to Palestinian manual labor, coupled with wage remittances from
the Gulf and elsewhere, helped the gross domestic product to quadruple
in the West Bank and triple in Gaza from 1968 to 1987.[26] In the mid-
1980s, however, the Arab regional oil boom collapsed, cutting worker
remittances from the Gulf. Recession and hyperinflation in Israel reduced
employment opportunities for Palestinians and further weakened the
dependent Gazan and West Bank economies.[27]

When the First Intifada and the closure of the West Bank and Gaza after
Desert Storm in 1991 created a labor shortage in Israel, Israeli employers
pressed the government to issue more guest permits. The number of such
permits grew from 8,000 in 1991 to almost 70,000 in 1993. Most of the
pressure for a rapid transition from Palestinian labor to foreign guest
workers arose from security concerns over armed infiltration into Israel.
But this was not the only critical component of Israel's long-term shift
toward guest workers. Growing labor mobility was making a vast pool of
cheap labor available for the first time, and many Israelis preferred to rely
on non-Palestinian guest workers who had no political agenda regarding
territorial claims. In this respect, economic incentives and security concerns
combined to erode Palestinians' living conditions in both the West Bank
and Gaza. Skyrocketing unemployment, in turn, contributed to Palestinian

anger over Israeli occupation, intensifying the security threat. That vicious cycle created fertile terrain for social agitation.[28]

Israel's increasing rejection of Palestinian workers—whose remittances were crucial to the Occupied Territories' economy—became even more destabilizing after Kuwait evicted 200,000 Palestinians following Desert Storm in 1991. Together, these events precipitated the Palestinian descent into wretched living conditions. In that context, it is not hard to see why the excitement brought about by the Oslo agreement in 1993 and Yasser Arafat's return to Gaza in 1994, after twenty-seven years in exile, faded so quickly. The PLO struggled to keep in check a fragmented and impoverished civil society. With over a quarter of its population living in poverty and revelations of scandalous PLO political corruption, Palestine's economic crisis fueled an intensifying ideological conflict. Meanwhile, the Israeli economy continued to grow. In Gaza and the West Bank, 25 percent of Palestinians lived below the poverty line—39 percent in Gaza alone.[29] These numbers also revealed the flip side of Israeli economic growth and help explain the popular disenchantment that later found expression in social uprisings.

The Oslo agreement and Arafat's jubilant arrival in Gaza seemed to promise Palestinians a new life, but that optimism would soon subside, leaving unresolved grievances that erupted into fury during the Second Intifada. Palestinian employment remained heavily dependent on the Israeli economy, but Israelis in the 1990s had access to Filipino, Nigerian, Indian, Chinese, and other workers—all of whom could compete with Palestinian labor without representing the same security threat. By 2006 there were nearly 200,000 foreign workers in Israel, including illegal workers.[30] During the same period, Palestinian employment in Israel dropped from 110,000 to 50,000, even as the migrant workforce doubled.[31]

The Second Intifada brought more repression and even steeper economic decline. Settlements were crowding into the West Bank, and the idea of a Palestinian state retreated from the imaginations of even the most ardent peacemakers. When Arafat died in 2004, bloody infighting ensued between Fatah loyalists and Hamas, culminating in Hamas's ascension to power in the Gaza Strip in 2006. Hamas thus completed its journey from a marginal grassroots movement to a major player in Palestinian politics.

THE EXTREME RIGHT TAKES HOLD

The sun of hope rose over Israel and Palestine during the Spring of Nations, but people in the Levant region were soon talking about an "Arab Winter" and a "Jerusalem Frost." The failed peace process, the intifadas, and economic hardship combined to darken the skies and harden right-wing movements on both sides. The consolidation of the extreme Right in Israel was accelerated by social fragmentation and political paralysis and the weakening of a left Zionist ideology in the face of greed and competitive materialist interests. The ineffectiveness and corruption of PA nationalist leaders amplified Hamas's call for the religious cleansing of Palestinian society. Arab sectarian war validated the fear that the world was going to fire and brimstone, and it convinced many Israelis that the "barbarians" must be kept outside the gates.

Social crises are experienced differently in a developed civil society like Israel than they are in developing societies like those in the West Bank and Gaza. Antonio Gramsci maintained that when the state in the West "trembled, a strong structure of civil society was at once revealed." In other words, even when the state apparatus weakened under economic shock and war, entrenched civil institutions were present to sustain the quivering foundation of the state. In the East, on the other hand, "the state was everything, civil society was primordial and gelatinous."[32] Gramsci was suggesting that underdeveloped civil societies are too embryonic and fragmented to prop up a state in crisis. Replacing the "West" with Israel and pre-revolutionary tsarist Russia with the Palestinian territories, this comparison holds with some historical license; it explains how independent and sufficiently developed civil societies, such as Israel's, can offer far better buffers against economic stress or internal conflict.

The upheavals in Tahrir, Tunis, Tripoli, and elsewhere were not only an Arab affair. Ripples of the Arab Spring reached Tel Aviv in July 2011 and Ramallah in September 2012. The global economic recession had dramatically inflated real estate prices and the cost of living, making the daily life of ordinary Israelis extremely difficult. Leftist Israelis called their response to the world economic crisis, domestic deregulation, and the ongoing social revolutions "Occupy Rothschild." As tents sprouted in the heart of Tel Aviv's financial district on Rothschild Boulevard, a wave of protest for economic justice, triggered by the rise of food prices, dominated Israeli politics for many months. Protesters brandished signs—"Egypt Is Here,"

"Tahrir Corner at Rothschild," and "The People Demand Social Justice" (mimicking the Egyptian slogan "The People Want the Fall of the Regime")—and protested through the night.[33] As the Israeli movement made a point of disentangling its demands from the perpetually volatile Palestinian question, some critics mockingly suggested that the Israelis wanted an Arab Spring without the Arabs.[34] The protesters' focus was clear: to lower the cost of living and increase pressure for affordable housing. The government averted more social agitation by promising a series of measures to resolve the housing deficit. The protesters went home quietly; civil society won.

Palestinians also took to the streets in 2012, denouncing their leaders from Bethlehem to Hebron and Ramallah for economic policies that were said to charge "a Scandinavian level of taxation for a Somali level of government services."[35] In Gaza and the West Bank, rising fuel prices, diminishing quality of life, and unpaid salaries of Palestinian governmental workers sparked waves of protests against Palestinian officials. Palestinians also marched in support of the Tunisian, Egyptian, and Syrian revolutions. In the streets, they shouted, "The people are the source of authority, and . . . [we] reject the use of violence against the Palestinian people by any and all hands."[36] Attempting to forestall the sort of popular rebellions experienced elsewhere in the MENA region, the PA announced its intention to hold elections. These electoral hopes were thwarted and finally suspended over internal conflicts between the PA and Hamas supporters. Palestinian civil society was fractured, unanchored, and unable to translate the protesters' demands into a unified political agenda.

Mirroring each country's social fragmentation, the political leadership in both Israeli and Palestinian territories became deadlocked. The Palestinian local election of 2012, held only in the West Bank and without the participation of Hamas, was the product of an ever deeper institutional crisis between the PA and Hamas. As long as the PA is the only recognized Palestinian entity and Hamas remains starkly at odds with it, there is little chance that open general Palestinian elections will take place. But if Hamas is willing to surrender to the PA leadership, the lingering political deadlock could improve ordinary operations in the West Bank and Gaza.[37]

Likud, after winning only the bare minimum of 61 seats in Israel's Knesset elections in 2015, formed a coalition with a bizarre amalgamation of ministers from the Jewish Home, United Torah Judaism, Shas, and Kulanu—the small right-leaning centrist party. Such a concoction of parties, barely sufficient to form a government, lacking a positive agenda, and held together primarily by fear, was a formula for political paralysis. This consolidation was facilitated by the collapse of the moderate Left, as Labor and Meretz together won only 16 of the 120 seats—the worst showing for the Left in Israeli history. The Left's decline was inevitable, as with each wave of immigration it failed to recruit newcomers to its cause. Both Mizrahim and Russian immigrants favored Likud, with the former also being drawn to Shas and the latter to Israel Beitanu.[38] These religious and right-leaning parties knew how to galvanize the frustrations of the marginalized, and they channeled popular insecurities against Palestinians and others. Following Ehud Barak's failure to bring peace at Camp David, the Labor Party fell from power and the Left was forced to retrench.

The dwindling power of the Israeli Left and the Palestinian Authority, coupled with ongoing political paralysis, gave strength to right-wing ideologies. With Zionism gradually shedding its socialist skin in the mid-1980s to reveal a more capitalist worldview, the portion of the Israeli population that was left behind—in effect banished from the garden of globalization—were the poor communities of Jewish Mizrahim and Haredim, and Arab Israelis. Add in the one million Russian Jews who migrated to Israel starting in the 1990s, an unresolved Palestinian question, and the shrinking ranks of the leftist parties, and the result is a cocktail of disenchanted people seeking to restore nationalist pride and yearning for both religious purity and economic security.[39]

Gramsci explained that political and institutional paralysis often gives rise to "Caesarism," a situation in which a charismatic personality is entrusted with unifying conflicting political forces otherwise headed toward catastrophe. As the German sociologist Max Weber tells us, "In radical contrast to bureaucratic organization, charisma knows no formal and regulated appointment or dismissal, no career, advancement or salary, no supervisory or appeals body, no local or purely technical jurisdiction, and no permanent institutions in the manner of bureaucratic agencies."[40] In Israel, political society is already highly developed and bureaucratized, and without a charismatic figure like a Ben Gurion, there is little likelihood that a leader will emerge with the capacity to unify the highly developed segments of the Israeli society.

Yet there can be a Caesarist solution without a Caesar.[41] The Israeli-Palestinian conflict lacks a clear Caesarist path, but there is an illiberal bloc that may take the place of the absent charismatic and unifying leader. Leaders of the Likud, Shas, Israel Beiteinu, and Halchud HaLeumi (National Union) Parties initially positioned themselves to provide a new cultural and strategic equilibrium—toward the right side of the political spectrum—in order to fill the ideological vacuum created by reciprocally destructive factionalism.[42]

In principle, the Caesarist phenomenon is more likely to emerge in the Palestinian territories, given their more malleable and less entrenched civil society. The charismatic leader Marwan Barghouti, who is said to be planning, in collaboration with Hamas, a nonviolent free Palestine even while jailed in Israel for murder, remains a popular choice. Israel, the UAE, and Egypt, however, seem to prefer the exiled former Fatah official Mohammed Dahlan as the next Palestinian leader. At present, Hamas and PA leaders remain divided despite repeated efforts toward reconciliation, and one could easily imagine that a splintered Palestinian leadership could give rise to an illiberal populist Caesar who exploits yearnings for Palestinian unity.

Jewish religious orthodoxy, seeking to implement claims of divine ownership over Greater Israel, is gradually redefining the secular character of the Israeli state. Under the Likud governmental coalition, the Jewish Home, Shas, and Israel Beiteinu have succeeded in swinging the political pendulum toward a populist extreme that is neither strictly conservative (from an economic perspective) nor progressive (from a universal human rights point of view). These parties, despite their differences, call on Israelis to follow higher Jewish religious (Halakhic) laws and to secure the de facto expansion of the Jewish community to the post-1967 borders. They brandish an unscrupulous religious nationalism that disregards the price imposed on Israeli democracy and human rights.

Religion offers tangible solutions in uncertain times. It is not that people have become suddenly spiritual or are in search of a God; what they look for is a greater sense of family, a grounded community that promises to be there no matter what and to offer something more reliable than abstract allegiance to universalist values. Hegel described, in *The Philosophy of Right*, the temptation of liberal states to oscillate between the *Rechtsstaat* and the *Volksstaat*, between the state of law and the state of

culture. The amalgamation of law and culture may be a necessary foundation of the liberal state, even a secular Zionist state, but it becomes
dangerous when the cultural expression is deified at the expense of the
universal rule of law. The liberal state is in peril when the elevation of
religious culture, spawned in Israel's case by its struggle to preserve the
state's Jewish character, competes with the state's original cosmopolitan
intent. In this way, democracies can become illiberal, retaining some
democratic processes while abandoning the fundamental democratic
commitment to universal human rights. Israel is in danger of joining the
list of countries, such as Poland and Hungary, that have recently embarked
on this dangerous path.

The Israeli intellectual historian Zeev Sternhell said, "We are at the
height of an erosion process of the liberal values on which our society is
based. Those who regard liberal values as a danger to the nation, the
homeland and the Jewish state are the ones currently in power. They are
striving to delegitimize the left and anyone who does not hold the view
that conquering the land and settling it through the use of force are the
fundamental foundations of Zionism. That's why universal values and
universal rights are enemies of the state, in their view."[43] Israel is,
however, also endowed with robust political institutions designed around
the rule of law and a system of checks and balances. Despite outbursts of
anti-Enlightenment activism in political society, the chance that Israel will
become a theocracy should be seen as possible but unlikely.

Nationalist and religious ideologies thrive on the idea that they are
threatened by powerful enemies from within and without. "For ultranationalists, the enemy is within—NGOs, the minorities, the courts,"
explains Moshe Halbertal, an Israeli professor of Jewish philosophy.
Within the Knesset, Israeli right-wingers have marginalized Arab parties
and hampered leftists and liberals. Outside it, the political climate has
turned menacing: fans of the Beitar Jerusalem football club, calling themselves La Familia, sing racist chants and are frequently involved in gratu-
itous violence against Arabs. The drift to illiberalism is so disconcerting
that even politicians from the old traditional Likud, such as President
Reuven Rivlin and former defense minister Moshe Arens, are troubled by
the emergence of open racism.[44]

On the Palestinian side, whereas Yasser Arafat was once seen
as the hero unifying the fragmented Palestinian political factions,

unemployment, corruption, and declining delivery of services brought his popularity down, from 65 percent approval in 1996 to 47 percent in 2000. Support for the PA dropped to 37 percent in 2000 and to 29 percent a year later.[45] Hamas steadily became the leading grassroots organization, boasting of its greater ability to offer basic services to the poor—albeit services delivered on a militantly religious plate. Islamism soon took center stage in Palestinian politics. Well before the global market economy made its impact on the Palestinian territories, radical religious groups like Hamas were already on the rise.

Hamas shook the world when it took 74 seats in the January 2006 election, with Ismail Haniyeh at its head, leaving Fatah, the previous ruling party, with 45 seats.[46] One cannot overstate the importance of Hamas's Islamism as a unifying force, given its early capacity, as its early ideologue Ahmed Yassin put it, to provide extensive welfare assistance and services to all Palestinians "without distinction of religious belief or political affiliation."[47] While high Palestinian Authority officials continued to live separately from their people in varying degrees of luxury, Hamas's leaders earned respect by living among the people and sharing their hardships without sinking into corruption. Hamas's principled posture, coupled with a refusal to negotiate with Israel or to recognize the Oslo agreement, contributed to its rising popularity in Palestinian civil society at the expense of its secular and nationalist competitor, Fatah.

Just as in Israel, Palestinian secular nationalism and religious fundamentalism can be perceived as contradictory: the former asserts earthly aspirations while the latter urges sacrifice for a better afterlife.[48] Against the national and secular aspirations once personified by the Palestinian Liberation Organization and Arafat, Hamas posited an Islamist unifying alternative, which gained momentum with the charismatic and religious radical Yassin. Under Yassin's influence, the fusion between fundamentalism and nationalism filled a widening ideological hollow within Palestinian civil society. In 2004, the Israeli security services assassinated Yassin for his and Hamas's involvement in the Second Intifada. This did not, however, stop the strengthening of Hamas's institutional base or the promotion of the ideological platform that gave Hamas its electoral victory in 2006.

In 2007, with the PA weakened after the election and Hamas viewed as a pariah by Israelis and Westerners, Palestinian politics fell further into political paralysis. The bloody feud between Hamas and the PA tore apart the union between secular nationalist Palestinians in the West Bank and Islamist followers in Gaza. In this fight, and in subsequent Israeli incursions into Gaza, Hamas was dramatically weakened. Egyptian President Abdel Fattah al-Sisi's efforts to reconcile Hamas and the PA by integrating Hamas government officials in a broader Fatah-led government is an effort to overcome the political impasse, which paralyzes Palestinian governance and leaves them unable to forge a common approach to negotiating with Israel.[49]

Unlike Israelis, the Palestinians do not even have a state, let alone a democratic one, and their civil institutions are much weaker. In the absence of a unified, viable, and recognized government, they are more likely to remain in a Hobbesian state of nature. Without creative designs for peace, present conditions could at best yield a Palestinian Leviathan with a strong security apparatus, the most appealing feature of which being that, like al-Sisi's government in Egypt, it averts political collapse. At worst, Palestinians could descend into "a war of all against all."[50] While Palestinians are an oppressed minority, Hamas has manipulated their anger at that oppression into a belligerent, anti-Enlightenment ideology. Its 1988 charter urged the killing of Jews—"the Day of Judgement will not come until Muslims kill the Jews" (Article 7)—and invoked the *Protocols of the Elders of Zion* as evidence of a Jewish conspiracy to control the world (Article 32). Despite having repudiated the most egregious anti-Jewish statements of the charter, Hamas continues to inculcate anti-Enlightenment religious fundamentalism in Gaza's schools, including the cult of death or martyrdom as a noble path for Palestinians.

Nationalism and religious fundamentalism feed on fear. They clearly identify scapegoats and undermine the humanity of the minorities who live in their midst. Political exclusion, the denigration of the other, was exacerbated by the recurrent failure of peace negotiations as well as by privatization, the socioeconomic chasm, and rising fear on both sides of the conflict. Fear can be real or imagined, a combination of both, or the vestige of a previous trauma. Stored fear can be unleashed at opportune times by shrewd leaders. In Israel, tragic wars with Arab neighbors may have helped perpetuate the collective historical trauma of the Holocaust, as did the Qassam missiles, launched from Gaza, that showered the sky of southern Tel Aviv in 2006 and again in 2014. Few Israelis died in these attacks, but thousands took refuge in shelters, driven there by the same sirens that shriek every year on the Day of the Remembrance of the Shoah. Throughout the country, the sirens' warnings remind Israelis of a long history of trauma, forcing them to set aside their mundane routines to enter a life on high alert. While one can debate the actual scale of current danger, popular fear bolstered the secular Right's claim that Jewish settlements and an expanded security zone had become essential. As hoarded fear is released like an Aeolian wind, peace with the Palestinians becomes an ever more distant proposition, receding before the specter of Hezbollah along the northern border and sectarian warfare destabilizing the Arab world. Continuous trepidations provide political ammunition for the growing religious and nationalist bloc.

For the Palestinians, tragic wars with their Israeli neighbor rekindle the collective historical trauma of Israel's War of Independence, known as al-Nakba, or "the catastrophe"—memories reanimated by the Israeli incursions into Gaza in 2006 and 2014. In all these episodes of violence, Palestinian casualties far exceeded Israeli losses. Thousands took refuge in vulnerable shelters while thousands of others were directly exposed to Israeli bombardment. Throughout the Palestinian territories, dislocation, restricted movement, checkpoints, and random stops interrupt daily routines, continually replaying trauma. Palestinian fears, more real than exaggerated, have been woven into vengeful anger by fundamentalist leaders. Peace with the Israelis is a quixotic project, particularly since the Palestinians have lost the support of much of the broader Arab world. Their sense of isolation has become the bastion of religious and secular nationalist zealots decrying heavenly or ungodly forces.

Nakba cannot be compared to the Holocaust, and Israeli anxiety pales in comparison to daily Palestinian life under siege or occupation. It is useless to compare moral claims when each side offers competing narratives of victimization. The point is that fear will be manipulated by extremists to fan anger, gain political leverage, and avert the more arduous path toward peace. A new competition of narratives—one that envisions the best path out of violence—is desperately needed, especially when progressives and moderates on both sides are losing hope. The novelist David Grossman, whose depictions of both peoples have inspired readers in Israel and beyond, concedes: "People feel really that they are doomed to live like that forever and the air of despair is so heavy that people just do not have the mental energy to start to envision how life of peace [*sic*] can look like. So we do need leaders and politicians and also intellectuals and writers to formulate the option of peace, to insist on revitalizing the option of peace that today is not existing at all."[51]

Even during this period of great despair, another wind is irresistibly propelling history into the future. This powerful wind, the German philosopher Walter Benjamin reminds us, is progress.[52] The world of the counter-Enlightenment is fearful, deeply distrustful, and dangerously belligerent. And yet in their afflictions, people yearn not only for revenge but also for harmony, peace, and new beginnings. One needs to reclaim Janus's insistence on maintaining peace during cycles of hostility; one needs to imagine warmer winds blowing in a different direction and toward different ends; one needs to recover Plutus's sight to promote prosperity for the common good; and one needs to toil with all available instruments for a Middle East where freedom of opinion, freedom of worship, freedom from fear, freedom from want, and freedom from sexual discrimination can sustain these aspirations.

The prospects of rerouting the Levant Express may seem dim if we only wait for providential goodwill or rely on the power of the sword to settle the dust of war. Intellectual resignation, the inertia of the status quo, and habitual pessimism can amount to self-fulfilling prophecies. Machiavelli reminds us that while fatality, or *fortuna*, is always in operation, *virtù*, a leader's courage and foresight informed by history, can still break us out of familiar yet destructive patterns.

PART THREE   REROUTING: FOUR FREEDOMS PLUS ONE

IN 2011, WHEN REBELLIONS SPREAD throughout the Middle East like a Khamsin storm and Arab regimes were collapsing like sandcastles from the Maghrebian desert to the Arabian Peninsula, expectations soared for a new era of human rights. Yet by 2013, the Levant Express was running in reverse. Hopes for a nascent Egyptian democracy slid back into fears, confirmed by greater suffering and repression. Throughout the region, struggles for human rights were thwarted by entrenched authoritarianism, religious extremism, and war. Hundreds of thousands were killed, tortured or displaced.

Many in the region have forgotten how to dream. If we were to envision a different situation amid the current tragedy, it would be a peaceful Middle East from the shores of Tunisia to Iran. All twenty-one national governments would be based on republican constitutions shaped by human rights, open to the criticism of a free press, with parliaments representing citizens who freely voice their opinions both in public conversation and in free and fair elections. Populations would interact peacefully through trade, investment, cultural exchanges and tourism, and the region would boast great universities. The spirit of Cordoba, in which Muslims, Christians, and Jews commingled peacefully, would be restored. Religion would be separate from the state. Women would walk freely in the streets, realizing their full potential in the household and in the public sphere. If only, if only . . .

REROUTING THE LEVANT EXPRESS

The poster, "Rerouting the Levant Express," features a mid-twentieth-century American locomotive blazing into a sunny future along water and sand, with five wagons and the presidential Pullman car in tow. From the rear platform of the Marco Polo, Franklin and Eleanor Roosevelt wave to a crowd. Each wagon bears an inscription from the president's famous Four Freedoms speech with one added. "Freedom of speech," on the first wagon, is followed by "freedom of worship," "freedom from want," "freedom from fear," and finally "freedom from sexual discrimination." On each wagon is the corresponding Middle Eastern reinterpretation of Norman Rockwell's original poster series. On the

How can the Levant Express be rerouted toward more promising horizons? How can we move from sectarian violence toward the hopeful state just imagined? Pessimists will say this is a chimera and that any involvement by outsiders in the Middle East, however well-intended, will only incite more violence. But the possibility of sustainable peace cannot be dismissed so easily, especially under the guise of a cautious and short-sighted pragmatism that improvises responses to particular crises while failing to grapple with underlying problems.

The similarities between current social and political conditions and those of other historical periods suggest possible paths that can enable the train to regain momentum. Those who claim that Europe followed a different path of democratization and human rights, and that it is a "civilized" continent essentially different from the tumultuous Middle East, forget that untold numbers were killed in Europe for being Protestant or Catholic during the Thirty Years' War. The carnage of religious war greatly damaged the fabric of European societies, creating a sea of refugees who fled their native lands. Captives were drawn and quartered, heretics were burned at the stake, and mass atrocities were commonplace. The flames of religious sectarianism engulfed the achievements of the Renaissance, stifling what had been a rebirth of cultural creativity, independent thought, and scientific inquiry. Such dark episodes did not end four hundred years ago. Still bloodier periods of history followed until the end of World War II. Despite these spasms of nationalist violence, Europe has mostly flourished in peace for the past seventy years. Why shouldn't we, confronting a similar descent into sectarian war in Syria, Iraq, Libya, and Yemen, imagine a Middle East future in which such despair is known only to students of history?

Freedom of Speech wagon, the Egyptian Internet activist Wael Ghonim gives a speech about freedom in front of a crowd in Tahrir Square; on the Freedom of Worship wagon, an interfaith gathering in Jerusalem prays for the ending of the drought; for the Freedom from Want wagon, a generous Iftar dinner celebrated with all; for the Freedom from Fear wagon, a refugee holding his toddler as he escapes merciless waters; for Freedom from Sexual Discrimination, a Middle Eastern woman resembling Rosie the Riveter drives the Levant Express toward Nablus, the West Bank, where an old man and a child sit waiting. Created by Brooke VanDevelder, 2017 (© 2017 Micheline Ishay).

What paths can the Middle East take to reclaim the fundamental human rights principles invoked during the Arab uprisings? Who will spearhead these initiatives? The US drove the locomotive of history after World War II. Over time, it lost steam before it could reach its liberal internationalist destination. Human rights were too often invoked as a rationale for self-serving economic and geopolitical interests. In a September 2016 talk at the University of Denver, Vice President Joe Biden pointed out that both the Republican and Democratic Parties were split between isolationist and interventionist forces, with isolationism fueled by the disastrous Iraq war and the concerns of American workers since the 2008 economic meltdown. Invoking an argument advanced by Franklin Roosevelt during World War II, Biden explained that a healthy economic recovery at home cannot be sustained unless it is combined with a viable liberal world order.

How might such a Rooseveltian position, which coincides with core pillars of human rights, address the problems of today's Middle East? We should note that the sectarian warfare in the Middle East, however tragic, pales in comparison to World War II. During the worst days of that war, as more than sixty million people were losing their lives, the Nazis ruled Europe, and Japan invaded China and much of Southeast Asia, Roosevelt used his January 1941 State of the Union speech to raise his voice against isolationism and proclaim America's commitment to four pillars of freedom: freedom of speech, freedom of worship, freedom from want, and freedom from fear. These Four Freedoms would later be encapsulated in the preamble to the Universal Declaration of Human Rights (1948). Roosevelt left a fifth freedom, freedom from sexual discrimination, unaddressed in his speech, but it was forcefully promoted by his wife and political partner, Eleanor Roosevelt. Following the Allied victory over fascism, these ideals found tangible expression in a comprehensive post–world war effort: the establishment of the United Nations, the Universal Declaration of Human Rights, the establishment of democracies in West Germany and Japan, the open and growing world economy made possible by the Marshall Plan, the International Monetary Fund, the World Bank, the General Agreement on Tariffs and Trade, and the security guarantee provided for Western Europe under NATO.

A similar mission in Arab civil societies would need to be built on the fundamental pillars of human rights, all of which are required to

Franklin D. Roosevelt waves from the vestibule of a railcar. From the Franklin D. Roosevelt Presidential Library and Museum.

uphold the structure of a new order. The remainder of this book is an extended thought experiment, envisioning constructive possibilities for the future of the Middle East. It argues for an invigorated democratic political discourse and outlines conditions for a revived Islamic Enlightenment; it promotes a New Deal economic strategy based on new security architectures; it explains how heightening social contradictions can lead to women's empowerment; and finally, it addresses a continuous lightning rod in the region, the Palestinian question, offering a human rights framework as a way forward in the midst of paralyzing disagreement and seemingly endless conflict.

CHAPTER FIVE

Vox Populi and the Islamic Enlightenment

FREEDOM OF SPEECH

In 1942, American artist Norman Rockwell was commissioned by the *Saturday Evening Post* to create a series of paintings based on Roosevelt's Four Freedoms. For freedom of speech, he portrayed a man in work clothes, standing tall and speaking fearlessly amid a better-dressed, yet respectful, even admiring, crowd. A contemporary Rockwell might portray a young man, modeled after the Egyptian Internet activist Wael Ghonim, standing on a stage in front of a crowded Tahrir Square in 2011, calling for freedom of speech.

The right to express oneself without interference is fundamental to democratization and human rights. It was proclaimed as part of the French Declaration of the Rights of Man and of the Citizen in 1789 and was adopted as part of the First Amendment to the American Constitution in 1791. Freedom of speech was further spelled out in the 1948 Universal Declaration of Human Rights: "Everyone has the right to freedom of opinion and expression; this right includes freedom to hold opinions without interference and to seek, receive, and impart information and ideas through any media and regardless of frontiers" (Article 19). Without such a right, there can be no fair path to political representation.

There have been times when free speech and critical thinking flourished in the Arab world. More recently, however, the right of free

Freedom of Speech, by Norman Rockwell. Printed by permission of the Norman Rockwell Family Agency; © 1943 the Norman Rockwell Family Entities. Illustration provided by Curtis Licensing.

expression has routinely been trampled upon. It flared briefly during the Arab uprising but was severely curtailed by the return of authoritarianism. How can it be resurrected in the Middle East? The Arab Spring sparked a yearning for a renewal of the Muslim Golden Age, stirred critical thinking, and developed new regionwide deliberative platforms as means of resistance that could open new paths toward democratization.

In Egypt, the short-lived freedom associated with the Arab Spring was already on trial soon after the revolution of 2011. On the fourth anniversary of the 2013 coup that overthrew the government of Mohamed Morsi, I met with a former Muslim Brother in a Cairo restaurant. He was obviously not commemorating the day, yet observed that "with Morsi in power, the Egyptians had already lost their famous sense of humor." He mentioned specifically the government's reaction to Bassem Youssef, a comedian and satirist who was charged with insulting Islam and making derogatory remarks about the newly elected president.

When Egyptian General Abdel Fattah al-Sisi overthrew President Morsi in July 2013, he championed a new constitution that guaranteed freedom of the press. The political ambiance, however, changed overnight. The new president put in place a system of counterterrorism laws that would purge the media of anyone sympathizing with the Muslim Brotherhood. In August 2015, three Al Jazeera journalists were imprisoned, and many others would soon meet the same fate. Khaled Dawoud, deputy editor of the newspaper *Al Ahram*, said, "We only have a chance to express ourselves in foreign media, but in the local media, we're being more attacked as Western agents. So . . . definitely, you know, the wide level participation in politics that marked the general scene in Egypt after January 25, 2011, has disappeared . . . and we're back into glorifying the leader."[1]

There was no corresponding military coup in Tunisia. Instead, with two general elections and a new constitution since the departure of Ben Ali, the Carthaginian spirit of tolerance and freedom of speech, which prevailed from 814 BCE to 146 BCE, created the Arab world's most democratic state—a rare beacon of hope. In 2015, however, following a series of Islamic extremist attacks, freedom of expression and basic civil rights confronted fresh challenges. In May of that year, two gunmen attacked the Bardo Museum in Tunis, killing twenty-one tourists and a security guard; in June, a jihadist rampaged through the Mediterranean resort of Sousse, murdering thirty-eight tourists; and in November, a suicide attack killed twelve presidential guards and wounded twenty others. In response, the Tunisian government declared a state of emergency, banning demonstrations that "could disrupt peace and order."[2] This flexing of executive power was not as excessive as in Egypt, but many Tunisian journalists and bloggers have been indicted for publishing critical information about the government.

The crackdowns were far harsher in the Gulf monarchies, where free expression has always been more constrained. The brutality of the Saudi Arabian ruling family was in full swing after 2011. It crushed the popular uprising in neighboring Bahrain, where the Saudi-backed government handed out sentences of one to seven years in prison to anyone who publicly insulted the king, the flag, or the national emblem. The Saudi suppression of free speech was demonstrated by the sentence given to

Shi'a blogger Raif Badawi: ten years in prison and one thousand lashes for publishing the website "Free Saudi Liberals," on which he allegedly committed apostasy against Islam. His fellow Shi'a activists experienced similar ordeals; some were tortured, and others received lengthy prison terms or even the death sentence.[3] More recently, the kingdom's intransigence toward freedom of speech was epitomized by the gruesome murder of Saudi journalist Jamal Khashoggi in Istanbul on October 2, 2018.

Even in more tolerant Gulf monarchies such as the UAE, Kuwait, and Oman, counterterrorism laws were issued to curtail the influence of Islamist sympathizers and members of Islah, a branch of the Muslim Brotherhood. The UAE authorities drafted regulations against acts such as "instigating hatred against the state" to prosecute and imprison dissidents. In 2014, additional laws were enacted to prescribe severe penalties, including death for people convicted of terrorism—a term applied not only to perpetrators of "acts of terror" but also to individuals acting disloyally toward the country's leadership.[4]

Kuwaiti authorities followed a similar course of action after the uprising, selectively using provisions in the constitution, national security laws against cybercrime, and other legislation to prosecute dissent. Between 2011 and 2015, over a dozen people were sentenced for using blogs, Twitter, Facebook, and other social media to criticize Emir Jaber al-Ahmad al-Sabah, the government, religion, or even the rulers of neighboring countries.[5] In Oman, national security laws were also enacted along with a citizenship law that allowed the government to revoke the citizenship of any individual who "embraces principles or ideologies that harm Oman's interest" or "works in favor of a hostile country that acts against the interests of Oman."[6]

Qatar, with one of the highest per capita GDPs in the world, experienced relatively little domestic dissent. During the Arab uprisings, Al Jazeera and other media outlets enjoyed great freedom as long as they did not criticize Qatari politics, becoming the envy of journalists in the region. At the same time, Qatar supported Egypt's Muslim Brotherhood government along with Ennahdha in Tunisia, Hamas, and Islamist opponents of the Syrian regime, including the al-Qaeda affiliated al-Nusra. Qatar saw in the Brothers a combination of religious organization and discipline that mirrored its own government, but neighboring leaders in Saudi Arabia, Bahrain, and the UAE, regarding political Islam as a revolutionary challenge to their own power, publicly rebuked Doha's vision and actions. The smooth transition of the emirship in 2013 from Sheikh Hamad bin Khalifa al-Thani to his son Sheikh Tamim bin Hamad al-Thani presumably represented Qatar's concession to this pressure, aligning the nation's foreign policy more closely to that of the other Gulf states. With $200 billion invested in hosting the 2022 World Cup, as well as pressure from regional and Western powers to synchronize Gulf efforts against radical Islamism, Qatar enacted new cybercrime legislation to stop those who were undermining the status quo. In 2017, however, deeming these concessions insufficient, the Saudis and Emiratis severed their ties with Qatar, accusing it of harboring and sponsoring terrorism and using its Al Jazeera media outlet to disseminate propaganda. As of May 2018, the International Monetary Fund (IMF) has demonstrated that the economic impact of the blockade on Qatar has been moderate due to the country's agile domestic and external fiscal policies. Whatever the long-term outcome of the Saudi-Qatar dispute, freedom of expression is now under greater scrutiny in Qatar than it was before the Arab Spring.[7]

Before 2011, the UAE and Qatar were striving to become hubs of Arab culture, with new universities; the construction of high-profile museums, such as the Guggenheim, the Louvre in Abu Dhabi, and the Museum of Islamic Art in Doha; and intellectual gatherings, such as the Doha Forum. During the uprisings, an exhibition in Qatar promoted the Muslim world's major accomplishments in the sciences from the eighth to the fifteenth century, displaying works by scientists, physicians, astronomers, engineers, artists, chemists, and architects from the Golden Age of Arab science. In his 2009 Cairo speech, President Barack Obama also offered a tribute to this period: "It was Islam that carried the light of learning through so many centuries, paving the way for Europe's Renaissance and Enlightenment. It was innovation in Muslim communities that developed the order of algebra; our magnetic compass and tools of navigation; our mastery of pens and printing; our understanding of how disease spreads and how it can be healed."[8] Science flourished in the Arab world in an atmosphere of great political and cultural tolerance,[9] but that era ended in the fifteenth century, and the Arab Golden Age was quickly overtaken by European exploration and innovation.

Invention and originality require an environment conducive to free and critical thought. The Emiratis with whom I worked while I was a visiting professor at Khalifa University encouraged free thinking, but mainly in the realm of science and technology. Teaching critical thinking there was not easy. Most of my students feared that classroom discussions would be over-heard, and they often hastened to clarify that the things they said in class did not represent their personal positions. Even on benign topics, they were not always comfortable expressing opinions for fear of offending the rulers.

In 2011 and 2012, political fears made these students even more reti-cent. Their caution was understandable: those who are free to think critically may envision a better government and perhaps put forward pernicious proposals for reform. Free thought was appealing and invigorating, but it was extremely dangerous in a region where, as one Emirati journalist told me, "the uprisings stripped us of our innocence." Open discussion remained sequestered behind private walls. I was regularly invited to teach political philosophy and discuss current events with members of the country's elite, but these conversations took place far away from the media and the masses. During the Arab Golden Age, in contrast, philosophers and scientists trav-eled freely and discussed ideas critically from one discipline to another. Intellectual freedom also flourished under the Ottoman Empire and in nineteenth-century Egypt. Sadly, the vital role of this freedom is rarely recog-nized in contemporary celebrations of Arab contributions to science and philosophy. It will require more than museums to revive the spirit of inquiry. An unrestrained and dedicated pursuit of scientific understanding, which has already begun in the Gulf countries thanks to their strong investment in education, will be essential to any new era of critical thinking.

Without robust institutional anchors, freedom of speech in academia or the press is jeopardized whenever authoritarian regimes fear losing their grip on power. Al-Sisi's Egyptian emergency and censorship laws are a reminder of this principle, as were Turkish President Recep Tayyip Erdogan's actions in July 2016, when he retaliated against a failed coup not just by arresting military officers but also by firing university officials, restricting the movement of academics, and imprisoning journalists.

With such a checkered history of tolerance and democracy in the Middle East, what can be done to cultivate a greater acceptance of freedom of speech? An important first step would be to encourage structures that contribute to a more robust civil society. This would require building on recent efforts like the Internet Social Forum (ISF), inaugurated in Tunis during the 2015 World Social Forum—a global meeting bringing together organizations opposed to neoliberalism, convened to discuss and promote ideas about democracy and human rights. The ISF declared its "commitment to a common goal of building a people's Internet from below and beyond borders: an Internet that works in the public interest and solidarity, where control is in the hands of people; an Internet based on human dignity, equality, social justice, freedom and people's communication rights,"[10] an Internet "free of surveillance, corporate dominance, and governmental abuse of power."[11]

Since today's voices of dissent are isolated and vulnerable, a regional organization with the willingness and ability to promote and protect free speech would be a great step forward. It could be developed based on such precedents as the International Workingmen's Association, formed by the European Left in 1864 as an outgrowth of the democratic revolutions of 1848. Just as the First International permitted labor representatives from various European states to meet for coordinated planning and action, a similar organization in the Arab world might bring together human rights representatives from each country to coordinate public action and articulate common principles. To the extent it achieved global visibility, it might also afford its members some protection. Alternatively, like other such networks in history, it could operate clandestinely for as long as was necessary.

Just as the French government operated in exile in London during the Vichy collaborationist government in World War II, so could a Middle East human rights institution, with appointed delegates known for their integrity. That body could have several functions: to educate Arab citizens on the theory and practice of human rights, provide policy recommendations, create free venues that encourage independent artistic and cultural expression, monitor human rights progress, and enlist the international community to provide economic rewards for countries that improve their human rights standards. It would create a forum of deliberative democracy within and between civil societies while bringing pressure against violating countries by "naming, shaming, and blaming." It would also allow for a sturdier and better-informed civil society in the Middle East, one that creates spaces for homegrown human rights activists and connects them with existing external human rights NGOs.[12]

Such an organization would be challenged by authoritarian regimes. One could hope, however, for the logistical and technological support of more open societies. Secure virtual communications would facilitate

Gustav Klimt's *The Kiss*, projected by Tammam Azzam on a bombed-out building in Syria, 2013. Courtesy of Tammam Azzam.

dialogue among members and disseminate information throughout the region. Such a forum might ultimately yield a new Declaration of Human Rights for the Middle East, to supplant the religiously tainted 1990 Cairo Declaration of Human Rights in Islam. Circumventing virtual censorship to secure freedom of speech will remain a challenge, as technology enables both communication and government surveillance. Nonetheless, as the Arab uprising revealed, technology and social media can create real possibilities for promoting freedom.

It would be a mistake to think that freedom of opinion has been totally extinguished. "If you want to understand the Middle East, ditch the think tank panels (in Washington, D.C.), and catch the photo exhibits and hip-hop shows by Arab artists," stressed BBC correspondent Kim Ghattas.[13] Where speech is censored, images and songs are irrepressible. "Since we don't have the freedom to express ourselves directly, we can put all our emotions in art," reports Libyan artist Faiza Ramadan, speaking for many in the region who see art as both therapy and a form of audience education.[14] The synergy of superimposed images, alternating rhythms and rapid-fire words in hip-hop songs leaves room for the imagination—and space for perpetuating resistance beneath the radar of censorship. The Arab uprising brought a flurry of artistic expression, particularly in such highly accessible popular forms as rap music and graffiti. The squares of revolutions—Tahrir, the Pearl Roundabout, and beyond—have been renovated to erase the memories of free speech and free association. But there is always a space for the committed artist. When Syrian artist Tammam Azzam superimposed Gustav Klimt's *The Kiss* on the façade of a building torn by the civil war in Damascus, the image went viral. Original songs evoking civil wars, the brutality of the army, and disappointment after the Arab Spring have been shared across the globe. With irrepressible forms of art, hope continues to suffuse subterranean terrains, defying old social conventions and reshaping religious mores.

FREEDOM OF WORSHIP

The concept of freedom of worship was fleshed out clearly, almost eight years after Roosevelt's 1941 speech, in the 1948 Universal Declaration of Human Rights: "Everyone has the right to freedom of thought, conscience and religion; this right includes freedom to change his religion or belief, and freedom, either alone or in community with others and in public or private, to manifest his religion or belief in teaching, practice, worship and observance" (Article 18). To honor this ideal, Rockwell painted people standing shoulder to shoulder, each praying according to his or her own beliefs. A similar scene occurred in 2010 in a valley near Jerusalem, when representatives of different faiths, each wearing distinctive religious attire, prayed together for the end of a seven-year drought. It was an encouraging but uncommon scene in a region known more for sectarian violence than for interfaith cooperation.

These hopeful images stand in contrast to our current dark times. The struggle for religious freedom has been waged throughout history; it was essential to every democratic revolution after World War II, and it gained new momentum after the Arab uprisings. But as we have seen, early revolutionary accomplishments often suffer setbacks. How can freedom of religion—and from religion—be reclaimed at a time when intolerance has so dramatically subverted the political culture? As the Arab Winter's cold winds swept the region, the authoritarian governments in relatively

Freedom to Worship, by
Norman Rockwell. Printed
by permission of the
Norman Rockwell Family
Agency; © 1943 the
Norman Rockwell Family
Entities. Illustration
provided by Curtis
Licensing.

stable countries, which had remained unshaken, quickly regained control over political and religious groups challenging their legitimacy. But a young generation, seeking more for their future, could rekindle the yearning for a new Islamic Enlightenment—one predicated on the free interpretation of religious texts, on reason, critical thinking, civic education, and the separation of religion and state. If widespread support for religious tolerance is to emerge, it must be in cosmopolitan cities, hubs of trade routes that welcome visitors and workers from all parts of the world. Why couldn't the Middle East reclaim its old centers of trade and foster the innovations and religious tolerance that once made it the cradle of civilization and the envy of the world?

The American and French Revolutions, which spurred a long series of democratic insurrections, established freedom of worship as a constitutional right. In World War II, the world was witness to the tragedy of six million Jews sent to their deaths simply because of their religious or ethnic background. One of the first resolutions passed by the newly constituted United Nations in 1946, presented for the General Assembly's consideration by the delegation from Egypt, declared that "it is in higher interests of humanity to put an immediate end to religious and so-called racial persecution and discrimination."[15] Likewise, the Convention on the Prevention of Genocide and the Universal Declaration of Human Rights, both adopted by the UN in 1948, reflected a determination that an event like the Holocaust would never again take place. Despite recent horrific massacres, such as Saddam Hussein's campaign against the Kurds or ISIS's against the Yazidi, religious persecution in the modern MENA region has not approached the Holocaust's scale of genocide, but freedom of religion has been intermittently repressed. Hindus and Buddhists have been seen as infidels, while Jews, Christians, and Shi'as, as people of the Book, have been generally tolerated as monotheists even if they were relegated to the sidelines of Arab societies.

With the establishment of the State of Israel in 1948, Jews native to the Levant who had long coexisted with Arab neighbors came to be seen as conspirators with the "Zionist entity." They were increasingly marginalized and ultimately evicted throughout the Arab world.[16] The Jewish Holocaust, so often invoked elsewhere to demonstrate the need for religious tolerance, is never openly discussed in Arab countries. Recognizing the Holocaust could be seen as conceding the necessity of a Jewish state, a counterargument to the plight of Palestinians and their yearning for national independence.[17] When I discussed this issue with young educated Emiratis, they often posed some form of the question "Why should the Arabs pay the price for a Jewish genocide under the hands of European imperialists?" More common, however, were cases like that of my students at Khalifa University. They were not even familiar with the term "Holocaust," though a few knew of Hitler's aggression. They did not question, let alone deny, the extermination of the Jews; they had simply never heard of it.

One of my female students asked if my reference to the Holocaust had to do with "that girl hiding in the attic." I told her it did and asked if she had read *The Diary of Anne Frank*. She said she had found it on her father's bookshelf and had been curious about it, but she did not know the whole story. Despite my awareness of the government's sensitivity to that issue, I brought two books to the next class: one released by Berlin's Topography of Terror museum, which documents Germany's extermination of the Jews,

and selections from Hitler's *Mein Kampf*. Without additional explanation,
I read selections from both books. The students were shocked. Their ignorance was unsurprising, since conspiracy theories about the Jews are taken
for granted in much of the Arab world, even among educated students and
the elite.

The question of religious freedom took center stage in Middle Eastern
human rights discourse after the repression of the Muslim Brothers and
the escalating Sunni and Shi'a sectarian conflict, which has dismantled
the very fabric of societies and states. From North Africa to the Arabian
Peninsula, states began strictly regulating religious activities in mosques
and civil societies in an effort to thwart political protests. The degree of
religious openness and control, however, varies across the region.
Morocco and Tunisia are relatively tolerant of religious diversity; even
Jews practice their religion more freely there than in other parts of the
MENA. Both countries offer constitutional protections for religious
freedom and religious minorities. In 2012, Tunisia's Islamist movement,
Ennahdha, under pressure from liberal forces, abandoned its early ambi-
tion to create an Islamic state and opted for an agenda in which conservative Muslims would be able to express their religious beliefs in ways that
had been banned under the Ben Ali regime. Tunisia's new constitution
states that the country's religion is Islam and the president must be a
Muslim, but it also stipulates that Tunisia is a civil state, responsible for
disseminating "the values of moderation and tolerance," securing holy
sites, and preventing punishment related to apostasy.[18] With the rise of
jihadists in the region, the minister of religious affairs was assigned the
responsibility of overseeing and controlling mosques. Following the mass
shootings at the Bardo Museum and in Sousse in 2015, the Tunisian state
shut down eighty mosques that it accused of promoting Islamist radicalism. By putting Tunisian Islamist operations under a siege of surveillance, the new liberal state revealed its vulnerability.[19]

In Egypt, the Muslim Brotherhood enjoyed a brief time in power
following its election victory in 2012, but it suffered a brutal crackdown
after al-Sisi came into power as a result of the 2013 coup-d'état. The new
government was far from secular, as the 2014 constitution continued to
identify Islam as the state religion. It also specified that Al-Azhar, the religious university in Cairo, would be "the main reference for religious
sciences and Islamic affairs."[20] The constitution declares that "freedom of

belief is absolute," but it grants freedom of religious practice only to the three monotheistic religions.[21] This paper freedom is hardly relevant for the forty or so Jews left in Egypt; but it has greater impact for the approximately 10 percent of the population that is recognized as Christian, 90 percent of whom are Coptic Orthodox.[22] In April 2017, the government declared a three-month state of emergency after ISIS claimed responsibility for two deadly attacks against Coptic churches. Assuring the Copts of government protection, President al-Sisi declared: "I won't say those who fell are Christian or Muslim; I will say that they're Egyptian."[23] Still, minority religious groups such as the Baha'is, and even Shi'a and Copts, remain under severe legal and cultural restriction, and the constitution does not recognize the freedom to convert. According to the US State Department's Religious Freedom Report, "Although religious conversion is not prohibited by law, the government does not recognize conversion from Islam in practice, and Muslim-born citizens who leave Islam for another religion may not change the religion field on their identity cards."[24]

The greatest problem for the Egyptian state today is its continuing struggle against the expanding influence of political Islam.[25] The Muslim Brotherhood, the one major Sunni group intermittently denied political freedom in Egypt since Nasser, was once again forced to go underground. After 2013, the new Egyptian authorities designated the Muslim Brothers as terrorists and barred them from political society, along with some 1,200 civil organizations sympathetic to their cause. Since August 2013, when more than 800 Muslim Brothers were massacred at Rabaa Square, thousands more have been imprisoned, leaving freedom of religion in greater jeopardy than before the revolution.[26] To offset the Muslim Brotherhood's influence, the government favored the Salafists, an ultra-conservative Islamist group that supported al-Sisi's coup and was less threatening to political power.[27] In Turkey, the political and religious Gulenist movement was banned as a threat to Erdogan's regime, and the Muslim Brothers were identified as allies. Had religion been separated from politics in the first place, both the Muslim Brotherhood and the Gulenists, one would hope, might have been accepted as contributing members of society, with the government encouraging their influence in social services and making their political ambitions less urgent. In that way, freedom of religion would prevail within the parameters of a constitution based on clear human rights principles.

In most Gulf nations, Islam is the state religion, but most religious minorities are free to practice their faith privately, and all religious denominations are expected to observe limits. Sermons (Khutbah) preached in the mosques are likely to be monitored by the state to curtail Islamist extremism. Shi'a Muslims enjoy religious rights but frequently experience harassment, particularly in Bahrain and Kuwait.[28] Life is more restrictive in Saudi Arabia, the most religiously intolerant country in the Arab world. A recent royal decree made atheism punishable by up to twenty years in prison. Sufi and Shi'a minorities are banned from religious practice, and apostasy carries the death penalty. Saudi Arabia remains a regional power, funding the ongoing Sunni sectarian war against Iran-backed Shi'a groups, as well as against the Muslim Brotherhood within its kingdom and beyond.[29] While Roosevelt's second freedom seems to be taking fragile root in some parts of the Arab world, it is a distant dream in others, particularly in Libya, Syria, and Yemen—countries immersed in proxy wars fueled by the rulers of Iran and Saudi Arabia.

Today, fatigued by decades of intolerance and religious warfare, the region desperately needs a new wave of Islamic Enlightenment, one even more robust than those that occurred under the Abbasid, Moghul, and Ottoman dynasties. Many Western analysts don't recognize that these empires showed an early commitment to religious tolerance and that Islamic philosophy and science made significant contributions to the Renaissance in Europe. The sixteenth-century Moghul emperor Akbar, borrowing his worldview from Sufism, a mystical interpretation of Islam based on divine love and wisdom in the world, broke from the domination of the clerics and professed the commonalities among religions. Similarly, from the capture of Constantinople in 1453 until World War I, the Ottomans provided formal recognition and state protection to Christian and Jewish communities (yet provided fewer rights for those groups than for Muslims). As the empire expanded, provinces large and small were added with continuous respect to religious diversity.[30] Gradually, the Ottomans declared civil equality between their Muslim and non-Muslim subjects; they outlawed the slave trade and challenged clerical opposition to anatomic dissection. Culture was modernized, with people electing secular over religious education.[31]

To reclaim that religious freedom and tolerance, the warring factions in today's Middle East must come to the conclusion reached by those who survived the Thirty Years' War or World War II: that freedom of religion can exist only when the state and religion are separate. A first step toward that objective must be to cultivate a climate of religious tolerance.[32] To this end, many have called for an Islamic Reformation,[33] but this term has been often used loosely, as not all reform movements embrace liberal ideals. Both Salafism and Wahhabism seek to reform, restore, and purify communities of faith by recovering essential religious and conservative principles—and we know all too well that so-called reformers sometimes advocate their beliefs with the sword.[34]

What, then, should a new Islamic Enlightenment resemble? In 1784, Immanuel Kant asked a similar question in a famous pamphlet called "Was ist Aufklarung?" ("What is Enlightenment?"). He maintained that people had to cut their umbilical cord to the past, having remained too long in darkness due to their "laziness and cowardice." "Sapere Aude!" he urged.[35] This slogan of the Enlightenment was translated in contemporary terms as "think for yourself." Yet reason is not simply an act of rebellion. If it were, Kant understood, we would end up in a state of anarchy, without a clear destination. Reason is both a deliberative instrument and a goal; it cultivates the capacity to see through multiple lenses, to acknowledge without encroaching on the rights and the dignity of each individual, and to strive to maximize the common good based on universal principles of rights (what Kant calls the categorical imperative).[36]

A reinterpretation of Islamic religious texts with tolerance in mind should coincide with the empowerment of individual interpretation, akin to the spirit of the Protestant Reformation, and a critical adherence to reason. In the Arab world, this would open the door to pluralism and religious freedom rather than dogmatism or unconditional faith. It would enable critical dialogue within Islam, as well as between Islam and other faiths—a process that could be fostered in schools, mosques, and the media. It could inspire the revision of civic education across the Arab world, foster separation between state and religion, and carve out the kind of secular space of tolerance that encourages economic cooperation, trade, and exposure to other cultures.

Empowering individuals in the MENA region to interpret religious texts is, however, not an easy proposition. Many times when I was teaching in the UAE, I was surprised by my students' inability to interpret Qur'anic texts in relation to current events. When I would allude to apparent contradictions in Qur'anic scriptures and ask for their views, they would typically quote higher religious authorities. One bright Emirati student who responded to my queries by deferring to a religious cleric told me she had memorized Qur'anic verses from a young age, but she resisted challenging the imams' often archaic interpretations. As the Arab Spring started to unravel, however, she began to find her voice, interpreting critical religious texts for herself.

Individual engagement with the meanings of texts might have felt rebellious to my students, but Kant saw it as a moral responsibility. In *Religion within the Limits of Reason Alone,* he showed that one could move beyond the prevailing Christian ideology by placing reason and duty at the center of one's moral universe and religion at the periphery. "Religion," he wrote, "is the recognition of all duties as divine commands."[37] In that sense, religion encourages the individual's best intention to attain the "summum bonum," the highest good, and universal rights across borders. Kant's philosophy of religion was a corollary of his moral ethic and his argument for the primacy of reason.

During the Arab uprising, I spoke often with a high-level Emirati royal who was particularly interested in these ideas and in the separation of state and religion. He was concerned about the place of religion in his highly conservative society, and he nurtured a private admiration for the Enlightenment thinkers. For him, Kant provided a compromise, a way not to rebuff religion but to subordinate it to reason while seeking what is best for all—a way to eradicate fanaticism without excising religion. In our conversations, he mused about the arrival of a pre-Enlightenment figure, an Arab Martin Luther (he was perhaps unaware of intolerant episodes attributable to Luther).

Such humanistic values, I told the prince, would be taught to children through civic education. To fulfill this aim, the state would need to take seriously its responsibility for education and for encouraging an individual and rational interpretation of the Qur'an outside the direct influence of clerics. This would not be easy to implement. Despite educational reforms in the Muslim and Arab world, civic education, vital to the teaching of religious tolerance, has remained weak. This problem was well illustrated by one of my Emirati students, a princess from a neighboring city-state who was working on her master's thesis under my supervision. Like many of her compatriots, she was a feisty young woman; she would always arrive late to class, usually blaming her chauffeur for underestimating the travel time needed to reach Abu Dhabi. She was always well covered with a black headscarf and *sheyla*, and her eyes flashed with passion during the class conversations. She was eager to discuss the Emirati national identity—a significant question for a postcolonial people, particularly in a nomadic society that had been catapulted from rags to riches.[38]

Three concurrent but dissimilar forces—none of which is sufficient by itself to provide a dominant narrative—have contributed to the region's confused sense of identity. Bedouin society belonged to a bypassed phase of history; Western consumerism was appealing but impersonal and anticommunal; and Islamism, still active in the Gulf despite being suppressed in Egypt since 1954, was an anachronistic counterforce to consumerism and globalization. These social contradictions were polarized during the Arab Spring. For my student, as for many educated Emiratis, some mediating alternative had to be found to create a common, modern Emirati identity. Civic education could shape such an identity, but when I asked her what sort of civic education was taking place in schools, she answered, "None."

This problem was not unique to the Emirates. Other Arab states, still very much under the yoke of authoritarianism, were reluctant to teach children critical thought and human rights. Not without cause, rulers feared that free critical thought as an integral part of public and civic education might be used to question their authority. While there are signs this reluctance may be easing,[39] there remains an unfortunate dissonance between intention and reality when it comes to civic and democratic education in the Arab world.[40] Educational reform is critical to fostering progress toward a tolerant environment. Should a strong program of civic education be developed, it would have to combine two narratives: the historical and cultural experience of particular nations and their peoples, and an appeal to a common future built on universal ethics and human rights. The former could be achieved with a knowledge of history, the latter with adherence to the method of critical thinking and tolerance of different viewpoints.

Many in the region became aware of the need for a robust civic education during the Arab uprising, and this awareness continued to surface at the Arab Tunisian Research and Policy Study meeting of May 2015, where the Rawlsian Tunisian philosopher Monir Kechaou spoke of the importance of secular civic education to sustain democracy and human rights in civil society.[41] The test of the success of civic education would be the degree of harmonious coexistence among different religions. Religious pluralism requires more than indulging religious diversity; it also demands a commitment to a shared future. As the Muslim interfaith leader Eboo Patel said, "Where diversity is a fact, pluralism is an achievement—it means deliberate and positive engagement of diversity; it means building strong bonds between people from different backgrounds."[42] A small step toward religious plurality occurred with the first exhibit at the Louvre in Abu Dhabi, where for the first time the public could see Muslim, Christian, and Jewish religious relics and art displayed side by side.[43]

Civic bonds are created through a sense of common cause and a shared identity that transcends religious and ethnic differences. For many Muslims, however, the dissociation of Islam from politics is tantamount to atheism and is seen as part of the curse of Western influence. After all, they maintain, Islam already provides answers for all moral questions and has been informed by laws tested throughout history.[44] Modern secularism, however, conforms to the tolerant voices of many religions, provided that they have abandoned the political exclusivism left over from their tribal beginnings. The health of the political body requires the separation of religion and state, as governments and faith communities have different constituents and different responsibilities toward them. Because there is no one Islam and no one interpretation of the Shari'a, governments that face conflicts between religious factions need to assert common values and prevent any one religious group from dominating politically at the expense of others. This means that civic membership must not be tied to the profession of religious beliefs, and while the right to a faith should be protected, religious forays into politics should be checked by a legitimate state.

When I was invited in fall 2010 to the American University of Sharjah, I engaged in a classroom discussion about the importance of human rights and the separation between the mosque and the state. Students were uncomfortable with this idea: they thought Islam provided a moral compass for social and political activities and could therefore not be severed from politics. They further suggested that atheism was Western and not consistent with core Muslim moral values. I tried to explain that the divorce between religion and state was a compromise reached by religious devotees who, after the wars of religion in the West, were seeking a civic space that could serve both sides. It was a strategy necessary for their own survival. Atheism is one of many possible responses to religious questions, but it was not the driving force behind the separation of state and religion in the West. I also described how, in his *Decisive Treatise*, the medieval Arab thinker Averroës provided—well before the European Enlightenment—a philosophical justification for the doctrine of separation between religion and state: "since it has been determined that the Law makes it obligatory to reflect upon existing things by means of the intellect, and to consider them; and consideration is nothing more than inferring and drawing out the unknown from the known ... and it is evident that this manner of reflection the Law calls for and urges is the most complete kind of reflection by means of the most complete kind of syllogistic reasoning and is the one called 'demonstration.'"[45] His vision, later shared later by European Enlightenment thinkers, has yet to be widely accepted in the MENA region.

Islam has a long history of religious cohabitation, encouraged within the Indian Moghul and Ottoman Empires and in the halcyon days of Cordoba, where a Moorish fortress houses a museum of the three religious cultures. Later, during the Ottoman era, religious dialogue and cultural diversity overcame conflict. This culture of tolerance spread among successful Arab trading centers from Tunis to Alexandria, to Beirut, to Damascus and Baghdad. These urban centers, scattered around the Mediterranean like an archipelago, all invented different expressions of the Islamic Enlightenment. Like Roman imperialists, the Ottomans also knew that the best way to sustain their empire was to give up some control, entrusting different religious groups with some degree of independence.

The call for clearer separation between state and religion historically has been related to the drive for mercantilist and capitalist ventures. Feudalism is based on agriculture and cooperative economic relationships between people under the converged authority of the church and the state. Capitalism, in contrast, favors all forms of competition, including economic rivalry with the state and with religious institutions, and the development of economic cooperation and contracts between trading peoples, states, and city-states—contracts that dissociate revealed and absolute morality from transparent rules governing business transactions based on mutual interest. In addition to trade partnerships, the scientific revolution and the Enlightenment yielded a new worldview that insisted on logical arguments based on facts and evidence.

It should not come as a surprise that the old spirit of Islamic religious tolerance coincided with a period of economic prosperity, commercial cooperation, and scientific development. In the postcolonial period, the push for a clear separation of religion and state may have been delayed by the late arrival of free enterprise. For a long time after World War II, economic policy in the Arab world consisted largely of Soviet-style five-year plans. Centralized collectivist worldviews, whether nationalist, communist, or Islamist, seem best suited to heavy-handed, state-sponsored economic approaches that neither rely on nor encourage free speech or freedom of religion. New economic trends, however, are advancing in much of the region, creating the preconditions for greater tolerance. Democratization requires many arduous steps. Just as religious conflicts within civil society demand a separation between religion and the state, the secular state must in turn be checked by a constitution based on human rights.

If the worst excesses of religious intolerance are now prevalent, there are noteworthy signs pointing toward new progressive endeavors. After the Arab uprisings began, many of my students, encouraged by a heady sense of imminent change, felt empowered to express individual freedom in all its dimensions, including religion. The uprisings gave confidence to skeptics and courageous atheists that they need not keep their beliefs private but could declare them in public or on social media. Many young people began moving away from religiosity.[46] For instance, "Black Ducks" episodes on YouTube grew in popularity as a forum for atheists and others seeking to build a secular society in the MENA region. Even in the conservative Arabian Peninsula, 19 percent of Saudis (four percentage points more than in Italy) admit in anonymous opinion polls to being "not religious"—this despite Saudi Arabia's criminalization of apostasy.[47] Two polarized spaces were opened by the Arab Spring: one secular, even atheist, and the other religiously extremist. The former still needs to be dissociated from the authoritarian secularism once imposed by Arab nationalist regimes; the latter lacked legitimacy on human rights. Between those two poles, religion must remain privatized; it should be neither the basis of legislation nor a tool to control the masses.

Despite the authoritarian structure of most Arab governments, one can aspire to a regional, deliberative democratic forum, the flourishing of popular art of resistance, and the revival of a new Islamic Enlightenment. If the Arab Winter has submerged hopes for reform, one should consider that since the uprisings, the widespread desire for freedom has been intensified with the experience of brutal religious repression and violence. One drive for freedom conjugates with another; the call for freedom of speech and religion is closely associated with freedom from want and fear. A new Islamic Enlightenment could be awakened by projects fostering commercial development and regional integration.

CHAPTER SIX

Sun, Sand, Water, and Shields

FREEDOM FROM WANT

Freedom from want was understood as an inalienable right by Enlightenment thinkers such as Jean-Jacques Rousseau, Immanuel Kant, and Thomas Paine. For Franklin Roosevelt it entailed "economic understandings which will secure to every nation a healthy peacetime life for its inhabitants—everywhere in the world."[1] That objective became a major focus of US foreign policy after World War II. Norman Rockwell illustrated Roosevelt's view with a classic image of American bounty. Drawing from his own family's experience of Thanksgiving, Rockwell painted his cook, an older lady in a white apron overseen by a gray-haired man, as she presents a large roasted turkey to her family around the table. The scene was culturally specific, but given our topic, one could likewise imagine a painting of an Arab feast: a family celebrating Eid al-Fitr at the end of Ramadan, their table filled with meze plates and sweets. This holiday is an occasion for generosity and collective charity (Zakat), and Muslim tradition encourages compassionate assistance. As stated in the Qur'an: "Whatever they should spend [in charity] . . . is good for parents, and kindred and orphans and those in want for wayfarers" (2:215).[2]

Four articles of the 1948 Universal Declaration of Human Rights acknowledged the significance of economic rights. Article 25, section 1, sums it up: "Everyone has the right to a standard of living adequate for the

Freedom from Want, by
Norman Rockwell.
Printed by permission of
the Norman Rockwell
Family Agency; © 1943
the Norman Rockwell
Family Entities.
Illustration provided by
Curtis Licensing.

health and well-being of himself and of his family, including food,
clothing, housing and medical care and necessary social services, and the
right to security in the event of unemployment, sickness, disability,
widowhood, old age or other lack of livelihood in circumstances beyond
his control."³ Could these rights ever be realized throughout the MENA
region after so much despair and conflict? If so, what steps would be
necessary to create a new Middle East whose entire population could
experience freedom from want? To put it another way, if large-scale
MENA conflicts ever end, what plans should be ready for the "day after"?
Beyond the immediate need for massive relief efforts in places like
Syria, Yemen, and Gaza, one would hope to see a broader framework for
addressing poverty and underdevelopment, a plan that would include
renewable energy, new transportation infrastructure, and desalination,
tailored to fit the region's unique constellation of sun, sand, and water.

Critics rightly argue that there is no shepherd leading lost flocks.
There is no one with Franklin Roosevelt's acumen and foresight to envision a Middle East beyond war, no American leadership in the world, and

hence no possibility for New Deal policies or major reconstruction efforts. If we look more closely, we will recognize four principles from which to begin. First, since early planning maximizes the prospects for postwar sustainable peace, failing to plan may mean that a fragile truce is followed by a renewed escalation of violence. Second, infrastructure developments already under way in the region—some based on renewable energy—represent expandable steps toward "freedom from want." Third, even assuming continued disengagement by the US, other countries may fill the gaps opened by the troubled American colossus. Fourth, to be viable, economic developments must (at least to some extent) coincide with progress in other dimensions of freedom.

Designing Economic Development Policies in Wartime
One should begin designing the peace during wartime—not after the war is over, when the absence of prior planning can unleash new dangers. I had the unusual opportunity to discuss this issue with a group of highly placed Emiratis whom I was tutoring in political philosophy during the Arab uprisings. We would meet on Friday evenings at a palace in Abu Dhabi, the flow of conversation enhanced by the guests' *shisha* (or water pipe) smoking. After a copious dinner, the royal convener would clear his throat over the laughter of his guests, then speak with a deeper, more serious voice as he directed everyone to a white marble classroom. As the group took their places in front of a smart board, our host would remind us, his troubled eyes gazing at the Gulf just beyond the palace windows, that the grim times called for sober conversation about the next steps for the UAE and the broader region.

On one such evening, our host admonished the group to engage with him more soberly. "This is not a joke," he said. "We are talking seriously here about what to do." I wondered what I was doing in the middle of such a gathering, but it was my turn to speak. I began by describing the failures of the 1919 Treaty of Versailles, outlining lessons for leaders who wished to avoid its example. The victors in World War I had set aside liberal principles of peacebuilding. Those who advocated principles such as minority rights, labor rights, and economic reconstruction based on free trade had to console themselves with unenforceable documents and an impotent League of Nations. Later tracing the rise of fascism to the failure at Versailles, Franklin Roosevelt presented his vision of a postwar world in

January 1941, during the "darkest hours" of World War II and before the United States was even formally at war. Europe had fallen to Hitler, the Nazi-Soviet pact was still in force, England stood alone, America remained mired in depression, and the "America First" movement reflected isolationism's popular appeal. That daunting situation did not deter Roosevelt from confidently announcing the postwar implementation of Four Freedoms as essential to averting yet another round of world war. In 1943, with the defeat of the Axis powers two long years in the future, Roosevelt and Churchill launched the process of detailed postwar planning. To effect the economic restoration of a liberated Europe, Roosevelt reprised the framework of his New Deal, which had already averted the rise of fascism and communism within the United States of the 1930s. "Is that history relevant to your situation?" I asked my noble Emirati gathering. "Yes, of course," my host responded. "We must lead the way toward progress in our region." His guests nodded in deferential agreement as they rose from their seats for a break, their countenances as grave as one might have seen in the historic war rooms of Europe.

A Middle Eastern New Deal
In spite of their country's great wealth, the Emiratis in that palace classroom understood the economic challenges facing the Middle East. When the group reconvened, smelling of *shisha* after the break, we discussed the possibility of new developmental projects for the MENA region on the scale of the Tennessee Valley Authority (TVA), which would stimulate growth while reducing unemployment. Created as a centerpiece of Roosevelt's New Deal in 1933, the TVA achieved an ambitious set of goals in parts of Alabama, Mississippi, Georgia, Kentucky, and Virginia by generating electricity, ensuring navigability of the Tennessee River, attracting industries, improving agriculture, reviving railroads, creating jobs, and generally uplifting a poor region through integration into the nation's broader economy. A Middle Eastern New Deal policy could incorporate the essential elements of sun, sand, and water to harness vast energy, link societies with railways across expanses of sand, and tap sufficient fresh water from the seas along the vast Arabian coasts. Such an integrated plan would address what my group of Emiratis saw as a major problem: the diversification of Middle Eastern economies. As one participant, a journalist from the *Gulf News*, illustrated on the white board for

the rest of the group, the economies of the Gulf states have been too centralized and controlled. They need more private investment and entrepreneurship.

Is it possible to diversify and integrate the region's economies simultaneously? The Middle East could adopt a free trade framework aimed at the success of one cluster of countries first, similar to the Coal and Steel Community of Belgium, the Netherlands, and Luxembourg established after World War II. This agreement was a stepping-stone toward the development of a broader European Common Market. It was clear to Jean Monnet and Robert Schuman, the founders of what would ultimately become the European Union, that the creation of a common entity to secure open European borders, facilitate interdependence, and implement human rights conventions was crucial to averting yet another war. I grew up attending European schools in Luxembourg and Brussels, where studying Monnet's and Schuman's practical vision for Europe was an important part of the curriculum. Are these lessons of European history applicable in today's Middle East? The people I have met in the region have not always seen the European experience as a point of reference, but all were intrigued by the question.

In a June 2016 conversation with Prince El Hassan bin Talal of Jordan, brother of the late King Hussein, I inquired about the future of the Jordanian economy. The prince told me about his hopes for the development of information technology and cooperative international agreements to stimulate manufacturing. We talked about the remnants of the Hejaz Railway, which once ran from Damascus to Amman and then on to Medina through the Hejaz region of Saudi Arabia. It also featured an offshoot line to Haifa, on the Mediterranean Sea. Might the dry bones of those tracks and cars live again? If the Hejaz train could be rebuilt, it would greatly benefit the Jordanian economy, carrying hundreds of thousands of pilgrims to Mecca and opening new markets for commercial sites along the way. Such a key infrastructure development could address many problems: improving regional transportation, creating jobs for local and refugee populations, integrating the region's economies, attracting new industries, stimulating trade, labor mobility and tourism, and hopefully contributing to sustainable peace.

The prince flashed a bemused smile, his eyes briefly unfocused in melancholic reverie, and then he described his familiarity with the railway and its historical importance. Though it operated for only twelve years after it was completed in 1908, it has never been forgotten in the Arab world. The Syrian writer Sheikh Ali al-Tantawi described the tragedy of the short-lived railway: "The line is there, but no train in motion, and the stations exist, but with no passengers. Here where they bid farewell and hello, witnessing hopes and expectations, people from every country and every race . . . with no distinction. . . . If tragic poets wept it with poems, the stations will remain the same and the rest of the poem will be erased by time, where each built wall and every stone in it are surviving lyrics of those poems. . . . Every block at every station weeps, and every window with torn padlocks, and every door . . . with no tomorrow."[4]

Today most of the Hejaz lies abandoned. There is no rail connection between Saudi Arabia and Jordan, the UAE, Qatar, or Iraq. No functioning rail system connects Jordan to Syria, Iraq, Egypt, Israel, or the West Bank. People and freight move by cars, trucks, buses, and planes, but none of these forms of transportation offer anything remotely approaching the capacity of rail to revive the regional economy. Recent railroad initiatives have been regularly thwarted by the volatile security environment and weak economies. Yet there have been encouraging developments, including a recent proposal for an industrial zone embracing Saudi Arabia, Jordan, and Egypt[5] and new cooperative planning for a railway link between Israel and Jordan.[6] This project, prompted by the need to route freight around the Syrian civil war, would boost the economies of these two Levantine countries and perhaps inspire a broader reconstruction of the railroad system throughout the region.

Less than two months after my conversation with Prince El Hassan bin Talal, Israel reinaugurated the Jezreel Valley Railway, retracing the old Hejaz line from Haifa to the Jordanian border. Yisrael Katz, the Israeli minister of transportation and intelligence, was clear about its implications: "This will connect Israel to Jordan and the rest of the countries of the Middle East."[7] After he began publicly promoting a rail link between Israel, Jordan, and Saudi Arabia, I sought a meeting with him in Jerusalem. Israel has no diplomatic relationship with Saudi Arabia, and Jordan has not offered an official response to his proposal, but Katz told me in June 2017 that a regional rail system is inevitable and will be a "game changer." The project indeed seems within reach. At the time of this writing, Saudi Arabia has nearly finished its own rail line to the

Jordanian border. Only 192 miles of track across Jordan would then connect the Israeli and Saudi railways, providing an unbroken rail connection between Riyadh, Amman, and the Mediterranean. By providing jobs and facilitating trade between regions, this network of steel would promote economic interdependence. One would also hope that the increase in people to people exposure would provide greater tolerance and help lay a foundation for viable peace.

Another positive development is the increasing investment in solar power. The Middle East has abundant solar energy resources that could economically empower the region's people. "The sun, with all those planets revolving around it and dependent on it," Galileo wrote, "can still ripen a bunch of grapes, as if it had nothing else in the universe to do."[8] In our meeting, Prince El Hassan bin Talal expressed chagrin that major solar power initiatives had not taken off in Jordan.[9] But there are positive developments elsewhere. Between 2008 and 2017, the total generating capacity of power plants and other installations using renewable energy in the Middle East increased by almost 60 percent, with solar energy clearly leading the way.[10] Morocco will soon have the world's largest concentrated solar power plant near the city of Ouazazate, which will reduce that city's carbon emissions by 760,000 tons per year and make it a model for the region.[11]

Projects in other regions have integrated railroad transportation and solar power, and this could also be in the cards for the Middle East. In 2011, Belgium launched Europe's first solar-powered train. With sixteen thousand solar panels on its roof, it runs from Belgium to Amsterdam, significantly reducing carbon dioxide emissions. Both France and Italy are looking into similar technology for their trains.[12] In 2016, Indian Railways launched a "Solar Mission" to reduce dependency on fossil fuels. The first pilot project was conducted in the Jodphur district of Bhadla with the creation of a solar park slated to provide one million megawatts of solar energy by 2022.[13] Solar bullet trains, potentially traveling 116 miles from Tucson to Phoenix in just thirty minutes, have been proposed as a pilot project in the Arizona desert.[14] With current technology, the price of completely solar-powered trains remains prohibitive, but technological progress is rapidly cutting prospective costs. Other possibilities, like hydrogen fuel cells, are also becoming more viable. Whether a major railroad in the Middle East is built along the route of the Hejaz, high-tech trains powered by renewable energy could greatly contribute to critical infrastructure development, boosting trade and tourism.

If the absence of railroad transport is one major source of underdevelopment, the most daunting obstacle is the lack of fresh water. The Middle East is one of the driest regions in the world. As early as the fourteenth century, the Arab historian Ibn Khaldun warned his peers that the decrease of water brings the decline of civilization.[15] When I was living in the UAE, a shiny icon of successful capitalism in the desert, the country's renewable water resources fell far below the UN water scarcity threshold. Some Emiratis claimed there were only three days of water in reserve, others insisted it was only thirty minutes. Would Dubai and Abu Dhabi, these Middle East outposts of urban civilization, come to ruin over something as simple as water? Emiratis joke that their water is more expensive than oil. On a visit to the Agra region of India, I saw many beautiful palaces built under the Moghul Empire and left desolate a few years after completion because of drought and lack of irrigation. Developing reliable sources of water is nowhere more vital than in the Middle East.

If the wealthiest countries of the Gulf are rightly concerned about the future of their water supply, the situation is even more dire in other Arab countries. It is estimated that by 2050, water availability per capita in the MENA will have fallen by 50 percent from today's level.[16] Desalination has proven to be an effective solution for water scarcity, but both distillation and membrane desalination depend on fossil fuel energy—an approach that seems especially costly given the global consequences of continuing greenhouse gas emissions. One could anticipate a future in which desalination is powered by solar energy.[17] Today, Gulf Arabs are adopting cleaner technologies and starting to harness their abundant sunshine to produce drinkable water from the sea.[18] On the final day of the World Government Summit, the CEO of Dubai Electricity and Water Authority announced plans for Dubai to be powered 75 percent through solar energy by 2050.[19]

Over time, the use of alternative energy to extract water or move trains will change the region's economy, making it less dependent upon oil either internally or for export. It would bring a significant boost in employment, since solar power is more labor intensive than the fossil fuel economy. The benefits of converting to cleaner forms of energy are well understood in the Gulf countries; they have already developed initiatives, such as UAE's Masdar, the Emirates Nuclear Energy Corporation, the

Qatar National Foundation, and Saudi Arabia's King Abdullah City for Atomic and Renewable Energy.[20]

Filling the Regional Vacuum

Facing the American selective disengagement that began under the Obama administration, Saudi Arabia and the UAE have become increasingly involved in their neighbors' politics. Today, US criticism of those monarchies' suppression of civil liberties, briefly emphasized by President George W. Bush and repeated more softly by President Obama, has simply stopped. For those who share aspirations for a progressive liberal order in the Middle East, and who even sensed its impending arrival with the 1989 destruction of the Berlin Wall, the 2016 election of Donald Trump seemed to signal a profound threat to that project. Right-wing nationalism is on the rise, abetted by Vladimir Putin's campaign of disinformation, cyberattack, and military aggression. Only a naïve optimist could wholly dismiss these threats to the survival of liberalism. Yet one should not assume that Middle East progress is at a standstill, waiting for another president to recommit the United States to global leadership. Other countries are already filling important gaps once occupied by the self-designated champion of democracy.

The troubled Middle East still has a compelling need for outside powers to envision steps toward a sustainable peace. Just as the regimes established by the Bretton Woods Agreement and the Marshall Plan enabled Europe's economic recovery, the Middle East now needs new financial structures to redirect resources from sectarian conflicts toward economic development. One could imagine a series of subregional Middle East economic initiatives, like the Coal and Steel Community in the Benelux countries that helped lay the foundation for the EU. These initiatives could serve as building blocks of a Mediterranean partnership or a revised version of Nicolas Sarkozy's 2007 proposal for a "Mediterranean Union." That now moribund proposal sought to accomplish three major aims: shared economic prosperity in the South Mediterranean region, better governance and steps toward democratic reform, and enhanced cultural exchanges and the strengthening of civil society.

What would it take, in the absence of American leadership in key parts of the Middle East, to revive similar initiatives in the Middle East? The economic landscapes vary dramatically from one region to another. The Gulf countries remain prosperous despite some economic uncertainties and may be able increasingly to help their neighbors. The Maghreb region has positioned itself to gain more financial help from its former colonial occupiers, and countries in the Fertile Crescent are beginning to invite investments from China, Europe, and the GCC states. With synchronized political will, these isolated enclaves of economic development could eventually create a more integrated economy that connects people within and between states across the region.

For instance, Tunisia, one of the Maghrebian states, suffered significant economic setbacks in the aftermath of the Arab uprisings. Despite a short-lived rebound in 2012, the country's postrevolutionary economy was slowed by domestic tensions, including terrorist attacks in 2015 that crippled the tourist industry.[21] Consequently, the International Monetary Fund approved a two-year arrangement under the Extended Fund Facility for $2.9 billion to support the country's economic and financial reform program. Tunisia's GDP was just under $40.26 billion in 2017, down from a high of $47.59 billion in 2014 and the nation's lowest production since 2007.[22] Moreover, unemployment in the latter half of 2018 stood at 15.5 percent and was significantly higher among the younger population.[23] Unemployment was 13 percent in 2010, and it has not been below 15 percent since the revolution.[24] Med Limem, a young professor at Tunis University, told me in May 2015, "We had our political revolution; what we need now is a social revolution."[25] "We need a New Deal," echoed Smaili Mongi, a member of Tunisia's General Labor Union, whom I interviewed in Tunis the same month. He maintained that the future belongs to a green economy. In Tunisia, he said, "We only see economic solutions in huge industrial projects. To stimulate a domestic green economy, Tunisia should . . . rather focus on small, local projects that involve desalination, solar panels, wind turbines, and water conservation." Mongi and other green economy advocates view those projects as an opportunity to expand employment while also protecting human rights.[26] In 2018, the IMF released an additional $257 million for Tunisia as part of its four-year, $3-billion loan agreement. This is far from the New Deal Mongi advocated, as IMF austerity measures have already provoked popular anger. Tunisia's economic transition is still uncertain, but Europeans, for a variety of reasons, including fear of more refugees, are concerned about the country's welfare. It is not surprising that they are investing in solar energy, exploring the possibility of a Maghreb Silicon

Valley, and developing railways, roads, and other infrastructure projects in an attempt to stabilize North Africa.

In Egypt, the IMF also recognized that despite al-Sisi's repressive policies, the country was becoming more politically stable. In 2016 they offered a $12-billion loan, lifting the spirits of business people.[27] Assessing progress in spring 2018, IMF deputy managing director David Lipton asserted that "macroeconomic stability and market confidence have been restored, growth has resumed, inflation has fallen, and the public debt ratio is expected to fall for the first time in nearly a decade."[28] Egyptian authorities hope this progress will continue and will contribute to social and political stability, though ongoing foreign investment is contingent upon Cairo's implementation of tough economic and structural reforms to address its currency crisis. Given the cumbersome and corrupt Egyptian bureaucracy, how much of the loan will filter down to ordinary people is unclear. Aid from the US to Egypt remains primarily military, and Egypt's massive deficits have compelled the government to reduce subsidies on fuel and other necessities, seriously affecting the less advantaged. While the IMF provisions spelled out ways for the government to expand its spending on vulnerable strata of the population, namely youth and women, its policies still cater primarily to the middle and upper classes connected to the Egyptian military.[29] The IMF loan, together with significant assistance from Saudi Arabia and the UAE since al-Sisi came to power, might help stabilize the Egyptian economy, but this is not enough. Freedom from want still remains a distant dream.

In the Gulf countries, the situation is different. After large fluctuations in the price of crude oil, which in 2016 reached a twelve-year low, Saudi Arabia was forced to reduce its massive domestic spending and foreign aid. Other members of the Gulf Cooperation Council are taking "austerity" measures, such as imposing taxes (a prospect hardly imaginable until recently), reducing fuel subsidies, and decreasing public sector jobs and salaries. At the time of this writing, oil prices are rising, and new US sanctions on Iran may increase them further, but this trend runs counter to long-term changes in the energy market.[30] The current higher price of oil will continue to encourage renewable energy efforts in oil-dependent countries.

The adage "prosperity favors democracy" does not seem to apply in oil-producing countries. With the exception of developed states such as

Norway, Denmark, and the UK—which were democracies long before they became oil exporters—the oil-producing countries have been plagued by authoritarian governance. Because oil production is not labor intensive, profits flow directly to the rulers, creating rentier states where citizens depend on governmental welfare subsidies.[31] A gradual shift to renewable energies and economic diversification would reshape the social contract within Saudi Arabia and other Gulf states. The weakening of the Saudi monarchy's economic leverage as oil income shrinks could stimulate that diversity, possibly making the monarchy more responsive to popular will. The recent efforts to consolidate the House of Saud under Mohammed bin Salman might move the country toward further modernization, but continuing human rights violations highlight the fragility of the regime.

When I asked my special students in the UAE what role their country might take in forging an economically integrated Middle East, they proudly mentioned Dubai. The rise of modern Dubai offers a model of how an ancient trading tradition can lay the foundation for a twenty-first-century global commercial hub; the airport in Dubai now ranks as the third busiest in the world. The group was equally eager to describe their nation's commitment to economic development in poor countries within and beyond the Middle East. The UAE has in fact intensified its investments in development projects in recent years; the Organisation for Economic Co-Operation and Development (OECD) now ranks it as the world's largest donor of official development aid relative to national income.[32] Much of that foreign assistance has served a political purpose of the UAE's ruling family: strengthening Sunni-led authoritarian regimes against challenges from ISIS, the Muslim Brotherhood, and secular democratic groups. Most notably, since the UAE-backed coup replaced Morsi and the Muslim Brotherhood with al-Sisi in Egypt, the UAE has given Egypt massive aid, including large investments in development projects. The combination of combatting poverty and quelling Islamism may eventually open space for political reform. For now, however, leaders in both the UAE and Egypt hope to resist that outcome.

By focusing on bilateral, politically influenced aid and development goals, the UAE is neglecting the broader aim that informed European reconstruction after World War II: the forging of regional economic interdependence. Other external powers, including the United States, the EU, China, and the IMF, seem to be making the same mistake. Trade between

Middle Eastern countries now constitutes only 9 percent of the region's overall trade.[33] Rebuilding the MENA's great trading tradition is crucial for cities like Tunis, Alexandria, and Baghdad; their reestablishment as leading commercial centers would help enhance domestic peace while improving economic growth and more inclusive prosperity.

Prioritizing Freedom from Want

Economic development does not necessarily bring democracy. Franklin Roosevelt's vision of sustainable peace appropriately integrated the four freedoms, but which one should take priority remains a subject of debate. The Emirati prince and the other leaders who attended my classes at the palace, like many economists I met in the region, tended to emphasize stable economic development, admiring the achievements and governance of Singapore with its efficiently managed economy. The governance of democratic India, on the other hand, was thought to be fatally flawed and to leave its people mired in poverty. Ironically, by giving priority to economic development over democracy, the Emiratis align themselves with orthodox Marxists, psychologists who embrace Maslow's hierarchy of needs, and right-wing neoliberal modernizers.

The prince who convened our class, eager to rationalize his emphasis on economic stability before democratic reforms, questioned the rush to elections during the Arab Spring. But he was intrigued by the popular appeal of human rights, as well as freedom of speech and elections, and he displayed a real interest in the history of democracy and the philosophical notion of justice. I had assigned Thomas Paine's *Common Sense,* which he and the others read while Arab revolutionaries marched in the streets. In the next class I reviewed Paine's eloquent arguments on universal rights and his support for the French Revolution. My intellectually curious host did not seem to be offended by Paine's harsh criticism of monarchies. By the time the Muslim Brotherhood came to power in Egypt, we were reading Edmund Burke's *Reflections on the French Revolution,* in which Burke criticized Paine's notion of universal natural law and the ideal of a tabula rasa created by the French revolutionaries. In Burke's opinion, these concepts were disrespectful of tradition and culture and would prove unsustainable. Unsurprisingly, my students found Burke more appealing than Paine. "What is the purpose of democracy or elections," the prince asked me, "if the representatives who are elected are antidemocratic or not deferential to binding traditions? If radical Islamists were to win an election, they would not care about human rights or the rights of women." "And if the Salafists won those elections," another attendee said to me impishly, "you would be beheaded." The history of elections that produced undemocratic leaders gave us all some pause. More important than elections, I was told, was economic welfare and stability.

I hastened to explain that democracy was not just about elections but had to include other freedoms. No one rebuffed my claim, but they pointed out that these transformations took a long time in Europe, and that the UAE was not ready for a post-Islamic tabula rasa. "Good governance," our host repeated, "is more important than democracy at this historical juncture." "So," I asked, "How do you ensure good governance?" Much like Sheikh Zayed, the founding father of his country, he answered, "We need to keep our ears close to the ground and listen to the people. Now more than ever."

Other attendees assured me that the country was making incremental democratic progress; it now had a parliament, with half the members elected by an approved (and growing) fraction of the electorate, and the other half by the royal families. They knew that the Federal National Council was almost powerless, but it constituted an increase, however small, in popular political participation. Progress, they emphasized, needs to be gradual and not revolutionary, just as Burke had written.

"Which do you prefer?" the prince asked me, "revolution or reform?" All eyes fixed on me, waiting for a response to his provocative question. I replied that real reforms, beneficial for the common good, were always preferable to violent revolution. My students liked that answer, as they were all betting that incremental reforms would succeed in the long run. They needed, however, to better understand the importance of a parliamentary system, even in a monarchy. For a final class, one that was ultimately canceled, I had assigned an excerpt from Max Weber's *On Economy and Society*. By doing so, I may have indirectly urged a future leader of the UAE to renounce his unchecked leadership role. Weber argued that, in Germany, the rule of Kaiser Wilhelm II would be delegitimized if better political representations were not put in place. Having seen the growth of mass politics in the late nineteenth century, he warned against the unorganized democracy of the street, writing that the danger "is strongest in countries with either a powerless or a politically discredited parliament, that means, above all, in countries without rationally organized parties."[34] Absent such institutions, bureaucrats are inclined to push their own agendas while losing sight of the whole, and advisors tend to say anything that will please the leaders they serve. Kings are not well served when they are surrounded by court jesters and public servants whose livelihood depends on royal approval. They are better served by a seasoned political class and organized parties. The only way to contain the unpredictable outbursts of the masses, Weber argues, is to elect true representatives, organized in parties able to filter and engage with dissent—those that can develop political acumen without fear of retaliation. These warnings were vindicated when the Weimar Republic in Germany crumbled under the pressure of angry masses and a weak parliament.

Freedom from want creates the opportunity to promote education and other freedoms, but such progress is far from inevitable. Wealth can be used to buy influence and quash freedom of speech, as when the Saudis co-opted protesters during the Arab Spring. Substantive democracy requires the synergistic implementation of the four freedoms, so that commerce may foster civil society, free speech, and religious tolerance. Without free speech there is no public corrective for ill-conceived economic development policies, wealth inequality, entrenched corruption, and the suppression of other freedoms in the name of security. "Those who would give up essential liberty, to purchase a little temporary safety," Benjamin Franklin reminds us, "deserve neither liberty nor safety."[35] In many places in the Middle East, there is neither liberty nor safety.

FREEDOM FROM FEAR

None of Roosevelt's first three freedoms can flourish without progress toward the fourth: freedom from fear. Thomas Hobbes, hoping to avoid the destructive passions that contributed to the Thirty Years' War, argued for the individual right to security. Later, Article 3 of the UDHR stated the more complete liberal vision plainly: "Everyone has the right to life, liberty and security of person." Rockwell's painting of Roosevelt's fourth freedom depicts two parents putting their children to bed, a folded newspaper in the father's hand bearing the headline: "Bombings . . . Horror." An updated version might feature a breathless Syrian refugee desperately clutching a toddler to his chest on a flimsy raft in a rough sea, seeking safety on a distant shore. Following World War II, the American, British, and French

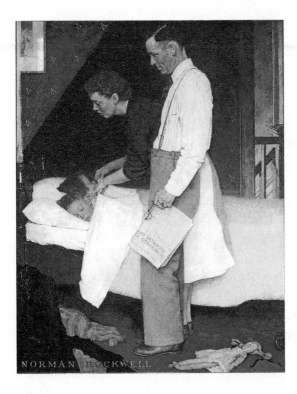

Freedom from Fear, by Norman Rockwell. Printed by permission of the Norman Rockwell Family Agency; © 1943 the Norman Rockwell Family Entities. Illustration provided by Curtis Licensing.

forces occupied what would soon become West Germany, providing the security underlying Germany's enduring transition to a prosperous, stable democracy. In 1949, ten Western European countries, plus the United States and Canada, formed the North Atlantic Treaty Organization in order to contain the new threat from Soviet Russia.

As I argued to my students in the Emirati palace, economic development without civil liberty is not enough. In the same way, I suggested, sustainable security requires equitable economic development. These lessons, which Roosevelt learned from the interwar period and that his successors applied to the reconstruction of Europe, seem largely forgotten today.

A Brief Historical Overview of Regional Security
Integrated human rights efforts have never been part of anyone's plan for the Middle East. Since before World War I, the region has been caught in a tug of war between outside powers driven by their own geopolitical and

economic interests and ruled by autocratic regimes at the expense of ordinary people. Today, especially in the absence of American leadership, it would be helpful to regard the region as composed of five distinct security theaters, each facing different challenges, and each connected historically to different outside powers. This approach, which emphasizes both the region's diversity and its multipolar influences, can provide critical guidance for mapping future possibilities.

The post-1945 order in the Middle East was devised to sustain American geopolitical and economic interests during the Cold War. America's opponent, the Soviet Union, had few real allies in the region, although many Arab rulers, following the lead of Egypt's Nasser, strove to remain nonaligned in the hope of preserving their self-determination while enjoying courtship from both sides. Neutrality proved difficult, however, and deep fault lines of Cold War antagonism ultimately persisted long after the fall of the Berlin Wall.

During the Cold War, the Soviet Union had little success extending its influence in the Middle East. After having supported the State of Israel early on, Moscow shifted its strategy in 1956, siding with Nasser's Egypt against Britain, France, and Israel during the Suez Crisis and becoming the champion of Arab nationalist leaders, who increasingly resented what they regarded as Western neocolonialism and its "lackey," Israel. In addition to Egypt, the Soviets supported Syria and Iraq, whose Ba'ath Parties made them, at least nominally, the first socialist regimes in the Arab Middle East. After the 1979 Camp David peace agreement between Egypt and Israel, the USSR built stronger ties with Iraq, Gaddafi's Libya, the Yemen Arab Republic, South Yemen, and the PLO. In 1979, it also attempted to preserve its influence in the region by invading Afghanistan to defend a puppet regime there against an Islamist insurgency, an effort that, in its failure, helped cause the demise of the USSR. Throughout its period of regional influence, the Soviet Union was preoccupied with geopolitics and efforts to export its own unsuccessful economic model; it offered the Arab people no path toward sustainable development.

As for the United States, from 1945 until September 11, 2001, its strategy in the Middle East focused primarily on the containment of threats: first from the Soviet Union, then Ayatollah Khomeini's Iran, and finally Saddam Hussein's Iraq. Another threat came from one of America's friends. Despite having allied with the US to support the anti-Soviet insurgency in Afghanistan and shared concerns about Iran, Saudi Arabia continued to export militant anti-Western Wahhabism, setting the stage for the September 11 attack on America. After that attack, the United States attempted, under President George W. Bush, a revolutionary transformation of the Middle East that was supposed to be achieved, somehow, by invading Iraq and toppling Saddam Hussein. Instead, these actions revealed American oil and geopolitical interests more than any commitment to the welfare of ordinary Iraqi people. Iraq turned into a battleground between al-Qaeda in Mesopotamia and militant Shi'a extremists largely controlled by Iran, yielding an illiberal democracy predicated on the disenfranchisement of Sunnis and Kurds. As the American presence became too costly, President Barack Obama pursued a strategy of military disengagement from 2009 until 2014, a policy that collapsed in the wake of the Arab uprisings, the war in Syria, and the rise of ISIS. First the Americans and then Russia were drawn into military reengagement in the Middle East.

In addition to the Cold War competition between superpowers, another regional power struggle began with Khomeini's takeover of Iran in 1979. From that point forward, Iran and Saudi Arabia pursued religious sectarian rivalries outside the interests of either superpower, sponsoring proxy wars that have intensified conflict in the region until today.

Multipolarity and Five Security Theaters
In the Middle East, one finds widespread fatalism about the persistence of conflicts fueled by external powers. America's historical reliance on dictators to protect its interests was widely seen as a lack of concern for the region's people, and Bush's attempt to shape a new regional order after September 11 made things worse. A promising exception was the 2015 nuclear agreement with Iran, negotiated under the Obama administration, which raised hopes of moderating Iran's support of terrorist groups and reducing tensions between Iran and the Sunni Arab states. Donald Trump's abrogation of the agreement in 2018 immediately set the region on edge and revived the specter of war between Iran and its enemies.

Assuming the continuing decline of American leadership, is there a regional organization currently active in the Middle East that could oversee a transition toward stability? The League of Arab States (or the Arab League) comes to mind; but it is an unlikely candidate for building a new security framework. Founded in March 1945, this loose union of twenty-two Arab nations, including Palestine, has the goal of advancing collaboration among its members on matters of common interest. Structured in reaction to postwar colonial divisions of territory, member states also united in their opposition to a Jewish state in Palestine. The League has long been condemned for poor governance, ineffectiveness, inability to corral uncooperative members, and accommodation of auto-cratic regimes. During the Arab uprisings, it briefly demonstrated a capacity to act—first in Libya, where it supported the air campaign culmi-nating in the ouster of Muammar al-Gaddafi, and then in Syria, where it orchestrated a fact-finding mission and called for the removal of President Bashar al-Assad after his murderous repression of protesters. Predictably, however, the League's sectarian and other divisions prevent it from exer-cising meaningful leadership in support of peace and stability.[36]

If regional security planning is beyond the reach of the Arab League and of little interest to the current US administration, other powers could make significant contributions, especially in smaller theaters where they have historical interests. The region may be sorted into five such theaters, starting with the more volatile and progressing to the more stable clusters of states. The theater most in need is one labeled "the humanitarian order." It is an area that includes Lebanon, Turkey, and Jordan and is currently aiding several million Syrian refugees, partly with subsidies from European countries that fear further arrivals. The second, the embat-tled states of Syria, Libya, Yemen and Iraq, are embroiled in or have just emerged from sectarian and tribal warfare fueled by Iran, Saudi Arabia, and other outside powers. The third, the Maghreb states of Tunisia, Algeria, Mauritania and Morocco, consists of former French colonies with relatively similar challenges. The fourth theater, the Fertile Crescent, consisting of Egypt, Jordan and Israel, shares a fragile peace reinforced by dependence on the US. The fifth, the Gulf Cooperation Countries of Saudi Arabia, Kuwait, Bahrain, the UAE, Oman, and Qatar, are rentier states with a common history of British and then American influence.

The Humanitarian Order

A new security framework is needed to address the needs of the individ-uals and countries most directly affected by the current refugee crisis, which has forced the movement of millions of people, particularly from

Humanitarian Order

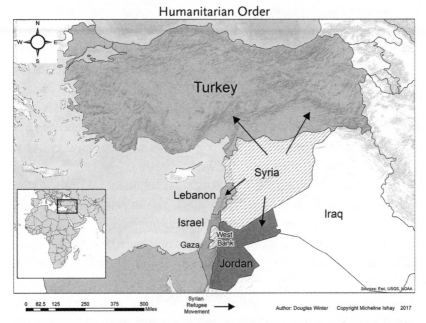

Refugee movement, designated as the humanitarian order. Map by Douglas Winter and Micheline Ishay (© 2017 Micheline Ishay).

Syria. At the 2016 Olympic Games in Brazil, ten athletes competed as a representative refugee team, part of an effort to raise global awareness of the crisis. One team member poignantly expressed their shared senti- ment: "We are equal now. We compete as human beings, like the others."[37] The Syrian refugee swimmer Yusra Mardini was cheered and applauded, yet many of those who celebrated her moment in the limelight would never dream of welcoming significant numbers of her displaced fellow citizens into their country.[38] Whereas some countries have closed their borders, other countries have taken on a deeply disproportionate share of the burden. How can we create a security regime in this first theater, which is in desperate need of humanitarian assistance, when the resources of host countries have been so taxed by the influx of refugees?

The refugee experience is tragic and all too common throughout history. Civil wars drive people to flee to adjacent countries. When those countries are too frail or unwilling to host them, refugees travel as far as they must to bring their families to safety. Along the way, they encounter people who prey on them or see them as rivals for scarce food or jobs. Dispossessed, the refugees are often demonized and dehumanized. Encountering indifference and hostility stirs their wrath, especially that of young people hopelessly trapped in transit camps. Often forced to live like animals without adequate shelter, they yearn for dignity, recognition, and sometimes revenge for the loss of their homes and their loved ones. These sentiments come to a boil in extremely precarious conditions. When reality lacks exit doors, youth often turn their last hopes toward dark alleys, embracing dogmatic prophecies in a last desperate *salto mortale*. At that point, the radicalized refugees of the Levant attract the full attention of the West.

As I write, refugees from Syria account for one-third of the entire refugee population worldwide. There are approximately 3.5 million refugees in Turkey, 1 million in Lebanon, 673,000 in Jordan, 250,000 in Iraq, and 165,000 in North Africa.[39] Europe as a whole has received a little more than 1 million Syrians. When they arrive, host countries act like emergency rooms, struggling to meet patients' immediate needs. "Our camps are humanitarian operations," Major Eyad al-Omari, the military administrator at Za'atari, told me when I visited the Jordanian camp near the Syrian border in June 2015. "This is a transit camp, and we cannot keep them here indefinitely. We are not in the triage business; we offer humanitarian relief for civilians and fighters alike." He was proud of his work; the camp provides shelter, food, water, medical care, education, and even small business opportunities for the refugees. To an outsider, however, these sites seem more like outdoor prisons. Once registered in the camp, residents may not go outside the fence without special permission and on the inside are vulnerable to gangs and violent attack. Even in smaller camps, residents feel homeless, powerless and purposeless. Radicalism easily gains a hearing.

Even when international financial aid reaches these camps, it has never been enough, and assistance rarely converts into real recovery from economic and security crises. Due to the continued unrest in Syria, thousands of people in distress have flooded across the borders to Jordan, Lebanon, and Turkey. As of January 2018, the EU has allocated an additional $25 million to support Syrian refugees in Turkey. According to the UN High Commissioner for Refugees (UNHCR), the international community has pledged $2.27 billion for the Regional Refugee Resilience Plan; as of this writing, however, the plan still falls short of its goal by $5.61 billion.[40] The European Union in particular understands that if these neighboring countries cannot absorb a fleeing population, or if they falter under economic pressure or domestic opposition, more people will reach Western shores by rail or by raft, or perish trying. The unstoppable flow of refugees poses multiple problems for Europe.

How can the international community help host countries turn their economic distress into new opportunities for refugees and local populations? Part of the answer would be an influx of multinational aid at the scale of the Marshall Plan. In 1948, that plan helped rebuild a war-devastated region as part of a broader campaign to remove trade barriers, restore Europe, and prevent the spread of communism. A similar endeavor in the Middle East could promote the region's reconstruction, stimulate trade between developing countries, and block the advance of jihadism. It could be done in a number of ways, including a focus on large-scale infrastructure projects that put people to work, supported by job-related education and training.

An additional step would be an international effort, under the flag of the United Nations, to build modern "cities of refuge," possibly on lands leased from host countries for an agreed-upon period. These "stateless cities" would be the responsibility of all UN member states and governed by the UN. A UN passport could be provided to vetted refugees. The economic infrastructure, and the newly constructed cities themselves—built at least partly by refugee labor—would revert to the local government at the end of the lease as a reward for its hospitality. One could entertain the idea of reviving the United Nations Trusteeship Council, a main organ of the UN from 1945 to 1994 in the administration of trust territories, to oversee the security and well-being of refugees (humanitarian needs, including permanent housing, health care, and education), economic development, and employment partnerships with the host country and other neighbors.

It is worth noting that Turkey initially proposed building "container cities" in Syria for the refugees. The mayor of Barcelona also suggested a chain of "refugee cities" to provide sanctuary and safety.[41] These and other proposals were not sufficiently developed as they did not address the host countries' need for sustained economic viability.[42] Such projects would require extensive planning and a wide spectrum of expertise. Of course, they would also require funding, and here it seems appropriate to turn first to the countries of the GCC. In 2017, GCC countries contributed over $62 million in public and private donations to the UNHCR, compared to more than $2.4 billion from the US, the EU, Germany, the UK, and Sweden. Japan, which has little direct interest in the current crisis, consistently ranks among the top five countries donating to the UNHCR.[43] The GCC countries have not been ungenerous, and Kuwait in particular often ranks high among donors per capita to UNHCR, but more will be needed to sustain an extensive international effort to buttress regional stability.

The Embattled States

Our second theater consists of four countries whose persistent internal conflicts have made them a fertile ground for violent Islamism: Libya, Syria, Iraq, and Yemen.

Because the wars here are proxy wars between outside powers, prospects for sustainable peace may be contingent on those countries' willingness to alter their roles. What would motivate them to do so? Concern for their survival as regional powers can compel long-standing enemies to seek détente and even rapprochement. For Saudi Arabia, Iran, Turkey, and

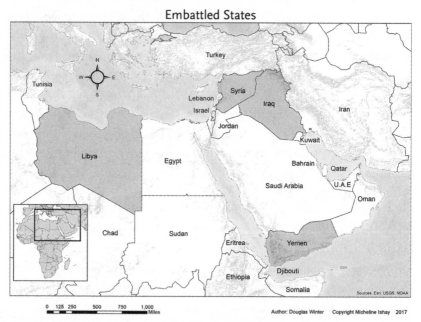

Designated territory of the embattled states. Map by Douglas Winter and Micheline Ishay (© 2017 Micheline Ishay).

Russia, the escalating costs of conflict, domestic discontent, and international pressure, particularly from Europe, could contribute to a change of
course. However the cessation of hostilities eventually comes, what would a
postwar environment look like for these embattled states? One can imagine
different forms of political arrangement, ranging from partition based on
sects, ethnicities, or tribes, to a fully cohesive state based on a power-sharing,
federal, or confederal arrangement. When economic and natural resources
are in dispute, some form of unity serves all parties better than partition.

Separation or Unity? When a territorial order collapses, those who have
endured civil war may yearn for separation; it is understandably difficult to
imagine living side by side with yesterday's visceral enemies. External
parties may also support separation. During World War I, the Sykes-Picot
Agreement of 1916 carved out new Middle Eastern states, managed by
imperial powers, even before the final collapse of the Ottoman Empire.
The British and French divided the Ottoman Arab provinces outside the
Persian Gulf into two areas of control. England claimed Jordan, Southern
Iraq, Palestine, and coastal strips along the Mediterranean Sea. France took
over Southeast Turkey, Northern Iraq, Syria, and Lebanon; and Russia
oversaw Istanbul, the Turkish Straits, and Armenia. After the Bolshevik
Revolution, the Russians lost their claim to Turkish territories, and France
and Britain, having drawn state boundaries within their respective areas of
influence, ultimately yielded control during the decolonization that
followed World War II.[44] The Sykes-Picot divisions remain greatly
contested in the Middle East over one hundred years later.

When the Soviet Union fragmented in 1991, forming fifteen states,
the European Union welcomed a number of Eastern European countries:
the Czech Republic, Hungary, Poland, Croatia, Bulgaria, and Slovakia, as
well as the three former Soviet republics of Latvia, Lithuania, and Estonia.
Secession from the USSR was a boon for these states, as they were integrated into a strong and prosperous European Union. There is currently
no similar regional entity that Middle Eastern countries could join, and
many observers have concluded that the partition into smaller states of
countries wrecked by civil war may be the best alternative to intractable
conflict. Although their sentiments are understandable, their reasoning
is flawed.

Secessionism was a powerful force during the late nineteenth and
early twentieth centuries. Addressing recurrent outbreaks of nationalism

and calls for self-determination in the Ottoman and Austro-Hungarian Empires and throughout Eastern Europe, leading Marxist thinkers Vladimir Lenin and Rosa Luxemburg took opposite positions. Lenin favored what he called "nationalism from below," for the sake of the people rather than leaders, born out of resistance to the unequal arrangements shaped by colonialism and capitalist greed. This type of oppression, he argued, warranted a tactical alliance between bourgeois nationalist elites and workers, in which secession should sometimes be regarded as an inescapable necessity. "To accuse those who support freedom of self-determination, i.e., freedom to secede, of encouraging separatism," Lenin wrote, "is as foolish and hypocritical as accusing those who advocate freedom of divorce of encouraging the destruction of family ties."[45] The Leninist position was popular during the anticolonial struggle and appeals to many in today's Middle East. Zikri Mosa, an advisor to Kurdistan's president Masoud Barzani, argues: "Sykes-Picot was a mistake, for sure; it was like a forced marriage. It was doomed from the start. It was immoral, because it decided people's future without asking them."[46] The boundaries established by Sykes-Picot are now being challenged, thanks to the rise of armed movements determined to erase those old borders.

Rosa Luxemburg, grappling with the question of Polish self-determination, warned of both the potential costs of secession for economically weak nationalities and the elitist trends of nationalist movements that showed little interest in the needs of ordinary peasants and workers. Any alliance between the working class and Polish nationalists, she contended, would subvert the establishment of human rights. The right to self-determination was an abstract one, she maintained, that never took into consideration "the material social conditions of the environment in a given historical epoch." It was as ridiculous and pointless a right as the "right of each man to eat off gold plates, which, as Nicholas Chernyshevski wrote, he would be ready to sell at any moment for a ruble."[47] The challenge is to define boundaries while being alert to the location of natural resources and other sources of wealth—given that inequitable resource distribution could favor one people's claim to self-determination while making another group's claim economically unsustainable. While the separation of people into new territories may look like an expedient response to existential distress, it is not by itself an enduring political solution. Whatever the ultimate political arrangement, some form of unified state would always be preferable to secession, as each territory offers particular advantages (ports, natural resources, and so on) from which all should benefit.

Rapprochement. The idea that Saudi Arabia and Iran might turn from confrontation in Syria and Yemen to a negotiated settlement may sound like a pipe dream. Hostility between Iranians and Saudis exists at the highest levels in both countries, and these conflicts are further complicated by the involvement of many other states whose interests do not align simply with one side or the other. Yet the financial and political costs may be growing unsustainable. Iran, which received around $100 billion when its frozen assets were released by the nuclear deal, appears to have applied that windfall to military buildup and foreign wars rather than to its declining domestic economy.[48] This decision caused widespread street protests in Iran in early 2018, reflecting growing popular resentment over the regime's priorities. In 2017, Saudi Arabia spent between $5 billion to $6 billion per month—as much as 10% of its monthly GDP—on its bombing campaign in Yemen. While some sources suggest this estimate is excessive, there is no doubt that the Saudi-led coalition has greatly stressed GCC economies over the war in Yemen.[49] The killing of thousands of Yemeni civilians is a deepening humanitarian catastrophe, and the cost of these wars has undercut Saudi Crown Prince Mohammed bin Salman's hopes to modernize the Saudi economy. The Saudis are not the only ones facing popular disillusionment with expensive foreign military campaigns in times of economic stagnation. Russia has deployed more than sixty thousand soldiers in Syria and was spending some $4 million a day during the heaviest airstrikes.[50] The US government has already spent over $30 billion on the Syrian war, and in 2018 the Trump administration asked Congress for another $13 billion.[51]

Like poker players who have bet too much to consider folding, these countries continue to invest in a costly game in which meaningful victory, even if it could be defined, is a remote prospect. As they raise the stakes, waiting for their opponents to blink, they also raise the danger of a military collision involving Russia, Iran, the US, Saudi Arabia, Turkey, and Israel. It would not be a novel story. Before both world wars, great powers pursued imperial ambitions while experiencing domestic tensions. They gambled on relieving domestic unrest through escalation and war, and all states involved suffered grievous losses. The powers hovering around

Damascus could, equally, be pulled into the vortex of a broader conflict as they test their strength, defend perceived interests, and rationalize the cost to their own citizens. No state will likely achieve its objectives, and the deaths of civilians and soldiers will grind on. The US and Russia could stop the descent into war and opt for de-escalation, if only to preserve their influence in the region.

The price of such influence should be helping to devise a stable and hopeful future for the Middle East. External intervention may begin with imperial ambitions, but calming the passions inflamed by the long conflict will require third parties to involve themselves in the demanding challenges of postwar peacebuilding. None of these efforts will succeed overnight, but they are the only antidotes to belligerent counter-Enlightenment world-views. Just as the devastation of the Thirty Years' War led to the Treaty of Westphalia, and World War II generated the complex planning that stabilized Europe, we can hope that the conflicts in Syria, Iraq, Libya, and Yemen lead to negotiated settlements with the cooperation of intervening powers. For each of these countries, a key question remains whether partition, reunification, or something else offers the best path to enduring peace.

Syria. Journalist Robin Wright recently identified three regions in Syria, each with its own flag and security forces, that she sees as the country's future: "a narrow statelet along a corridor from the south through Damascus, Homs and Hama to the northern Mediterranean coast controlled by the Assads' minority Alawite sect. In the north, a small Kurdistan, largely autonomous since mid-2012. The biggest chunk is the Sunni-dominated heartland."[52] If an agreement to end the civil war involves a partition among Sunnis, Kurds, and Alawites, these new entities would benefit best from a confederal or federal arrangement in which all ethnic groups would contribute to the national army and to common economic development projects. One would hope that these steps would progressively blur parochial allegiances and set the stage for deepening interdependence. Whether President Donald Trump decides to withdraw all US forces from Syria or not, an end to hostilities will require the support of its neighbors and the powers that have fueled the conflict: Saudi Arabia and other Sunni Gulf states, Iran, Turkey, Iraq, Israel, the US, and Russia. All have a stake in such an agreement. Russia, which has supported the Assad family since the Soviet era, is particularly key to major power cooperation in Syria.

Iraq. US National Security Advisor John Bolton has made a case for the partition of Iraq.[53] The Kurds in the north, approximately 20 percent of the population, clearly want out, as confirmed by the Kurdish referendum in September 2017, in which 92 percent of voters opted for independence. The Sunni Arabs in the west, also about 20 percent of the population, resisted the Shi'a-dominated sectarian government in Baghdad, and many among Iraq's Shi'a majority remain fearful of the Sunni minority's return to control. To the extent that current fractures seem beyond repair, partition may be the best option. "If they want a divorce," writes journalist Michael Totten, "for all of our sakes—let them have it."[54]

Today, however, after the defeat of ISIS and the army's rapid occupation of Kirkuk and surrounding areas following the Kurdish independence referendum, Iraq is struggling to reconstitute itself as a unified state. There were hopeful signs in the May 2018 elections, as new political movements, running on a pledge of "Iraq First" and fighting corruption, drew many voters away from traditional divisions.[55] The ultimate impact of the vote remains to be seen, but it may have signaled a popular yearning for an end to sectarian warfare in favor of a unified Iraq. The reintroduction of US forces in 2014 and their key role in defeating ISIS have also revitalized hopes for that outcome, which had collapsed in the wake of the US withdrawal four years earlier. Even some long-standing opponents of the American occupation now seem open to a limited US role in strengthening the current precarious peace.

Libya. There have been similar partitionist proposals for Libya. The ongoing east-west conflict, internal tribal divisions, and deepening reach of jihadist groups in the east have created three Libyan territorial zones: Tripolitania in the west, Cyrenaica to the east, and Fezzan in the south. After years of civil war following the 2011 revolution, many believe it may be time for these provinces to go their own way according to their respective social, religious, and political origins.[56] There are problems, however, with resolving civil wars by creating new borders. The example of Sudan teaches us that dividing an oil-producing country can bring disaster. Proponents of partition need to consider the question Rosa Luxemburg asked about Poland's secession from Russia: whether each of the new states thus created would be able to thrive. The same concern was recently echoed by Mahmoud Jibril, interim prime minister of Libya in the 2011 National Transitional Council. "A partition," Jibril pointed out, "will not benefit everyone!"[57]

Despite episodes of civil war in Libya since the Arab uprisings, and the establishment of ISIS in Sirte in 2014, hopeful signs point toward a peaceful and unified Libya. The country has never had strong state institutions, but the four ports of Es Sider, Zawya, Ras Lanuf, and Zueitina give it the potential to compete with Qatar and Indonesia in export capacity. Oil profits could provide the foundation for nationwide economic development.[58] Should current internationally mediated negotiations between competing factions succeed in implementing steps toward reunification, the National Oil Corporation's resources and the army would form the backbone of a central government, whether or not Libya is compartmentalized into three or more territories with some degree of autonomy. If it can invest its oil revenue in a diversified economy, Libya, like Iraq, has the potential to achieve stable domestic peace and inclusive prosperity. As with the other countries in this security theater, progress toward those goals may require some degree of shared power among aggrieved groups, along with institutionalized human rights mechanisms, to transcend what are now deep social divisions. Outside support will be also necessary if such efforts are to succeed. European powers have shown a strong interest in Libyan stability, both to secure the flow of oil and to prevent the flow of refugees. With US help, they organized a seven-month campaign that drove ISIS from Sirte in 2016,[59] and the European Union joined the League of Arab States, the African Union, and the United Nations in pledging to support Libya's democratic transition. In spite of its recent devastation, Libya is hosting conversations to hold elections in early 2019 that may usher in an era of considerable hope for progress toward a stable and prosperous state.

Yemen. Yemen's civil war is rooted in a long and troubled history complicated by colonialism and tribalism, which led to a partition, lasting from 1967 to 1990, between the communist People's Democratic Republic of Yemen in the south and the Yemen Arab Republic in the north. Their subsequent reunification was soon marred by tribal feuds, heightened by the actions of al-Qaeda (later al-Qaeda in the Arabian Peninsula) beginning in 2000 and then by the Arab uprisings of 2011, which escalated into a proxy war between Iran and Saudi Arabia in 2015.

Yemen suffers from two interlocked sources of instability: deep poverty driven by a lack of resources, and a strategic location that invites intervention by outside powers. Before the Arab uprising, 54.5 percent of

Yemen's population was estimated to be living in poverty.[60] Since 2015, the war has created one of the world's worst humanitarian crises. The unofficial death toll of more than fifty thousand does not capture the scale of the disaster, which has left 22.2 million people (three-quarters of the population) in desperate need of aid and protection, yet both sides have blocked delivery of food in order to starve their enemies.[61] In 2017, Yemen experienced the worst cholera epidemic in world history.[62] The situation in Yemen has been further exacerbated by a devastating man-made food security crisis with over 15 million people facing starvation; according to UN Secretary General Antonio Guterres, nearly half of Yemeni children under five years old are chronically malnourished, "resulting in a child dying every ten minutes of preventable causes."[63]

The conflict has been fueled by the strategic ambitions of outside powers to control the strait of Bab-el-Mandeb, the choke point between the Horn of Africa and the Middle East where the Red Sea meets the Indian Ocean. Currently, neither the Iranians nor the Saudis and Emiratis are willing to allow their adversaries to control access to the Red Sea. The strait is so highly coveted that Djibouti, on the western side, now resembles Casablanca circa 1940, with numerous external forces, including France, Japan, China, and Saudi Arabia, maintaining a military presence there.[64]

Given the vast amounts both the Iranians and the Saudis have already spent, ending the conflict in Yemen will necessarily require an agreement between Riyadh and Tehran. Any power-sharing agreement between the proxies will also require the involvement of outside actors, including the United States, on whom the Saudis rely for logistical support. A goal of negotiations should be to transform the area surrounding the strait (including Aden) into an internationally protected transport hub that will attract foreign investment, contribute to Yemen's development, and protect the interests of all parties.

The Maghreb Union

The Maghreb Union in North Africa—Algeria, Libya, Morocco, Mauritania, and Tunisia—is more stable than the other theaters. The Maghreb countries share a history of European colonialism, and with the exception of Libya, they confront similar security and economic challenges: the threat of violent Islamism and a lack of security that has stalled economic development and trade. All of these problems directly affect the

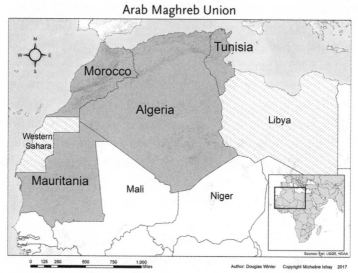

Reconfigured countries of the Arab Maghreb Union. Map by Douglas Winter and Micheline Ishay (© 2017 Micheline Ishay).

EU, especially as the Maghreb has become a staging point for migration into Europe. The EU, Qatar, and Turkey have all been deeply involved in the region, expanding their influence on multiple levels.[65] At the same time, the Arab Mahgreb Union (AMU), weakened by traditional rivalries between members, most prominently the dispute between Morocco and Algeria over the status of Western Sahara, has proven unable to address the region's chronic economic stagnation, high unemployment, and political unrest.

Insecurity and underdevelopment are interlocked; insecurity stifles economic progress, and economic stagnation can threaten prevailing security arrangements. That interconnection informed the initial proposal in 1956, shortly after Tunisia and Morocco gained independence from France, for an economic union among North African nations, leading to establishment of the AMU in 1989. Members were to negotiate both expanded trade and improved diplomatic relations within their union, leading to a common market in which people, products, and capital could circulate freely. These promises have yet to materialize. Between 1980 and 2017, the AMU's share of world exports plummeted from 2 percent to less than 0.5 percent and it is estimated that member countries have lost at least $8.5 billion of potential income.[66] The report also estimates that if the economies of the five states were fully integrated, each country could achieve annual GDP growth of at least 5 percent.[67] The union has been largely dormant for more than a decade, and the border between its two most prominent members, Algeria and Morocco, has been closed since 1994. Economic development projects could reinvigorate the AMU, especially if Morocco and Algeria can resolve their political differences enough to reestablish the direct flow of goods between their countries.[68] There is pressure from both countries' business sectors to do so.[69] Major infrastructure projects, such as a proposed high-speed train linking Morocco, Tunisia, and Algeria, would create significant employment and draw investment to the region.[70] Investment in renewable energy is growing, and synergies among regional railways, solar power, and desalination projects could trigger a rapid rise in employment and economic growth.

Drawn into North Africa by its 2011 bombing campaign against Muammar al-Gaddafi, NATO has moved toward long-term engagement in the wake of the anarchy and violence that followed his downfall; it now affirms its interest in expanded security cooperation with Tunisia, Morocco, and Mauritania to address the root causes of instability.[71] This is an important development, given the strategic importance of the Maghreb in blocking terrorist access to Europe. Tighter security cooperation among the states of the Maghreb, secured by regional and Western actors, could help the AMU become a new outpost of stability and prosperity.

The current efforts fall far short of Rooseveltian endeavors, but there are growing domestic pressures within the AMU for greater security and economic cooperation based on infrastructure investment and expanded intraregional trade. A revived AMU could also help stabilize Libya; restoring Libyan oil output could in turn further accelerate integrated regional development. Before the 2010 uprisings, a great number of Tunisian and Egyptian workers were employed in Libya's oil fields, one indicator of Libya's potential as an economic hub of North Africa and beyond, as Egypt forms a bridge from the African Arab countries to their nearest Asian neighbors, Israel and Jordan.

The Fertile Crescent

The Fertile Crescent historically stretches from the Nile Valley through modern Israel, Palestine, Lebanon, Jordan, Syria, and Iraq, all the way to the western fringe of Iran. In terms of our fourth theater, however, "fertile

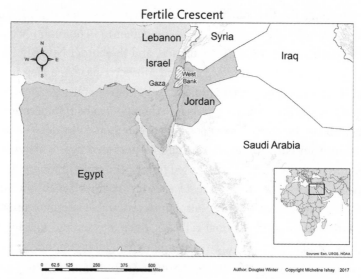

Selected territories of the Fertile Crescent. Map by Douglas Winter and Micheline Ishay (© 2017 Micheline Ishay).

crescent" refers only to three core countries that today constitute a natural geographic bloc for advancing cooperation: Egypt, Israel, and Jordan. Israel signed a peace agreement with Egypt in 1979 and with Jordan in 1994. Since the Arab uprisings, the leaders of these three countries have deepened their security cooperation. Egyptian and Jordanian leaders now see Israel as an important and powerful ally, especially for sharing military intelligence in their struggles against ISIS and the Muslim Brotherhood.[72]

Yet official and unofficial voices within both Egypt and Jordan continue to question the existence of the Jewish state. Despite recent textbook changes acknowledging peace with Israel, Egypt's school curricula continue to be influenced by hatred of the "Zionist entity," and many in the Jordanian population, particularly those of Palestinian origin, stand in solidarity with their brethren on the other side of the Jordan Valley.[73] Each of these countries has domestic problems: the al-Sisi regime's ongoing efforts to suppress the Muslim Brotherhood and defeat jihadists in the Sinai reveal its vulnerability; Jordan's economy is stretched to the breaking point by the flow of Syrian refugees; and Israel is seemingly in a state of denial, as if hoping the Palestinian problem will fade away. Can stable security cooperation advance human rights for all people in these countries?

Stronger security cooperation alone is not sufficient to ensure real stability. Lasting peace will require that the current triangular security arrangement coincide with an economic partnership that benefits all. As mentioned earlier, a significant first step would be to rebuild the old Palestinian Railways from El Kantara, Egypt, to Haifa, Israel, from there to Amman, Jordan, and from Amman back to Egypt via Aqaba and Eilat. Cooperation could be further expanded through joint economic projects involving shared technology, and major investments in solar power and desalination could serve the people of all three states. Greater economic cooperation would feed a virtuous cycle of investment, employment, and a reduction in the appeal of extremist groups. In the long run, shared prosperity creates pressure for wider political participation while increasing everyone's stake in greater social harmony. These synergies may be partial and uneven, but they could galvanize the will to address the political, social, and economic sources of conflict and radicalization. For these three countries of the Levant, a sustainable security regime will require sound economic development policies.

It is always easier to address thorny security issues, such as the Palestinian question, when people on all sides are experiencing growing freedom from want. A successful economic union between the Egyptians and the Jordanians would undermine the popularity of Islamism. With its borders less threatened by terrorist attacks, Israel would be more receptive to restarting the peace process with the Palestinians. With infrastructure development providing jobs and linking the Palestinians with each other and to the broader world, Palestinian societies will be better able to marginalize Islamist belligerence.

Donald Trump's 2018 decision to move the US Embassy from Tel Aviv to the contested city of Jerusalem surrendered any US claim to diplomatic evenhandedness. America's absence as a mediator, however, has not prevented the emergence of a new regional dynamic, the tacit anti-Iranian alliance among Israel, Saudi Arabia, and the UAE. Many argue that Saudi/ Emirati reliance on Israel's military strength has led them to downplay the plight of the Palestinians, but this may be shortsighted. Political reform in both Gulf states, the likely long-term consequence of their modernization campaigns, could leave them more vulnerable to the strong pro-Palestinian sentiments of the "Arab street." As those pressures mount, Israel's need for positive relations with Sunni Arab regimes, together with intensified

Gulf Monarchies

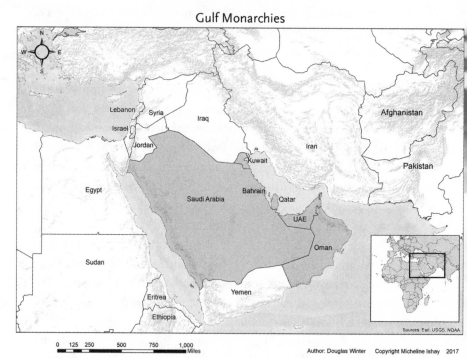

Gulf monarchies. Map by Douglas Winter and Micheline Ishay (© 2017 Micheline Ishay).

Saudi-UAE insistence on an equitable Israeli-Palestinian settlement, may enable those states to assume the "honest broker" role the United States has abandoned. Those Arab states might also have greater leverage over Palestinian leaders than the US could ever achieve.

The Gulf Cooperation Council

Our fifth theater, the GCC states, includes one active constitutional monarchy (Kuwait), two nominal constitutional monarchies (Qatar and Bahrain), two absolute monarchies (Saudi Arabia and Oman), and one federal monarchy (the UAE, composed of seven members, each with its own emir). Jordan and Morocco were invited to join the alliance after the 2011 uprisings, but both countries' membership remains on hold. Since it was established in 1981, the main purpose of the GCC has been to achieve greater unity among its members, based on political and cultural identities rooted in Islamic beliefs. To counter the Iranian revolution and its growing regional influence, the GCC also developed a defense planning council to coordinate military cooperation among member countries.

The GCC states are bound by two compelling shared interests. The first is defending the legitimacy of monarchy as a basis of governance. That concern led to increased repression in the wake of the Arab uprisings, including the joint Saudi-UAE occupation of Bahrain to defend its Sunni ruler, Hamad bin Isa al-Khalifa, against demands for democracy by Bahrain's Shi'a majority population. The same principle led the Sunni monarchies (except for Qatar) to suppress their domestic Muslim Brotherhood parties following Morsi's electoral victory in Egypt and to intensify their repression of secular democratic groups.

The second binding GCC interest is the need to resist any outside power attempting to seize their oil fields. That interest in containing outside threats ties them to the United States, whose postwar determination to protect the capitalist world economy corresponded with the oil monarchies' desire to preserve their regimes and oil fields. Beneath these unifying forces, however, lie powerful divisions. One concerns the threat posed by Iran. The Saudi and Emirati regimes see Iran as a mortal danger, whereas the Qataris, who share a major natural gas field with Iran and who resist domination by their Saudi neighbor, pursue those strong incentives for cordial relations with Iran. Finally, the weak state of Oman has chosen neutrality as its best option, refusing the Saudis' request to join their military coalition in Yemen and facilitating the initial meetings that culminated in the 2015 nuclear deal between the US and Iran.

Given the deep hostility between Iran and the two most powerful Gulf Arab states, is there any room for a de-escalation of the geopolitical and sectarian divisions between Sunni and Shi'a? In spite of appearances to the contrary, both sides are attentive to the dangers of continuing toward unlimited war. Demographic realities place inescapable limits on Iran's reach into the Sunni Arab world, and the Saudi regime's paralyzing symbiosis between an extremist strand of Sunni Islam and a vast, conflict-ridden ruling family leave them unable to assemble a military capable of a decisive offensive against Iran and its Shi'a allies. Both sides face the escalating costs of an unwinnable confrontation, the dangers the conflict poses to their own regimes, and the potential for apocalyptic war. They may awaken to the wisdom of de-escalation and even détente. Serious coordinated efforts toward economic diversity and integration within and beyond the Gulf oil states would help prod decision makers to recalculate the relative advantages of war and peace.

Following an April 2016 summit between President Obama and the leaders of the GCC, the US pledged in a joint communiqué to protect member states against external aggression and to "support GCC efforts to diversify their economies, provide more effective governance, and adapt to economic challenges posed by low oil prices and changing demographics."[74] Those commitments, however disrupted by the policies of the current US administration, outline a sensible framework for the relationship between the US and the GCC states. As the Trump administration's flirtation with regime change in Iran leaves the US internationally isolated and the Iran-Saudi confrontation unresolved, steps to promote reconciliation are likely to intensify. Those efforts will necessarily focus on the diplomatic improvisations born of immediate challenges, but they should be framed by broader plans to strengthen regionwide security, economic development, and human rights.

Those reluctant to explore alternatives to the current maelstrom should recall an even darker period, when a worldwide depression and a failed international order under the League of Nations contributed to the rise of fascist movements with global ambitions. When Franklin D. Roosevelt gave his speech presenting the Four Freedoms in January 1941, continental Europe was almost entirely under Nazi control. His own country, on which he called for leadership in liberating Europe and the wider world, was mired in the decade-long Great Depression. Many Americans greeted Roosevelt's human rights vision with a cry of "America First," invoking isolationism, economic protectionism, nativism, and scorn for the concept of a liberal world order. Just five years later, Western Europe found itself on a path to political freedom, prosperity, free trade, social justice, and unity. That zone of liberalism later grew to include the long-imprisoned nations of Eastern Europe. At the time of Roosevelt's speech, all this seemed wildly improbable.

The echo of Roosevelt's Four Freedoms, rooted in Enlightenment ideals, resonates despite the dark shadows now cast across the Middle Eastern deserts. The conviction that we can make serious, creative inquiry into possible steps forward is an important precondition of progress. In a time when the hatred unleashed by years of warfare rages unabated, idealistic prescriptions for freedom of speech, freedom of religion, freedom from want, and freedom from fear are not vain imaginings but pragmatic necessities. To escape from endless war and poverty, the Middle East nations will have to apply historical lessons to their conflicts and foster a broad political vision that favors human rights while remaining sensitive to different cultural and historical contexts.

The struggle for universal human rights, a surging popular hope during the Arab Spring, has been momentarily defeated. The contagious revolutions of 1848, the postcolonial struggles after World War II, the Prague Spring of 1968, the Latin American revolutions of the 1970s, and the "velvet revolutions" of 1989 show us that all revolutions suffer setbacks, yet the forces of human rights have always resurfaced, especially among the young. History is not amnesic; it recalls both mistakes and successes. In the Middle East, those who were prepared to gamble their lives on their hopes for an Arab Spring represented not an end but another beginning.

After years of derailment, war fatigue, regional powers' domestic and external pressures, and humanitarian disasters, the Levant Express is poised to be rerouted onto new tracks, galvanizing those who yearn for freedom of speech and of worship, for freedom from want and freedom from fear. Possibilities for embarking on that reclamation of human rights are part of a long-term process which has already begun, as the Gulf countries, European states, and China are turning their attention to major infrastructure development projects in the region. It is time for responsible leaders, those with relevant academic expertise, and far-sighted actors in the private sector to balance understandable pessimism over the current Middle East with the imagination to pursue the more ambitious framework discussed in this chapter. As Eleanor Roosevelt reminds us: "We gain strength, and courage, and confidence by each experience in which we really stop to look fear in the face . . . we must do that which we think we cannot."[75] But to stop looking fear in the face, she could have added, we also need to strive for yet another freedom "which we may think we cannot." That other freedom, which I call the "fifth freedom," focuses on women's efforts to dismantle the well-entrenched—yet vulnerable—Middle Eastern patriarchal structure. As many Arab women understood during the Arab uprising, echoing Eleanor Roosevelt, human freedom begins in the family, expands to civil society, and then grows politically and internationally. With only a little imagination, closer attention to subterranean change, and more resolve, we will see the Levant Express gaining speed and moving toward a new destination, toward freedom from sexual oppression.

CHAPTER SEVEN

The Female Time Bomb

INTERWAR COUNTER-ENLIGHTENMENT worldviews, such as fascism and Nazism, attempted to reverse the progress made by women's movements earlier in the century. After the war, Eleanor Roosevelt could be counted as a modern Enlightenment figure as she lent her considerable influence to the improvement of women's rights, fighting for a limitation on the number of hours an employer could force a woman to work and striving to remedy the unsafe and exploitative conditions in many male-dominated workplaces. With her leadership in the first UN Human Rights Commission, women's rights gained recognition as a key pillar of universal human rights. Women in the Western world are still pushing for equal rights. While they have made significant progress in recent decades, the gap between aspiration and practice remains, and nowhere is it wider than in today's Middle East. Freedom from gender discrimination is a "fifth freedom" whose attainment is crucial to regional economic development and peace in that region.

Norman Rockwell's 1943 cover for the *Saturday Evening Post* depicted a new female image that quickly became an American cultural icon: Rosie the Riveter. Introduced a year earlier in a popular song, Rosie represented the millions of women who went to work in factories and shipyards during World War II, sustaining the wartime production essential to battlefield victories. Rockwell's image of Rosie toured the country along

Rosie the Riveter, by Norman Rockwell. Printed by permission of the Norman Rockwell Family Agency; © 1942 the Norman Rockwell Family Entities. Illustration provided by Curtis Licensing.

with his Four Freedoms paintings to sell war bonds. Sitting against the background of a waving American flag, she holds on her lap a rivet gun and her lunch box. Her visor and goggles are pushed back, and she chews her sandwich self-assuredly, casually resting her feet on a copy of Hitler's *Mein Kampf.* Rockwell gave her painted fingernails, lipstick, and tidy red curls to convey her half-concealed femininity.

There were many real-life Rosies during the Arab uprisings who joined male companions in the streets of revolution; they were fellow travelers fighting for better tomorrows. Why were their struggles thwarted after the uprisings? What are the lingering social, political, economic, and religious tensions that could rekindle a new feminist wave? As in many other wars and revolutions, women were sent home after the fighting to avert competition with men in the workforce and restore the patriarchal stability often associated with social order. In this chapter, I argue that despite these postrevolutionary setbacks, women in the Middle East have gained a taste for freedom that will linger until the next wave of struggle. As their free speech and religious freedom are further censored, their economic opportunity curbed, and their safety threatened, women's political consciousness simmers, ready to explode in a female time bomb.

Historically, despite reversals, women's rights advancement has proven resilient. In 1915, more than a thousand women representing a dozen countries converged on The Hague for an international congress. Protesting the Great War and advocating for women's suffrage and equality, they formed what would later become the Women's International League for Peace and Freedom (WILPF). Despite many setbacks, eighty years later, that organization's international congress met in Helsinki. Soon after, members left on a Peace Train for the United Nations' Fourth World Conference on Women in Beijing. As they traveled across Europe and Asia, the 224 women and 10 men traveling together, ranging in age from eighteen to eighty-two, educated each other on the situations in their countries and discussed concerns about the environment, nuclear testing, and women's rights with local groups in many cities. In 2001, following the example of WILPF, another women's peace train traveled from Kampala to Johannesburg for the Second Preparatory Committee of the United Nations World Summit for Sustainable Development.[1] Crossing seven countries in ten days, the African women who participated emphasized that they were tired of bearing the brunt of war, and they met with government officials along the way to advocate for peace and stability.

At the Beijing conference on women, Hillary Clinton made famous the phrase "Women's rights are human rights." She was echoing a sentiment invoked in the nineteenth century. Real revolutionary changes in civil society, Karl Marx and Friedrich Engels argued, can only be gauged by "women's progress towards freedom, because here, in the relation of woman to man, of the weak to the strong, the victory of human nature over brutality is most evident. The degree of emancipation of woman is the natural measure of general emancipation."[2] After World War II, Eleanor Roosevelt deplored the omission of women's rights from the struggle for human rights. "I believe in active citizenship, for men and women equally, as a simple matter of right and justice," she said.[3] For her, human rights were both the work and the privilege of every individual. "Where, after all," she claimed, "do universal human rights begin? In small places, close to home. . . . Such are the places where every man, woman, and child seeks equal justice, equal opportunity, equal dignity without discrimination. Unless these rights have meaning there, they have little meaning anywhere."[4] Similar calls for equality in both the private and public realms resonated throughout the Arab world during the rebellions of 2011, yet the experience of women in the Middle East resembles that of Western women during the Industrial Revolution and after World War II, when persistent resistance to their aspirations brought deep and widespread frustration that eventually burst out in collective public action. Transformation may well come to the Middle East through such a female time bomb.

THE TRIALS OF SPRING

The highly regarded 2015 documentary *The Trials of Spring* is composed of six short films that tell the stories of nine women from Egypt, Tunisia, Libya, Syria, Bahrain, and Yemen during the uprisings and crackdowns of the Arab Spring.[5] Each narrative offers a conduit to the women's initial hope for change, later quashed by increased repression. The Syrian segment, for example, follows four women, known as the Brides of Peace, from their sense of empowerment as they protested the Assad regime in wedding gowns to their month of imprisonment by the regime they had defied. In Egypt, Hend Nafea found her voice among the protesters in Tahrir Square, only to be assaulted by police and locked up at home by her family. In Bahrain, Dr. Nada Dhaif was tortured in prison after helping wounded protesters. Such stories echoed throughout the region—a thousand and one tales of empowerment and repression.

As early as January 2011, photos and accounts of women taking over the streets and squares became familiar images of the Arab Spring. From Tunisia to Yemen, the increased involvement of women in Arab civil society was unprecedented, even in Gulf countries where conservative religious forces were long all-powerful. In Tunisia, where women had already attained greater equality with men, they protested with their male counterparts from the outset of the revolution, and in broad daylight—street associations seen as *haram* (sinful, forbidden) by guardians of the faith. This was even more the case in Egypt, where women were also prominent in the demonstrations. In Syria, women marched in the face of Assad's murderous soldiers and tanks, demanding the release of their imprisoned husbands.[6] Tawakkol Karman, a leader of Yemen's democracy movement and a role model for women of the region, shared in the 2011 Nobel Peace Prize for her courageous advocacy of free speech and human rights.

Although many Arab women had assumed an active role during the nationalist movements against European domination, the 2011 uprisings were also remarkable in the sheer scale of women's participation and in their revolutionary call for genuine equality. Despite a pattern of sexual assaults in Cairo's Tahrir Square—recurrent offenses that came to the world's attention through an attack on CBS reporter Laura Logan—courageous, unarmed women faced down armed pro-Mubarak thugs.[7] Social media often highlighted their critical role in the revolution.

Even more striking, on February 20, 2011, women from conservative Gulf countries became a force of change. From the Pearl Roundabout in Bahrain to the Sultanate of Oman, thousands of women stood shoulder to shoulder with men as they protested against the government and demanded their rights. In Yemen, when President Saleh suggested that antigovernment protesters in the capital violated Islamic law by allowing women to mix with men, his comments stirred an even greater uproar and further emboldened female protesters, who burned their veils in rage in the streets of Sanaa. There were signs of progress even in Saudi Arabia, where the late King Abdullah bin Abdulaziz Al Saud surprised many in 2011 by announcing that women would be allowed to vote in the 2015 municipal elections and be included on the Shura Advisory Board. In September 2017, King Salman bin Abdulaziz Al Saud issued a decree granting women the right to drive cars in 2018. While the right to vote means little under the authoritarian Saudi monarchy, the right to drive may signal a deeper cultural transition—small steps toward gender equality in the most male-dominant society on earth.

Unfortunately, these steps forward can be thwarted and women find themselves back where they started. In May 2018, just weeks before the Saudi ban on women's driving was to be lifted, seven women's rights activists were arrested. All had campaigned against the driving ban and called for other reforms, such as an end to the guardianship system. A government spokesperson said the women wanted to "destabilize the kingdom and breach its social structure and mar the national consistency."[8] This should not be surprising, since the oppression of women has for centuries served as the lynchpin of authoritarianism, employed to maintain or restore despotic stability. Despots kept their populations in servitude, in part, by allowing ordinary men to become masters in their homes, thereby appeasing male anger against their regimes.[9] This symbiosis between tyranny and patriarchy has been well evidenced in the history of women's rights. In the seventeenth century, the British feminist writer Mary Astell highlighted the hypocrisy of men protesting against the monarchy in the name of equal rights. "If the authority of the husbands . . . is sacred and inalienable," she wrote, "why not that of the Prince?"[10] That sarcastic question recognizes the repression of women as a fundamental pillar of authoritarianism. As long as men can still subjugate or legally discriminate against women, their own frustration, due to unemployment or repression, can be more easily appeased or vented at home instead of defying their rulers. Put another way, when a man's home is his castle, the prince is safer on his throne.

Even after tyrants are removed, women's subjugation persists. In the early days of the American Revolution, Abigail Adams was aware that women's support might ultimately bring freedom only for the men. She wrote a letter to her husband, John Adams, asking him to "remember the ladies": "I long to hear that you have declared an independency. And, by the way, in the new code of laws which I suppose it will be necessary for you to make, I desire you would remember the ladies and be more generous and favorable to them than your ancestors. Do not put such unlimited power into the hands of the husbands. Remember, all men would be tyrants if they could. If particular care and attention is not paid to the ladies, we are determined to foment a rebellion, and will not hold ourselves bound by any laws in which we have no voice or representation."[11] Adams's fears were well-founded, but her determined resistance would take a long time to bear fruit. Women were not granted the right to vote in the United States for another 144 years.

Women have always had to work against a double repression: patriarchal and political. During the final act of the French Revolution, Louis Marie-Prudhomme, a Jacobin who initially urged female citizens of all ages to join the revolution, remarked that once "the country is purged of all these hired brigands, we will see you [women] return to your dwellings to take up once again the accustomed yoke of domestic duties."[12] Similar regressions were experienced after the Bolshevik and Chinese Revolutions. Later, as feminist scholars Nawal El Saadawi, Nikki Keddie, and others have documented, many women fought for independence against colonial rule under the banner of Arab nationalism, only to return to more traditional roles after national liberation was achieved.[13] Given such historical precedent, it should not be surprising that women's rights opportunities also began to dwindle after the Arab uprisings of 2011.

The Arab women who took their grievances to the streets were protesting as citizens, not as women, but political differences emerged despite their unified front during the uprisings. "Women United by Revolution May Be Divided by Politics" was the title of a Gulf newspaper article.[14] The goals of Islamic feminists and secular feminists began to diverge. This split between women facilitated the marginalization of women's rights after the revolution. In the push for pluralism, resurgent Islamist groups, previously censored, dedicated themselves to defeating not just the entrenched Arab governments but also the agenda of secular feminists and progressive revolutionaries in general. They advocated for elections but not for the rights of women. Many secular participants in the revolution once again invoked the notion of women as the moral anchor of the family, especially as social chaos reinforced the appeal of domestic order. Women were reminded that the hijab kept them safe, that virginity before marriage was sacred, that they were in need of vigilant protection. As a spokesperson of the Morsi government in Egypt told me in Cairo in January 2013: "We are for women's rights! We want to help them fulfill their role as child bearer and caretaker without the types of distraction that are imposed on them elsewhere. They should earn the right to be mothers rather than become politicians. These are human rights as well!"[15] These traditional arguments were consistent with a familiar historical reality: the sacrifice of women's liberation on the altar of postrevolutionary regimes.

FREEDOM FROM SEXUAL DISCRIMINATION

The post-uprising era brought intensified repression—in some cases by both sides in sectarian civil wars—that pushed women back to the lower levels of the social echelon. In such times, it is important to remember that even when revolutions are not successful, they should not be written off as futile. Despite significant setbacks, Arab women had raised their political consciousness. They demonstrated that they could take to the streets, defy the highest authorities of their lands, fight enemies in combat, and assume positions previously occupied by men. In doing so, they now continue in the tradition of Olympe de Gouges during the French Revolution, the Pankhursts of the Industrial Revolution,

Alexandra Kollontai of the Bolshevik Revolution, Tcheng Hsiu in China, Gloria Steinem in the US, Nawal El Saadawi from Egypt, and Sherin Ebadi in Iran. As did their predecessors in the West or under communist dictatorships, Arab feminists continue to hone their skills, speak more freely, and reclaim their sexual identity within and outside religious realms. They are increasingly prepared to become new agents of progress and critical forces of a new Arab Enlightenment.

The Arab Spring revolutions were either crushed or unfinished for everyone, but women, in particular, were left frustrated. No less than men, women aspire to freedom of speech, freedom of religion, freedom from want, and freedom from fear. For them, however, those freedoms will not be realized without a fifth freedom: the freedom from sexual discrimination. First, social media empowered women's digital voices, and later their freedom of expression was suppressed in the political sphere; second, they sought a more liberal interpretation of the Qur'an, and later they remained sexually discriminated against by both religious and secular authorities; third, they became more educated, and later they suffered from increasing economic inequality; and fourth, they overcame the duress of revolutions and wars, and later they remained vulnerable— seeking greater freedom from fear at home and beyond.

The Struggle for Freedom of Speech
Ideally, women's freedom of speech will be protected by constitutions consistent with the Universal Declaration of Human Rights; they will have free access to the press; and they will be active participants in politics. In reality, women's speech thrives in the digital world of the Internet and social media, but it continues to be restricted in physical public spaces. It should not come as a surprise if Arab women continue to translate messages from the private realm of their laptops and cell phones into concerted public action.

Amidst regional war, Arab women have achieved, in two cases, constitutionally guaranteed freedom of speech as well as other fundamental rights. Tunisia and Egypt, the two initiators of the Arab revolutions, have completed their postrevolution constitutional processes, creating legal foundations for the possibility of genuine change for women. These countries' 2014 constitutions, though revised and enacted at the same time, resulted in different outcomes. Egypt has, to a large extent, fallen back into the structure of the 1971 constitution and will likely continue to restore its historically authoritarian presidency, especially as the armed forces play such a dominant role in the political and constitutional life of the country. In Tunisia, a balanced institutional framework provides substantial checks on executive power. Both countries affirm women's right to hold senior public offices, but Tunisia secured women's rights more forcefully. When Tunisia's Article 45 passed, guaranteeing the protection of women's rights, equal opportunity between men and women, and parity for women in elected bodies—a first in the Arab world and one of the most progressive constitutional articles in Arab history—the parliament rose as one and sang the national anthem. While the Egyptian constitution established a much lower quota for women's representation, to be enforced only within local councils,[16] Tunisia has set the standard for women and men in the Arab world.

Limited as they are, these constitutional protections are clearly a step in the right direction, but legal mechanisms are not sufficient in themselves. Lenin anticipated that equal rights for women under the law would, in itself, be insufficient to overcome prevailing male chauvinism in the Soviet Union.[17] The revolutionary Soviet government began to enact new legislation in 1918, granting women equal civil rights, voluntary marriage and divorce, legal contraception and abortion, state-supported childcare, employment rights, and maternity leave provisions. But after 1920, and particularly after the ascent of Stalin, women's rights suffered a setback as a result of an entrenched Russian patriarchal culture. Many of the rights granted to women and families in the 1918 Family Code were reversed: abortion was banned, divorce was curtailed, and the rights of illegitimate children revoked.

As in the early days of the Bolshevik Revolution, the elite and educated Arab revolutionary women who advocated for their rights during anticolonial rule and nationalist movements were at first rewarded with well-funded state-affiliated women's organizations throughout the region (for example, the Arab Women Organization and the US–Middle East Partnership Initiative [MEPI]). Women's endeavors, however, were soon co-opted by the state, and over time their issues became a political cosmetic veneer, easy to dismiss. To counter long-standing political negligence and cultural stereotypes, a number of independent women's organizations—such as the Tunisian League of Women Voters, the Egyptian

Center for Women's Rights, the Libyan Women's Platform for Peace, and the association Equality and Parity—mushroomed after the Arab revolutions. Women were now utilizing independent spaces that allowed them to exercise their skills and work against discrimination beyond the rigid, hierarchical, and authoritarian structure of the state.[18]

Using mobile phones, women were able to shroud themselves behind a veil of privacy and communicate beyond the control of parents, male relatives, or husbands.[19] They could disseminate information across neighborhoods, cities, and states, creating a pulse of energy that swept through the region. The Internet and social media gave them new outlets to express their frustrations, fears, and hopes. Feminist tweeters and bloggers, such as Egypt's Gigi Ibrahim and Mona Seif,[20] contributed to activist groups, for example, "No to Military Trials of Civilians." Lina Ben Mhenni's blog, *A Tunisian Girl*,[21] attracted readers from all over the world; at the time of this writing, her Twitter account has more than 340,000 followers. Even in highly repressive Saudi Arabia, the hashtag #StopEnslavingSaudiWomen[22] was created by women protesting the oppressive male guardianship law. In Yemen, Afra Nassar's blog has made a significant impact in a highly patriarchal society.[23]

According to an Egyptian joke, "In Egypt, there is freedom of speech, but no freedom after speech." Strict censorship continues to impede the free flow of information, but women continue to find ways to circulate information to a virtual community in the absence of other social or state protection. They are following the pattern of Western suffragettes from the late nineteenth and early twentieth centuries, who made good use of the press to promote their cause through a number of journals, such as *The Una, The Woman's Journal, The Revolution, Woman's Tribune,* and *Woman's Column.*[24]

The Internet and social media triggered new forms of feminist engagement with an intensity that could not have been imagined a generation ago, and political and religious leaders were not prepared for it. "Muslim sexuality is territorial," the Moroccan feminist and sociologist Mernissi explains. "Its regulatory mechanisms consist primarily in a strict allocation of space to each sex and an elaborate ritual contradictions [sic] arising from the inevitable intersections of spaces."[25] Already segregated in the public sphere, women were experiencing a second schizophrenic reality, between a virtual space that offered greater freedom and a shrunken

Celui qui n'a pas (The One Who Does Not Have), sculpture by Nadia Jelassi, protesting the stoning of women. Courtesy of Nadia Jelassi.

public space where they continued to feel repressed. Authoritarian governments have tried to monitor and restrict online outlets in the name of security, heightening the political exasperation of citizens and intensifying the pressure cooker of patriarchal control, all but ensuring a new feminist outburst, more seasoned and resolute than the previous one.

Freedom of Religion

Women in the Middle East also have been denied the right to challenge, reinterpret, or free themselves from their religion. After what was for many an overture of sexual freedom during the Arab Spring, the reassertion of religious expectations regarding women's traditional role in society frustrated their call for equality and sexual emancipation and stirred further discontent. All persons, male and female, whether they reject religion or embrace some form of it, need safe social environments where religious authority is clearly separate from the state. It is the nature of religious authority, however, to pull in the opposite direction, seizing greater control by merging the two spheres. No wall was erected between the mosque and the state, and religious control came back with a vengeance during the Arab Winter.

All civilizations, Sigmund Freud tells us, control sexuality; repressive regimes limit it firmly, and religious societies discipline it severely. After all, a central role of all religions is to organize family dynamics and regulate marriage, sexual reproduction, and gender division. "Religion," the German sociologist Max Weber stated, not only wishes "to eliminate the sexual orgy (the 'whoredom') experienced in early times," but also "to eliminate all free sexual relationships in the interest of religious regulation and the legitimation of marriage."[26] The religious desexualization of marriage is consistent with the establishment of an economic institutional structure for the reproduction and the rearing of children.[27] To this end, traditional religion, in the service of the state, generally maintains an antiquated subordination of women to their husbands and other male relatives in order to stabilize an internal patriarchal order aligned with external social stability. Religion perpetuates women's familial role and economic dependence on their husbands' position and earnings and thus helps avert male rebellion against authoritarian power.

During revolutions, pent up sexual repression is unleashed and expressed alongside progressive calls for change. With anarchy on the rise and social mores in disarray, Eros is unbound. During the Arab uprisings, many women felt sexually liberated, reclaimed freedom over their bodies, picked up sexual partners on virtual sites, called for the right to abortion and an equal right of inheritance, arranged temporary Islamic marriages for purposes of pleasure, and removed their veils.[28] Others made it a point to uphold traditional standards of dress and decorum even while calling for revolution, deflecting accusations of dishonor to those who might arrest or oppose them.[29] Either way, they acted out of a new sense of freedom. When Eros is reanimated in revolutionary times, the struggle to preserve new freedoms converges into solidarity, competition gives way to cooperation, hierarchy to equality, power to truth, and restraint to pleasure.

That spirit does not often last. A postrevolutionary restoration of order, as in the aftermath of the French and Russian Revolutions, requires new forms of discipline, and deep cultural traditions often come surging back, reestablishing religious control. Such enduring traditions are powerful in the MENA. "Running right across [the Arab world] is a hard and fast rule," Shereen El-Feki writes, explaining that "the only publicly-accepted sexuality is strict heteronormativity, its cornerstone family-endorsed, religiously-sanctioned, state-registered marriage. Anything outside this context is *haram* (forbidden), *illit adab* (impolite), *'ayb* and

hchouma (shameful)—a seemingly endless lexicon of reproof."[30] In
Tunisia, where women's rights flourished the most after the Arab Spring,
in 2013 89 percent of citizens told pollsters that sex before marriage is
morally wrong.[31] Sexually active women often seek hymenoplasty to
remanufacture their virginity before marriage, lest they bring everlasting
shame to their families and perhaps even harm to themselves.[32]

In this volatile environment, some Arab feminists choose individually to reinterpret the Qur'an in order to remain within the faith; others
concluded that they needed to step away from it entirely. Such divergent
approaches recall earlier women's rights champions and their strategies
against religious opposition. American suffragist Elizabeth Cady Stanton
reinterpreted biblical texts to support demands for political reforms, and
others, like the British socialist suffragist Sylvia Pankhurst, rejected religion in toto. In the face of religious prejudice, feminists like the members
of Musawah, a global movement advancing rights for women in Muslim
contexts,[33] have grounded their demands in a narrative of women's liberation that appeals to fresh, nonpatriarchal interpretations of the Qur'an as
a primary source.[34] Other, more secular feminists, like Nawal El Saadawi,
reflect a modern liberal discourse of women often associated with secular
nationalism.[35] Islamic feminists have accused secular feminists of
throwing out the baby with the bathwater, taking Qur'anic passages liter-
ally and then rejecting them, rather than recognizing the spirit of the text.
The Qur'an, they claim, should be valued as a source of authority in the
development of a non-Western and postcolonial type of Muslim feminism, in sync with Middle East culture. Secular feminists often find the
notion of "Islamic feminism" an oxymoron, regarding Islam (and perhaps
religion in general) as antithetical to women's rights.[36] In a way, coming
from different fronts, they are still unified against both the legacy of
Western imperialism and the patriarchal restrictions of their state and
religious institutions.

I witnessed many iterations of feminism in the United Arab
Emirates, where a great number of women from a variety of Arab and
cultural backgrounds reside. The Arab uprisings empowered women
across the region; many felt at ease to discuss their experiences within the
framework of Islam, and others reacted against their religious upbringing.
These sentiments conflicted with spatial and segregative dynamics sanc-
tioned by religious customs. The "protective" separation of women was

strictly enforced in government offices, hospitals, and buses, ensuring that single men (as opposed to men with their wives and families) were never in the proximity of single women. As in the American South under Jim Crow, these cultural patterns of segregation persisted regardless of written code or legal sanction.

I had a Lebanese colleague at Khalifa University, an assistant professor from the upper middle class who dressed in modern, sophisticated attire and spoke forthrightly. She was Muslim, but also a secular feminist. School events and ceremonies inevitably segregated women, seating them on one side or in the back of the room, but it was not difficult for my colleague to talk me into sitting with her in the male rows. Our presence stirred male indignation more than once, prompting some men to relocate farther away from us. Our rejection of separation was pointed. We knew that winds of freedom were sweeping across the region, whether the men in their privileged seats recognized it or not.

Women more religious than my Lebanese colleague began to rise up against entrenched traditions. One of my Muslim students hid her face behind large glasses and covered her hair in a tight headscarf, but as the events of the Arab rebellions unfolded, she was one of many women who grew more daring. She and other Islamic feminists believed that the Qur'an was a source of liberation for women and that many misinterpreted it. She offered me a book, The Ideal Muslimah, on the good standing of the "Muslim woman" and tried to convince me that the Prophet was concerned about equality between men and women.[37] When I asked about her views on polygamy, she glanced around nervously before intimating that polygamy could never be acceptable. She was so angry at the idea, she confided, that she vowed never to get married, to be sure that she would never be one of a man's multiple wives.

Polygamy remains a contested subject among most Muslim women. The Qur'an states that a man can marry up to four wives as long as he can provide for all of them. Polygamous marriages were once justified as a means to protect widows and their children who could not support themselves, yet that is rarely the objective when well-to-do men today legally marry more than one wife. The desire for a new wife tends to take precedence over economic necessity, and it does not take a staunch feminist to object to that practice, as many women, suddenly demoted by the new wife, find themselves competing for the diminished attention of the patriarch. Despite her more progressive understanding of the Qur'an, my student believed that becoming highly educated and remaining single was the only way for her to escape this fate.

The women I knew, religious or not, were most frustrated with the issue of legal guardianship. Under most interpretations of Islamic law, while a woman cannot be coerced into an unwanted marriage, she cannot get married without a guardian (a father or other male relative, even a mature son). Similar traditions can be found throughout monotheism, though they are not now legally enforced in Christianity or Judaism. The rationale behind guardianship—that a woman needs the contractual protection of a man to secure her well-being—continues to infantilize women, enabling men to claim dominion over every important public detail of families' lives. In the countries of the Arabian Peninsula, particularly in Saudi Arabia, male guardianship remains an important obstacle to the progress of women's rights. Adult women must obtain the permission of a male guardian to travel abroad, marry, get health care, or be released from prison. In the case of divorce, women will almost certainly lose the custody of any children who are not of a very young age, as the father remains their primary guardian.[38]

An Emirati from a royal family struck up a conversation about the custody issue with my mother and me in an Abu Dhabi mall. Sitting at an adjacent coffee table, she told us about her life quandaries. For over two hours, she lamented about her husband, who had recently married an Egyptian woman while on a short trip abroad. She was perturbed and was looking for support. Her husband, she explained, was not intellectually or financially her equal, yet she had to ask his permission to renew her driver's license or leave the country. She wanted a divorce, but was powerless and desperately afraid of losing the custody of her children. "This is simply unfair," she told me in despair.

If a woman is not her own guardian, her body does not really belong to her. She is essentially someone else's property, and she is, at best, a third of a person, with limited rights. In many Arab countries, particularly in the Gulf, she can take off her headscarf and walk without her *sheyla* only in her household, and only if any men present are her relatives. After all, as the Qur'an (24:30–31) spells out, "They should draw their head covering over their bosoms and not display their beauty except to their husbands." Today, this view is rationalized as an important cultural protection against unfamiliar male predators. While many women would still wear the veil if given a choice, there is widespread resentment about being compelled to do so.

With respect to the covering of the body, Islamic and secular feminists tend to disagree. In one of my tutorials in a royal setting, an appointed female parliamentarian from the Federal National Council (FNC) asked my opinion regarding a new policy that would prevent women from wearing shorts in the malls, an obvious temptation for Western visitors in hot climates. In the UAE, the dress code instructed expatriate women and others to wear clothes that cover the knees and shoulders. I questioned whether she thought this was an appropriate law to legislate on the floor of the FNC. With pride in her eyes, she retorted that the French president Nicolas Sarkozy had supported the banning of headscarves in schools and veiling women's faces in public areas. "Why was that different than our legislative discussions?" she asked. "We are also concerned about decency; tourists and expatriates should adjust to our customs, just as we have to accommodate to the French customs." The point was plausible, but I suggested that there was too much preoccupation with women's bodies, especially compared to men's, and that, overall, women should be able to choose what parts of their bodies to reveal. Her face showed mixed feelings; she was content with the way my remark had empowered women in that important male audience, but annoyed by yet another Westerner's critique of local customs. Our regal host was bemused by the conversation, pointing out that he was, as usual, wearing gym shorts while his guests were all dressed up in formal white *dishdashas* (traditional robe for men) or black *sheylas* (customary dress for women). I replied with a smile, "Sir, your knees have been a source of distraction for me, and this for several months since I began teaching these lessons." Everyone burst into laughter, but the point regarding a prevailing double standard had been registered.

Another participant in the gathering referred to scientific studies showing that men sexually fantasized about women constantly throughout the day, justifying the argument for hiding women's bodies. "Assuming you are right and that men are more biologically predisposed to predatory acts and lack of control," I replied, "then why can the testimony of men in your courts weigh three times that of women, and why should they be entrusted with the reign of power? And why shouldn't power be handed over to the gender capable of greater self-control?

Shouldn't society be protected from men's erratic and childish behavior?" My noble host, who had a penchant for Socratic rebuttal, enjoyed the exchange, but we both knew the time was not yet ripe for radical steps toward gender equality.

Outside such palace settings, the discourse about the inconsistent treatment of women is not always so polite, especially in countries where secular feminism has sunk deeper roots, such as in Egypt or Tunisia. "My body is my own and not the source of anyone's honor," wrote a Tunisian woman on her bare chest, protesting topless with others from the feminist group Femen.[39] Such demonstrations evoke familiar scenes from the feminist movement of the 1970s, when women tore off and burned their bras in the streets of London, Paris, Rome, and New York, while the Catholic Church decried them as indecent, even calling them whores. In North Africa, the Salafists reacted far more menacingly, calling for the feminist protestors to be stoned to death and forcing them into hiding. Some women were accused of being mentally ill,[40] like the European suffragettes who were institutionalized for anorexia nervosa or hysteria when they tried to regain control of their bodies and refused to submit to abusive husbands.[41]

Patriarchal control over the body can be both physically coerced and internalized by willing participants, as is often the case with female genital mutilation (FGM). Among feminists, whether religious or secular, few today would champion genital cutting. Eighty-seven percent of women in Egypt, however, are victims of this practice, which is also experienced by 19 percent of women in Yemen, 8 percent in Iraq, and 87 percent in Sudan.[42] Despite recent laws against FGM, it has continued to be defended as a means of beautification, necessary for a woman's marriageability. In fact, it is an act of violence against female sexuality, enabling male sexual pride and authority to remain untouched while enforcing the ideal of a woman's frigidity.[43] Sadly, older women who have experienced genital mutilation themselves are generally the ones most likely to impose it on the girls in their families, in a feudal exchange of bodily control for marital and economic protection.

Women's sexual repression and the internalization of male sexual dominance, typically regulated by religious practice, manifests everywhere, even without the brutal sexual control of genital mutilation. In the West, the path-breaking 1953 Kinsey study of female sexual behavior reported that 50 percent of women were sexually inhibited by "the church, the home, and the school." These regulating forces contributed collectively to the "distaste for all aspects of sex, the fear of physical difficulties that may be involved, [and] the feelings of guilt . . . which many females carry with them into marriage."[44] Just as in 1950s America, sex and orgasm are rarely discussed in the Arab world. Sexuality is subjected to an external or internal religious police that disciplines, even extinguishes, desire. It is not surprising that in this land of sexual misery, "paradise and its virgins are a pet topic of preachers, who present these otherworldly delights as rewards. . . . Dreaming about such prospects, suicide bombers surrender to a terrifying, surrealistic logic: The path to orgasm runs through death, not love."[45] Sex is repressed, but everywhere present and sought after. It is the unspoken undercurrent of public order, manifested in the demand that women veil their heads and cover their bodies, relentless male sexual harassment in public spaces, and obsession with the sanctity of hymens as another way males mark their control. Unsurprisingly, in conservative societies of the Gulf countries, such as in Abu Dhabi, cable television might carry at least a dozen stations combining soft porn videos with images of seductive women, along with a number to call for sexual favors.

A society that opts for segregation also indirectly promotes homosocial and homosexual relations, as long as they remain in the private sphere. I learned how taboo that subject was when I was summoned to the office of one of the deans at Khalifa University and reprimanded for a class discussion about an article on homosexuality in Southeast Asia before imperialism. None of the other politically charged topics I covered in the class prompted so much indignation. "You know very well," the dean told me, "that we condemn homosexuality in Islam; it is *haram!*" I replied that our discussion was not religious and I felt compelled to cover the topic because of then-current discussions at the UN General Assembly. I also noted the tension between religious or legal restrictions and popular practice. Homosexuality may be *haram,* but out on the Corniche, the beachfront promenade in Abu Dhabi, gays walk together in full public view. Homosexuality was remarkably present on our own campus, too, and lesbianism was well known in dorms at the University of Sharjah. Exasperated, the dean told me I could not talk about it in class, as these were the orders from above. But silencing the discussion did not change the fact that many Arab men, even those married with one or more wives, still enjoyed homosexual relationships. Early European homosexual men had likewise hidden their sexuality by becoming husbands and fathers. There remains a world of difference in the Middle East between what is admitted publicly and tolerated privately, particularly on the subject of sexuality.

This rigid patriarchal model may have benefits for men, but, over time, it is burdening for them as well. I recall an Egyptian driver from Alexandria who, like many other Arab men, still lived with his parents because he could not afford marriage. He had to postpone marriage ad infinitum and either repress his sexuality or indulge privately in forbidden sex, soliciting favors from women but more easily from other men. Marriage in the Arab world typically requires men to have a steady income; assume legal, moral, and economic responsibility; and stifle women's libidos in their households. By repressing women, men ultimately repress themselves. The disciplinarian always has to discipline himself, struggling to become a stoic model. When this role becomes unbearable, men may look for alternatives to this type of masculinity. Particularly in the midst of social distress, revolution, and sectarian warfare, it is not surprising that some men are increasingly seeking to share household responsibility with their wives, while others dream of being allowed to have casual sex without being shamed as philanderers or adulterers. As men give voice to their own sexual frustration and sexual dissonance, they could become, just as many Western men in the 1970s did, supporters of a new feminist movement. In the Arab world, that movement has temporarily receded since 2011, but the next revolutionary moon may well illuminate freer sexual paths for both women and men.

It is not surprising that in human rights struggles, women's rights and gay rights are often supported or repressed simultaneously. A gay Saudi student once asked me if he could write a thesis on women's repression in Saudi Arabia. When I inquired why he would not write about gay rights as well, he smiled shyly and told me in a quiet voice that women's progress would help advance gay rights as well. As in nineteenth-century Western capitals, when urban homosexuality became more visible as women were redefining themselves as active citizens, and in the 1970s, when gay protest movements peaked alongside the women's liberation movement, gay rights and women's rights constitute a tandem threat to

masculine dominance in the MENA. Such renegotiation of sexual identity tends to disrupt order within the family, creating instability and chaos,
and it undermines authoritarianism and extreme forms of nationalism.[46]
In the MENA region, homosexuality is criminalized, and, in many countries, homosexuals face the threat of execution.[47] Even in more tolerant
countries, such as Lebanon, Tunisia, and Egypt, the LGBT community's
calls for the right to privacy are often met with popular outrage.[48]

Freedom from Want

"The claim of women to be educated as solidly, and in the same branches
of knowledge, as men," John Stuart Mill wrote, "is urged with growing
intensity and with a great prospect of success, while the demand for their
admission into professions and occupations hitherto closed against them
becomes every year more urgent."[49] In 1869, this important father of
liberalism anticipated that education would enhance women's professional opportunities. Still, over a century and a half later, women in the
Arab world who seized the opportunity to graduate from college have
found themselves in the same economic and domestic predicament as
their far less educated mothers and grandmothers. With few job opportunities, and confronted with the painful realization that their acquired
knowledge is financially worthless, some find partial solace in maternal
responsibilities, but a growing number recognize that their lot will not
improve if they are forced to rely economically on equally impoverished
husbands. The women I have met in the MENA, from students and
would-be professionals to activists and young mothers, are becoming less
comfortable with traditional roles. Their heightened sense of self-worth,
mixed with denied opportunities, has morphed into a powerful political
consciousness, pushing them one step closer to the boiling point of social
transformation.

Women have, at times in the past, mobilized en masse, entering the
workforce during wartime. Like Rosie the Riveter, women during World
War II were gaining strength, developing new skills, and showing independence. They were crucial for the war effort, but American women still
earned 50 percent less than their male counterparts, and at the end of the
war, many had to give up their jobs. It would take another generation for
the political discourse to change. As described in Betty Friedan's *Feminine
Mystique*, women were generally expected to return to their homes,

assume the role of housewives, and cook for their heroic men. The 1950s were challenging for American women; many harbored resentments over the traditional gender role that they had to reoccupy once the national danger had passed. Resigned, sexually dissatisfied, and armed with lasting memories of their capacity and potential, these women raised a new generation of girls who, entering university in the 1960s, became far more empowered than their mothers, ready to fight for their overdue rights. The journey of Western women's emancipation did not evolve in a straight line, but in a zigzag.

Overall, women in the Arab world have experienced high growth rates across key development indicators like literacy, life expectancy, and reduced infant mortality rates than in most other developing regions.[50] The education level of Arab girls today equals that of boys. Most remarkably, Arab women have reversed the gender gap in the key sector of tertiary education, where women now outnumber men.[51] At Khalifa University in the UAE, women make up more than half of the student body, with double the percentage of female enrollment in engineering compared to the global average.[52] At first glance, these signs forecast better times for women in their struggle for freedom from want and independence. However, despite the rising level of education for Arab women, eleven of the fifteen countries with the lowest rates of women's participation in their labor force are in the MENA region.[53] Yemen has the world's lowest rate of working women, with Jordan, Iran, Morocco, Saudi Arabia, Algeria, Lebanon, Egypt, Oman, Tunisia, Mauritania, and Turkey not far behind. In several of these countries, the number continues to decline.[54]

There is a wide gender gap in the labor force. In the center of the Maghreb, 63 percent of Tunisian men take part in the workforce, but only 23 percent of women.[55] Women are often better qualified, but men are given preference in hiring, leaving difficult and low-paying jobs, such as farming and textile work, to women. With few job opportunities, women in the Arab world who have college degrees find themselves with limited options. Some find partial reward in maternal responsibilities, but many others recognize that they cannot rely financially on their husbands, who use their control over household finances as a means of dominance in a precarious job market.

Their frustration reaches new heights when the economic structure of the pater familias erodes. "The authority-promoting effects of the family depend essentially on the man having the decisive role he does," writes the German thinker Max Horkheimer, "and his domestic power depends in turn on his being a provider. If he ceases to earn or possess the money, if he loses his social position, his prestige within the family is endangered."[56] This does not mean, however, that the patriarchal structure fades away with the disappearance of the father's income. Role divisions between men and women are deeply entrenched. Patriarchy is oppressive, but women often continue to perpetuate their subordination, accepting their own shackles despite their educational liberation. "The most dangerous shackles are the invisible ones," writes Nawal El Saadawi, "because they deceive people into believing they are free. This delusion is the new prison that people inhabit today, north and south, east and west. . . . We inhabit the age of the technology of false consciousness, the technology of hiding truths behind amiable humanistic slogans."[57] Saadawi's remark resonates loudly in a more developed feminist culture like Tunisia's, illustrating how the patriarchal worldview inevitably makes a comeback over liberal values during economic crises. In Arab countries, it is commonly believed that unemployed men should have priority in getting jobs and that women should make way for them by staying at home. Citing the Arab Human Development Report, Muntaha Banihani and Jawad Syed write, "Arabs support and stand with gender equality in education but not in employment, and in the case of scarce jobs men have the priority over women."[58]

In the early 1930s, when millions of American men lost their jobs, great efforts were made to prevent them from feeling emasculated, including the widespread expectation that working women would yield their positions voluntarily so men could work. It was unsettling for many women, and the feeling intensified as their absorption into the wartime workforce was reversed when soldiers returned home after 1945. Simmering resentment amplified over the next two decades, until it burst into the women's rights movement of the late 1960s. With women making up 60 percent of university students in Tunisia and outperforming male students, the failure to utilize their enormous skills is producing similar feelings.[59] To turn indignation toward social transformation, women from the Maghreb will need to assert their right to gender parity not just in parliament but also in hiring and promotion in the private sector and in governance.

Women in the Fertile Crescent confront predicaments similar to those in the Maghreb. Egyptian women have a significantly lower level of participation in the formal economic sector than men (23 percent versus 78 percent) and lower literacy (65 percent for women versus 82 percent for men).[60] On the other side of the Nile, Jordanian women are far more likely to be literate, as the nation's literacy rate of 85 percent easily leads the region, but they are just as likely to be employed, with only 23 percent in the labor force.[61] Gender discrimination is perpetuated by, among other factors, women's sole responsibility for children coupled with the high cost of childcare and their lack of control over land, bank accounts, pensions, and other economic assets.[62] Women are often not seen as their own guardians for basic economic transactions, and they are usually barred from passing their nationality to family members.[63] Gender equality will clearly require reforms on multiple fronts.

In comparison, Israel's 1948 Declaration of Independence affirms that the country "will ensure complete equality of social and political rights to all its inhabitants irrespective of religion, race or sex."[64] Israeli law prohibits all forms of discrimination based on gender in employment and wages, and in 2017, 59 percent of Israeli women participated in the workplace.[65] Yet as in other industrialized countries, wage disparities between men and women remain a source of frustration for Israeli women; in 2017, Israel had the fourth widest wage gap among the fifteen OECD countries surveyed, with Israeli women receiving a salary 78 percent less than their male counterparts.[66]

When one considers the gap between Jewish and Arab Israelis, a different picture emerges. Arab Israeli women find far less opportunity in the workforce than their Jewish counterparts.[67] Within Israel, where 71 percent of Jewish-Israeli women are in the workforce, employment for Arab-Israeli women remains below 23 percent.[68] In the West Bank and Gaza, the percentage of Palestinian women in the workforce is 17.4 percent.[69] Further, when they are employed, Palestinian women most commonly work in the low-income agriculture and service industries.[70] Palestinian women's rights are regularly overshadowed by the overarching goal of Palestinian national liberation and the continuing Israeli-Palestinian hostilities. Neglected politically and economically and fragmented geographically between Israel, the West Bank, and Gaza, Palestinian women are inclined to see patriarchal oppression as the result of Israeli occupation. It is conceivable that this fragmentation could be transcended if they made common cause with liberal Jewish Israeli feminists. Recent efforts, like the women's peace march of October 2016, uniting Palestinian and Israeli women, demonstrate the possibility of broader cooperation.

The gap between education and employment is as great in the Gulf as in other MENA regions. In the UAE, women are almost twice as likely as men to enroll in higher education, but men are twice as likely as women to participate in the labor market. Explanations for this disparity sound familiar: family responsibilities, gender bias, and problems with mobility, exacerbated by the expectation that women, despite some recent relaxation of the guardianship law, should be accompanied by a male relative when traveling.[71] In Saudi Arabia, women account for nearly 60 percent of university graduates, and they typically perform better than men in math and science, but less than 20 percent of women enter the workforce after graduation.[72] Nevertheless, there are positive developments in the Gulf. The UAE is trying more aggressively to increase women's ability to work by providing childcare, at least in large government offices.[73] Thanks to the dominance of foreign labor in most Gulf countries, female nationals are more often solicited to become part of the workforce. Emiratization, Omanization, and Bahrainization have enabled women to enter the higher levels of public administration despite an entrenched patriarchal structure that continues to favor men over women, both in business and in the bloated public sector.

Women in the Gulf are still underrepresented on corporate boards and in other executive-level positions, and the gender gap in entrepreneurship remains greater in that region than in any other,[74] but, with the exception of Saudi Arabia, they are entering the labor force at a rate approximately double that of other MENA states, particularly in the UAE (with 46 percent participation), Kuwait (44 percent), and Qatar (51 percent).[75] Perhaps most significant, yet often overlooked in the prevalent coverage of Saudi suppression of women's rights, is the fact that women from the GCC not only rank significantly higher in educational attainment and employment, but, compared to other women in the MENA region, they are far wealthier.[76] Put another way, they already have latent economic power.

As economically empowered women in the GCC attain growing levels of responsibility and achievement, they will become an increasingly integral part of these nations' social capital and could well be in a position to push for greater liberal reforms despite Islamist resistance. Religion remains a major hindrance to women's social progress, but for many that opposition also motivates them to strive for higher educational and work accomplishments. Wealthy women are in a better position to make sustainable demands for equal rights, especially as they gain greater financial independence. They could become the unexpected leaders of a female sexual revolution and a drive for secularization.

In oil-producing countries, female empowerment will require a context of broader economic development. Large infrastructure development projects (such as rail, solar energy, and desalination) could include a 50 percent recruitment quota for women, reducing women's dependence upon men, while stimulating sluggish economies. More women in the workspace would also help keep radical Islamists at bay. An International Monetary Fund report highlighted the way gender inequality in the workforce hurts economic growth. Closing gender gaps in the labor market, the report estimates, would raise GDP in the United States by 5 percent, in the United Arab Emirates by 12 percent, and in Egypt by 34 percent.[77]

A focus on raising women's employment rates does not address broader obstacles to the improvement of their economic rights. As early as the nineteenth century, August Bebel explained in *Women and Socialism* that employers would hire more women because women are accustomed to settling for less, driven, in part, by a concession to the possibility that they will become pregnant and have to care for their families. Because they are often compelled to accept poorer jobs and lower wages than men, it is possible to hire women without improving substantially their economic well-being.[78] Bebel also argued, just as many feminists after him, that corporate profits would benefit from competition between men's work and women's work, which would send salaries into a downward spiral. Families with two small incomes would experience greater distress in childrearing, increasing the likelihood of divorce. Europeans have recognized that problem better than Americans, integrating socialized childcare as an important aspect of advancing human rights and preserving stable democratic societies. As feminists in the West have long understood, freedom from want requires freedom from the assumed obligation of childcare.

By raising their level of education, women from Tunisia to the Arabian Gulf have taken a major step forward. Women from the Maghreb and the

Fertile Crescent need broader reforms, including major investment in economic development, the enforcement of equal rights in employment, generous maternity leave laws, and state-sponsored childcare.[79] One should not discount Gulf women and their capacity to enact change. Through their relative economic advantage, and despite high religious barriers, it would not be surprising if the next Arab feminist outburst begins in those countries. While women across the MENA raised their voices in the streets of the Arab Spring revolutions, the women of the oil-rich Gulf states have alone gained economic power. Others in the region can draw on that strength, as it gains expression, in a unified, transnational women's movement that overcomes the fear inspired by economic vulnerability.

Freedom from Fear

Arab women confront fear in three realms: the home, with threats of domestic violence; the public sphere, with threats of sexual harassment and governments' lack of protection; and the state of war. Since the publication of Naguib Mahfouz's *Palace Walk* in 1956, depicting wives' fearful submission to their husbands in the post–World War I era, modern Arab women have evolved: they entered universities, they challenged traditional roles, and many espoused one form of feminism or another. Patriarchalism did not disappear, however, and in most cases, the cultural or legal notion of male guardians with ultimate authority in the household prevails. The authoritarian state proved to be a poor guardian of women's safety, relegating that task to the men of each family, who are free either to respect or to abuse females, with little or no consequences. With spreading revolutions and wars, the world has become less certain, and women's fears grow exponentially. Nonetheless, in arduous situations, women gain new competencies that can provide enduring power in the long run.

As their revolutions derailed, Arab women suffered from a rise in gender-based violence, even in the relatively more peaceful countries of the Maghreb, the Fertile Crescent, and the Gulf. Women's advocates interpret the increase in rape and sexual assault as a form of collective punishment for women's public role in the revolutions and a deterrent to scare them away from public spaces.[80] Similar explanations were offered for increased domestic violence, as men reasserted their authority at home.

These actions were consistent with the Qur'an (4:34), which, in its literal reading, permits a man to hit his wife if she does not do as he asks.[81] Allegedly, the beating is intended as a last resort after verbal abuse and abandonment and it is to stop if the woman complies with her husband's demands, but abusive men take full advantage of religious sanction and respect few boundaries in their justification of violence. They rationalize even murder in cases of social disgrace, as family members attempt to reclaim their honor by killing women suspected of prohibited sexual contact—women whose bodies plainly were not their own turned into scapegoats to purify the family shame. In some cases, women who have simply claimed their legal inheritance have been said to shame their families and have been subjected to honor killings. It is no wonder that women often waive their property rights—to preserve not just their family harmony but their lives.[82]

In an effort to draw attention to the problem of domestic violence, the Moroccan actress Maisa Maghrabi wore dark glasses during a 2015 interview on a Saudi TV station. In front of the camera, she slowly removed her glasses, revealing a purple eye, where her ex-husband had struck her. Domestic violence is generally kept hidden in the Middle East, and showing the dirty laundry in public to outsiders is considered shameful. "Don't hide the violence towards you," Maghrabi told her audience as pictures of her battered face were later disseminated on Instagram and Twitter across the region.[83]

Violence against women (VAW) is rampant. The 2014 MENA regional report for the Due Diligence Project states, "VAW is not just a phenomenon in the region; it is a defining norm of power dynamics and the relationships between men and women."[84] In the MENA region, approximately 30 percent of ever-partnered women have experienced physical violence at some point,[85] and 94 percent of unmarried females report that they are sexually harassed daily.[86] In Egypt, upwards of 43 percent of interviewed women experienced physical intimate partner violence, and over 80 percent of men admitted to using emotional violence towards their partners.[87] These numbers are particularly disturbing considering that child marriage is relatively common in the MENA region, where one in five girls are married before the age of eighteen, with the highest rates of child marriage in Yemen.[88] Abuse is vastly underreported due to the shame involved in going to the authorities, and many don't report acts of domestic violence for fear of being shamed. Despite condemnations of excessive acts of brutality, governmental agencies show almost complete negligence in combating such crimes.[89] In Jordan, for example, where the number of women who have experienced physical violence at least once since the age of fifteen is reported to be as high as 44 percent,[90] legislative and judicial protections still lag far behind in addressing the problem of domestic violence.[91]

The abuse of female migrant workers is even more likely to go unnoticed. Typically working without contracts and lacking legal protection, more than 18 percent of foreign domestic workers surveyed in Tunisia indicated their employers had sexually assaulted them.[92] A recent study of Nepali women working in the Middle East found that more than 50 percent of those working in Saudi Arabia and Lebanon had experienced physical violence on the job, and as many as 15 percent had been sexually abused.[93] Migrant women working in the Gulf (from India, Bengal, Philippines, and so on) often live in continual fear. A Human Rights Watch researcher stated: "I have interviewed scores of women working in Gulf states who told me that their employers confiscated their passports, withheld their salaries, forced them to work up to 21 hours a day without rest and no day off, confined them to the employer's home, deprived them of food, provided inadequate sleeping conditions, and subjected them to psychological, physical, and sexual abuse."[94] Despite recent legislation granting some of the GCC's twenty-five million migrant workers minimal protections with regard to contracts, governments still give employers far too much control over their domestic workers, who, largely excluded from labor laws for citizens, are vulnerable to all forms of abuses.[95] The laws that should protect them are either not in place or not enforced.

One would expect a better situation in the Maghreb, where women's rights have a longer history. On Avenue Bourguiba, the main street of Tunis, many women can be seen wearing miniskirts or tight jeans and walking alongside others wearing headscarves and long dresses. Even though political rights were largely moot for all Tunisians under the dictatorship of Ben Ali, with the country's first free elections taking place after the revolution in 2011, the country has long prided itself on women's equality.[96] More than sixty years ago, Tunisia's Personal Status Code banned polygamy and took steps to eliminate forced marriages. It also demanded that marriage contracts take place between consenting partners, not guardians, and set a minimal legal age for marriage.[97] The Personal Status Code gave women the right to vote, be elected to the parliament, and initiate divorce. In 2014, in what was seen as a landmark for women's rights, Tunisia publicly withdrew all prior reservations to the Convention on the Elimination of All Forms of Discrimination against Women (CEDAW).[98]

It seems, however, there is always a loophole. When Tunisia formally adopted the convention, it created a broad religious exemption and declared that the state will not enforce any elements of the convention that conflict with Islam, the recognized state religion (as codified in chapter 1 of the Tunisian Constitution). Likewise, rapists have been able to escape prosecution by marrying their young victims, and women who file claims of sexual assault are often shamed by their families and rendered liable to charges of public indecency and defamation.[99] Protective laws have thus far been inadequate and unenforceable, and it remains to be seen whether new legislation will bring the substantial change for which human rights organizations have campaigned.[100] In a state where nearly half the women surveyed indicate that they have suffered physical violence at the hands of their male partners, more needs to be changed than the penal code.[101] After a long struggle, feminists scored a major victory in June 2017 when the Tunisian parliament legislated a new gender parity law, criminalizing, among other issues, sexual harassment at work and in public and also marital rape.[102]

Many hoped that Egypt would offer greater legal protections for women under a new government. When President al-Sisi seized power, he stated: "Women have always taken part in writing the history of our nation. They have shown their ability, responsibility and strength, in building our country."[103] Under his government, women would, at least in principle, be able to hold senior positions in both the public and private sectors. The 2014 constitution affirmed the equality of the sexes, and after 75 women won seats in the 596-member parliament in 2015, the president appointed 14 more. Unfortunately, this was the same al-Sisi who had infamously defended the so-called virginity tests inflicted on female protesters during the 2011 upheaval. When detained, women were beaten and subjected to forced vaginal examinations. Al-Sisi's warning to women was clear: they would be seen as "loose," and they would be publicly shamed and mistreated if they did not support his government.[104]

Egypt has lived in a constant state of political instability since 2010, with two presidents ousted and two constitutions revisited, but one constant has been the government's inability—or unwillingness—to combat violence against women and girls. The Egyptian penal code permits violations committed in the good faith observance of Shari'a, allowing domestic violence to continue virtually unrestrained.[105] But there is at least one positive sign of attitudinal change. In 1995, 69 percent of Egyptian women believed it was justifiable for a man to beat his wife in the midst of a disagreement. By 2005, just over 37 percent of Egyptian women agreed, and by 2008, less than 15 percent of female respondents would excuse such violence.[106] In Egypt, the road to equal rights still has a long way to go, but women no longer accept the status quo.

Legal protections obviously require the rule of law, and women in failed or warring states find themselves in even greater jeopardy. In the West Bank and the Gaza Strip, Palestinian penal law is a pastiche of inconsistent Jordanian, Egyptian, Palestinian, Ottoman, and British laws—a situation not aided by the paralysis of the Palestinian parliament since 2007—and it does not adequately protect women and girls from domestic and sexual violence.[107] Women are punished more severely than men for the same offenses, and existing laws also protect rapists who marry their victims, along with men who commit honor killings on the basis of "local customs."[108] Women are not protected from rape or sexual harassment, and victims of incest can be treated as offenders.[109] In August 2017, Jordanian women earned a small victory when the parliament abolished the law that allowed rapists to avoid jail by marrying their victims.

For female refugees, the situation gets even worse. Millions have entrusted their lives and those of their children to unscrupulous smugglers in order to cross the Mediterranean Sea or to find another path to safety. Others experienced harsh conditions and prolonged uncertainty in the refugee camps of Lebanon, Turkey, and Jordan. "Whether they are underpaid at work or living in dirty, rat-infested, leaking homes, the lack of financial stability causes immense difficulties for women refugees and encourages people in positions of power to take advantage of them," reported Kathryn Ramsay from Amnesty International.[110] Since Lebanese authorities have stopped registering refugees, women in that country have been made even more vulnerable to sexual assaults and rape, as they are in the country illegally and unable to report to the police. Child marriage predated the Syrian civil war—13 percent of girls under the age of eighteen were married—but in the camps the forced marriage of Syrian girls has increased significantly, possibly even doubled.[111] With scarce resources available to Syrian families, and few economic opportunities, many families regard the marriage of young girls as a way to avert sexual violence and ease their own economic burden. Married to much older men, these young brides are all but enslaved; they lack power and are at great risk of violence or other forms of exploitation.[112]

The situation for women still surrounded by battle—in Libya, Syria, Iraq, and Yemen—is even more disturbing. Women have been the spoils of war, often beaten and raped by more than one faction in the same conflict. Whether women are Sunni, Shi'a, Kurdish, Christian, or Druze, they have suffered at the hands of perpetrators from every side. A March 2018 UN report features interviews of 454 Syrian refugees and demonstrates that "no one [is] unaffected by sexual and gender-based violence in [the] Syrian conflict."[113] Rape serves as a particularly devastating weapon of war, and it is important to note here that sexual-based gender violence (SBGV) is not only directed toward women. In a 2017 UNHCR report a group of interviewed refugee women estimated that 30 to 40 percent of the men in their community had experienced sexual violence while detained in Syria.[114] Sexual- and gender-based violence must not be dismissed as an unfortunate consequence of conflict; it is a violent strategy of control, a process of humiliating women and their loved ones to subjugate a population.[115] In the former Yugoslavia, the International Criminal Tribunal (ICTY) played a historic role in the prosecution of similar acts of sexual violence, forging a way toward the more robust adjudication of such crimes worldwide. A third of those convicted by the ICTY were found guilty of crimes involving sexual violence.[116]

Among the great number of female victims, there are many courageous women showing the path toward a better future. Of special notice are the Kurdish female soldiers, who have taken up arms against ISIS along the border between Turkey and Syria. These Peshmerga fighters follow a tradition of Kurdish women warriors; in 1996, Kurdish women joined combat units in opposition to Saddam Hussein. Today, they are fighting Islamic State extremists. Their goal is to protect Kurdistan—but also to show the world that they are equal to men, swelling front-line units, special forces, and SWAT teams. These units of female combatants know all too well that they are feared by fundamentalists, who believe, by a strict interpretation of the Qur'an, that a soldier killed by a woman is barred from Paradise.[117]

One would hope that the Arab women who suffered through war and who have occupied traditionally male roles would become standard-bearers for a new generation of women unwilling to accept the affliction visited on their mothers. With men fighting in trenches or absent from the home, the number of Syrian female-headed households in Jordan has doubled in recent years and is approaching 50 percent. After traveling thousands of miles over many months with their families, many of these female refugees wish to integrate into their host societies, to learn new languages and find new jobs. Where possible, they are entering the work-force and starting small businesses. Having survived tumultuous jour-neys under horrid circumstances, they are ready to claim an active role in the private sector and the public sphere.[118] Syrian women may follow the path of their Iranian sisters, whose station was paradoxically improved when half a million Iranian men died in the 1980–1988 war with Iraq.[119] Joining universities in full force, they became critical political voices during the Iranian Green Movement of 2009 and once again, after the repression of that movement, their voices were heard nine years later, as they took their griefs to the street, unveiled against religious oppression. Those who now imagine them as permanently subdued have a very short-sighted view of history. One can expect Syrian women, as well, to rise up as strong survivors, part of a new force for social change and peace based on the realization of human rights.

Such a force may also be materializing in other places, such as the Women Wage Peace movement, a group of Israeli and Palestinian women that came together after the 2014 war in Gaza. Their two-week March of Hope across Israel and the West Bank in 2016, from Rosh Hanikra on the Lebanese border to Prime Minister Benjamin Netanyahu's home in Jerusalem, swept up thousands of like-minded women. "We cannot count on men to create peace," said one participant. "We have to do it ourselves."[120] At the front of the line of marchers was Nobel Peace Prize laureate Leymah Gbowee, who, as a Liberian social worker, had led a women's movement of nonviolent resistance that helped end her coun-try's civil war and oust its dictator, Charles Taylor. Like her Liberian foot soldiers, the Palestinian and Israeli women were dressed all in white, proclaiming that they wanted peace now.[121] Women have been instrumental in bringing about peace in many regions of the world, and perhaps they will now rekindle in civil society the moribund peace process in the Middle East, amidst lingering defeatism and political cynicism. In 2000, UN Security Council Resolution 1325 directly linked, for the first time, women's experience of conflict to the international peace and security agenda, stressing the importance of women's equal and full participation in conflict prevention and conflict resolution. Women's voices are needed now more than ever.

Even in areas less characterized by organized violence, women are actively demanding their own rights. In Saudi Arabia and in other Gulf countries, where men control women's lives from birth until death, women's rights activists have relentlessly called on the government to abolish the male guardianship system, and they are seeing some success. The Saudi government agreed to changes in 2009 and again in 2013, after the Universal Periodic Review of the United Nations Human Rights Council.[122] Women are fearlessly turning to social media to raise awareness.[123] Many men have joined their fight, as the system of guardianship is a burden that many no longer wish to assume. A sign that their fight would finally be vindicated came in May 2017, with the partial abolition of the Saudi system of legal guardianship. Although there is still a vast distance to travel, the relaxing of this oppressive rule is a move in the right direction.[124]

Rationalizations for oppressing women, couched in terms of cultural relativism or backwardness compared to the West, are losing relevance. As long as a patriarchal social and religious system keeps women silent in the public sphere, sexually dissatisfied and disempowered in the family, impoverished despite their increased level of education, and living in fear despite their growing skills of resilience, pressures will build toward a new women's rights contagion, and a new sexual revolution, occurring in the Arab world—one that would reorder families and destabilize autocratic regimes. It may well be women who reroute the temporarily derailed Levant Express toward new democratic pastures. It may also be women, history suggests, who finally break the impasse of seemingly intractable conflicts. If there is one place in the region crying out for women from every quarter to work together for peace and human rights, it is in the heart of the Levant, in the disputed land of promise.

CHAPTER EIGHT

Remembering the Future

IN THE FILM *THE CITY OF LOST CHILDREN*, French directors Marc Caro and Jean Pierre Jeunet tell the story of mad scientists who kidnap children from a port city to steal their dreams because the adults are no longer able to dream for themselves. In places like Gaza, generations of conflict have similarly stolen children's dreams. Palestinian children reside in limbo, torn between hopes and sorrows, fearing exile and yearning for promised lands, pulled forward toward uncertain futures yet drawn back to a mythologized past. Hamid Ahmed, a Palestinian from Gaza, now seventy-five, recalls that between 1959 and 1965, when Palestinians could travel freely, he often took the train from Shujaiya, his neighborhood in Gaza City, to Cairo.[1] These trips were a pure joy. Today, Gaza is cut off from the world, and travel restrictions make such simple trips a distant dream.[2] Most dreams of freedom have faded away, leaving it to poets to voice any remaining hopes. The Palestinian poet Mahmoud Darwish (1941–2008) wrote:

> Quickly the train passed by
> Passed by me and I am
> Like the station, not knowing whether
> To bid farewell or greet the people;
>
> ....

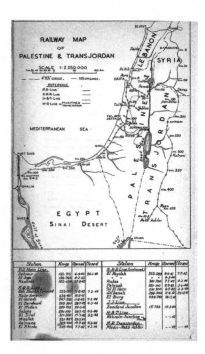

Map of Palestine and Transjordan Railway, 1925. Courtesy of the Israel Railway Museum, Haifa.

Quickly, the train passed by
Passed by me
And I am still waiting.[3]

Can a peace process based on human rights be forged, one that overcomes the shortfalls of both one- and two-state solutions? Recent academic writings on the Israeli-Palestinian conflict have begun to integrate a human rights approach, but they tend to privilege one cluster of rights at the expense of another. By contrast, Roosevelt's Four Freedoms provide a vision for a comprehensive path forward that can be expressed in tangible mechanisms for implementing human rights. In that spirit, in this chapter I argue for a confederative solution, incorporating interim human rights milestones in the transition to a final peace settlement.

The situation in the heart of the Levant is grim. The dreams of too many Israelis and Palestinians have been drowned in sorrow and anger. It is easy to see why Palestinians' hopes have faded, and why, after decades of missed opportunities and futile peace talks, so many Israelis have concluded that a political settlement with Palestinians is not achievable or sustainable. Many Israeli government leaders seem to have decided that their best hope is to prolong the status quo, postponing indefinitely any arrangement with the Palestinians. They claim that since the split between Fatah and Hamas in 2007, there has been no legitimate negotiating partner on the Palestinian side, and the political turmoil following the Arab uprisings only emphasized the need to base policies on unilateral national security and stability. In the 2015 elections, Prime Minister Netanyahu retained his office, in part, by appealing to conservatives with an eleventh-hour promise that he would never allow a Palestinian state. After his surprising victory, Netanyahu quickly reintroduced the possibility of a two-state solution, saying he had meant only that it was not possible at the present time. Meanwhile, Jewish settlements continue to expand in the West Bank and any real movement on Palestinian issues remains indefinitely on hold.

Other Israelis regard the postponement of the Palestinian issue as a dangerous oversight—one that, according to former Israeli intelligence chief Ami Ayalon, will only hasten the crisis of Israeli democracy and Jewish national identity.[4] From this perspective, no democratic country can deny the civil, political, and socioeconomic rights of a people subject to its control without eroding its legitimacy as a democratic state.

Jordanian Prince El Hassan bin Talal told me that while the region's attention has been absorbed by the wars in Syria, Iraq, and Yemen, the resolution of the Palestinian question remains essential to achieving a comprehensive peace in the region. Without entering into detail, he favored a confederal solution—one of the options to be discussed below— and thought outsiders should assist the transitional management of a Palestinian territory. A sustainable peace between Israelis and Palestinians would not resolve the region's other conflicts, but it would surely reenergize the sense of possibility. Such dreams of the future, however, need to be translated into clear and viable strategies. To that end, I argue for four integrated freedoms for both Israelis and Palestinians. After briefly reviewing entrenched obstacles associated with ideal forms of one- or two-state solutions, I argue for the institutional protection of human rights, focusing on a confederative structure.[5]

FOUR FREEDOMS FOR ISRAELIS AND PALESTINIANS

Franklin Roosevelt's Four Freedoms coincide with what the 1948 Universal Declaration of Human Rights identified as the main families of rights: civil-political, religious and cultural, socioeconomic, and security—principles that can be understood only as inalienable and indivisible. Israel and, more recently, the Palestinian Authority have agreed to international human rights agreements, but competing narratives continue to divide them, and both sides favor certain rights while ignoring others. An all-encompassing framework, including individual and collective rights, might address these differences and enable negotiators to formulate the steps necessary for a viable peace.

In its 1948 Declaration of Independence, Israel stressed its commitment to universal human rights: "The State of Israel will foster the development of the country for the benefit of all its inhabitants; it will be based on freedom, justice and peace, as envisaged by the prophets of Israel; it will ensure complete equality of social and political rights to all its inhabitants irrespective of religion, race or sex; it will guarantee freedom of religion, conscience, language, education and culture; it will safeguard the Holy Places of all religions; and it will be faithful to the principles of the Charter of the United Nations."[6]

In 1991, Israel acceded to several human rights conventions, including the International Covenant on Civil and Political Rights and the International Covenant on Economic, Social and Cultural Rights. A year later, the Knesset passed the Basic Law: Human Dignity and Liberty, which declared, among other things, that "all persons are entitled to protection of their life, bodily integrity and human dignity." This should have created an opening for a new, shared emphasis on the rights, needs, and aspirations of all, with both Israel and Palestine formally accountable to the international community.[7] As an occupying power since 1967, however, Israel has deprived Palestinians of fundamental rights.[8] Life in Gaza and the West Bank is far removed from that envisioned by the Universal Declaration of Human Rights and the subsequent covenants.

Aside from Israel's failure to live up to its own words, placing human rights concerns at the center of peace negotiations would have pressured Palestinian leaders to accept norms that they had not often practiced toward their own people, let alone in their relationships with others. The 1988 Palestinian Declaration of Independence might be seen as a step in the right direction: "Palestinian Governance [will be] based on principles of social justice, equality and non-discrimination in public rights of men or women, on grounds of race, religion, color or sex, and the aegis of a constitution which ensures the rule of law and an independent judiciary."[9]

Ultimately, since negotiations have always been directed toward separation of the two peoples, the protection of human rights was treated as
each side's internal matter. The only human rights provision agreed upon
by Israel and the PLO is Article 19 of the Agreement on the Gaza Strip
and Jericho Area (May 4, 1994), which states: "Human Rights and the
Rule of Law: Israel and the [Palestinian] Council shall exercise their
powers and responsibilities pursuant to this Agreement with due regard
to internationally-accepted norms and principles of human rights and the
rule of law." After gaining non-member observer state status in the UN
General Assembly in 2012, the Palestinian Authority, too, agreed to the
major human rights conventions. Yet life in the territories controlled by
the PA (and, unsurprisingly, Hamas) shows that human rights principles
have little relevance to Palestinians' daily realities. The PA and Hamas
have both engaged in arbitrary arrest, torture, denial of due process,
summary executions, and detention of journalists.[10] Hamas, whose religiously derived laws are harsher than those of the West Bank, punishes
"unnatural intercourse," understood as homosexuality, with up to ten
years in prison.[11]

Past approaches to peace have treated human rights as little more
than a marginal concern.[12] There are a number of explanations for this
oversight. Israelis and Palestinians have diametrically opposed narratives
regarding the causes of the conflict and the events that led to the present
impasse, and these differences lead to different understandings of human
rights issues. Each side sees itself as the victim. Focusing on specific
human rights would force them to confront these opposing narratives. In
1967, Isaac Deutscher eloquently offered an interpretation of the way a
group of victims can victimize others, leading to a battle of self-righteous
narratives:

> A man once jumped from the top floor of a burning house in
> which many members of his family had already perished. He
> managed to save his life; but as he was falling he hit a person
> standing down below and broke that person's legs and arms.
> The jumping man had no choice; yet to the man with the broken
> limbs he was the cause of his misfortune. If both behaved ratio-
> nally, they would not become enemies. The man who escaped
> from the blazing house, having recovered, would have tried to

help and console the other sufferer; and the latter might have
realized that he was the victim of circumstances over which
neither of them had control. But look what happens when these
people behave irrationally. The injured man blames the other for
his misery and swears to make him pay for it. The other, afraid
of the crippled man's revenge, insults him, kicks him, and beats
him up whenever they meet. The kicked man again swears
revenge and is again punched and punished. The bitter enmity,
so fortuitous at first, hardens and comes to overshadow the
whole existence of both men and to poison their minds.[13]

Israeli decision makers have vacillated between purely pragmatic and
extreme nationalist approaches to the peace process, generally avoiding
questions of justice or remedies for past human rights violations. For
them, placing human rights at the center of negotiations could be regarded
as a concession to the Palestinians. Israeli leaders may also have feared
that a human rights discourse would highlight the most delicate and difficult issue—the "right of return," or the rights of Palestinians who fled
Israel during the 1948 war to reclaim their former homes. The Israelis
believe there is no possible agreement on this question. They have also
countered that the Palestinian leadership has little human rights record of
its own, except in using human rights discourse as a tool to discredit Israel.

After so many years of promoting their own political programs in the
midst of conflict, Israelis and Palestinians have not developed a sense of
their common destiny. The universal protection of human rights could
provide both sides, as well as outside actors interested in promoting peace
in the area, with a shared set of principles for achieving a common goal.
To reach it, each side will have to recognize the other's historical plight,
and each side will have to make hard compromises. Naked power that is
insensitive to issues of justice and human rights can never settle the
conflict in a way that will command lasting legitimacy. Likewise, institutional mechanisms or power-sharing models must first delineate shared
principles before anyone can attempt to enforce them. These common
standards, if they are to be viable, are best articulated in the language of
universal, inalienable, and indivisible rights.

The universal aspirations of human rights are clear: individuals hold
these rights simply by being part of the human species, regardless of sex,

race, religion, ethnicity, nationality, or economic background. They are universal in content and recognize no borders. An important contribution of the first Commission on Human Rights, under the leadership of Eleanor Roosevelt, was the affirmation that human rights are to be embraced as a whole; one cannot take them piecemeal. Fragmented views of human rights have contributed directly or inadvertently to the rise of exclusive group interests. For instance, while Israelis have emphasized their fundamental right to be free from fear, the Palestinians reply that they still lack equally essential freedoms.

Further, the rights of one person or group cannot be preferred over the rights of other persons or groups. By 1966, when the two international covenants were adopted, group rights were recognized in Common Article 1: "All peoples have the right of self-determination. By virtue of that right they freely determine their political status and freely pursue their economic, social and cultural development."[14] Both Jews and Palestinians understandably invoke their particular histories of oppression to vindicate their respective rights of self-determination. Existential fears of group vulnerability and collective demands for political independence and cultural autonomy need to be addressed as an essential component of universal rights.

Recognition of group rights inevitably raises the possibility that they will clash with individual rights. For instance, a Palestinian might call for sexual freedom as a fundamental individual right, but his or her group would likely restrict or prohibit it. The desire for self-determination is a collective response to colonialism, oppression, occupation, or genocide. In circumstances of collective suffering, when the individual is merged with the persecuted tribe, it becomes hard for that person later to reclaim individual rights against the group. Any form of dissent—by journalists, human rights advocates, gays, or others—may be seen as weakening the group's cohesion. Many states that were established out of conflict in order to fulfill a people's right to self-determination commit extensive violations of individual rights. There may be no way to resolve these competing claims without external involvement by some supranational body. Any attempt by such a body, however, to enforce individual rights against those of the majority risks energizing nationalist, illiberal sentiments and could thus be self-defeating.

Any framework for peace that reconciles competing visions of justice must employ confidence-building measures that advance the implementation of rights without relegating any to some final stage.[15] There can be no sequential formula privileging one set of rights over another. For instance, the right to security is clearly central to progress as in all other realms of human rights, but creating sustainable economic opportunities may be a prerequisite for long-term security. Neither democratic institutions nor developed economies can be established overnight, especially given the wide disparity between Israel and Palestine in these realms. Neither the one- nor the two-state proposals currently under discussion satisfy this criterion.

THE CHALLENGES OF ONE- AND TWO-STATE SOLUTIONS

Both partitionists, who advocate the two-state approach, and unionists, who favor the one-state approach, can marshal isolated aspects of human rights to support their views. The partitionist approach focuses on the centrality of group rights to self-determination, security, and culture. Its most obvious advantage is that it allows both Israeli Jews and Palestinian Arabs to exercise their right to self-determination through political independence. Isaac Herzog, the Israeli Labor opposition leader, urged a negotiated two-state solution to allow Israel to preserve its Zionist democratic union.[16] Likewise, despite Israel's renewed construction of Jewish settlements in 2017, Palestinian leader Mahmoud Abbas has continued to call for restarting talks aimed at a two-state solution. "Peace in the world can be secured by the realization of the two-state solution, Palestine and Israel, living side by side on the pre-1967 borders in peace and security. The creation of the State of Palestine will undermine the driving force of terror and extremism, and we are a part of the international system combating terrorism," he claims.[17]

A unionist approach, on the other hand, emphasizes individual rights, which should never be subordinated to group or religious rights. In a unitary state, the group affiliations of individuals would be privatized, as in the French and South African models, where the only common denominator recognized by the state is citizenship. Ethnic, religious, or national identities are the private affair of citizens. Avraham Burg, former Speaker of the Israeli Knesset, advanced that position, proposing that "[the] next diplomatic formula that will replace the 'two states for two peoples' will be a civilian formula. All the people between the Jordan and the sea have the same right to equality, justice and freedom. In other words, there is a very reasonable chance that there will be only one state between the Jordan and the sea—neither ours nor theirs but a mutual one."[18] This view was echoed by Saree Makdisi, an American scholar of Palestinian descent, who called for "the cooperative integration of Israelis and Palestinians in one common state. . . . Israel and the occupied territories [*sic*] already constitute a single geopolitical entity, even if it's not labeled that way. . . . That state would join two peoples whom history has thrust together into one democratic, secular and self-governing community of truly equal citizens."[19]

I need not enumerate the long list of obstacles that continue to block both the two-state and the one-state approach. Israeli settlements on the West Bank, doubling in number over the last two decades, have punctured the feasibility of a Palestinian state with contiguous borders. West Bank unification with Gaza seems equally daunting, given that Hamas and Fatah are divided not just by geography but by a deep ideological rift. Further, the growing economic gap between Israel and the Palestinian state could become a permanent security hazard for both countries. A one-state solution also remains both politically and viscerally challenging. Given memories of the persecution that engendered Zionism, few Israeli Jews would agree to become a vulnerable minority in a unified state. Simultaneously, many Palestinians are frightened by the prospect of a Jewish hegemony that could use an already powerful state to reinforce its interests. Years of conflict have created deep psychological barriers and collective distrust. One can only believe that the widening gap in educational and economic skills between the two peoples will lead to prolonged social and economic tensions like those seen in post-apartheid South Africa.

Given the near impossibility of both unitary and partitionist approaches, it is understandable why so little has changed and why those who continue to stall or sabotage the peace process succeed so easily year after year. Both options are incomplete: each secures only a portion of the comprehensive human rights corpus. No solution will be adequate if it does not incorporate interim processes and institutional mechanisms built upon a comprehensive human rights framework.

A CONFEDERATIVE SOLUTION

If neither one state nor two is capable of ensuring the full range of human rights, we are left with something between the two: a confederative structure. Unlike a federation, which usually involves a constitutional division of power in a single state between central and regional governments, a confederation comprises two or more sovereign states that have agreed to allocate defined powers to a supranational institution. The best modern example is the European Union. Recently, the concept of a confederation as a structure for the relations between Israelis and Palestinians has gained traction within various intellectual and political circles.[20] In an interview with the Israeli newspaper *Yedihot Ahronot*, the Israeli president, Reuven Rivlin, suggested that in the absence of open borders between Israel and its neighbors, the two sides should explore a borderless Israeli-Palestine confederation.[21]

The tremendous mutual distrust between Israelis and Palestinians necessitates the presence of international partners, as multiple cycles of violence easily cause security imperatives to override other human rights concerns, exacerbating distrust and stalling efforts toward peace. Without interim efforts toward broad human rights progress, a sustainable Israeli-Palestinian agreement may never get off the ground. How can we build interim human rights efforts that will not be derailed by violent spoilers from either side? Short of a final confederative structure, some legitimate entity must have the authority to monitor, protect, and promote human rights. Although neither side is likely to trust an international broker to be impartial, it is difficult to envision tangible human rights progress without a legitimate third party.

Such an international partner (whether one state or several) would be required to allay these fears and persuade the two sides that negotiation is beneficial to all. Given the present political impasse, exacerbated by new settlement construction in the West Bank, states really interested in advancing a political settlement should not simply demand that the parties return to the negotiating table to rehash all the well-known issues. Instead, they should emphasize both sides' obligations to respect and ensure human rights and propose a mechanism for monitoring human rights, which would include representatives of both sides working together with well-respected outsiders.

Some Israeli policy makers question the relevance of implementing human rights standards because they perceive the other side as contemptuous of these norms. Moderate Israelis also dismiss the idea, but for a different reason: under the principle of self-determination, they say, it is none of Israel's business what type of regime Palestinians choose. Others support the inclusion of human rights criteria in order to preclude an authoritarian government in Palestine, since such regimes reliably invoke outside enemies to deflect domestic opposition. Ensuring the democratic stability of one's neighbor can only contribute to one's own security. As Machiavelli and many subsequent thinkers have pointed out, stability relies on a system of checks and balances—a system that contains feuds and conflicts.

Secular Palestinians tend to favor democracy and are worried about a Hamas-led Palestinian government. When I led a class of American graduate students on a trip to Israel and the Palestinian territories in the summer of 2017, we listened to an affable Palestinian activist in Nazareth condemning the Israeli occupation in the West Bank, deploring what she called her second-class citizenship. When a student asked her if she, as a Palestinian with Israeli citizenship, would move to Palestine if it were granted independence, she gently reprimanded him, telling him the question was unfair. Palestinians had not yet demonstrated their capacity to live in a democracy, she said hesitantly, and as a citizen she was not about to forego the benefits of the Israeli welfare state. Her feelings are echoed by many Palestinian intellectuals, who share her concern about the viability of a Palestinian state and its ability to live up to human rights ideals.

By ensuring that the two sides take steps to further protect human rights, a confederal entity could both mitigate human rights violations in the Occupied Territories and help anchor a pluralist, democratic Palestinian state. The promotion of human rights and the establishment of a legitimate Palestinian sovereign state that could join a confederation are best devised in tandem. Even as specific disputes, including interminable fights over land and water, take longer to settle, enhanced protection of human rights might provide the trust and security needed for a confederative agreement. If it is currently unrealistic to launch such a project in Gaza under Hamas's leadership, the West Bank, under the control of the Palestinian Authority, might be more receptive to a process that advances individual Palestinian rights. In November of 2018, Egypt attempted to revive the stalled reconciliation process between Hamas and Fatah. Could their preliminary reconciliation agreement present a viable avenue for such progress?[22] The obstacles are significant, but the stakes are too high to overlook this possibility.

Whatever the shape of a final confederative structure, its human rights standards will require the two sovereign entities to agree on several key provisions. First, there must be a commitment from all levels of government, within the entities and within the confederal institutions, to respect and ensure the human rights enshrined in the international conventions to which both Israel and Palestine are parties. Second, a confederal human rights commission should be established that conforms to the 1993 Paris Principles on National Human Rights Institutions. Third, a human rights tribunal should be established to adjudicate complaints from individuals who have exhausted domestic remedies. In order to strengthen both the human rights commission and the tribunal and to prevent power struggles between Israelis and Palestinians, these bodies should incorporate significant international elements.

In short, from initial pressure on both sides to move beyond current impasses, to the creative process of developing an integrated rights-based approach, to the design of an overseeing mechanism to guide the transition to a more permanent solution predicated upon human rights, any initially fragile alliance between Israelis and Palestinians will need the strong and consistent engagement of an international coalition to back their efforts. How will a confederal structure address major human rights issues?

Freedom of Speech

The right to freedom of speech, including a free press, is an essential foundation of democracy. It provides a check on politicians in and out of power, counters governmental corruption, disseminates popular opinions to elected officials, and contributes to sustainable peace. Governments, however, recognizing their vulnerability in times of conflict and uncertainty, often attempt to preserve power by suppressing free speech. Both Hamas and the Palestinian Authority have arrested journalists and activists who criticized their policies.[23] Less fragile but equally concerned, Israel too has imposed restrictions on Palestinian media.[24] How can freedom of speech prevail in volatile times like these?

The Israeli Supreme Court has affirmed that freedom of speech is an essential human right. Nowhere else in the Middle East is this freedom so well entrenched, with established legal precedents dating back to the Yishuv—Jewish political institutions created before the state was founded. For decades, the Ottoman government had allowed the Jewish press considerable freedom of expression, extending even to the criticism of officials, and this freedom increased after the Young Turk Revolution of 1908.[25]

Despite its link to the Western (and Ottoman) tradition of press freedom, the Israeli government has sometimes imposed restrictions on journalists on the basis of the 1948 Prevention of Terrorism Ordinance. The state has also banned incitement to violence and restricted groups that call for the destruction of Israel.[26] Unfortunately, the government's understanding of incitement has broadened to allow the gagging of journalists who simply report on disturbing Israeli practices. In addition, Israel has developed a governmental media program, *Hasbara*, to explain and legitimize Israeli action in the world. While it is true that Israel's human rights shortcomings are disproportionately covered and much of the international media hold it to seemingly impossible standards, *Hasbara* is itself selective and sometimes completely misleading. By deflecting Israel's responsibility to correct abuses in the Occupied Territories, *Hasbara* detracts from the otherwise free and powerful independent press that Israelis enjoy.[27]

Like its Israeli counterpart, the Palestinian Basic Law guarantees a free press and prohibits government censorship. In practice, however, Palestinian authorities routinely suppress news that undermines the "general system," "national unity," or public "morals."[28] Political pressure has been allowed to undermine the freedom of the press, and journalists are often harassed or prosecuted for criticizing Palestinian officials. The problem is significantly worse in Gaza. For instance, Mohamed Othman, a Palestinian journalist who had criticized Hamas, reported that he was detained for a day and a half, beaten, deprived of food, and forced into painful positions.[29] In an independent Palestinian state, dissenting political speech like his would have to be protected. This standard might be difficult to establish, however, given the tension between Hamas and Fatah supporters, meaning that the region's best chance for freedom of speech may be a confederacy model.

A confederacy model would enforce a high standard of freedom of speech, drawing on the standard provided by the Israeli free press while providing financial support for the development of strong media outlets in the Palestinian state. In such a conflict-filled, transitional environment, the media would also have to take on the additional role of fostering mutual trust and cooperation among feuding groups. The confederacy and its international overseeing body would face a challenging balancing act: how to preserve truth-telling while minimizing the sort of speech that triggers violence.[30] A free media culture would need to curb such incitements, which are real issues in post-conflict areas, while still reporting on abuses of power in the name of national security. John Stuart Mill offered an interesting early contribution to the subject of speech as incitement of violence: "An opinion that corn dealers are starvers of the poor, or that private property is robbery, ought to be unmolested when simply circulated through the press, but may justly incur punishment when delivered orally to an excited mob assembled before the house of a corn dealer, or when handed about among the same mob in the form of a placard. . . . It is desirable, in short, that in things which do not primarily concern others, individuality should assert itself."[31] In 1969, the US Supreme Court established a clear standard for incitement, ruling in *Brandenburg v. Ohio* that the violence advocated must be intended, likely, and imminent. Both Israeli and Palestinian authorities have restricted speech far beyond this standard, abusing what has become a widely accepted definition of incitement.

Under a confederal arrangement, free speech would require uniform legal protections, equally applicable in both states. Against unchecked government interference in the name of security, charges of incitement would need to follow an accepted standard such as the *Brandenburg* test. Difficult as it may be for authoritarian governments to accept, freedom of speech in a post-conflict setting should not be rescheduled for some undetermined future. As a vital component of sustainable peace, it must be incorporated into initial negotiations or the peaceful future will remain a mirage.

Freedom of Religion

Freedom of religion is closely linked to freedom of speech and would likewise benefit from confederal oversight. In Israel, religious orthodoxy occupies a significant political stronghold in an otherwise secular state, and Islamism prevails in Palestinian-controlled areas. Partitionists often argue that once freed from tension over religious and ethnic identity, each of the two states would secure the full range of religious freedom recognized by international law. Both Israel and Palestine have ratified the major human rights covenants, and both address religious freedom in their Basic Law standards, but the states would not be freed from religious issues requiring special attention in a partitionist model.

According to Israeli Supreme Court rulings, the Basic Law: Human Dignity and Liberty protects freedom to practice religious beliefs, including freedom of conscience, faith, religion, and worship, regardless of an individual's religion. The Israeli court, following the Ottoman millet court, recognized Judaism, Christianity, Islam, the Druze, and the Baha'i. Free practice and government recognition of religions, however, does not constitute equal treatment under the law.[32] Though 50 percent of Muslim imams in Israel are supported by the government, the proportion of the state budget allotted to Jews for religious activities remains greater than that for other communities of faith. It does not, however, extend to all Jews.[33] In Israel, the Chief Rabbinate recognizes only the Orthodox as Jews, so Reform and Conservative Jewish activities are not funded. The disproportionate influence of Orthodox Judaism creates social inequalities and conflicts with both secular forces and minority religions. The Orthodox enjoy great privileges, including exemption from military duty and substantial financial support, and they have an inordinate influence in politics and civil society, including the enforcement of kosher rules, the regulation of business activities on Shabbat, and, perhaps most significantly, jurisdiction over family law. The Basic Law consigns domestic concerns to relevant religious authorities, and, in general, women's rights (particularly in divorce) are not equally protected under rabbinical law.

This division also exists between different practices of Judaism. For example, Prime Minister Netanyahu's promise to Reform Jews that there will be an unsegregated praying space for both women and men at the Western Wall was delayed in 2017 under pressure from Orthodox Jews, who have legal and political monopoly over religious questions in the country. Despite official recognition of religious freedom and minority rights, freedom of religion in Israel does not match that of other Western societies. Some of the shortcomings can be traced to the establishment of the state itself, when religious groups and the secular government clashed over what constitutes a "Jewish state" and over the scope of financial assistance to non-Jewish minorities.

A similar situation exists in the PA-controlled territories, where recognized religious groups have jurisdiction over matters of personal status and the religious courts' rulings are legally binding. The Palestinian Basic Law identifies Islam as the official religion and Shari'a as the main source of legislation, though all other monotheistic religions are respected. Mosques and Islamic institutions receive government support, as do some churches, but such favor does not extend to Jews (now funded by the

Israeli state) or non-monotheistic religions. Under Hamas's rule in Gaza, religion is even more restricted than in the West Bank. Hamas officials restrict women's rights in accordance with a stricter observance of Shari'a law. Though they generally ignore the Christian minority population, they have continued to incite violence toward Jews. Such behavior is reflected in the 1988 Hamas Charter: "The Day of Judgement will not come about until Moslems fight the Jews (killing the Jews), when the Jew will hide behind stones and trees. The stones and trees will say O Moslems, O Abdulla, there is a Jew behind me, come and kill him."[34] Despite a 2017 policy document that avoids such language, the 1988 charter remains in force, and it is unlikely the views it represents would simply wither away under a sovereign Palestinian state. Such a state will not be immune from destructive fundamentalist forces unless Islamist laws are abandoned in favor of a unified charter consistent with international human rights law.[35]

A unionist approach would seemingly avoid these dangers: everyone would be a citizen under a democratic secular constitution predicated upon a strong bill of rights, perhaps along the lines of the South African constitution. No one religion would receive preferential treatment, and a clear separation between state and religion would need to be enforced uniformly to secure the rights of all citizens, particularly women. Israelis would need to relinquish the favored status granted to the state's Jewish population. Such a secular and pluralistic model may seem ideal in many ways, but the experience of other ethnically or religiously divided societies does not inspire confidence that carefully conceived constitutional protections would effectively guard the rights of all individuals and groups.[36] In this case, that approach is even less viable, as it does not take into account the historical reality that the Jews claim to have built their national identity on the ashes of the Holocaust, while Palestinians center theirs on the Nakba or "disaster," their exile into refugee camps that accompanied Israel's independence.

A hybrid confederative model involving both constitutional protection and supranational supervision based on international human rights law has a better chance of leveling potential discrepancies of religious freedom within each state while retaining both the Jewish and democratic character of Israel and the Muslim and democratic character of a new Palestinian entity. A direct two-state solution would not bring about the complete separation of the two peoples, as some Jewish settlers would almost certainly remain within Palestinian territory,[37] and Palestinian Israelis would likely remain in their homes. The peaceful cooperation that would accompany a confederal solution would make coexistence all the more secure, and each minority would be entitled to established rights under international law.[38] The provisions of the Framework Convention for the Protection of National Minorities adopted by the Council of Europe in 1995 could serve as a further guide. Under the terms of this convention, members of national minorities must be guaranteed full and equal rights in the state, which is obligated to "promote the conditions necessary for persons belonging to national minorities to maintain and develop their culture, and to preserve the essential elements of their identity, namely their religion, language, traditions and cultural heritage."[39] A confederal solution would have greater capacity to secure free and equal access to disputed religious spaces in Jerusalem and beyond. Both states would be parties to all major international human rights conventions, and the confederal human rights institutions would help ensure that these constraints are respected.

Freedom from Want

Freedom from want would also be enforced most effectively by a confederal architecture. The protection of socioeconomic rights presents a major obstacle to both partitionist and unionist solutions, given the significant inequality between the two peoples. The absence of a viable local economic infrastructure originally forced Palestinians from the West Bank and Gaza to become low-wage transient workers in Israel. When most of these workers were later excluded from Israel, the resulting high unemployment and mobility restrictions contributed to increased violence.[40] Palestinians found themselves dependent on the charity of foreign state donors and humanitarian organizations.[41]

In a partitionist model, the protection of social and economic rights would be the responsibility of each of the two states, whose very different points of departure would mean a wide discrepancy in their respective abilities to manage this responsibility. Given the historical and geographical connection between the two states, any agreement on a two-state solution would have to include mechanisms for reducing this disparity. It is unclear, however, what role the two small Palestinian economies in Gaza and the West Bank would fill alongside the large and energetic Israeli economy.

Under a unionist vision, following the guidance of the International Covenant on Economic, Social and Cultural Rights, the state would "take steps, individually and through international assistance and cooperation, especially economic and technical, to the maximum of its available resources, with a view to achieving progressively the full realization of the rights recognized in the present Covenant by all appropriate means."[42] The wide disparity between the economic rights now enjoyed by Israelis (Jewish and Arab) and Palestinians in the West Bank and Gaza would surely hinder achievement of this goal. A united state would arguably provide greater opportunities for growth in the Palestinian sector, but it would likely produce tensions among poor Israelis, who would feel that their social mobility was delayed by the state's attention to even poorer and in some areas less educated Palestinians. This feeling that outsiders are "cutting ahead of them in line" could exacerbate the existing tensions between members of both national groups.

To avert violence caused by economic despair, a hybrid approach, strengthened by supranational arrangements, would need to narrow the socioeconomic gaps between the two peoples. It could do this by focusing on two economic trajectories: one targeting the developmental challenges confronting Palestinians as a group, and the other providing opportunities for the most disadvantaged within each side.[43] The need to transcend the grievances of historically disadvantaged nations and groups has long pointed toward collective rights approaches to economic development. The challenge of combining an integrating free market with protection of the initially disadvantaged is as old as the "infant industries" arguments of Alexander Hamilton and Friedrich List, who in the eighteenth century sought ways for the United States and Germany, respectively, to close the industrialization gap with the British. The same strategy is represented today by the provisions for preferential treatment for developing countries built into the global free trade regime and in American affirmative-action policies.[44]

More important, a dual-track economic approach based on economic interdependence and integration, and supervised by a confederal institution, would benefit from the development policies for the Middle East discussed in chapter 6: increased freedom of movement, improved mass transportation, rising reliance on solar energy, and a joint strategy for ensuring universal access to clean water. Palestine Railways was the largest employer of urban workers in Palestine until World War II, with an Arab and Jewish workforce that peaked at 7,800 in 1943.[45] It soon became a target for militant groups, however, in the developing conflict over Palestine: the tracks were attacked and blown up during the Arab Revolt of 1936–1939, and the Jerusalem station was bombed in 1946 by the right-wing Zionist group, the Irgun Stern Leumi. After 1948, the Jerusalem station resumed operation under Israeli rule but with regular trains running only to Tel Aviv (the Jaffa station was abandoned).

Israelis have moved forward in recent years to develop a modern rail infrastructure within their 1967 borders and have made significant progress with respect to water reclamation and desalination, but those technologies have not brought similar benefits to the Palestinian territories. The Israeli Ministry of Transportation has plans for a railway that would link the Israeli-Palestinian town of Jenin to the Jezreel Valley Railway, running from Haifa to Beit She'an. It would be an important first step toward improving the Palestinian economy. The shortage of clean water remains a critical problem in the West Bank and Gaza, a problem for which Palestinians blame Israel.[46] With a shared strategy for transportation, energy, and water infrastructure under a confederal government, one could envision a growing rail network, bolstered by the effective use of solar power, and a revitalized agriculture sector—all fueling economic growth through the greater circulation of goods and improved labor mobility for both Israelis and Palestinians. As Palestinians enjoy more economic power, their stake in shared prosperity could make walls and checkpoints obsolete.

Freedom from Fear

The main object of political Zionism was for Jews to gain control over their own destiny and security. Despite claims to the contrary, the Jews never enjoyed full equality in Muslim states,[47] and the insecurity of religious minorities under Islamist governments hardly encourages confidence that they would enjoy adequate protection today. Rhetoric from Palestinian and Arab media, along with documents like the Hamas Charter, does not allay Jewish fears.[48] Palestinians in the West Bank and in Gaza obviously have very different security concerns. Having been subject to oppression, domination, and occupation, they neither will, nor should, agree to continued dominance by a militaristic state. Partitionists argue that a two-state solution would best provide individual and collective security to both peoples. Israeli Jews would not become a vulnerable minority in a hostile environment; Palestinians would be freed from occupation and theoretically could protect their own security. In reality, however, a simple separation into two states would leave the Palestinians utterly unable to balance Israel's overwhelming military advantage, and Israel could remain subject to bombardment by militants, prompting disastrous military responses like Operation Protective Edge in Gaza.

Unionists argue that a political and constitutional regime that guarantees protection of individual rights would ensure the security of Jews and Arabs alike. In theory, they may be right. Expecting such a regime to provide adequate security were the Jews to become a minority would require a leap of faith on the part of Israeli Jews. At present, very few Israeli Jews would willingly take that leap, just as very few Palestinians would willingly serve with Israeli Defense Forces' soldiers after years of oppression at their hands. This presents a major stumbling block for unionists. Unless they can come up with credible mechanisms for ensuring group and individual security, they have little chance of persuading Israeli Jews and Palestinians to discuss, let alone adopt, a unionist model.

A confederal vision would side with partitionists in supporting group rights to national security, but it would place security within the broader context of human rights for all. All agreements regarding the Israeli-Palestinian conflict have put the onus on the Palestinians to increase Israeli security before Palestinian political and economic aspirations can be realized. According to the Oslo agreement, for instance, "The Council will establish a strong police force, while Israel will continue to carry the responsibility for defending against external threats."[49] The same point was forcefully reiterated in the Wye River Memorandum, which demanded that the Palestinians combat terrorism in cooperation, where needed, with the Israelis.[50] In the Road Map, phase 1 aimed at "ending [Palestinian] terror and violence."[51] Building a democratic Palestinian state was not to begin until phase 2, and only in phase 3 would steps be taken to address cooperative economic development, the status of Jerusalem, the fate of the settlements, and the refugee question.[52]

Making the achievement of Israeli security a first and separate step, with Palestinian political and economic rights relegated to some distant point in the future, may have contributed to the vicious cycle of growing extremism and ever-harsher countermeasures that seemed to confirm both sides' darkest interpretations of the other's objectives. While security understandably comes first in the minds of Israeli Jews, security arrangements can be sustainable only if both sides' political, economic, cultural, and security rights are also addressed. The protection of fundamental rights is an essential component of security, not a prize to be awarded after security has been ensured.

Within the supranational framework envisioned above, what mix of independence and integration would be desirable? In domestic security, it makes sense for police forces to reflect the demographic realities of their jurisdictions. Israel has long recognized the right and need for Palestinians on the West Bank to enforce public order and safety within their own neighborhoods and cities. A confederated state, however, should also establish joint police units responsible for intercommunal policing. A joint unit trained, and possibly commanded, by EU law enforcement personnel could serve as a beginning. Other civilian services, in which individuals could enlist in lieu of military service, and in which both sides have equal participation, may follow suit. With EU support and international training, some integrated emergency response teams are already in place.[53] As the efforts of both Israeli and Palestinian paramedics are hindered by continuing belligerence, the cooperation afforded by a formal joint organization of services would be immediately beneficial to both sides.[54]

The question of external security will remain a pressing issue for Israelis. Since a joint military force is unrealistic, at least at present, the confederation's external security would almost certainly be Israel's responsibility, with the rights of both peoples protected. Whether this would change in the future would depend on the success of the model in changing the relationship between Israelis and Palestinians, as well as on developments in the region and their security implications. A Palestinian democracy that protects human rights could be seen as threatening to authoritarian or theocratic states in the region; an Israeli-Palestine confederation, ready to defend those principles, could inspire and lend practical support to a more sustainable Spring of Nations.

If sustainable peace was *à l'ordre du jour*, one should draw once again from the lessons of post–World War II reconstruction efforts. Then, Western leaders understood that only new economic orders based on both independent and integrated economies could provide enduring security in Europe. A similar strategy is required in the Middle East, and the Fertile Crescent could be an epicenter for the enduring peace that has long eluded the region. That is not to suggest that change will come easily. Just as Europeans were immersed in hypernationalist fervor fanned by two world wars, most ordinary people of Jordan, Egypt, and the Palestinian territories are deeply hostile toward Israel. At the same time, Egyptians, Israelis, and Jordanians have never been as close, in terms of shared security concerns, as they have been since the Arab Spring. All three governments face threats from violent Sunni Islamists, a factor that has undercut support for Hamas and promoted counterterrorism cooperation among the three states. There is also a de facto coalition between Israel and the Sunni Arab states in confronting Iran. Just as Europeans were able to move forward through a Common Market that buried decades of nationalist animosities, one would hope a similar economic strategy for the Middle East would assuage fears on each side, promoting freedom from want for all, in the Jewish, Christian, Sunni, and Shi'a worlds. This may be a necessary condition for developing mutual understanding and confidence building, which must underlie advances in security and all other human rights. With greater economic opportunities in Palestine, the question of Palestinian refugees would be easier to address.

Refugees and the Right of Return

Most Israeli Jews, even those who have long favored the establishment of a Palestinian state around Israel's pre-1967 borders, believe the return of Palestinian refugees to Israeli territory would be incompatible with Israeli Jews' right to self-determination. In a partitionist model, refugees would have the right to return to the Palestinian state. Article 28 of the Palestinian Basic Law states that no Palestinian shall be prevented from returning to the homeland. In a partitionist model, one could envisage a "law of return" granting Palestinians the legal right to enter Palestine, reside there, and acquire citizenship. Many Palestinians outside of Israel proper who claim an individual right to return to the homes of their parents, grandparents, or great-grandparents might find this agreement unacceptable. In theory, their claim of a right of return would pose no problem in a unionist model, since both Palestinians and Israelis would have access to the whole territory. But in reality, Jewish homes previously inhabited by Palestinians would surely be contested. Further, the prospect of mass return to such a state would further weaken the negligible support for such a model among Israeli Jews as it would guarantee that they would quickly become a shrinking minority in that state.

In a confederative approach, the conflicting narratives of rights could be connected to the issue of settlements. Israeli resistance to the return of Palestinian refugees to Israel itself, which rests on the Jews' right to self-determination in their own state, cannot go hand in hand with the demand that all settlements remain in the West Bank. Tying these issues together under a confederative model may help to forge imaginative solutions that could involve evacuation of some settlements and acceptance of some refugees in Israel. In other words, if Palestinians must accept limits to the right of return, Israel must make reciprocal concessions, such as withdrawing from settlements and committing to Palestinian economic development and economic integration throughout the confederacy.

A one-state solution is widely rejected on both sides, yet the two-state solution has proven to be a mirage, though vivid enough to propel endless futile efforts. Notwithstanding some of the achievements of the Oslo process, decades of negotiations over borders, refugees, settlements, and the status of Jerusalem have not drawn the parties nearer to a political resolution. A new approach would focus on both transitional and final aims, promoting a settlement that will protect the rights of all persons: Jews and Arabs, Israelis and Palestinians. It requires all participants to recognize the interdependence of security, sustainable economic development, and political freedom for these two peoples.[55]

The pure two-state and one-state models are both unrealistic. No person sensitive to human rights and long-term stability, however, could support the indefinite continuation of the present situation, in which Palestinians living under occupation are denied fundamental rights. The real question, then, is what alternative would offer adequate protection to the group and individual rights of Jews and Arabs who live side by side. Admittedly, when asked how such a model would work in the present political and social context, any preliminary answer is certain to expose new difficulties. Unlike both the two- and one-state solutions, a confederative model based on the centrality of human rights—the four freedoms (with a fifth freedom, as discussed in chapter 7, for Israeli and Palestinian women)—provides an alternative that could ensure lasting peace. It offers an agenda for continuing discussion in which security, political, economic, cultural, and civil rights can be addressed synergistically. To the extent that Israeli Jews and Palestinians are reluctant to initiate such a comprehensive dialogue, outside parties could and should play a positive role.

Overall, the framework presented here is not a blueprint for a comprehensive settlement of the conflict. It is not meant to address fully all of the specific areas of contention that have blocked negotiations in the past, especially the status of Jerusalem, the settlements, and return of the refugees. This architecture assumes the need to advance protection of group and individual rights for all—standards that not only represent moral criteria but also act as constraints on what is practical and durable in the peace process. Universal protection of human rights, as a common starting point and a common goal, can provide hopeful direction toward overcoming the present impasse.

Can the Levant Express be rerouted to break this stalemate? It was not long ago, still in the early twentieth century, that a growing railway system connected most of the Middle East. That railway was gradually destroyed by the conflicts that roiled the region. Trains and tracks were blown up during World War I by T. E. Lawrence, then again during the Arab revolt of 1936–1939, and yet again in 1946 by violent Zionists. Some tracks were never rebuilt, and people who once traveled freely have been walled off from each other by fear and distrust. Lack of imagination about paths toward peace created time bombs of resentment and hostility that have exploded again and again. The region begs for a new cartography of peace. The Levant Express can be revived on the tracks of the old Hejaz Railway and beyond, allowing Israelis to connect with the Arab world while giving Palestinians mobility beyond walls and checkpoints. The future should be placed in the hands of those prepared to pursue the complexities of postwar planning: those seeking to bridge differences, exchange ideas freely, improve religious tolerance, and promote economic development under regionwide security arrangements. Israelis and Arabs "cannot collaborate with despair," claimed the Israeli novelist David Grossman, echoing the late Palestinian poet Mahmoud Darwish, who maintained that "hope is neither something tangible nor an idea. It's a talent."[56]

Conclusion

HUMAN RIGHTS IN AN AGE OF COUNTER-ENLIGHTENMENT

"WHEN AND IF FASCISM COMES to America it will not be labeled 'made in Germany'; it will not be marked with a swastika; it will not be called fascism; it will be called, of course, 'Americanism.'" Halford E. Luccock spoke these words at Yale in 1938.[1] Today, the specter of fascism is again haunting Europe, the US, and the Middle East. Resisted by democratic institutions, it may not yet have sunk deep roots in Western soil, but fascism shows alarming vitality as populism, in its right-wing variant, progresses on both sides of the Atlantic and in the Middle East. Today, the counter-Enlightenment is advancing, and human rights are in retreat.

The Universal Declaration of Human Rights was inaugurated on December 10, 1948, at the General Assembly of the United Nations. Eleanor Roosevelt suggested that it could become a new Magna Carta for all people in a world that had just buried fascism. The rights invoked in the Declaration would provide the framework for lasting peace in postwar Europe. In 2018, however, the seventieth anniversary of the UDHR was celebrated in a very different climate, as resurgent populism and fascism threatened the very notion of universal rights. Whereas 1948 was lifting its face toward the future with renewed hope and a sense of urgency to rebuild societies from the ashes of war, 2018 turns an amnesic gaze toward the darkening clouds of the 1930s.

In this book, I have set out to address possible paths toward progress in the Middle East maelstrom of the Arab Winter. I believe the problems of the Middle East and North Africa region are best understood through the lens of human rights, and that the same human rights strategies that rebuilt Europe after World War II can be reclaimed to counter the waves of counter-Enlightenment ideology and economic despair that have swept over the Levant. These are not unrealistic and empty ideals, as ill-informed critics of human rights sometimes suggest. Over the past two and a half centuries, the struggle for human rights, despite setbacks, has reshaped world politics while fulfilling practical objectives along pathways validated by historical experience. Those achievements provide an enduring demonstration that human rights principles can, amidst turmoil, guide progress toward a Middle East freed from censorship, religious conflict, poverty, insecurity, and sexual discrimination.

I conclude this book with several observations. Isolationist or unilateralist impulses in the West, together with an apparent lack of progress toward peace, have fed a sense of fatigue with regard to the Middle East and a skepticism toward struggles for human rights more generally. This fatigue is dangerous because it abdicates responsibility in the face of increasing nationalism and populism. To counter populist and fascist trends both in the Middle East and the West, the promotion of comprehensive human rights strategies, as understood by realists like FDR, is crucial now and will remain so for decades to come. With European doors now closed to further mass migration, this approach can rebuild the capacity for MENA countries to meet the material needs of their populations while advancing their inalienable rights.

MIDDLE EAST FATIGUE

The global community's prolonged failure to resolve the Middle East crisis has fueled nationalist resentment and liberal fatigue. If this persists, with continuing missed opportunities to bring real change to hellish conditions in the Levant, populist and fascist trends will gain traction, and the West, too, will suffer the consequences of its neglect. ISIS may not have retained its hold on territories, but without new efforts to bring political and economic stability, the same radicalism under different names will thrive again in societies devastated by war, and it will inevitably resume its spread to Western shores. Despite their historically close relationship to the Middle East, the US and the European Union have seen popular attention move away from the region in favor of domestic politics and trade wars. The Levant is on the back burner, and many who have been invested in the region seem ready to surrender to a dangerous hopelessness.

"What would you do if you were a Palestinian?" One of my American students asked that question of Israel's deputy minister of intelligence, Chagai Tzuriel, while participating in an educational tour I led in Israel and the West Bank in June 2018. Tzuriel let out a long, exasperated sigh—directed not at the student but at the problem. He is not an ideologue but simply acknowledged that the Palestinians' current approach was going nowhere. The current demonstrations along the border fence in Gaza, he said, are acts of violence in the garb of peace. "Israelis are used to these kinds of eruptions," he said. "We know how to stop them." As for what Gazans should do instead, another sigh. For Tzuriel, as for many other Israelis, there was little hope for Palestinians. The conflict in Gaza may have dissipated for now, but for how long?

Later during the same trip, another student asked Moshe Raz, a Knesset member from Meretz, the social-democratic and green political party in Israel, "What are the strategies through which the secular Left might regain seats in the Knesset?" Raz's voice turned flat, recognizing that his party had been seen for too long as representing only the affluent liberals of Tel Aviv. How could they change that perception? He admitted that his response was not sufficient but offered no answers and seemed to concede to the forces of nationalism he deplored. The same week, a notable Israeli scholar greeted me at a restaurant in Jerusalem: "Welcome to this quiet part of the world! As you can see, *plus ça change, plus c'est la même chose.*" He was a renowned political scientist, an adamant opponent of Israeli settlements in the West Bank, and the author of an inspiring book on Theodor Herzl, the nineteenth-century Zionist leader whose movement encouraged Jews to escape anti-Semitism by establishing a new state in their ancient home. My colleague did not exude much optimism, deploring instead the crisis of the country's democracy and admitting that he could see no way out for either Palestinians or Israelis.

A week later, at a cafe in Ramallah, I asked a Palestinian politician, "What would you do if there was an election tomorrow?" She conveyed an increasingly familiar sense of tiredness. "It would be unclear if Hamas or

Fatah would win. . . . The people are fed up with the political situation. There are no charismatic Palestinian leaders on the horizon—no one who will show us a way forward anyway, and there is no real reconciliation between Hamas and Fatah. The current Palestinian establishment is not inspiring the youth." She shrugged and smiled: "We might need a charismatic populist . . ." After a brief pause, laughing at her own thought, she added, "Perhaps we need someone like Trump!" The Palestinians understand that no Arab Messiah is about to come. Many realize that the political situation for some of their neighbors, like Syria, Yemen, or Iran, is even worse than their own, but they feel abandoned by the world. The Arab countries of the Gulf focus on their own problems; an American president backs the Israeli Right; and the Europeans continue to play only a marginal role.

Later, at a bistro on the Left Bank in Paris, a senior foreign correspondent from a leading French newspaper told me, "I am tired of the Middle East." For many years, he had covered Arab dictatorships, the Arab Spring, and then the Arab Winter. His latest work had focused on the Syrian refugee crisis. But now he wanted to move on to "more pressing issues," like the upcoming NATO summit. His briefcase contained a thick red accordion folder filled with articles questioning NATO's survival. "Trump will still be president after the 2020 election," he said resignedly. He dug through his bag for another article, which conveyed Trump's high approval rate among Republican voters. "I feel as if I have lost my American father," he said, referring to the United States. "What is left?" He stared into his coffee as if looking for an answer. "Emmanuel Macron is leading alone. We voted for him, but Angela Merkel is now unable to help him because of her own weak government. Where is Europe going? Look at the rise of authoritarianism and nationalism in Poland and Hungary. This is a calamity!" He seemed to have forgotten that Western policy failures in the Middle East, spawning new waves of terrorism and innocent refugees, had helped erode European democracies and bolster the populist movements he now feared.

POPULISM, NATIONALISM, AND THE MIDDLE EAST CRISIS

My conversation with the French journalist was interrupted by the sudden outburst of loud singing and chanting in the evening streets: "On est à la finale! On est à la finale!" For a moment, France's cultural divisions had vanished as Gallic French, blacks, and immigrants—a nation of soccer fans—joined in cheering their team, Les Bleus, in the final match of the World Cup. Sports-induced solidarity is fleeting and generally benign; the darker variants of nationalism require constant, more pernicious reminders of "us" versus "them." Which form of national pride would prevail? Would it be that of Marianne, the symbol of the French Revolution, celebrated for her universal ideas? Or Joan of Arc, the heroic young woman who defeated France's enemies during the Hundred Years' War and was later reclaimed by nineteenth-century French nationalists? A virulent nationalism is on the rise in the West: the Party of Freedom in the Netherlands, Alternative for Germany, Golden Dawn in Greece, the National Front in France, Jobbik in Hungary, the Sweden Democrats, the Freedom Party in Austria, the People's Party in Slovakia, the Lega in Italy, the Tea Party and Alt-Right in the United States. These movements are all antiestablishment, anti-immigrant, anti-European, anti-globalist, antiliberal, and anti–human rights.

In the US, nationalism and the counter-Enlightenment are back with a vengeance. It should be noted that democracy was already in crisis before Donald Trump came to power. Despite a significant economic recovery under the Obama administration, many still felt marginalized and excluded from the American social contract. Candidate Trump fed on the widespread sense, prevalent among working-class whites, that their lot had changed for the worse and that minorities and immigrants were cutting ahead of them in line for the benefits of economic recovery. American civil society is increasingly fragmented, with no clear champion offering a unifying and inclusive vision of the increasingly elusive American dream. Neither major party has brought forward viable economic and social solutions for unifying these disparate groups. Nationalist and religious fervor fills the political void, and the Trump administration shows an alarming affiliation with the nationalists and racists. Trump is following the formula of right-wing populists during the interwar period, mixing calls for national unity with the marginalization of excluded groups. His slogan, "Make America Great Again," unifies much of the white Christian working class, while selected minorities are depicted as threatening that narrowed conception of American solidarity.

Whenever the spirit of internationalism and human rights fails to deliver on its promise, people tend to revert to the certain, the familiar, the community, and the nation. The Middle East has proven no exception.

The combination of weak state structures and divided civil societies created fertile ground for the appearance of new strongmen who claim that only they can transcend the conflicts tearing society apart. Western and Middle Eastern populism and illiberalism mimic each other, creating an ironic alliance among authoritarian leaders like Trump, Putin, Erdogan, al-Sisi, and Netanyahu, who foment popular fear and accrue power by promising security to "the people."

To connect fragmented segments of society, popular appeals to cultural pride, the myth of the "nation," or religious identity are asserted over more personal interests, inspiring a broad yet thin sense of national unity. Right-wing and religious movements step in to galvanize the poor and the disenfranchised, resurrect traditional communities, and restructure politics according to nationalist or divine interpretations. All of these anti-Enlightenment movements call to unite their nation but convey a more sinister message: that the persecution or exclusion of certain minorities is essential to cleanse the "true people" from alleged spoilers. While the elixir of nationalism unifies people, xenophobia rises against foreigners, particularly Muslims, who are depicted as spoilers stealing the jobs of Westerners, as carriers of infectious disease, as exploiters of the welfare state, or as terrorists. But waves of refugees seeking safe haven will continue as long as the perilous transit brings less fear than staying home. Inevitably, frustration will drive some toward despair, from despair into anger, and from anger into terror.

Terror and forced migration are symptoms of problems that must be addressed at their source. To be enduringly successful, counterterrorism must include serious efforts to grapple with the political, social, and economic factors that nurture it, lest the Middle East continue to destabilize the world. Confronting self-serving foreign policies in the Middle East that help foster intractable conflicts, learning from the successful endeavors of history, and promoting a full spectrum of human rights remain robust antidotes against populism and fascism.

UNIVERSAL HUMAN RIGHTS AGAINST POPULISM

Western liberals felt betrayed after the election of Trump, just as they did after Brexit and every other movement seeking to fragment the European Union. But neither liberals nor progressives in the West have offered an alternative to populism and nationalism. Many view this period as a farce, hoping it will simply go away, perhaps through another election. From Putin to al-Sisi, Trump seems eager to forge a new axis among illiberal rulers. Meanwhile, America's long-standing allies are wondering how they will absorb the next blow, and Trump's own party cringes as he defies the liberal alliance in front of a worldwide audience.

Followers of post-Marxist theorists, such as Chantal Mouffe and Ernesto Laclau, have reaffirmed that the vox populi in civic engagement is essential to the revitalization of democracy—a perspective that has been embraced by left-wing populist parties like Podemos in Spain and Syriza in Greece. On the positive side, they support racial equality and bring to the table concerns shared by a broad segment of the population, for example, the lack of well-paying jobs and affordable health care. Yet if left-wing populism seems promising as a first act, it is dangerous as a second. Initially, it can mobilize the grass roots for protest and even social upheavals, but by favoring an antiestablishment and anti-isolationist message, it quickly dissipates its potential political impact at home and abroad. Isolationism dangerously merges left-wing populism with its right-wing cousin. In a world of "our workers" or "our interests" versus "theirs," the line between Right and Left blurs under the flag of the nation.

No walls or isolationist policies can prevent the global impact of conflict in a region that connects three continents and produces vast quantities of oil. If wealthy countries fear the inflow of refugees, building fences or turning their back on the problem will only make it worse. They will be better off helping to resolve the crisis on Middle Eastern soil, especially since they helped to create it. Western leaders have too often brandished the torch of democracy with one hand while placating dictators with the other, choosing their interest in oil or geopolitics over the lives of ordinary Middle Easterners.

I argue for a universal human rights approach that opposes both the racism and xenophobia of right-wing populism and the anti-internationalist myopia of left-wing populism. It is a perspective that cannot be sustained without a reorganized liberal order. Should that order be revisited, it would need to subscribe to principles that have never been expressed more powerfully and simply than in Roosevelt's Four Freedoms and that are encapsulated in the preamble to the Universal Declaration of Human Rights. International law recognizes that human rights work best if understood as inalienable and indivisible, irrespective of difference in race, sex, or cultural background. These core values have for centuries advanced human cooperation and prosperity, shamed abusive governments, and at best, averted war and promoted peace—a history that realist critics often seem to forget. Overall, human rights are fundamentally internationalist and antithetical to isolationism—whether it stems from a realist or a populist worldview. Ignoring large-scale human rights violations in as critical a region as the Middle East will trigger a time bomb that will again impact the West. If the crisis of the Middle East had a significant impact on the rise of populism in the West, one could conversely argue that the advance of human rights in the Levant should advance the improvement of democracy in the West and the restoration of a liberal order. These five ideals are not dated; they can regain momentum in this time of amnesia.

Today, the right to free expression is under attack even in the US, as ideas are shouted down by both the Right and the Left and deliberation, so vital to democracy, is challenged relentlessly by relativism, fake news, and the routine labelling of truthful reporting as lies. Informed understanding has been reduced to superficial arguments shaped by personal preferences. Without the respectful and rational exercise of free speech, political discourse will not be distinguishable from propaganda that feeds the populist leaders' cult of personality. Free expression is a right that Westerners take for granted, forgetting how countless young people in the Middle East confronted repressive power, rapping their rage and flaunting their freedom of expression through social media. The subsequent repression of speech in the Middle East should remind Westerners how quickly fundamental rights can be curtailed, closing the path to political representation.

Freedom of worship is also under attack in the bastions of liberal democracy. In the US and Europe, it is not uncommon to hear people complaining about the corrupting religious influence of Muslim refugees, elitist multiculturalism, and secular humanists. For many, the preservation of cultural identity (and imagined anti-Christian prejudice) is at least partially rooted in the fear of losing economic privilege. The refugee influx from the Middle East made Western democracies even more intolerant of religious minorities. In the Middle East, freedom of (or from) worship was briefly celebrated with a burst of interfaith and secular activities during the Arab uprisings, particularly when Copts, Muslims, and nonreligious Egyptians joined hands to overthrow the Mubarak government. After the Arab Spring, some Arab authoritarians justified their own religious intolerance by pointing to Western Islamophobia, evidenced by American attempts to restrict Muslim immigration. Religious intolerance knows no border; it hinders both social harmony and socioeconomic interdependence within and across borders.

Freedom of speech and religion cannot thrive without freedom from want. With the Reagan administration's attack on the legacy of Roosevelt's New Deal and then with the fall of the Soviet Union, the human rights tradition gave way to a neoliberal expression of internationalism, in which the benefits of free trade were thought to outweigh the costs of neglecting workers' rights. Many on the Left have since come to regard human rights as nothing more than hyper-neoliberalism, and human rights rhetoric simply a rationalization of Western imperialism. Human rights, however, cannot be reduced to unfettered globalization or the harmonious confluence of different cultural or religious identities. Earlier, I proposed an expanding program of economic integration in the Middle East that would include transportation networks, new financial structures, and a commitment to renewable energy across vast expanses of sun, sand, and water. The same programs, if applied to the West, would greatly aid its economic malaise. Large-scale infrastructure investment, better systems of financial governance, and conversion to renewable energy could invigorate economies and promote economic welfare. Protectionist trade wars do not alleviate, but instead worsen, the lot of the disenfranchised. The global economy is significantly more interdependent than it was after World War II. New large-scale investment that promotes employment and renewable energy in the Middle East could make equal sense for the West. Renewable energy is gathering momentum; it will not only provide new jobs and improve trade, but will improve our ecosystem for generations to come.

Only in a climate free from fear can the other rights materialize. The world must not forget the images of Syrian refugees clutching scared toddlers against life vests while crossing pitiless waters, forced by the relentless catastrophe of war to take unimaginable risks just to survive. The refugee crisis has rocked the liberal order in the West and heightened fear across Europe and the US. To restore safety to Middle Eastern populations and to create a more peaceful order, new security architectures will be needed, modeled on the creation of NATO. The Trump administration's threatened divestment from NATO and the UN in the name of nationalism has created worldwide insecurity. Our need is not to dismantle such institutions but to reform and strengthen them, drawing greater involvement from the developing world and refocusing their mission to connect economic growth with human security.

Finally, as long as a patriarchal social and religious system keeps women silent in the public sphere, sexually dissatisfied, disempowered in the family, impoverished despite their education, and living in fear despite their growing resilience, pressure will build toward a new women's rights contagion—an overdue revolution that will almost certainly reorder families and destabilize autocratic regimes. This simmering feminist consciousness could explode at any moment in the Middle East, where Arab women may be the actors most likely to reroute the Levant Express toward democratic frontiers. With the viral influence of the #MeToo movement and the reawakening of feminism after the election of Donald Trump, sisterhood seems to be global once again. Even for those who did not favor Hillary Clinton's candidacy, the election of Trump—despite his misogynist history—came as a shock. Before that election, women's rights were in stagnation, if not retreat, but it has brought renewed energy to rally against sexual harassment and reduce the gender wage gap across global capitals and even in rural Iran.

A new liberal order will require popular agency from within, and the renewed women's movement has the critical capacity to galvanize a broad progressive human rights program nationally and internationally. Politically, therefore, it makes sense to build on a movement that has brought the women's rights question to renewed prominence across class, race, and culture. Reinvigorating democracy and human rights requires, as Eleanor Roosevelt reminds us, that we start at home. At the same time, if it begins at home, that struggle has to occur everywhere. That is, as long as women are the conduit of a comprehensive human rights agenda, they may well carry the torch of democratization and become the antidote to populism, the new engineers of the Levant Express.

This book began with the idea of a metaphorical train carrying the flame of freedom throughout the Middle East. Counter-Enlightenment forces derailed it, but there is reason to believe it can be rerouted toward new possibilities for human rights. If that metaphor has sparked the imagination, it may provide the impetus for a new cartography: a Middle East connected by railways, roads, and trade routes, uniting financial, commercial and governmental interests. A project like this would serve the interests of every country in the region. A short additional link between the expanding internal rail networks of the UAE and Saudi Arabia would effectively connect the UAE directly to the Mediterranean, providing significant incentive for completion of the regional Gulf Railway, which is now on hold. This railway would link the Jordanian kingdom to its neighbors and help pull that country out of economic distress. The Israeli government supports this proposal because it will spur economic development and integration with the Arab world. A short extension into the West Bank, already planned, will provide an outlet for Palestinians. It is not difficult to imagine branches to Baghdad, Damascus, Aqaba, Cairo, Mecca, Dubai, and perhaps even Tehran. Such a project would not require the resolution of long-standing conflicts, but it should build confidence among all the nations in the region. This project could be a reality if the political will could be aligned for the greater good of humanity.

The Palestinian poet Mahmoud Darwish, nostalgic of past trains, may well be a prophet of the future:

> The train moved like a peaceful snake from Syria to Egypt
> Its whistling hid the hoarse bleating of goats from the wolves'
> voracity
> As if it was a mythical time to tame the wolves to befriend us.
> Its smoke billowed over the fire in the villages
> which were blossoming like trees.
>
> ....
>
> The train was a wild ship docking . . . and carrying us
> to the realistic cities of imagination
> whenever we needed some innocent play with destinies.
> The windows of the train have the status of the magical in
> the mundane:
> everything runs. Trees, thoughts, waves and towers run
> behind us.
> The scent of lemons, the air and all things run.
> So does the yearning for an ambiguous distant. The heart runs.[2]

The Levant Express still runs fiercely as an undying myth in the hearts of those left behind in desolate railway stations. Dreams of a better future prevail well beyond uprisings or crackdowns. They are transmitted from one historical epoch to another, petrified as sediments of collective memory. The rubble of human tragedy inspires new myths, visions pave new paths, and tracks lay out practical possibilities. With necessity as the combustion engine of invention, the locomotive, whistling and taming the wolves of war, bursts into the future, amidst lemon scent and olive trees, securing fundamental freedoms across sun, water, and sand.

NOTES

PART I. DEPARTURE

1. Marx and Engels, *18th Brumaire of Louis Bonaparte*, 1.

1. RAILROADS AND REVOLUTIONS

1. Dobbin, *Forging Industrial Policy* (1994).
2. Hugo, *Les Misérables (1887)*, part V, book I, chapter 1.
3. Marx, "Defeat of June, 1848," in *Class Struggles in France* (1964).
4. Engels, "June Revolution" (1848).
5. See for an interesting discussion Bronner, *Socialism Unbound* (1990), 12ff.
6. Hobsbawm, *Age of Revolution* (1962), 55.
7. Ishay, *History of Human Rights* (2008), 332, note 38.
8. Ibid., 117–155.
9. Trevelyan, *British History in the Nineteenth Century* (1922), 292.
10. Barak, *On Time* (2013), 5.
11. Gandhi, *Hind Swaraj* (1998), 1.
12. Ibid., 6.
13. Ishay, *History of Human Rights* (2008), 315–355.
14. All Empires, "Britain's Post-War Decline" (2015).
15. Ibid.
16. This should not suggest that were no examples whatsoever of social protest; for example, see Isaacman, "Peasants and Rural Social Protest" (1990), 1–120.
17. Minh, *Declaration of Independence, Vietnam* (1945).
18. *New York Times*, "Amin Praises Hitler for Killing of Jews" (1972).
19. Butcher, *Blood River* (2008), 249.
20. Robinson, "Sino-Soviet Border Dispute" (1972), 1175–1202.
21. Svec, "Prague Spring" (2006), 981.

22. Pogash, "At Berkeley, Free (though Subdued) Speech" (2014).
23. Havel, *Power of the Powerless* (1979), 1.
24. Navrátil, ed., *Prague Spring 1968* (2006), 177–181.
25. Ibid., 477.
26. Walton, "Debt, Protest, and the State in Latin America" (1989), 306.
27. For an interesting discussion on this topic, see O'Donnell, *Modernization and Bureaucratic-Authoritarianism* (1979).
28. BBC News, "Chile Recognises 9,800 More Victims of Pinochet's Rule" (2011).
29. North American Congress on Latin America, "Former Dictator Arrested for Stealing Children" (2007).
30. Ruddle and Hamour, "Statistical Abstract of Latin America" (1970), 54–55.
31. Kenez, *Birth of the Propaganda State* (1985), 59, 342.
32. Wasik, "Inside the Forgotten Ghost Stations of a Once-Divided Berlin" (2017).
33. Arrighi et al., "1989, the Continuation of 1968" (1992), 221–242.
34. Ibid., 230–231.
35. Tismaneanu, "Revolutions of 1989" (2009), 281.
36. Ibid., 107–111.
37. Bush, "Remarks at the 20th Anniversary of the NED" (2003).
38. Bronson, "Where Credit Is Due" (2005), 108.
39. Thomas Jefferson to James Madison, Paris (January 30, 1787). *Founders Online*. National Archives. Accessed July 14, 2017. https://founders.archives.gov/documents/Jefferson/01–11–02–0095.

2. THE LEVANT EXPRESS AND THE ARAB SPRING OF NATIONS

1. Perkins, *History of Modern Tunisia* (2014), 66.
2. "French in Tunis" (2015).
3. Khaleej Times, "Shops Sacked, Train Station Burned in Tunisia" (2015).
4. Ishay, "Spring of Arab Nations?" (2013), 373–383.
5. Reuters, "Four Algerians Set Selves on Fire, Echoing Tunisia" (2011).
6. Achcar, *People Want* (2013), 10–23.
7. Achy et al., "Arab Youth Unemployment" (2011).
8. Ahmed et al., "Youth Unemployment in the MENA Region" (2012).
9. Assaad and Roudi-Fahimi, *Youth in the Middle East and North Africa* (2011), 6–7; Beehner, "Effects of 'Youth Bulge' on Civil Conflicts" (2007).
10. Paciello, "Tunisia: Changes and Challenges of Political Transition" (2011), 2.
11. Ibid.
12. Ahmed Rock, "Down with Military Rule" (2011), translated by Fouad Alkhouri.
13. World Bank, "Unemployment, Youth Total" (2017).
14. Thabit, "Al-Soo-al" ("The Question") (2011). The translated lyrics are provided by kind permission of Freemuse, an independent international organization advocating for and defending freedom of artistic expression, freemuse.org.
15. Huebler and Weixin, *Adult and Youth Literacy* (2013), 31.
16. World Bank, "Unemployment, Youth Total" (2017).
17. Rais, "Syria under Bashar Al Assad" (2004), 144–168.

18. Scheer, "Bashar al-Assad and the 'Damascus Spring'" (2010).
19. Freemuse, "Protest Singer Ibrahim Kashoush Had His Throat Cut" (2011); Yassin-Kassab, "Sound and the Fury" (2015).
20. Sotloff, "Bahrain's Shia Crackdown" (2010).
21. Holodny, "27 Countries Where Young People Are Living in an Unemployment Crisis" (2015); Barrett, "Bahrain Emerging as Flashpoint in Middle East Unrest" (2011); Broomhall, "Bahrain and Oman Have Highest Gulf Unemployment Rates" (2011).
22. Freedom House, "Freedom of the Press: Bahrain" (2010).
23. Phillips, *Carnegie Papers* (2007), 17–18.
24. Atia, "Paradox of the Free Press in Egypt" (2004); Khamis, "Role of New Arab Satellite Channels" (2007), 39–51.
25. Lynch, "Assessing the Democratizing Power of Satellite TV" (2005), 150–155.
26. Atia, "Paradox of the Free Press in Egypt" (2004).
27. Friedman, "Virtual Mosque" (2017).
28. Fnaire Band, "Maktish Bladi" (2005), produced by Mohine Tizaf, written by Achraf Aarab and Khalifa Mennani, www.facebook.com/Fnaire, www.instagram.com/fnaire_official/. Reprinted by permission.
29. Lyrics by Youssra Oukaf (Soultana), reprinted by permission; also quoted in Wright, *Rock the Casbah* (2011), 123.
30. See Ishay, *History of Human Rights* (2008), 315–355.
31. Ishay, "Spring of Arab Nations?" (2013), 373–383.
32. Langohr, "Labor Movement and Organization" (2014), 183.
33. Ibid., 185.
34. Kirkpatrick and Cowell, "Egyptian Government Figures Join Protestors" (2011).
35. Ardic, "Understanding the 'Arab Spring'" (2012), 8–52.
36. Amin, *Whatever Else Happens to the Egyptian?* (2004), 158–168.
37. Dawoud and Whitaker, "370 Die in Egypt's Speeding Inferno" (2002).
38. El Masry, "Egypt's Railways" (2013).
39. Willis, "Lessons from Algeria's 'Dark Decade'" (2014); Al Jazeera, "Algeria: The Revolution That Never Was" (2012).
40. Lewis, "Why Has Morocco's King Survived the Arab Spring?" (2011).
41. It should be noted that the Qatari monarchy supported the Muslim Brotherhood in Egypt, and elsewhere, leading to a rift between Qatar on one side, and Saudi Arabia and the UAE, on the other side.
42. Kipling, "White Man's Burden" (2008).
43. Malik, "Proposing Ground Rules for Committee Debates on Human Rights" (1947).
44. Jacobson, *Ambassador Charles Malik* (2008), 3.
45. Nasser, quoted in Morgan, "Sunday Times Reporter Interview" (2017).
46. Maududi, *Human Rights in Islam* (1976), 39.
47. Moghadam, "Women, Citizenship and Civil Society in the Arab World" (2006), 100.
48. United Nations, *Arab Human Development Report 2009*.
49. Hegel, *Philosophy of Right* (1967), 13.

PART II. DERAILMENT

1. Joseph de Maistre, *Études sur La Souveraineté,* chapter 10, 377 (author's translation).

3. ARAB WINTERS

1. Eddy and Johannsen, "Migrants Arriving in Germany Face a Chaotic Reception in Berlin" (2015).
2. Hirsh, "Team Trump's Message" (2016).
3. Gramsci, *Selections from the Prison Notebooks,* 245–246.
4. Hobsbawm, *Age of Extremes* (1994), 119.
5. Halliday, "1967 and the Consequence of Catastrophe" (1987).
6. Ibid.
7. Clawson and Rubin, *Eternal Iran* (2005), 82.
8. See Kraft, "Letter from Iran" (1978).
9. Lacey, *Inside the Kingdom* (2009), 5.
10. MacFarquhar, "Economic Frustration Simmers Again in Tunisia" (2012).
11. Almosawa et al., "Islamic State Gains Strength in Yemen" (2015).
12. McElroy, "Rome Will Be Conquered Next" (2014).
13. Naji, *Management of Savagery* (2006).
14. Goldfischer and Ishay, "Belligerent Fundamentalism and the Legacy of European Fascism" (2008). Part of this section has been revised and updated from this source and from Ishay, "Violent Islamism beyond Borders" (2016).
15. Sternhell, "Fascist Ideology" (1976).
16. Bush, "President Discusses War on Terror" (2005).
17. Laqueur, *Fascism* (1996), 14.
18. Steigmann-Gall, "Nazism and the Revival of Political Religion Theory" (2005), 94: Among his many invocations of Christianity, Hitler said in 1928, "We tolerate no one in our ranks who attacks the ideas of Christianity . . . in fact our movement is Christian." For a study of the heavy reliance of the fascist Romanian Iron Guard on Christian faith, see Ioanid, "Sacralised Politics of the Romanian Iron Guard" (2005), 125–160.
19. Laqueur, *Fascism* (1996), 147. Laqueur argues that that the potential for such movements to be based on religious fundamentalism—the phenomenon he calls "clerical fascism"—was already noted by the early 1920s, and he cites a 1924 article, "Faszismus und Fundamentalismus in den USA," as an early account of that linkage.
20. Griffin, "Fascism," in *Encyclopedia of Fundamentalism,* ed. Brasher (2001), 171–178.
21. Linehan, "British Union of Fascists" (2005), 105.
22. See Ishay, *History of Human Rights* (2008), 117–172.
23. Berlet, "Christian Identity" (2005), 175–212.
24. Mussolini, "Fascism" (1995), 226.
25. Quoted in Smith, ed., *Mussolini's Roman Empire* (1976), 54.
26. Naji, *Management of Savagery* (2006).
27. Ibid., 52.

28. BBC News, "Islamic State Releases 'Al-Baghdadi Message'" (2015).
29. Mussolini, "Fascism" (1995), 227.
30. Al-Zarqawi, "Democracy Is the Very Essence of Heresy" (2005).
31. Al-Baghdadi, "Message to the Mujahidin" (2014).
32. Mussolini, "Fascism" (1995), 226–227.
33. Wright, *Looming Tower* (2006), 14.
34. Naji, *Management of Savagery* (2006), 81.
35. The Covenant of the Islamic Resistance Movement, Article 22 (1988).
36. Ibrahim, *Al Qaeda Reader* (2007), 66.
37. Ibid., 144.
38. Isseroff, "Biography of Hassan Nasrallah" (2007).
39. Bronner, *Bigot* (2014).
40. Gjelten, "State Department Declares ISIS Attacks" (2016).
41. Hitler, "Mein Kampf" in Dahbour and Ishay, eds., *Nationalism Reader* (1995), 233.
42. Ibid.
43. Al-Baghdadi, "Even If the Disbelievers Despise Such" (2015).
44. Allen-Ebrahimian and Dreazen, "Real War on Christianity" (2015).
45. Callimachi, "ISIS Enshrines a Theology of Rape" (2015); Human Rights Watch, "Iraq: ISIS Escapees Describe Systematic Rape" (2014); Amnesty International, "Iraq: Yezidi Women and Girls" (2014).
46. Ibid.
47. Callimachi, "ISIS Enshrines a Theology of Rape" (2015).
48. Mroue, "Islamic State Publicly Kills Gays'" (2015).
49. Oosterhuis, "Medicine, Male Bonding and Homosexuality" (1997), 190.
50. Ibid., 194.
51. United States Holocaust Memorial Museum, "Persecution of Homosexuals in the Third Reich" (2016).
52. Arendt, "Origins of Totalitarianism" (2007), 273.

4. FROST IN JERUSALEM

1. Harkov, "PM: Jewish Killer of Palestinian Family Also Deserves Death Penalty" (2018).
2. French, "Palestinian Reasoning" (2015).
3. Occupy Rothschild was a 2011 Israeli protest held in the Rothschild Boulevard at the center of Tel Aviv.
4. Snitkoff, "Gush Emunim" (2017); see also Avineri, *Making of Modern Zionism* (1981), 187–197.
5. Center for Israel Education, "Israel's Allon Plan Is Unilaterally Presented" (2017); Gross, "After Six Day War, Cabinet Debated West Bank's Future" (2017).
6. Sprinzak, "Israeli Radical Right" (1989).
7. Jewish Virtual Library, "Israeli Settlements" (2008).
8. Khalidi, *Brokers of Deceit* (2013), 7–11.
9. Barsamian, "Interview with Edward Said" (1993).

10. Arafat, "Nobel Lecture" (1994).

11. Said, "Morning After" (1993), 3–5.

12. International Crisis Group, "Radical Islam in Gaza" (2011).

13. Wiener, "Bridging the Divide" (2007).

14. Pedahzur, *Triumph of Israel's Radical Right* (2012), 158–159.

15. Baumgart-Ochse, "Opposed or Intertwined?" (2014), 401–420.

16. Fanon, *Wretched of the Earth* (2004), 24.

17. Filc and Lebel, "Post-Oslo Radical Right in Comparative Perspective" (2005), 87.

18. Hanieh, "From State-Led Growth to Globalization" (2003), 6.

19. Middle East Quarterly, "Shimon Peres" (1995), 75–78; Shimon Peres, "Full Text of Peres Speech to European Parliament" (2017); see also Peres and Naor, *New Middle East* (2014).

20. French, "Palestinian Reasoning" (2015).

21. Ram, "Promised Land of Business Opportunities" (2000); Shafir and Peled, "Peace and Profits" (2000), 221.

22. Furstenberg, "Israeli Life" (2001).

23. Gramsci, *Selections from the Prison Notebooks* (1971), 210.

24. Sinai, "Poverty Level Holds Steady" (2007).

25. One should keep in mind that these numbers are relatively high due to the employment gap between men and women. Women in Jewish Orthodox communities and men in Palestinian communities tend to be compensated for their work outside home while their respective spouses study at Yeshivas or stay at home.

26. Arnon and Gottlieb, *Economic Analysis of the Palestinian Economy* (1993), see appendix, table 1.

27. Diwan and Shaban, *Development under Adversity* (1993), 2–3; Kleiman, "Conditions of Economic Viability" (2007).

28. B'Tselem, *Closure of the West Bank and Gaza Strip* (1993), 4.

29. Beaumont, "Gaza Economy 'on Verge of Collapse'" (2015).

30. Wagner, "Migrant Workers in Israel" (n.d.), 6; Friedberg and Sauer, "Effects of Foreign Guest Workers in Israel" (2003); World Bank, *Poverty in the West Bank and Gaza after Three Years of Economic Crisis* (2003), F258; World Bank, *West Bank and Gaza—Medium-Term Development Strategy for the Health Sector* (1998), 2.

31. Kav LaOved, "Population of Labor Migrants in Israel" (2006), chart 6. Cf. Israel Population and Immigration Authority, "Labor Migration to Israel" (2016).

32. Gramsci, *Selections from the Prison Notebooks* (1971), 238.

33. Monterescu and Shaindlinger, "Situational Radicalism" (2013).

34. Burris, "In Tel Aviv, an Arab Spring That Ignores the Arabs" (2011).

35. International Monetary Fund, *West Bank and Gaza* (2014), 6: Gaza's 2014 poverty rate was approaching 45 percent, and the West Bank's 2014 poverty rate was around 16 percent; Kershner, "Support for Palestinian Authority Erodes as Prices and Taxes Rise" (2012).

36. Al Jazeera, "Palestinians Stage Protests in the West Bank" (2012).
37. Ragson, "Leaked" (2017); Hatuqa, "What Not to Expect from a Palestinian Unity Deal" (2017).
38. Cohen, "Israel: The Collapse of the Left" (2013).
39. One should note that a section of the Russian population would ultimately contribute to the Israeli economic boom and achieve a high level of propaganda for themselves.
40. Weber, *Sociology of Religion* (1991), 1112.
41. Gramsci, *Selections from the Prison Notebooks* (1971), 222–223.
42. Filc and Lebel, "Post-Oslo Radical Right in Comparative Perspective" (2005), 85–97.
43. Eldar, "Is Israel Inching Closer to Fascism?" (2016).
44. The Economist, "Politics in Israel Is Increasingly Nationalist" (2017).
45. Arens, "Israel's Arabs Can Still Identify with the Jews' Tragic Fate" (2015).
46. BBC News, "Palestinian Election: Results in Detail" (2006).
47. Quoted in Hroub, "Hamas after Shaykh Yassin" (2002), 22.
48. Israeli, "State and Religion in the Emerging Palestinian Entity" (2002), 238–240.
49. Lieber, "Hamas Said to Accept Egyptian Plan for Palestinian Unity, Fatah Holding Out" (2017).
50. Hussein and Khalidi, "End of This Road" (2017).
51. Kumar, "David Grossman" (2016).
52. Benjamin, *Illuminations* (2007), 257–258.

5. VOX POPULI AND THE ISLAMIC ENLIGHTENMENT

1. Siegel, "Journalist" (2015).
2. Human Rights Watch, "Tunisia: Events of 2015" (2016).
3. Amnesty International, *Amnesty International Report 2014/15* (2015), 314.
4. Ibid., 387–389.
5. Ulrichsen, "Pushing the Limits."
6. Human Rights Watch, "Oman: Events of 2015" (2016).
7. International Monetary Fund, "Qatar: Staff Concluding Statement" (2018). See further Human Rights Watch, "Qatar: Events of 2015" (2016); Dickinson, "Case against Qatar" (2014).
8. NPR, "Transcript: Obama Seeks 'New Beginning' in Cairo" (2009).
9. Ofek, "Why the Arabic World Turned Away from Science" (2011).
10. Internet Social Forum, "Tunis Resolution" (2015).
11. Internet Social Forum, "About Us" (2018).
12. See Offe, "Referendum vs. Institutionalized Deliberation" (2017) for a similar discussion on deliberative democracy.
13. Foreign Policy, "Art Is a Window to the Arab World's Soul" (2016).
14. Hajjaji, "Libya Art Exhibit Paints Bleak Picture of Post-Arab Spring Society" (2017).
15. United Nations, Resolution 103(I): Persecution and Discrimination (1946). There was some suspicion, explicitly denied before the vote by Egyptian

delegate Bahgat Badaoui Bey, that Egypt intended by this resolution to oppose Zionism indirectly (Jewish Telegraphic Agency, "General Assembly Places Resolution on Religious Persecution on Agenda" [1946]).

16. Jewish Virtual Library, "Fact Sheet: Jewish Refugees from Arab Countries" (2015); Aderet, "Israel Marks First-Ever National Day" (2014); Freedman, "Are Jews Who Fled Arab Lands to Israel Refugees, Too?" (2003).
17. Achcar, *Arabs and the Holocaust* (2011).
18. United States, Department of State, *Tunisia 2014 International Religious Freedom Report* (2014), 2; Human Rights Watch, "Tunisia: Events of 2015" (2016).
19. Freedom House, *Freedom on the Net: Tunisia* (2015), 10.
20. Egyptian Parliament, Constitution of the Arab Republic of Egypt (2014), Article 7.
21. Ibid., Article 64.
22. United States, Department of State, *Egypt 2017 International Religious Freedom Report* (2017), 3.
23. Samaan and Walsh, "Egypt Declares State of Emergency" (2017).
24. United States, Department of State, *Egypt 2014 International Religious Freedom Report* (2014), 6, 4.
25. Nosset, "Free Exercise after the Arab Spring" (2014), 1655.
26. Fayed, "Is the Crackdown on the Muslim Brotherhood Pushing the Group Toward Violence?" (2016).
27. Inanc, "Salafis and the Muslim Brotherhood" (2014).
28. Freedom House, *Freedom in the World* (2013), 336, 386.
29. Lynch, "Why Saudi Arabia Escalated the Middle East's Sectarian Conflict" (2016).
30. Hourani, *Arabic Thought in the Liberal Age* (1983), 930.
31. See also Ishay, *History of Human Rights* (2008), 66–69.
32. Al-Hussein, "Tolerance Is Not Enough" (2017); Niebuhr, *Beyond Tolerance* (2008).
33. Khader, "We Need a Muslim Reformation" (2017); Rumi, "Islam Needs Reformation from Within" (2015); Ali, *Heretic: Why Islam Needs a Reformation* (2015); Khalaf, "Search for a Muslim Martin Luther" (2015).
34. Hasan, Mehdi. "Why Islam Doesn't Need a Reformation" (2015).
35. Kant, *An Answer to the Question "What Is Enlightenment?"* (1784), 1.
36. Ishay, *Internationalism and Its Betrayal* (2005), 58.
37. Kant, *Religion within the Limits of Reason Alone* (1960), 142.
38. Al-Fahim, *From Rags to Riches* (1998).
39. Faour, "Review of Citizenship Education in Arab Nations" (2013).
40. Waghid and Davids, "On the (Im)possibility of Democratic Citizenship Education in the Arab and Muslim World" (2014), 346.
41. Kchaou, *Le juste et ses normes* (2007).
42. Patel, *Sacred Ground* (2012), 70–71.
43. Times of Oman, "300 Masterpieces Set for Louvre Abu Dhabi" (2014).
44. Hashemi, *Islam, Secularism and Liberal Democracy* (2009), 136.

45. Averroës in *Decisive Treatise and Epistle Dedicatory*, trans. Butterworth (2001), 3–4.
46. Benchemsi, "Invisible Atheists" (2017).
47. Ibid.

6. SUN, SAND, WATER, AND SHIELDS

 1. Roosevelt, "The Four Freedoms" (2008), 403–406.
 2. Ali, *Meaning of the Holy Quran* (1989), 86.
 3. Universal Declaration of Human Rights G.A. Re. 217A (1948), III.
 4. Saudi Arabia: Permanent Delegation of Saudi Arabia to UNESCO, "Hejaz Railway" (2015).
 5. Torchia, "IMF Endorses Saudi Plan for $500 Billion Business Zone" (2017).
 6. Hirschauge and Jones, "Israel Builds Railway in Hope of Boosting Commerce with Arab Neighbors" (2016).
 7. Staff, "Restored Northern Railway Sees Historic Maiden Voyage" (2016).
 8. Galilei in "Dialogue Concerning the Two Chief World Systems" (1953).
 9. El Hassan bin Talal, in conversation with the author (June 2016).
 10. Alagappa, "Garden of Eden 2.0" (2014); International Renewable Energy Agency, *Renewable Capacity* (2018), 14, 33.
 11. Domonoske, "Morocco Unveils a Massive Solar Power Plant in the Sahara" (2016); Parke and Giles, "Morocco's Megawatt Solar Plant" (2018).
 12. Carrington, "High-Speed Euro Train Gets Green Boost from Two Miles of Solar Panels" (2011).
 13. Prasad, "Railways to Start Trial Runs of Solar Train in Sunny Jodhpur" (2016); Sinha, "Catching the Sun at Bhadla Solar Park" (2017); Sinha, "Morocco's Megawat Solar Plant" (2018).
 14. Woodhouse, "Feds Pick Preferred Route for Possible Tucson-Phoenix Passenger Railway" (2017).
 15. Khaldûn, in *Muqaddimah,* ed. Dawood (2015).
 16. Immerzeel et al., *Middle-East and Northern Africa Water Outlook* (2011).
 17. World Bank, *Renewable Energy Desalination* (2012).
 18. Stanley, "How the Sun Might Help Solve a Looming Water Crisis in the Arab Gulf" (2018).
 19. Holtham, "Solar Energy to Generate 75 Percent of Dubai's Power by 2050" (2018).
 20. Wright, "Five Benefits of Solar Energy" (2016).
 21. Trading Economics, "Egypt Unemployment Rate"; Adly and Meddeb, "Why Painful Economic Reforms Are Less Risky in Tunisia Than Egypt" (2017); Trading Economics, "Tunisia Unemployment Rate" (2017).
 22. World Bank. "Tunisia: Data" (2018).
 23. Tunisian National Institute of Statistics (INS), *Monthly Report (Bulletin Mensuel de Statistique)* (2018), 5.
 24. Statista, "Tunisia: Unemployment Rate" (2018).
 25. Med Limem, in conversation with the author, Tunis University (May 2015).
 26. Yaros, "Is Tunisia Ready for a Green Economy?" (2012).

27. International Monetary Fund, "IMF Executive Board Approves US$12 Billion Extended" (2016).

28. Waheesh, "Half Way There" (2018).

29. Momani, "Egypt's IMF Program" (2018).

30. West, "Just How Low Can Oil Prices Go?" (2016); Wells, "Saudi Arabia Struggles to Cope with Cheap Oil" (2016); Heath, "Oil Prices Creep Higher as OPEC Wrestles Trump's Call" (2018).

31. Ross, *Oil Curse* (2013), 3–4.

32. The National, "UAE Is World's Top Donor of Development Aid in 2017" (2018); Organisation for Economic Co-Operation and Development, "Development Aid" (2018), 4.

33. International Trade Center News, "What Did the Middle East Trade?" (2018).

34. Weber, *Economy and Society* (1978), 1393–1395.

35. Franklin, "Pennsylvania Assembly: Reply to the Governor" (2017).

36. Masters and Sergie, "Arab League: Backgrounder" (2016); Khanna, *Connectography* (2016), 105.

37. BBC News, "Rio Olympics 2016" (2016).

38. United Nations High Commissioner for Refugees (UNHCR), "Syria Regional Refugee Response" (2017); the latest number of registered Syrian refugees is more than 5,300,000.

39. Connor, "Most Displaced Syrians Are in the Middle East" (2018); Kanter and Higgins, "E.U. Offers Turkey 3 Billion Euros" (2015); UNHCR, *Global Trends: Forced Displacement in 2017* (2017), 14; UNHCR, *Operational Update: Turkey* (2018), 1; UNHCR, *Registered Persons of Concern Refugees and Asylum Seekers in Jordan* (2018), 1; UNHCR, *Operational Portal: Refugee Situations* (2018).

40. UNHCR, "EUR 25 Million to Support Turkey" (2018); UNHCR, *3RP: Regional Refugee and Resilience Plan* (2017–2018), 7; UNHCR, *Regional Refugee and Resilience Plan 2018 Progress Report* (2018), 4.

41. Camarasa, "'Appeal to Affection and Empathy'" (2015).

42. Tastekin, "Davutoglu Proposes Refugee 'Container City'" (2015).

43. UNHCR, "Contributions to UNHCR, 2016" (2017).

44. Graham, "How Did the 'Secret' Sykes-Picot Agreement Become Public?" (2015).

45. Lenin, "Right of Nations to Self-Determination" (1972), 66.

46. Wright, "How the Curse of Sykes-Picot Still Haunts the Middle East" (2016).

47. Luxemburg, *National Question* (1976), 123.

48. Sanger, "Iran Complies with Nuclear Deal" (2016).

49. Riedel, "In Yemen, Iran Outsmarts Saudi Arabia" (2017); Cordesman, *Military Spending* (2018).

50. BBC News, "Russia Says 63,000 Troops" (2018); *Moscow Times*, "Calculating the Cost of Russia's War" (2015).

51. Bremmer, "Why the Syrian Civil War Is Becoming Even More Complex" (2018).

52. Wright, "Imagining a Remapped Middle East" (2013); CNN News, "On GPS: Landis on a Syria Solution" (2014).

53. Bolton, "John Bolton: To Defeat ISIS, Create a Sunni State" (2015).
54. Totten, "Let Iraq Die" (2016). It should be noted that this claim hopes that ISIS Sunni-controlled territories will disappear on their own.
55. Coker and Gladstone, "Iraqi Voters Strengthen Hand of Militia Leader Who Battled U.S." (2018); Coker, "U.S. Takes a Risk" (2018); Cambanis, "Can a Shiite Cleric Pull Iraq Out of the Sectarian Trap?" (2018).
56. Fasanotti, "Confederal Model for Libya" (2016).
57. Jibril, "Making Sense of Libya" (2016).
58. Ibid.
59. Libya-Business News, "NOC Chairman Explains Unity Agreement" (2016).
60. The World Bank, "Facing the Hard Facts" (2012).
61. Cockburn, "Yemen War Death Toll" (2018); Council on Foreign Relations, "War in Yemen" (2018).
62. Reuters, "Yemen's Cholera Epidemic" (2018).
63. Nikbakht and McKenzie, "Yemen War Is the World's Worst Humanitarian Crisis" (2018); BBC News, "Yemen 'Could be Worst Famine in 100 Years'" (2018); Oxfam America, *Missiles and Food* (2017).
64. Reel, "Djibouti Is Hot" (2016).
65. Center for Strategic and International Studies, "Maghreb Rising" (2015).
66. NATO: "The Arab Maghreb Union" (2018), 2.
67. Hamza, "Maghreb Union Is One of the World's Worst-Performing Trading Blocs" (2017); World Bank, "Trade Offers Path to Growth and Integration" (2012); United Nations Economic Commission for Africa, "AMU-Trade and Marketing Integration" (2016); Menas Associates, "Hopes for Re-Opening of Algeria-Morocco Border" (2016).
68. Ghilès, "Doubts Remain about Reopening the Algeria-Morocco Border" (2015).
69. Weber, *Economy and Society* (1978), 1460.
70. Guizani, "Train from Tunis to Casablanca" (2015).
71. Morocco World News, "NATO Determined to Reinforce Security Cooperation with Morocco, White House" (2016).
72. Caspit, "Israeli-Egyptian Love Affair" (2016).
73. Lynfield, "New Textbook Bodes Well for Egypt-Israeli Relations" (2016).
74. United States, Office of the Press Secretary, "United States-Gulf Cooperation Council Second Summit Leaders Communique" (2016). The joint communique also stated: "The United States policy to use all elements of power to secure its core interests in the Gulf region, and to deter and confront external aggression against its allies and partners, as it did during the Gulf War, is unequivocal."
75. Roosevelt, *You Learn* (1960), 98.

7. THE FEMALE TIME BOMB

1. Musyimi-Ogana, *True Story of Women Peace Train* (2015).
2. Fourier, as quoted in Marx and Engels, "Holy Family" (1956), 258–259.
3. Roosevelt, "U.N. Deliberations on Draft Convention on the Political Rights of Women," 180.

4. Roosevelt, "Where Do Human Rights Begin?" (1953).

5. Reticker, dir, *Trials of Spring* (2015).

6. Law, "Bahrain Protests Prompt Global Concern" (2015); Donger, "Why Protesting Sexim Is Taboo" (2011).

7. Kingsley, "80 Sexual Assaults in One Day" (2013).

8. El Sirgany and Clarke, "Saudi Arabia Arrests Female Activists" (2018).

9. Horkheimer, "Authority and the Family" (1982), 83.

10. Astell, "Some Reflections upon Marriage" (1995), 563.

11. Abigail Adams to John Adams, Braintree, MA (March 31, 1776). Accessed November 18, 2016. https://history.hanover.edu/courses/excerpts/165adams-rtl.html.

12. Marie-Prudhomme, "On the Influence of the Revolution on Women" (1791).

13. Keddie, *Women in the Middle East* (2006); Moghadam, *Modernizing Women* (2013); El Saadawi, *Nawal El Saadawi Reader* (1997), ch. 22.

14. Al Yafai, "Women United by Revolution May Be Divided by Politics" (2011).

15. Freedom and Justice Party official, in conversation with the author, Zamalek, Cairo (January 15, 2013).

16. Egyptian Legislature, 2014 Constitution of the Arab Republic of Egypt, Article 180 calls for 25 percent of local council seats to be filled by women, the same percentage that is to be filled by "youth" under the age of thirty-five.

17. See Ishay, *History of Human Rights* (2008), 231–232.

18. Gheytanchi and Moghadam, "Women, Social Protests, and the New Media" (2014), 6.

19. Sreberny, "Women's Digital Activism in a Changing Middle East" (2015), 357–361.

20. Bronstein, "For Egyptian Online Warrior, Father's Torture Fueled Activism" (2011).

21. Ryan, "Tunisian Blogger Becomes Nobel Prize Nominee" (2011).

22. England, "Saudi Women Are Campaigning Online against 'Enslavement'" (2016).

23. Nasser, "Yemen: Women Must Be in the Peace Talks."

24. See Solomon, ed., *Voice of Their Own* (2004).

25. Mernissi, "Meaning of Spatial Boundaries" (2003), 489.

26. Weber, *Economy and Society* (1978), 604.

27. Ibid., 605.

28. Guidère, *Sexe et Charia* (2014); see also Mahdavi, *Passionate Uprisings* (2006).

29. Hafez. "Bodies That Protest" (2014), 23.

30. El-Feki, "Arab Bed Spring?" (2015), 38–44.

31. Pew Research Center, *World's Muslims* (2013), 80.

32. Bocchi, "Manufacturing Virginity" (2017).

33. See Musawah, "For Equality in the Muslim Family," http://www.musawah.org/.

34. Moghadam, "Islamic Feminism and Its Discontents" (2002), 1135–1171; Segran, "Rise of the Islamic Feminists" (2013); Najmabadi, "(Un)Veiling Feminism" (2000), 29–45; Tohidi, "'Islamic Feminism'" (2003); Mir-Hosseini, "Beyond

'Islam' vs. 'Feminism'" (2011), 67–77; Moghissi, "Islamic Feminism Revisited" (2011); Mojab, "Theorizing the Politics of 'Islamic Feminism'" (2011), 124–146; Shahidian, "Saving the Savior" (1999), 303–327; Barlas, *Believing Women" in Islam* (2002); Wadud, *Qur'an and Woman* (2011).

35. Badran, "Between Secular and Islamic Feminism/s" (2005), 6–28.
36. Barlas, "Qur'an, Sexual Equality, and Feminism," lecture, University of Toronto, Toronto, Canada, January 12, 2004.
37. Al-Hashimi, *Ideal Muslimah* (2005).
38. Rafiq, "Child Custody in Classical Islamic Law" (2014).
39. Daily Mail, "Feminist Protesters Strip Off in Tunisia" (2013).
40. Tayler, "Tunisian Woman Sent to a Psychiatric Hospital" (2013).
41. United Kingdom Science Museum, "Women and Psychiatry" (2017).
42. United Nations International Children's Emergency Fund, "Female Genital Mutilation" (2018).
43. Rouzi, "Facts and Controversies on Female Genital Mutilation and Islam" (2013), 10–14.
44. Scheinfeld, "Social Scientist's Evaluation of Kinsey's Study of Female Sex Behavior" (1953).
45. Daoud, "Sexual Misery of the Arab World" (2016).
46. See also Mosse, *Nationalism and Sexuality* (1995).
47. Bearak and Cameron, "Here Are the 10 Countries" (2016); for additional information, see Leveille, *Equaldex, Collaborative LGBT Rights Knowledge Base* (2017).
48. Chamas, "Fight Goes On" (2015); McCormick-Cavanaugh, "Is Homophobia at an All-Time High?" (2016); Jankowicz, "Jailed for Using Grindr" (2017); see also Michaelson, "LGBT People in Egypt Targeted" (2017).
49. Mill, "Subjection of Women," in *"On Liberty" and Other Writings*, ed. Collini (1989), 131.
50. World Bank. *Opening Doors* (2013), 31–33; World Bank, "Life Expectancy at Birth, Female" (2018); World Bank, "Mortality Rate, Infant" (2018); World Bank, "Literacy Rate, Adult Female" (2018).
51. El-Swais, "Despite High Education Levels"; World Bank, *Opening Doors*, 34–45 (2013); World Bank, *Progress towards Gender Equality*, 29–30.
52. Abu Dhabi e-Government, "Khalifa University Top Rankings in UAE" (2016); Rizvi, "UAE Bucks Global Trend as Women Lead the Way" (2018).
53. World Economic Forum, *Global Gender Gap Report* (2016); World Bank, "Labor Force Participation Rate, Female" (2018).
54. European Bank for Reconstruction and Development, *Enhancing Women's Voice* (2015), 25; World Bank, "Labor Force Participation Rate, Female: MENA" (2018).
55. Organisation for Economic Co-Operation and Development, *OECD Economic Surveys* (2018), 49.
56. Horkheimer, "Authority and the Family," in *Critical Theory: Selected Essays* (1982), 122.
57. El Saadawi, *Memoirs from the Women's Prison* (1986), 200.

58. Banihani and Syed, "Macro-National Level Analysis of Arab Women's Work Engagement" (2017), 136.
59. Ellouze, "Work Is Freedom" (2014).
60. Organisation for Economic Co-Operation and Development, *Women's Economic Empowerment in Selected MENA Countries* (2017), 27.
61. World Bank, "Women in Jordan—Limited Economic Participation" (2014).
62. Ibid.
63. In Egypt, women gained the right to pass their nationality to their children in 2008. UN Women, "Spring Forward for Women Program: Egypt" (2014), 3.
64. Jewish People's Council, "Declaration of the Establishment of the State of Israel" (1948).
65. World Bank, "Labor Force Participation Rate: MENA" (2018).
66. Organisation for Economic Co-Operation and Development, *Pursuit of Gender Equality* (2017), 154. According to the World Bank, female labor force participation in Israel reached 47 percent in 2017, putting it ahead of Germany and France (World Bank, "Labor Force Participation Rate, Female" [2017]). However, just 31 percent of managerial positions in the top 100 companies were held by women in 2013, see Weisberg, "31% of Israel's Top 100 Company Directors Are Women" (2014).
67. Jahal, "New Initiative Aims to Protect Palestinian Working Women" (2016).
68. Sa'ar, "Palestinian Women in the Israeli Workforce" (2015), 15.
69. UN Women, "Facts and Figures: Economic Empowerment" (2013); Ma'an News Agency, "Report: Palestinian Female Labor Participation among World's Lowest" (2015).
70. Thrope, "War on Women in Israel" (2015).
71. Salhab et al., *View from the Top* (2016), 22; Human Rights Watch, "Saudi Arabia: 'Unofficial' Guardianship Rules Banned" (2017).
72. Young, "Small Victories for GCC Women" (2015); Organisation for Economic Co-Operation and Development, *Pursuit of Gender Equality* (2017), 115.
73. Salama, "UAE Government Offices Need Childcare Facilities" (2010).
74. More than 20 percent of Fortune 500 board members are female, but in the GCC the numbers are much lower, ranging from 7 percent in Saudi Arabia and Qatar to 14 percent in Kuwait. See Willen et al., *Power Women in Arabia* (2016), 4.
75. World Bank, "Labor Force Participation Rate" (2017).
76. World Economic Forum, *Global Gender Gap Report 2016* consistently ranks each of the GCC states higher on female education than on female employment; Duncan, "Young, Rich, and Female" (2015).
77. Elborgh-Woytek et al., *Women, Work, and the Economy* (2013), 4.
78. Bebel, *Woman and Socialism* (1910), 211. Evidencing this reality, women in the MENA devote six to eight times more time to household chores and one to two more hours to total work than men each day; European Bank for Reconstruction and Development, *Enhancing Women's Voice* (2015), 29.
79. Willen et al., *Power Women in Arabia* (2016).

80. European Bank for Reconstruction and Development, *Enhancing Women's Voice* (2015), 65, 70.

81. Ali, *Meaning of the Holy Quran* (1989), 195; see also, Chaudhry, *Domestic Violence and the Islamic Tradition*.

82. European Bank for Reconstruction and Development, *Enhancing Women's Voice* (2015), 48.

83. Bar'el, "Arab Women Breaking Silence on Domestic Violence" (2015).

84. Due Diligence Project, *Due Diligence and State Responsibility to Eliminate Violence against Women* (2014), 7.

85. UN Women, "Global Database on Violence against Women" (2017).

86. European Bank for Reconstruction and Development, *Enhancing Women's Voice* (2015), 63.

87. Tashkandi and Rasheed, "Wife Abuse" (2009); Promundo, *Understanding Masculinities* (2017), 81.

88. United Nations International Children's Emergency Fund, "Child Marriage in Middle East and North Africa" (2016).

89. Al-Arabiya English, "Domestic Violence Cases on the Rise" (2016).

90. Fareed, "Saudi Social Media Users Break Silence on Violence against Women" (2017); see also European Bank for Reconstruction and Development, *Enhancing Women's Voice* (2015), 66.

91. For a comprehensive report on violence against women in Jordan and efforts to combat it, see United Nations, *Violence against Women*. To date, attempted legal protections have lacked adequate definitions and have contained enough loopholes to be virtually unenforceable. Promundo, *Understanding Masculinities* (2017); report highlights similar discrepancies in law and in practice in Morocco, Egypt, Lebanon, and Palestine.

92. European Bank for Reconstruction and Development, *Enhancing Women's Voice* (2015), 71.

93. Gurung and Khatiwada, *Nepali Women in the Middle East* (2013), 56.

94. Begum, "Gulf States Fail to Protect Domestic Workers" (2015); cf. Human Rights Watch, "*I Already Bought You*" (2015).

95. Gulf Research Center, "Gulf Labor Markets" (2016).

96. This in spite of gross violations by the state itself under the security apparatus of Ben Ali; Zaki, "Tunisia Uncovered a History of State Sexual Violence" (2016).

97. The minimum legal age for marriage was raised to seventeen in 1964; see Islamopedia, "Personal Status Code" (2017).

98. Tunisia: Withdrawal of the Declaration (2014).

99. Amnesty International, *Assaulted and Accused* (2015), 1, 3.

100. Sherwood, "Tunisian Coalition Party Fights for Women's Rights with Gender Violence Bill" (2016).

101. Amnesty International, *Assaulted and Accused* (2015), 17.

102. McCormick-Cavanagh, "New Tunisian Law Takes Long Stride" (2016).

103. Amnesty International, *Circles of Hell* (2015), 5.

104. Wilson, "From Virginity Test to Power" (2012).

105. Egyptian Parliament, Egypt Penal Code (1937), Article 60; cf. Due Diligence Project, *Due Diligence and State Responsibility to Eliminate Violence against Women* (2014), 19.

106. United Nations, *World's Women 2015*, 155. Unfortunately, statistics on male attitudes to this same question were not available.

107. Women's Centre for Legal Aid and Counseling (WCLAC), *Palestinian Women and Penal Law* (2012).

108. Ibid.

109. UN Women, "Facts and Figures: Ending Violence against Women" (2017).

110. Amnesty International, "Lebanon: Refugee Women from Syria Face Heightened Risk of Exploitation and Sexual Harassment" (2016).

111. Amnesty International, "Lebanon: Refugee Women" (2016).

112. Save the Children, *Too Young to Wed* (2014).

113. United Nations Office of the High Commissioner for Human Rights, "Report: No One Unaffected" (2018); UNHRC, *I Lost my Dignity* (2018); Miles, "U.N. Aided 38,000 Victims of Syrian Gender-Based Violence in 2013" (2014); UN Women, "Snapshot of UN Women's Work in Response to the Crisis in Syria" (2016). As of 2016, it should be noted, UN Women has successfully established protective "safe spaces" for refugee women and girls in two of the largest Syrian refugee camps, located in Jordan. Through the Oasis Project, in Za'atari Camp alone, more than five thousand refugee women and girls are aided per month.

114. United Nations High Commission for Refugees, *We Keep It in Our Heart* (2017), 6.

115. Batha, "World Is Failing Former Yazidi Sex Slaves" (2016); Omar, "Women in the Middle of the War" (2015).

116. Rome Statute of the International Criminal Court (1998), Article 54.

117. Wagtendonk, "Female Kurdish Fighters Take Arms" (2014); Costello, "ISIS in Iraq: The Female Fighters That Strike Fear into Jihadis" (2016).

118. Batha, "Syrian Refugee Crisis Is Changing Women's Roles" (2016).

119. Kurzman, "Death Toll of the Iran-Iraq War" (2016).

120. Price-Gibson, " 'We Cannot Count on Men to Create Peace' " (2016).

121. Ettinger, "Thousands Finish Women's Peace March with Plea for Action at Netanyahu's Door" (2016).

122. Human Rights Watch, "Boxed In" (2016).

123. For an example in the Tunisian context, see Al-Bawaba, "Check Out This Striking Campaign" (2016).

124. Human Rights Watch, "Saudi Arabia: 'Unofficial' Guardianship Rules Banned" (2017).

8. REMEMBERING THE FUTURE

1. Eltarabesh, "When Will the Train Return to Gaza?" (2016).

2. Ibid.

3. Darwish, "The Train Passed" (2006), 66–68. Reprinted by permission of the Darwish Foundation.

4. Ayalon, "Why the Iran Nuclear Deal Is Good for Israel" (2015).

5. This chapter is drawn from Ishay and Kretzmer, "Reclaiming Human Rights" in *Israel and Palestine: Alternative Perspectives on Statehood* (2016), 77–94. It has been revised and expanded. I take sole responsibility for the additional statements and revisions that may not reflect David Kretzmer's position.

6. Jewish People's Council, The Declaration of the Establishment of the State of Israel (1948).

7. Montell, "Palestine and Human Rights Treaties" (2015).

8. The modes of occupation have changed over time, and following the disengagement from Gaza, many claim that Israel is no longer an occupying power. Yet, the essential features of control have remained the same: the lives of the Palestinians remain subservient to Israeli interests; see Gordon, *Israel's Occupation* (2008); Ophir, Givoni, and Hanafi, eds., *Power of Inclusive Exclusion* (2009); Kretzmer, "Law of Belligerent Occupation as a System of Control" (2013), 31.

9. Palestinian Declaration of Independence (1988).

10. Human Rights Watch, *Internal Fight: Palestinian Abuses in Gaza and the West Bank* (2008).

11. Human Rights Watch, "Palestine: Crackdown on Journalists" (2016).

12. Bell, *Peace Agreements and Human Rights* (2000).

13. Deutscher, *Non-Jewish Jew* (1968), 136–137.

14. International Covenant on Civil and Political Rights, 14668 U.N.T.S. 999, Article 1 (1976); International Covenant on Economic, Social and Cultural Rights, 14531 U.N.T.S. 993 (1976).

15. Kuttab, "Confidence-Building Measures Needed for Israel-Palestine Talks" (2013).

16. Herzog, "Only Separation Can Lead to a Two-State Solution" (2016).

17. Lazaroff, "Abbas at UNHRC" (2017); see also Oz, "For Its Survival, Israel Must Abandon the One-State Option" (2015); Sharon, "Half a Loaf" (2015); Smooha, "Model of Ethnic Democracy," (2002), 475; Sharon, "One State Delusion" (2016), 115–132.

18. See Burg, "Now It's Your Turn" (2011).

19. See the following chapters in Ehrenberg and Peled, eds., *Israel and Palestine* (2016): Farsakh, "The One-State Solution and the Israeli-Palestinian Conflict," 201–221; Lustick, "Making Sense of the Nakba," 17–40; and Jamal, "Beyond Traditional Sovereignty Theory," 337–364. See also Abunimah, *One Country* (2006); Segal, "Case for Binationalism" (2001); Tilley, *One State Solution* (2005).

20. Serious work on such a model of governance has been done in Israel by a group called Two States One Homeland. See http://2states1homeland.org/.

21. Middle East Monitor, "Israel's Rivlin Proposes 'Confederation' with Palestinians" (2015); Avnery, "Israeli-Palestinian Federation Is Still the Way" (2013); Ellis, "Yossi Beilin's Back to the Future Confederation" (2015); Bell, "Israel and Palestine" (2014); Lake, "Confederation in Israel-Palestine?" (2015); Yiftachel, "Colonial Deadlock or Confederation for Israel/Palestine?" (2013); Har-El, "Sharing Land for Peace" (2013).

22. Al Jazeera, "Mahmoud Abbas in Egypt" (2018). Beaumont, "Hamas and Fatah Sign Deal" (2017).

23. Human Rights Watch, "Palestine: Crackdown on Journalists" (2016).

24. Kuttab, "Palestinian Journalists Facing Dual Restrictions" (2016).

25. Ben-Bassat, "Rethinking the Concept of Ottomanization" (2009), 463.

26. Freedom House, *Freedom of the Press Report 2016: Israel.*

27. Pfeffer, "Israel Is More Focused on 'Hasbara' Than It Is on Policy" (2012).

28. Freedom House, *Freedom of the Press Report 2016: West Bank and Gaza Strip.*

29. The Economist, "Gagged in Gaza" (2016).

30. Cf. Rediker, "Incitement of Terrorism on the Internet" (2015), 321–351.

31. Mill, "On Liberty," in *J. S. Mill: "On Liberty" and Other Writings*, ed. Collini (1989), 56–57.

32. Sapir and Statman, "Minority Religions in Israel" (2015), 67.

33. United States, Department of State, *International Religious Freedom Report* (2015), 15–16.

34. The Covenant of the Islamic Resistance Movement (1988), Article 7.

35. It should be noted that Hamas has abandoned some problematic language about killing the Jews, but it still does not adhere to international human rights law, as it still condones "resisting the occupation by all means and methods"; see The Islamic Resistance Movement (Hamas), "Document of General Principles and Policies" (2017).

36. Cohen, "Mandela's Economic Legacy Threatened by S. Africa Inequality" (2013): "Almost twenty years after apartheid, the president of the 2.2-million-member Congress of South African Trade Unions said: 'We still have racial unemployment, racial poverty and racial inequality. Our country is still in white hands." See also Rabushka and Shepsle, *Politics in Plural Societies* (1972).

37. Erekat, "As Long as Israel Continues Its Settlements, a Two-State Solution Is Impossible" (2016).

38. E.g., International Covenant on Civil and Political Rights (1976), Article 27.

39. Framework Convention for the Protection of National Minorities H (95) 10 (1995), Article 5.

40. Ishay, "Globalization, Religion, and Nationalism in Israel and Palestine" (2011), 69–84.

41. Arnon, "Israeli Policy Towards the Occupied Palestinian Territories" (2007). 573; Samara, "Globalization, the Palestinian Economy, and the 'Peace Process'" (2000), 20–34; Hanieh, "From State-Led Growth to Globalization" (2003), 5–21.

42. International Covenant on Economic, Social and Cultural Rights (1976), Part 2, Article 2.

43. Naqib, "Economic Aspects of the Palestinian-Israeli Conflict" (2003), 499–512.

44. Weingast, "Economic Role of Political Institutions" (1995), 1–31.

45. Gendzier, *Dying to Forget* (2015), 16.

46. Estrin, "West Bank Water Crisis" (2016).

47. Stillman, *Jews of Arab Lands* (1979); Ye'or, *Dhimmi: Jews and Christians under Islam* (1985).

48. The Covenant of the Islamic Resistance Movement (1988); Wistrich, *Muslim Anti-Semitism* (2002).

49. Declaration of Principles on Interim Self-Government Arrangements (1993), Article 8.

50. Israeli Knesset, Wye River Memorandum (1998).

51. United Nations, "Performance-Based Roadmap to a Permanent Solution" (2003), 2.

52. Naor, "Security Argument in the Territorial Debate in Israel" (1999), 150–177; Levy, "Militarizing Peace" (2008), 145–159; Peri, "Political-Military Complex" (2005).

53. Siegel-Itzkovich, "BGU and Partners to Create Emergency Response Teams" (2014).

54. Dali-Balta, "Palestine Red Crescent Society on Alert as Violence Spreads" (2015).

55. Peled and Rouhana, "Transitional Justice" (2004), 317–332.

56. Cooke, "David Grossman" (2010); Darwish, "Talent for Hope" (2009), 26.

CONCLUSION

1. New York Times, "Disguised Fascism" (1938).

2. Mahmoud Darwish, "At the Station of a Train Which Fell Off the Map" (2008). Reprinted by permission of the Darwish Foundation.

Abd Rabou, Ahmed. *Civil-Military Relations in the Middle East: Comparing the Political Role of the Military in Egypt and Turkey.* Paris: Arab Reform Initiative Publications, 2016.

Abdel-Samad, Hamed. *Islamic Fascism.* New York: Prometheus Books, 2016.

Abu-Lughod, Lila. *Local Contexts of Islamism in Popular Media.* Amsterdam: Amsterdam University Press, 2006.

Abunimah, Ali. *One Country: A Bold Proposal to End the Israeli-Palestinian Impasse.* New York: Metropolitan Books, 2006.

Achcar, Gilbert. *The Arabs and the Holocaust: The Arab-Israeli War of Narratives.* New York: Metropolitan Books, 2011.

———. *The People Want: A Radical Exploration of the Arab Uprising.* Translated by G. M. Goshgarian. Berkeley: University of California Press, 2013.

Achy, Lahcen, Nada Al-Nashif, Ibrahim Awad, Mongi Boughzala, Hana El-Ghali, Nacer Eddine Hammouda, Nader Kabbani, et al. "Arab Youth Unemployment: Roots, Risks, and Responses." Carnegie Endowment for International Peace, February 10, 2011. Accessed July 27, 2017. http://carnegieendowment.org/2011/02/10/arab-youth-unemploymenat-panels-i-and-ii-roots-risks-and-responses-event-3158.

Aderet, Ofer. "Israel Marks First-Ever National Day Remembering Jewish Exodus from Muslim Lands." *Haaretz*, November 30, 2014. Accessed August 23, 2017. http://www.haaretz.com/jewish/.premium-1.629226.

Adly, Amr, and Hamza Meddeb. "Why Painful Economic Reforms Are Less Risky in Tunisia Than Egypt." Carnegie Middle East Center, March 31, 2017. Accessed September 1, 2017. http://carnegie-mec.org/2017/03/31/why-painful-economic-reforms-are-less-risky-in-tunisia-than-egypt-pub-68481.

African Manager. "Tunisia: Growth Rate Has Almost Doubled Compared to 2016." African Manager, August 16, 2017. Accessed September 1, 2017. https://africanmanager.com/site_eng/tunisia-growth-rate-has-almost-doubled-compared-to-2016/?v=947d7d61cd9a.

Agha, Hussein, and Ahmad Samih Khalidi. "The End of This Road: The Decline of the Palestinian National Movement." New Yorker, August 6, 2017. Accessed August 10, 2017. http://www.newyorker.com/news/news-desk/the-end-of-this-road-the-decline-of-the-palestinian-national-movement.

Ahmed, Leila. A Quiet Revolution: The Veil's Resurgence, from the Middle East to America. New Haven: Yale University Press, 2011.

Ahmed, Masood, Dominique Guillaume, and Davide Furceri. "Youth Unemployment in the MENA Region: Determinants and Challenges." Washington, DC: International Monetary Fund, June 13, 2012. Accessed November 5, 2015. https://www.imf.org/en/News/Articles/2015/09/28/04/54/vc061312.

Ahmida, Ali Abdullatif. Forgotten Voices: Power and Agency in Colonial and Postcolonial Libya. New York: Routledge, 2005.

Akhavi, Shahrough. The Middle East: The Politics of the Sacred and Secular. New York: Zed Books, 2009.

Al-Arabiya English. "Domestic Violence Cases on the Rise in Saudi Arabia." Al Arabiya English, March 2, 2016. Accessed December 30, 2016. http://english.alarabiya.net/en/variety/2016/03/02/Domestic-violence-cases-on-the-rise-in-Saudi-Arabia.html.

Al-Baghdadi, Abu Bakr. "Even If the Disbelievers Despise Such." Audio address, May 14, 2015. English translation online at https://pietervanostaeyen.com/2014/11/14/audio-message-by-abu-bakr-al-baghdadi-even-if-the-disbelievers-despise-such/. Accessed December 9, 2018.

———. "A Message to the Mujahidin and the Muslim Ummah in the Month of Ramadan." Al-Hayat Media Center, July 1, 2014. Accessed November 24, 2017. https://scholarship.tricolib.brynmawr.edu/bitstream/handle/10066/14241/ABB20140701.pdf?sequence=1.

Al-Bawaba, "Check Out This Striking Campaign Combatting Violence against Women in Tunisia." Al-Bawaba, December 21, 2016. Accessed May 21, 2017. https://www.albawaba.com/loop/check-out-striking-campaign-combatting-violence-against-women-tunisia-917554.

Al-Diri, Muhammad. Arab Christians and the Islamic-Christian Co-existence. Amman: Royal Institute for Inter-Faith Studies, 2012.

Al-Fahim, Mohammed. From Rags to Riches: The Story of Abu Dhabi. Abu Dhabi: I. B. Tauris, 1998.

Al-Hashimi, Muhammad Ali. The Ideal Muslimah. Riyadh: International Islamic House, 2005.

Al-Hussein, Feisal. "Tolerance Is Not Enough: Why 'Active' Tolerance Is Needed Now More Than Ever." Huffington Post, November 16, 2015. Accessed November 3, 2017. https://www.huffingtonpost.com/hrh-prince-feisal-al-hussein/tolerance-is-not-enough-w_b_8575320.html.

Al-Rasheed, Madawi. *A Most Masculine State: Gender, Politics, and Religion in Saudi Arabia*. New York: Cambridge University Press, 2013.

Al Yafai, Faisal. "Women United by Revolution May Be Divided by Politics." *The National*, March 8, 2011. Accessed November 5, 2015. https://www.thenational. ae/women-united-by-revolution-may-be-divided-by-politics-1.418858.

Al-Zarqawi, Abu Mus'ab. "Democracy Is the Very Essence of Heresy, Polytheism, and Error." Audio address, January 23, 2005. English excerpts online at Middle East Media Research Institute, Special Dispatch 856, January 31, 2015. Accessed November 21, 2017. https://www.memri.org/reports/ zarqawi-and-other-islamists-iraqi-people-elections-and-democracy-are-heresy.

Alagappa, Harish. "The Garden of Eden 2.0: How Renewable Energy Is Changing the Landscape of the Middle East." *Energy Future* 2, no. 1 (2014): 12–21.

Albright, Madeleine. *Fascism: A Warning*. New York: HarperCollins, 2018.

———. *Madam Secretary: A Memoir*. New York: Miramax Books, 2005.

Alexander, Anne, and Mostafa Bassiouny. *Bread, Freedom, Social Justice: Workers and the Egyptian Revolution*. London: Zed Books, 2014.

Alhassen, Maytha, and Ahmed Shihab-Eldin. *Demanding Dignity: Young Voices from the Front Lines of the Arab Revolutions*. Ashland, OR: White Cloud Press, 2012.

Ali, Abdullah Yusuf. *The Meaning of the Holy Quran, with Revised Translation and Commentary*. Beltsville, MD: Amana Publications, 1989.

Ali, Ayaan Hirsi. *Heretic: Why Islam Needs a Reformation*. New York: HarperCollins, 2015.

Al Jazeera. "Algeria: The Revolution That Never Was." Al Jazeera, May 17, 2012. Accessed November 6, 2015. http://www.aljazeera.com/programmes/ peopleandpower/2012/05/2012516145457232336.html.

———. "Mahmoud Abbas in Egypt to 'Discuss Hamas-Fatah Reconciliation.'" Al Jazeera, November 3, 2018. Accessed December 9, 2018. https://www. aljazeera.com/news/2018/11/mahmoud-abbas-egypt-discuss-hamas-fatah-reconciliation-181103082641674.html.

———. "Palestinians Stage Protests in the West Bank." Al Jazeera, July 3, 2012. Accessed November 3, 2017. http://www.aljazeera.com/news/middleeast /2012/07/201273214025301804.html.

All Empires. "Britain's Post-War Decline, 1945–50." *All Empires*. Accessed December 9, 2018. http://www.allempires.com/article/index.php?q= Britains_Post-War_Decline_1945–50.

Allen-Ebrahimian, Bethany, and Yochi Dreazen. "The Real War on Christianity: In the Middle East, the Islamic State Is Crucifying Christians and Demolishing Ancient Churches. Why Is This Being Met with Silence from the Halls of Congress to Sunday Sermons?" *Foreign Policy*, March 12, 2015. Accessed March 28, 2016. http://foreignpolicy.com/2015/03/12/ the-real-war-on-christianity-iraq-syria-islamic-state/.

Almosawa, Shuaib, Kareem Fahim, and Eric Schmitt. "Islamic State Gains Strength in Yemen, Challenging Al Qaeda." *New York Times*, December

15, 2015. Accessed August 4, 2017. https://www.nytimes.com/2015/12/15/world/middleeast/islamic-state-gains-strength-in-yemen-rivaling-al-qaeda.html?_r=0.

Alsharekh, Alanoud, ed. *The Gulf Family: Kinship Policies and Modernity.* Beirut: London Middle East Institute at SOAS, 2007.

Amar, Paul, and Vijay Prashad, eds. *Dispatches from the Arab Spring: Understanding the New Middle East.* Minneapolis: University of Minnesota Press, 2013.

Amin, Galal. *Whatever Else Happens to the Egyptian?* Cairo: American University in Cairo Press, 2004.

Amnesty International. *Amnesty International Report 2014/15: The State of the World's Human Rights.* London: Amnesty International, 2015.

———. *Assaulted and Accused: Sexual and Gender-Based Violence in Tunisia.* London: Amnesty International, 2015.

———. *Circles of Hell: Domestic, Public and State Violence against Women in Egypt.* New York: Amnesty International, 2015.

———. "Iraq: Yezidi Women and Girls Face Harrowing Sexual Violence." Amnesty International, December 23, 2014. Accessed March 16, 2016. https://www.amnesty.org/en/latest/news/2014/12/iraq-yezidi-women-and-girls-face-harrowing-sexual-violence/.

———. "Lebanon: Refugee Women from Syria Face Heightened Risk of Exploitation and Sexual Harassment." Amnesty International, February 2, 2016. Accessed December 9, 2016. https://www.amnesty.org/en/latest/news/2016/02/lebanon-refugee-women-from-syria-face-heightened-risk-of-exploitation-and-sexual-harassment/

Arafat, Yasser. Nobel lecture, December 10, 1994. Translated by D. Karara. Accessed November 21, 2017. https://www.nobelprize.org/nobel_prizes/peace/laureates/1994/arafat-lecture.html.

Ardic, Nurullah. "Understanding the 'Arab Spring': Justice, Dignity, Religion, and International Politics." *Afro Eurasian Studies* 1, no. 1 (2012): 8–52.

Arendt, Hannah. "The Origins of Totalitarianism." In *The Human Rights Reader,* 2nd ed., edited by Micheline Ishay, 373–375. Abingdon, UK: Taylor and Francis Group, 2007.

Arens, Moshe. "Israel's Arabs Can Still Identify with the Jews' Tragic Fate." *Haaretz,* April 27, 2015. Accessed August 20, 2017. http://www.haaretz.com/opinion/.premium-1.653592.

Arnon, Arie. "Israeli Policy Towards the Occupied Palestinian Territories: The Economic Dimension, 1967–2007." *Middle East Journal* 61, no. 4 (2007): 573–595.

Arnon, Arie, and Daniel Gottlieb. *An Economic Analysis of the Palestinian Economy: The West Bank and Gaza, 1968–1991.* Jerusalem: Bank of Israel Research Department, 1993.

Arrighi, Giovanni, Terence K. Hopkins, and Immanuel Wallerstein. "1989, the Continuation of 1968." *Review (Fernand Braudel Center)* 15, no. 2 (1992): 221–242.

AsiaNews. "At the Louvre Abu Dhabi, Christian, Muslim and Jewish Religious Art Are Side by Side." *AsiaNews*. Accessed August 23, 2017. http://www.asianews.it/news-en/At-the-Louvre-Abu-Dhabi,-Christian,-Muslim-and-Jewish-religious-art-are-side-by-side-27741.html.

Assaad, Ragui, and Farzaneh Roudi-Fahimi. *Youth in the Middle East and North Africa: Demographic Opportunity or Challenge?* Washington, DC: Population Reference Bureau, 2007. Accessed December 9, 2018. https://www.prb.org/wp-content/uploads/2007/04/YouthinMENA.pdf.

Astell, Mary. "Some Reflections upon Marriage." In *The Portable Enlightenment Reader*, edited by Isaac Kramnick, 560–567. New York: Penguin Books, 1995.

Atia, Tarek. "Paradox of the Free Press in Egypt." Presentation, USEF Expert Panel Discussion. Washington, DC, 2004.

Attali, Jacques. *Une brève histoire de l'avenir*. Paris: Fayard, 2006.

Averroës. *Decisive Treatise and Epistle Dedicatory*. Translated by Charles E. Butterworth. Salt Lake City: Brigham Young University Press, 2001.

Avineri, Shlomo. *The Making of Modern Zionism: The Intellectual Origins of the Jewish State*. New York: Basic Books, 1981.

Avnery, Uri. "An Israeli-Palestinian Federation Is Still the Way." *Haaretz*, August 8, 2013. Accessed January 10, 2017. https://www.haaretz.com/opinion/1.540551.

Ayalon, Ami. "Why the Iran Nuclear Deal Is Good for Israel." Presentation, University of Denver, Denver, CO, August 17, 2015.

Badeeb, Saeed. "Iran's Dispute with the UAE over Three Gulf Islands." *Washington Report on Middle East Affairs*, March 1993. Accessed September 2, 2017. https://www.washingtonreport.me/1993-march/iran-s-dispute-with-the-uae-over-three-gulf-islands.html.

Badious, Alain. *The Rebirth of History*. Brooklyn: Verso, 2012.

Badran, Margot. "Between Secular and Islamic Feminism/s: Reflections on the Middle East and Beyond." *Journal of Middle East Women's Studies* 1, no. 1 (2005): 6–28.

Baker, Luke. "As Israeli Election Nears, Peace Earns Barely a Mention." Reuters, March 11, 2015. Accessed November 3, 2017. http://www.reuters.com/article/uk-israel-election-peace/as-israeli-election-nears-peace-earns-barely-a-mention-idUKKBN0M717T20150311.

Banihani, Muntaha, and Jawad Syed. "A Macro-National Level Analysis of Arab Women's Work Engagement." *European Management Review* 14, no. 2 (2017): 133–142.

Barak, On. *On Time: Technology and Temporality in Modern Egypt*. Berkeley: University of California Press, 2013.

Bar'el, Zvi. "Arab Women Breaking Silence on Domestic Violence." *Haaretz*, December 1, 2015. Accessed December 11, 2016. https://www.haaretz.com/middle-east-news/.premium-1.689336.

Barkey, Henri. *Iraq, Its Neighbors, and the United States: Competition, Crisis, and the Reordering of Power*. Washington, DC: United States Institute of Peace, 2011.

————. *Reluctant Neighbor: Turkey's Role in the Middle East.* Washington, DC: United States Institute of Peace, 1997.

Barlas, Asma. "Believing Women." In *Islam: Unreading Patriarchal Interpretations of the Qu'ran.* Austin: University of Texas Press, 2002.

Barrett, Raymond. "Bahrain Emerging as Flashpoint in Middle East Unrest." *Christian Science Monitor*, February 15, 2011. Accessed December 9, 2018. https://www.csmonitor.com/World/Middle-East/2011/0215/Bahrain-emerging-as-flashpoint-in-Middle-East-unrest.

Barsamian, David. "Interview with Edward Said." *The Progressive*, November 16, 2001. Accessed November 21, 2017. http://progressive.org/dispatches/interview-edward-w.-said/.

————. "Interview with Edward Said." *Z Magazine*, September 27, 1993, 52.

Bassiouni, M. Cherif. *Chronicles of the Egyptian Revolution and Its Aftermath, 2011–2016.* New York: Cambridge University Press, 2017.

Batha, Emma. "Syrian Refugee Crisis Is Changing Women's Roles: Aid Agency." Reuters, September 9, 2016. Accessed December 21, 2016. http://www.reuters.com/article/us-syria-refugees-women/syrian-refugee-crisis-is-changing-womens-roles-aid-agency-idUSKCN11G00W?il=0.

————. "World Is Failing Former Yazidi Sex Slaves: Amnesty International." Reuters, October 9, 2016. Accessed December 9, 2016. http://www.reuters.com/article/us-iraq-yazidi-survivors/world-is-failing-former-yazidi-sex-slaves-amnesty-international-idUSKCN12A00D.

Baumgart-Ochse, Claudia. "Opposed or Intertwined? Religious and Secular Conceptions of National Identity in Israel and the Israeli-Palestinian Conflict." *Politics, Religion and Ideology* 15, no. 3 (2014): 401–420.

BBC News. "Chile Recognises 9,800 More Victims of Pinochet's Rule." BBC, August 18, 2011. Accessed June 5, 2018. https://www.bbc.com/news/world-latin-america-14584095.

————. "Islamic State Releases 'al-Baghdadi Message.'" BBC, May 14, 2015. Accessed November 21, 2017. http://www.bbc.com/news/world-middle-east-32744070.

————. "Palestinian Election: Results in Detail." BBC, February 16, 2006. Accessed November 3, 2017. http://news.bbc.co.uk/2/hi/middle_east/4654306.stm.

————. "Rio Olympics 2016: Refugee Olympic Team Competes as 'Equal Human Beings.'" BBC, August 21, 2016. Accessed August 25, 2016. http://www.bbc.com/sport/olympics/37037273.

————. "Russia Says 63,000 Troops Have Seen Combat in Syria." BBC, August 23, 2018. Accessed December 5, 2018. https://www.bbc.com/news/world-middle-east-45284121.

Bearak, Max, and Darla Cameron. "Here Are the 10 Countries Where Homosexuality May Be Punished by Death." *Washington Post*, June 16, 2016. Accessed November 1, 2017. https://www.washingtonpost.com/news/worldviews/wp/2016/06/13/here-are-the-10-countries-where-homosexuality-may-be-punished-by-death-2/?utm_term=.3fcc37085ibf.

Beaumont, Peter. "Gaza Economy 'on Verge of Collapse,' with World's Highest Unemployment." *The Guardian*, May 22, 2015. Accessed June 10, 2016. https://www.theguardian.com/world/2015/may/22/gazas-economy-on-verge-of-collapse-jobless-rate-highest-in-world-israel.

———. "Hamas and Fatah Sign Deal over Control of Gaza Strip." *The Guardian*, October 12, 2017. Accessed November 16, 2017. https://www.theguardian.com/world/2017/oct/12/hamas-claims-deal-agreed-fatah-control-gaza-strip.

Bebel, August. *Woman and Socialism*. New York: Socialist Literature, 1910.

Beehner, Lionel. "The Effects of 'Youth Bulge' on Civil Conflicts." Council on Foreign Relations, April 13, 2007. Accessed November 1, 2015. https://www.cfr.org/backgrounder/effects-youth-bulge-civil-conflicts.

Begum, Rothna. "Gulf States Fail to Protect Domestic Workers from Serious Violence." Human Rights Watch, October 16, 2015. Accessed December 30, 2016. https://www.hrw.org/news/2015/10/16/gulf-states-fail-protect-domestic-workers-serious-violence.

"Belgium Launches Europe's First Solar Train." EuroNews, June 16, 2011. Accessed August 8, 2016. http://www.euronews.com/2011/06/16/belgium-launches-europe-s-first-solar-train.

Bell, Christine. *Peace Agreements and Human Rights*. London: Oxford University Press, 2000.

Bell, John. "Israel and Palestine: Two States and the Extra Step." Al Jazeera, May 14, 2014. Accessed January 10, 2017. http://www.aljazeera.com/indepth/opinion/2014/05/israel-palestine-two-states-ex-2014513111110913958.html.

Bellaigue, de C. "Stop Calling for a Muslim Enlightenment." *The Guardian*, February 19, 2015. Accessed August 23, 2017. https://www.theguardian.com/world/2015/feb/19/stop-calling-for-a-muslim-enlightenment.

Ben-Bassat, Yuval. "Rethinking the Concept of Ottomanization: The *Yishuv* in the Aftermath of the Youth Turk Revolution of 1908." *Middle Eastern Studies* 45, no. 3 (2009): 461–475.

Benchemsi, Ahmed. "Invisible Atheists: The Spread of Disbelief in the Arab World." *New Republic*, April 23, 2015. Accessed August 23, 2017. https://newrepublic.com/article/121559/rise-arab-atheists.

Benjamin, Walter. *Illuminations: Essays and Reflections*. Edited by Hannah Arendt. Translated by Harry Zohn. New York: Schocken Books, 2007.

Berlet, Chip. "Christian Identity: The Apocalyptic Style, Political Religion, Palingenesis and Neo-Fascism." In *Fascism, Totalitarianism and Political Religion*, edited by Robert Griffin, 175–212. New York: Routledge, 2005.

Biden, Joseph R., and Leslie Gelb. "Unity through Autonomy in Iraq." *New York Times*, May 1, 2006. Accessed August 8, 2016. http://www.nytimes.com/2006/05/01/opinion/01biden.html.

Bin Talal, El Hassan. "Memories of The Future: On the Anniversary of the Balfour Declaration." *HuffPost*, November 2, 2017. Accessed April 20, 2018. https://www.huffingtonpost.com/entry/the-anniversary-of-balfour-declaration_us_59fb1a70e4b0b0c7fa3866f7.

Bocchi, Alessandra. "Manufacturing Virginity: The Tunisian Women Choosing to 'Repair Their Honour.'" *New Arab*, June 29, 2017. Accessed November 1, 2017. https://www.alaraby.co.uk/english/society/2017/6/29/manufacturing-virginity-tunisian-women-choosing-to-repair-their-honour.

Bolton, John R. "John Bolton: To Defeat ISIS, Create a Sunni State." *New York Times*, November 24, 2015. Accessed May 23, 2018. https://www.nytimes.com/2015/11/25/opinion/john-bolton-to-defeat-isis-create-a-sunni-state.html.

Borschel-Dan, Amanda. "Western Wall Egalitarian Area Used Daily for Gender-Segregated Orthodox Prayer." *Times of Israel*, July 19, 2018. Accessed December 10, 2018. https://www.timesofisrael.com/western-walls-egalitarian-area-is-used-daily-for-sex-segregated-orthodox-prayer/.

Bowen, Jeremy. *The People Want the Fall of the Regime: The Arab Uprisings.* London: Simon and Schuster, 2012.

Bradley, John R. *After the Arab Spring: How Islamists Hijacked the Middle East Revolts.* New York: Palgrave Macmillan, 2012.

Bremmer, Ian. "Why the Syrian Civil War Is Becoming Even More Complex." *Time*, April 9, 2018. Accessed May 24, 2018. http://time.com/5229691/syria-trump-putin-saudi-arabia/.

Brinton, Crane. *The Anatomy of Revolution.* New York: Random House, 1965.

Bronner, Stephen E. *The Bigot: Why Prejudice Persists.* New Haven: Yale University Press, 2014.

———. *Peace Out of Reach: Middle Eastern Travels and the Search for Reconciliation.* Lexington: University Press of Kentucky, 2007.

———. *A Rumor about the Jews: Antisemitism, Conspiracy, and the Protocols of Zion.* Oxford: Oxford University Press, 2003.

———. *Socialism Unbound.* London: Routledge, 1990.

Bronson, Rachel. "Where Credit Is Due: The Provenance of Middle East Reform." *National Interest* 80 (2005): 107–111.

Bronstein, Scott. "For Egyptian Online Warrior, Father's Torture Fueled Activism." CNN News, June 16, 2011. Accessed May 29, 2017. http://www.cnn.com/2011/WORLD/meast/06/16/arab.unrest.irevolution/index.html.

Broomhall, Elizabeth. "Bahrain and Oman Have Highest Gulf Unemployment Rates." *Arabian Business*, July 7, 2011. Accessed July 20, 2017. http://www.arabianbusiness.com/bahrain-oman-have-highest-gulf-unemployment-rates-409116.html.

Brynen, Rex, Pete Moore, Bassel Salloukh, and Marie-Joëlle Zahar. *Beyond the Arab Spring: Authoritarianism and Democratization in the Arab World.* Boulder, CO: Lynne Rienner Publishers, 2012.

B'Tselem. *The Closure of the West Bank and Gaza Strip: Human Rights Violations against Residents of the Occupied Territories*, B'Tselem. May 1993. Accessed December 9, 2018. https://www.btselem.org/download/199304_closure_eng.doc.

———. *The Occupation's Fig Leaf: Israel's Military Law Enforcement System as a Whitewash Mechanism.* Jerusalem: B'Tselem, 2016.

Bureau of Democracy, Human Rights and Labor. *International Religious Freedom Report for 2015: Israel and the Occupied Territories*. 2015. US Department of State. Accessed February 22, 2017. https://www.state.gov/documents/organization/256481.pdf.

Burg, Avraham. "Now It's Your Turn." *Haaretz*, December 23, 2011. Accessed February 20, 2017. https://www.haaretz.com/now-it-s-your-turn-1.403059.

Burgat, François. *Islamism in the Shadow of Al-Qaeda*. Austin: University of Texas Press, 2008.

Burris, Greg. "In Tel Aviv, an Arab Spring That Ignores the Arabs." *Electronic Intifada*, September 14, 2011. Accessed August 10, 2017. https://electronicintifada.net/content/tel-aviv-arab-spring-ignores-arabs/10374.

Bush, George W. "President Discusses War on Terror." Speech. Chrysler Hall, Norfolk, VA, October 28, 2005. Accessed December 9, 2018. https://georgewbush-whitehouse.archives.gov/news/releases/2005/10/20051028-1.html.

———. "Remarks at the 20th Anniversary of the National Endowment for Democracy." Speech. United States Chamber of Commerce, Washington, DC, November 6, 2003. Accessed December 9, 2018. https://www.ned.org/remarks-by-president-george-w-bush-at-the-20th-anniversary/.

Butcher, Tim. *Blood River*. New York: Vintage Books, 2008.

Cafiero, Giorgio. "Oman Breaks from GCC on Yemen Conflict." *Al-Monitor*, May 2015. Accessed September 28, 2016. http://www.al-monitor.com/pulse/originals/2015/05/oman-response-yemen-conflict.html.

Calhoun, Craig. *Nations Matter: Culture, History and the Cosmopolitan Dream*. New York: Routledge, 2007.

Callimachi, Rukmini. "ISIS Enshrines a Theology of Rape." *New York Times*, August 13, 2015. Accessed March 15, 2016. https://www.nytimes.com/2015/08/14/world/middleeast/isis-enshrines-a-theology-of-rape.html?_r=0.

Camarasa, Violeta. "An 'Appeal to Affection and Empathy': Barcelona's Mayor Wants Spain's Cities to Welcome Refugees." *Global Voices*, September 5, 2015. Accessed September 2, 2017. https://globalvoices.org/2015/09/05/an-appeal-to-affection-and-empathy-barcelonas-mayor-wants-spains-cities-to-welcome-refugees/.

Cambanis, Thanassis. "Can a Shiite Cleric Pull Iraq Out of the Sectarian Trap?" *New York Times*, May 11, 2018. Accessed May 23, 2018. https://www.nytimes.com/2018/05/11/opinion/moktada-al-sadr-iraq.html.

Carrington, Damian. "High-Speed Euro Train Gets Green Boost from Two Miles of Solar Panels." *The Guardian*, June 6, 2011. Accessed November 3, 2017. https://www.theguardian.com/environment/2011/jun/06/tunnel-solar-belgium-rail.

Caspit, Ben. "The Israeli-Egyptian Love Affair." *Al-Monitor*, February 2016. Accessed September 2, 2017. http://www.al-monitor.com/pulse/originals/2016/02/israel-egypt-security-ties-cooperation-sinai-is-hamas-sisi.html#ixzz4JaxRQ8bg.

Center for Israel Education. "Israel's Allon Plan Is Unilaterally Presented."
    Center for Israel Education, July 26, 2017. Accessed August 10, 2017.
    https://israeled.org/allon-plan/.
Chamas, Sophie. "The Fight Goes on for Lebanon's LGBT Community."
    Al-Monitor, June 15, 2015. Accessed May 29, 2017. https://www.al-monitor.
    com/pulse/originals/2015/06/lebanon-lgbt-gay-rights-article-534-helem-
    legal-agenda.html.
Chaudhry, Ayesha. *Domestic Violence and the Islamic Tradition*. Oxford: Oxford
    University Press, 2013.
Chorin, Ethan. *Exit the Colonel*. New York: PublicAffairs, 2012.
Clawson, Patrick, and Michael Rubin. *Eternal Iran: Continuity and Chaos*. New
    York: Palgrave Macmillan, 2005.
Cleveland, William, and Martin Bunton. *A History of the Modern Middle East*, 4th
    ed. Philadelphia: Westview Press, 2009.
CNN News. "On GPS: Landis on a Syria Solution." *Fareed Zakaria GPS*,
    November 8, 2014. Accessed September 2, 2017. http://www.cnn.com/
    videos/bestoftv/2014/11/08/exp-gps-landis-sot-syria.cnn.
Cockburn, Patrick. "The Yemen War Death Toll Is Five Times Higher Than We
    Think—We Can't Shrug Off Our Responsibilities Any Longer." *Independent*,
    October 26, 2018. Accessed December 9, 2018. https://www.independent.
    co.uk/voices/yemen-war-death-toll-saudi-arabia-allies-how-many-killed-
    responsibility-a8603326.html.
Cohan, A. S. *Theories of Revolution: An Introduction*. New York: John Wiley and
    Sons, 1975.
Cohen, Lauren. "Israel: The Collapse of the Left." *Fair Observer*, January 20,
    2013. Accessed November 3, 2017. https://www.fairobserver.com/region/
    middle_east_north_africa/israel-collapse-left/.
Cohen, Mike. "Mandela's Economic Legacy Threatened by S. Africa Inequality."
    Bloomberg, December 6, 2013. Accessed December 9, 2018. https://www.
    bloomberg.com/news/articles/2013-12-06/mandela-free-market-legacy-
    imperiled-by-south-african-inequality.
Coker, Margaret. "U.S. Takes a Risk: Old Iraqi Enemies Are Now Allies." *New
    York Times*, May 11, 2018. Accessed May 23, 2018. https://www.nytimes.
    com/2018/05/11/world/middleeast/iraq-iran-election-enemies.html.
Coker, Margaret, and Rick Gladstone. "Iraqi Voters Strengthen Hand of Militia
    Leader Who Battled U.S." *New York Times*, May 14, 2018. Accessed May
    23, 2018. https://www.nytimes.com/2018/05/14/world/middleeast/iraq-
    election-moktada-al-sadr.html?rref=collection%2Ftimestopic%2FIraq%20
    Elections&action=click&contentCollection=timestopics&region=stream&mo
    dule=stream_unit&version=latest&contentPlacement=1&pgtype=collection.
Coleman, Isobel. *Paradise Beneath Her Feet*. New York: Random House, 2010.
Connor, Phillip. "Most Displaced Syrians Are in the Middle East, and about a
    Million Are in Europe." Pew Research Center, January 29, 2018. Accessed
    May 23, 2018. http://www.pewresearch.org/fact-tank/2018/01/29/where-
    displaced-syrians-have-resettled/.

Cooke, Rachel. "David Grossman: 'I Cannot Afford the Luxury of Despair.'"
The Guardian, August 28, 2010. Accessed October 7, 2015. https://www.
theguardian.com/books/2010/aug/29/david-grossman-israel-hezbollah-
interview.

Cordesman, Anthony. *Military Spending: The Other Side of Saudi Security.*
Washington, DC: Center for Strategic and International Studies, March 13,
2018. Accessed December 5, 2018. https://csis-prod.s3.amazonaws.
com/s3fs-public/publication/180311_Saudi_Military_Spending.pdf?
ZiUodawlrCwU76RaQH_sAygDb_xL3FjB.

Costello, Norma. "ISIS in Iraq: The Female Fighters That Strike Fear into
Jihadis—Because They'll Rob Them of Paradise." *The Independent*, April 10,
2016. Accessed December 11, 2016. http://www.independent.co.uk/news/
world/middle-east/isis-in-iraq-the-women-kurd-and-yazidi-fighters-that-put-
the-fear-into-jihadis-because-theyll-rob-a6977761.html.

Council of Europe. Framework Convention for the Protection of National
Minorities H (95) 10, Council of Europe (February 1995). Accessed
December 9, 2018. https://rm.coe.int/16800c10cf.

Council on Foreign Relations. "Global Conflict Tracker." December 7, 2018.
Accessed December 9, 2018. https://www.cfr.org/interactives/global-conflict-
tracker?cid=ppc-Google-grant-conflict_tracker-031116&gclid=CjwKEAiAj7TC
BRCp2Z22ue-zrj4SJACG7SBEH9uE_raTezcIufDr28x3vGe1FFlO2Y7kt4
ui1PzWKxoCO5Tw_wcB#!/conflict/war-in-yemen.

Covenant of the Islamic Resistance Movement 1988, in *The Avalon Project:
Documents in Law, History and Diplomacy.* Lillian Goldman Law Library,
Yale Law School. Accessed October 11, 2015. http://avalon.law.yale.edu/20th_
century/hamas.asp.

Daily Mail. "Feminist Protesters Strip Off in Tunisia in Support of Local Girl
Who Muslim Leaders Demanded Should Be Stoned to Death for Posing
Topless." *Daily Mail*, May 29, 2013. Accessed November 1, 2017. http://
www.dailymail.co.uk/news/article-2332776/Feminist-protesters-strip-
Tunisia-support-local-girl-Muslim-leaders-demanded-stoned-death-posing-
topless.html.

Dalacoura, Katerina. *Islam, Liberalism, and Human Rights.* New York: I. B. Tauris,
2003.

Dali-Balta, Soraya. "Palestine Red Crescent Society on Alert as Violence Spreads
across the Occupied Palestinian Territory." International Federation of Red
Cross and Red Crescent Societies, October 21, 2015. Accessed March 20,
2017. http://www.ifrc.org/en/news-and-media/news-stories/middle-east-
and-north-africa/palestine/palestine-red-crescent-society-on-alert-as-violence-
spreads-across-the-occupied-palestinian-territory-69518/.

Danahar, Paul. *The New Middle East: The World after the Arab Spring.* New York:
Bloomsbury Press, 2013.

Daoud, Kamal. "The Sexual Misery of the Arab World." *New York Times*,
February 12, 2016. Accessed December 10, 2016. https://www.nytimes.
com/2016/02/14/opinion/sunday/the-sexual-misery-of-the-arab-world.html.

Darling, Linda. *A History of Social Justice and Political Power in the Middle East: The Circle of Justice from Mesopotamia to Globalization*. New York: Routledge, 2013.

Darwish, Mahmoud. "At the Station of a Train Which Fell Off the Map." *Middle East Research and Information Project* 248, Fall 2008. Accessed July 11, 2017. http://www.merip.org/mer/mer248/station-train-which-fell-map.

———. "A Talent for Hope," in *A River Dies of Thirst* (Brooklyn: Archipelago Books, 2009), 26.

———. "The Train Passed," in *Why Did You Leave the Horse Alone?* Translated by Jeffrey Sacks. Brooklyn: Archipelago Books, 2006, 66–68.

Darwish, Nonie. *The Devil We Don't Know: The Dark Side of Revolutions in the Middle East*. Hoboken, NJ: John Wiley and Sons, 2012.

Dawisha, Adeed. *The Second Arab Awakening: Revolution, Democracy, and the Islamist Challenge from Tunis to Damascus*. New York: W. W. Norton, 2013.

Dawoud, Khaled, and Brian Whitaker. "370 Die in Egypt's Speeding Inferno." *The Guardian*, February 20, 2002. Accessed July 20, 2017. https://www.theguardian.com/world/2002/feb/21/brianwhitaker.

Declaration of Principles on Interim Self-Government Arrangements (the Oslo Accords) Distr. General A/48/486-S/26560, United Nations General Assembly (October 11, 1993). Accessed December 9, 2018. https://unispal.un.org/DPA/DPR/unispal.nsf/0/71DC8C9D96D2F0FF85256117007CB6CA.

Desai, Meghnad. *Rethinking Islamism: The Ideology of the New Terror*. New York: I. B. Tauris, 2007.

Deutscher, Isaac. *The Non-Jewish Jew: And Other Essays (Radical Thinkers)*. Edited by Tamara Deutscher. London: Oxford University Press, 1968.

Diamond, Larry, Marc Plattner, and Daniel Brumberg. *Islam and Democracy in the Middle East*. Baltimore: Johns Hopkins University Press, 2003.

Dickinson, Elizabeth. "The Case against Qatar." *Foreign Policy*, September 30, 2014. Accessed July 24, 2016. http://foreignpolicy.com/2014/09/30/the-case-against-qatar/.

Diwan, Ishac, and Radwan Shaban. *Development under Adversity: The Palestinian Economy in Transition*. Washington, DC: World Bank, 1993.

Dobbin, Frank. *Forging Industrial Policy, The United States, Britain and France in the Railway Age*. New York: Cambridge University Press, 1994.

Domonoske, Camila. "Morocco Unveils a Massive Solar Power Plant in the Sahara." NPR, February 4, 2016. Accessed September 28, 2017. http://www.npr.org/sections/thetwo-way/2016/02/04/465568055/morocco-unveils-a-massive-solar-power-plant-in-the-sahara.

Donger, Elizabeth. "Why Protesting Sexism Is Taboo in a Land of Endless Protests." *Broad Recognition*, February 23, 2011. Accessed September 3, 2017. http://www.broadrecognitionyale.com/2011/02/23/why-protesting-sexism-is-taboo-in-a-land-of-endless-protests/.

Doumato, Eleanor Abdella, and Marsha Posusney. *Women and Globalization in the Arab Middle East: Gender, Economy, and Society.* Boulder, CO: Lynne Rienner Publishers, 2003.

Due Diligence Project. *Due Diligence and State Responsibility to Eliminate Violence against Women—Region: Middle East and North Africa.* Due Diligence Project (2014).

Duff, Mark. "The Italian Jews Deported from Milan's Hidden Platform." BBC News, March 3, 2011. Accessed July 21, 2017. http://www.bbc.com/news/world-europe-12618452.

Duncan, Gillian Sarah. "Young, Rich, and Female: Private Banks Respond to Wealthy Women Clientele in the U.A.E. and G.C.C." *Gulf News Focus*, November 20, 2015. Accessed December 11, 2016. http://gulfnews.com/gn-focus/personal-finance/investment/young-rich-and-female-1.1629129.

Economist, The. "Gagged in Gaza." *The Economist*, September 24, 2016. Accessed February 22, 2017. https://www.economist.com/news/middle-east-and-africa/21707540-hamas-and-fatah-try-silence-press-gagged-gaza.

———. "Politics in Israel Is Increasingly Nationalist." *The Economist*, May 20, 2017. Accessed August 10, 2017. https://www.economist.com/news/special-report/21722031-israels-politicians-promote-religion-and-intolerance-politics-israel-increasingly.

Eddy, Melissa, and Katarina Johannsen. "Migrants Arriving in Germany Face a Chaotic Reception in Berlin." *New York Times*, November 27, 2015. Accessed February 24, 2016. https://www.nytimes.com/2015/11/27/world/europe/germany-berlin-migrants-refugees.html.

Egyptian Parliament. Constitution of the Arab Republic of Egypt (2014). Accessed October 31, 2017. https://www.constituteproject.org/constitution/Egypt_2014.pdf.

———. Egypt Penal Code, No. 58 (August 1937). Accessed October 31, 2017. http://www.refworld.org/docid/3f827fc44.html.

Ehteshami, Anoushiravan. *Dynamics of Change in the Persian Gulf: Political Economy, War and Revolution.* New York: Routledge, 2013.

El-Aref, Nevine. "Egypt's Railway Museum Inaugurated after Major Renovation." *Ahram Online*, March 3, 2016. Accessed July 21, 2017. http://english.ahram.org.eg/NewsContent/9/44/190083/Heritage/Museums/Egypts-Railway-Museum-inaugurated-after-major-reno.aspx.

Elborgh-Woytek, Katrin, Monique Newiak, Kalpana Kochhar, Stefania Fabrizio, Kangni Kpodar, Philippe Wingender, Benedict Clements, and Gerd Schwartz. *Women, Work, and the Economy: Macroeconomic Gains from Gender Equity.* Washington, DC: International Monetary Fund, September 2013.

Eldar, Akiva. "Is Israel Inching Closer to Fascism?" *Al-Monitor*, May 10, 2016. Accessed August 10, 2017. http://www.al-monitor.com/pulse/originals/2016/05/zeev-sternhell-holocaust-fascism-nationalistic-education.html#ixzz4otvhZ3ZC.

El-Feki, Shereen. "The Arab Bed Spring? Sexual Rights in Troubled Times across the Middle East and North Africa." *Reproductive Health Matters* 23 (2015): 38–44.

———. *Sex and the Citadel: Intimate Life in a Changing Arab World.* New York: Random House, 2013.

El Feki, S., B. Heilman, and G. Barker, eds. *Understanding Masculinities: Results from the International Men and Gender Equality Survey (IMAGES)—Middle East and North Africa.* Cairo and Washington, DC: UN Women and Promundo-US, 2017.

Ellis, Marc. "Yossi Beilin's Back to the Future Confederation." *Mondoweiss*, May 15, 2015. Accessed January 10, 2017. http://mondoweiss.net/2015/05/beilins-future-confederation/.

Ellouze, Maître Donia Hedda. "Work Is Freedom: Tunisian Women Step Up." *HuffPost*, March 23, 2014. Accessed December 16, 2016. https://www.huffingtonpost.com/maatre-donia-hedda-ellouze/work-is-freedom-tunisian-_b_5017264.html.

El Masry, Sarah. "Egypt's Railways: Past, Present, and Future?" *Daily News Egypt*, May 8, 2013. Accessed December 9, 2018. https://dailynewsegyptcom-mokannggxlave7h.stackpathdns.com/2013/05/08/egypts-railways-past-present-and-future/.

El Saadawi, Nawal. *Memoirs from the Women's Prison.* Berkeley: University of California Press, 1986.

———. *The Nawal El Saadawi Reader.* New York: Zed Books, 1997.

Elshahed, Mohamed. "Is Cairo's Railway Museum Lost?" *Cairobserver*, August 24, 2012. Accessed November 3, 2017. http://cairobserver.com/post/30117632943/is-cairos-railway-museum-lost#.WglF_ROPK8p.

El Sirgany, Sarah, and Hilary Clarke. "Saudi Arabia Arrests Female Activists Weeks before Lifting of Driving Ban." CNN, May 21, 2018. Accessed December 9, 2018. https://www.cnn.com/2018/05/20/middleeast/saudi-women-arrests—-intl/index.html.

Elster, Jon, Claus Offe, and Ulrich K. Preuss. *Institutional Design in Post-Communist Societies: Rebuilding the Ship at Sea (Theories of Institutional Design).* Cambridge: Cambridge University Press, 1998.

El-Swais, Maha. "Despite High Education Levels, Arab Women Still Don't Have Jobs." Washington, DC: World Bank, March 9, 2016. Accessed December 29, 2016. http://blogs.worldbank.org/arabvoices/despite-high-education-levels-arab-women-still-don-t-have-jobs.

Eltarabesh, Hamza Abu. "When Will the Train Return to Gaza?" *Electronic Intifada*, March 14, 2016. Accessed February 20, 2017. https://electronicintifada.net/content/when-will-train-return-gaza/15996.

Engels, Friedrich. "The June Revolution: The Course of the Paris Uprising." *Neue Rheinische Zeitung* 32 (July 2, 1848). Translated by the Marx-Engels Institute. Accessed June 9, 2018. https://www.marxists.org/archive/marx/works/download/Marx_Articles_from_the_NRZ.pdf.

England, Charlotte. "Saudi Women Are Campaigning Online against 'Enslavement,'" *Yahoo News*, August 31, 2016. Accessed November 3, 2017. https://www.yahoo.com/news/saudi-women-campaigning-online-against-060000513.html.

Erekat, Saeb. "As Long as Israel Continues Its Settlements, a Two-State Solution Is Impossible." *Washington Post*, October 24, 2016. Accessed May 29, 2017. https://www.washingtonpost.com/news/global-opinions/wp/2016/10/24/as-long-as-israel-continues-its-settlements-a-two-state-solution-is-impossible/?utm_term=.2a7c14ab744d.

Estrin, Daniel. "West Bank Water Crisis: Palestinians Put Blame on Israel." NPR, July 26, 2016. Accessed February 17, 2017. https://www.npr.org/2016/07/30/488027731/west-bank-water-crisis-palestinians-put-blame-on-israel.

Ettinger, Yair. "Thousands Finish Women's Peace March with Plea for Action at Netanyahu's Door." *Haaretz*, October 20, 2016. Accessed May 21, 2017. https://www.haaretz.com/israel-news/.premium-1.748288.

European Bank for Reconstruction and Development. *Enhancing Women's Voice, Agency and Participation in the Economy: Studies in Egypt, Jordan, Morocco, Tunisia and Turkey*. London: European Bank for Reconstruction and Development, 2015.

European Commission. "EU Launches New Humanitarian Programme for the Integration and Accommodation of Refugees in Greece." European Commission press release, July 26, 2017. Accessed December 9, 2018. https://ec.europa.eu/echo/news/eu-launches-new-humanitarian-programme-integration-and-accommodation-refugees-greece_en.

Fanon, Frantz. *The Wretched of the Earth*. Translated by Richard Philcox. New York: Grove Press, 2004.

Faour, Muhammad. "A Review of Citizenship Education in Arab Nations." Carnegie Endowment for International Peace, May 20, 2013. Accessed July 31, 2016. http://carnegieendowment.org/2013/05/20/review-of-citizenship-education-in-arab-nations-pub-51771.

Fareed, Aisha. "Saudi Social Media Users Break Silence on Violence against Women." *Arab News*, February 13, 2017. Accessed October 31, 2017. http://www.arabnews.com/node/1053516/saudi-arabia.

Farsakh, Leila. "The One-State Solution and the Israeli-Palestinian Conflict: Palestinian Challenges and Prospects." *Middle East Journal* 65, no. 1 (2011): 55–71.

Fasanotti, Frederica. "A Confederal Model for Libya." Brookings Institute, July 6, 2016. Accessed August 7, 2016. https://www.brookings.edu/blog/order-from-chaos/2016/07/06/a-confederal-model-for-libya/.

Fayed, Ammar. "Is the Crackdown on the Muslim Brotherhood Pushing the Group toward Violence?" Brookings Institute, March 23, 2016. Accessed August 23, 2017. https://www.brookings.edu/research/is-the-crackdown-on-the-muslim-brotherhood-pushing-the-group-toward-violence/.

Feldman, Noah. *After Jihad: America and the Struggle for Islamic Democracy.* New York: Farrar, Straus and Giroux, 2003.

Fernea, Elizabeth Warnock. *Women and the Family in the Middle East: New Voices of Change.* Austin: University of Texas Press, 1985.

Filali, Azza. *Les Intranquilles.* Tunis: Éditions Elyzad, 2014.

Filc, Daniel, and Udi Lebel. "The Post-Oslo Radical Right in Comparative Perspective: Leadership, Voter Characteristics, and Political Discourse." *Mediterranean Politics* 10, no. 1 (2005): 85–97.

Filiu, Jean-Pierre. *The Arab Revolution: Ten Lessons from the Democratic Uprising.* London: C. Hurst, 2011.

Fischer, Stanley, Patricia Alonso-Gamo, and Ulric Erickson von Allmen. "Economic Developments in the West Bank and Gaza since Oslo." *Economic Journal* 111, no. 472 (2001): 254–275.

Foley, Sean. *The Arab Gulf States: Beyond Oil and Islam.* Boulder, CO: Lynne Rienner Publishers, 2010.

Foran, John. *Taking Power: On the Origins of Third World Revolutions.* Cambridge: Cambridge University Press, 2005.

Foreign Policy. "Art Is a Window to the Arab World's Soul." *Foreign Policy,* May 3, 2016. Accessed August 23, 2017. http://foreignpolicy.com/2016/05/03/art-is-a-window-to-the-arab-worlds-soul/.

Foss, Daniel, and Ralph Larkin. *Beyond Revolution: A New Theory of Social Movements.* South Hadley, MA: Bergin and Garvey Publishers, 1986.

Fraihat, Ibrahim. *Unfinished Revolutions: Yemen, Libya, and Tunisia after the Arab Spring.* New Haven: Yale University Press, 2016.

Franklin, Benjamin. "Pennsylvania Assembly: Reply to the Governor, 11 November 1755." Founders Online, National Archives. Accessed September 1, 2017. https://founders.archives.gov/documents/Franklin/01-06-02-0107.

Freedman, Samuel. "Are Jews Who Fled Arab Lands to Israel Refugees, Too?" *New York Times,* October 11, 2003. Accessed August 23, 2017. http://www.nytimes.com/2003/10/11/arts/are-jews-who-fled-arab-lands-to-israel-refugees-too.html?mcubz=0.

Freedom House. *Freedom in the World: Anxious Dictators, Wavering Democracies: Global Freedom under Pressure.* Washington, DC: Freedom House, 2016. Accessed July 27, 2016. https://freedomhouse.org/report/freedom-world/freedom-world-2016.

———. *Freedom in the World: Democratic Breakthroughs in the Balance.* Washington, DC: Freedom House, 2013. Accessed July 27, 2016. https://freedomhouse.org/report/freedom-world/freedom-world-2013.

———. *Freedom of the Press Report 2010: Bahrain.* Washington, DC: Freedom House, 2010. Accessed July 4, 2018. https://freedomhouse.org/report/freedom-press/2010/bahrain.

———. *Freedom of the Press Report 2016: Israel.* Washington, DC: Freedom House, 2016. Accessed October 31, 2017. https://freedomhouse.org/report/freedom-press/2016/israel.

————. *Freedom of the Press Report 2016: West Bank and Gaza Strip* (2016). Washington, DC: Freedom House, 2015. Accessed October 31, 2017. https://freedomhouse.org/report/freedom-press/2016/west-bank-and-gaza-strip.

————. *Freedom on the Net: Tunisia*. Washington, DC: Freedom House, 2015. Accessed November 3, 2017. https://freedomhouse.org/sites/default/files/resources/FOTN%202015_Tunisia.pdf.

Freemuse. "Protest Singer Ibrahim Kashoush Had His Throat Cut." *FreeMuse*, July 6, 2011. Accessed September 20, 2015. https://freemuse.org/news/syria-protest-singer-ibrahim-kashoush-had-his-throat-cut/.

French, David. "Palestinian Reasoning: Yield to Our Crazy Religious Intolerance or We'll Kill You." *National Review*, October 13, 2015. Accessed June 15, 2016. http://www.nationalreview.com/article/425498/palestinian-reasoning-yield-our-crazy-religious-intolerance-or-well-kill-you-david.

"French in Tunis, The." *Argus* (Melbourne), 1881. Accessed September 23, 2015. http://trove.nla.gov.au/ndp/del/article/11523985.

Friedberg, R., and R. M. Sauer. "The Effects of Foreign Guest Workers in Israel on the Labor Market Outcomes of Palestinians from the West Bank and Gaza Strip." Jerusalem: Maurice Falk Institute for Economic Research in Israel, 2003.

Friedman, Thomas. *Thank You for Being Late: An Optimist's Guide to Thriving in the Age of Accelerations*. New York: Farrar, Straus and Giroux, 2016.

————. "The Virtual Mosque: Moderates in Iran Turn to Facebook and Twitter." *New York Times*, June 16, 2009. Accessed July 21, 2017. http://www.nytimes.com/2009/06/17/opinion/17friedman.html.

Furstenberg, Rochelle. "Israeli Life: Who Gets to Be a Millionaire?" *Hadassah Magazine* 82, no. 6 (February 2001).

Galilei, Galileo. "Dialogue Concerning the Two Chief World Systems." 1632. Translated by Stillman Drake, condensed by S. E. Sciortino, 1953. Accessed September 4, 2017. https://math.dartmouth.edu/~matc/Readers/renaissance.astro/7.3.DialogueDay3.html.

Gandhi, M. K. *Hind Swaraj or Indian Home Rule*. Edited by Jitendra Desai. Ahmedabad: Navjivan Publishing House, 1998.

Gelvin, James. *The Arab Uprisings: What Everyone Needs to Know*. New York: Oxford University Press, 2012.

Gendzier, Irene. *Dying to Forget: Oil, Power, Palestine, and the Foundations of U.S. Policy in the Middle East*. New York: Columbia University Press, 2015.

Gheytanchi, Elham, and Valentine Moghadam. "Women, Social Protests, and the New Media Activism in the Middle East and North Africa." *International Review of Modern Sociology* 40, no. 1 (2014): 1–26.

Ghilés, Francis. "Doubts Remain about Reopening the Algeria-Morocco Border." Barcelona Centre for International Affairs, January 2016. Accessed August 21, 2017. https://www.cidob.org/en/publications/publication_series/opinion/mediterraneo_y_oriente_medio/doubts_remain_about_reopening_the_algeria_morocco_border/(language)/eng-US.

Gjelten, Tom. "State Department Declares ISIS Attacks on Christians Constitute Genocide." NPR, *All Things Considered*, March 17, 2016. Accessed August 4, 2017. http://www.npr.org/2016/03/17/470861310/state-department-declares-isis-attacks-on-christians-constitute-genocide.

Glendon, Mary Ann. *A World Made New: Eleanor Roosevelt and the Universal Declaration of Human Rights*. New York: Random House, 2002.

Goldfischer, David, and Micheline Ishay. "Belligerent Fundamentalism and the Legacy of European Fascism." *Fletcher Forum of World Affairs* 32, no. 1 (2008): 63–82.

Goldschmidt, Arthur, Jr., and Lawrence Davidson. *A Concise History of the Middle East*, 9th ed. Philadelphia: Westview Press, 2010.

Goldstone, Jack, ed. *Revolutions: Theoretical, Comparative, and Historical Studies*, 3rd ed. Ontario: Thomson Wadsworth, 2003.

Gordon, Neve. *Israel's Occupation*. Berkeley: University of California Press, 2008.

Graham, David. "How Did the 'Secret' Sykes-Picot Agreement Become Public?" *The Atlantic*, May 2015. Accessed September 10, 2016. https://www.theatlantic.com/international/archive/2016/05/sykes-picot-centennial/482904/.

Gramsci, Antonio. *Selections from the Prison Notebooks*. Edited by Quintin Hoare and Geoffrey Nowell Smith. New York: International Publishers, 1971.

Griffin, Roger. "Fascism." In *Encyclopedia of Fundamentalism*, edited by Brenda Brasher, 171–178. New York: Routledge, 2001.

Gross, Judah. "After Six Day War, Cabinet Debated West Bank's Future—and Charles de Gaulle's Nose." *Times of Israel*, May 28, 2017. Accessed August 10, 2017. http://www.timesofisrael.com/after-six-day-war-cabinet-debated-west-banks-future-and-charles-de-gaulles-nose/.

Grossman, David. "An Israel without Illusions." *New York Times*, July 14, 2014. Accessed February 28, 2017. https://www.nytimes.com/2014/07/28/opinion/david-grossman-end-the-grindstone-of-israeli-palestinian-violence.html.

Guidère, Mathieu. *Sexe et Charia*. Monaco: Éditions du Rocher, 2014.

Guizani, Emna. "Train from Tunis to Casablanca, New High-Speed Link between Morocco, Algeria and Tunisia." *TunisiaLive*, April 27, 2015. Accessed September 2, 2017. https://www.railwaynews.net/new-high-speed-link-between-morocco-algeria-and-tunisia.html.

Gulf Research Center. "Gulf Labor Markets and Migration." Gulf Research Center, April 20, 2016. Accessed December 9, 2018. http://gulfmigration.org/gcc-total-population-percentage-nationals-foreign-nationals-gcc-countries-national-statistics-2010-2016-numbers/.

Gurung, Ganesh, and Padma Khatiwada. *Nepali Women in the Middle East: A Situation Report*. Kathmandu: Nepal Institute of Development Studies, 2013.

Haas, Mark, and David Lesch, eds. *The Arab Spring: Change and Resistance in the Middle East*. Boulder, CO: Westview Press, 2013.

Haddad, Bassam, Rosie Bsheer, and Ziad Abu-Rish, eds. *The Dawn of the Arab Uprisings: End of an Old Order?* London: Pluto Press, 2012.

Hafez, Sherine. "Bodies That Protest: The Girl in the Blue Bra, Sexuality, and State Violence in Revolutionary Egypt." *Signs: Journal of Women in Culture and Society* 40, no. 1 (2014): 20–28.

Hajjaji, Danya. "Libya Art Exhibit Paints Bleak Picture of Post-Arab Spring Society." *Al-Monitor*, April 19, 2017. Accessed November 3, 2017. https://www.al-monitor.com/pulse/originals/2017/04/libya-tripoli-art-exhibition-warning.html.

Halliday, Fred. *Islam and the Myth of Confrontation: Religion and Politics in the Middle East*. New York: I. B. Tauris, 1995.

———. "1967 and the Consequences of Catastrophe." *Middle East Research and Information Project* 17, no. 146 (1987). Accessed November 21, 2017. http://www.merip.org/mer/mer146/1967-consequences-catastrophe.

Hammond, Andrew. *Popular Culture in the Arab World: Arts, Politics, and the Media*. Cairo: American University in Cairo Press, 2007.

Hamza, Wadia. "The Maghreb Union Is One of the World's Worst-Performing Trading Blocs. Here Are Five Ways to Change That." Cologny, Switzerland: World Economic Forum, June 2017. Accessed August 21, 2017. https://www.weforum.org/agenda/2017/06/five-ways-to-make-maghreb-work/.

Hanieh, Adam. "From State-Led Growth to Globalization: The Evolution of Israeli Capitalism." *Journal of Palestinian Studies* 32, no. 4 (2003): 5–21.

Har-El, Shai. "Sharing Land for Peace: Revisiting Israel-Palestine's Confederate Future." *World Policy Blog*, February 5, 2013. Accessed November 17, 2015. http://www.worldpolicy.org/blog/2013/02/05/sharing-land-peace-revisiting-israel-palestines-confederate-future.

Harkov, Lahav. "PM: Jewish Killer of Palestinian Family Also Deserves Death Penalty." *Jerusalem Post*, January 3, 2018. Accessed May 4, 2018. https://www.jpost.com/Arab-Israeli-Conflict/PM-Jewish-killer-of-Palestinian-family-also-deserves-death-penalty-532750.

Hasan, Mehdi. "Why Islam Doesn't Need a Reformation." *The Guardian*, May 17, 2015. Accessed July 29, 2016. https://www.theguardian.com/commentisfree/2015/may/17/islam-reformation-extremism-muslim-martin-luther-europe.

Hashemi, Nader. *Islam, Secularism and Liberal Democracy*. Oxford: Oxford University Press, 2009.

Hashemi, Nader, and Danny Postel, eds. *The People Reloaded: The Green Movement and the Struggle for Iran's Future*. Brooklyn: Melville House Publishing, 2010.

———. *Sectarianization: Mapping the New Politics of the Middle East*. New York: Oxford University Press, 2017.

———. *The Syria Dilemma*. Cambridge: MIT Press, 2013.

Hashemite Kingdom of Jordan. *Amman Message*. Amman: Hashemite Kingdom of Jordan, 2004.

Hashimi, Muhammad Ali. *The Ideal Muslimah*. Riyadh: International Islamic Publishing House, 2005.

Hastedt, Glenn. *Understanding the War in Iraq: Insights from History, International Politics, and American Foreign Policy*. New Jersey: Pearson Prentice Hall, 2004.

Hatuqa, Dalia. "What Not to Expect from a Palestinian Unity Deal." *The Atlantic*, October 13, 2017. Accessed October 31, 2017. https://www.theatlantic.com/ international/archive/2017/10/palestinian-unity-deal/542754/.

Havel, Vaclav. *The Power of the Powerless*. New York: M. E. Sharpe, 1979.

Heath, Thomas. "Oil Prices Creed Higher as OPEC Wrestles with Trump's Call to Increase Production." *Washington Post*, September 27, 2018. Accessed December 10, 2018. https://www.washingtonpost.com/business/2018/ 09/27/oil-prices-creep-higher-opec-wrestles-with-trumps-call-increase-production/?noredirect=on&utm_term=.a2df6758bbd5.

Hegel, G. W. *The Philosophy of Right*. Translated by T. M. Knox. Cambridge: Oxford University Press, 1967.

Herzog, Isaac. "Only Separation Can Lead to a Two-State Solution." *New York Times*, February 28, 2016. Accessed February 20, 2017. https://www.nytimes. com/2016/02/29/opinion/international/only-separation-can-lead-to-a-two-state-solution.html.

Hirschauge, Orr, and Rory Jones. "Israel Builds Railway in Hope of Boosting Commerce with Arab Neighbors." *Wall Street Journal*, June 22, 2016. Accessed August 5, 2016. https://www.wsj.com/articles/israel-builds-railway-in-hope-of-boosting-commerce-with-arab-neighbors-1466614190.

Hirschman, Albert, "Political Economics and Possibilism." In *A Bias for Hope: Essays on Development and Latin America*, 1–34. New Haven: Yale University Press, 1971.

Hirsh, Michael. "Team Trump's Message: The Clash of Civilizations Is Back." *Politico*, November 20, 2016. Accessed July 20, 2017. http://www.politico. com/magazine/story/2016/11/donald-trump-team-islam-clash-of-civilizations-214474.

Hobsbawm, Eric J. *The Age of Extremes: A History of the World, 1914–1991*. New York: Vintage Books, 1994.

———. *The Age of Revolution, 1789–1848*. London: Weidenfeld and Nicolson, 1962.

Holodny, Elena. "47 Countries Where Young People Are Living in an Unemployment Crisis." *Business Insider—Markets*, December 3, 2015. Accessed July 20, 2017. https://www.businessinsider.com/countries-with-worst-youth-unemployment-2015-11.

Holtham, Alice. "Solar Energy to Generate 75 percent of Dubai's Power by 2050." *What's On*, February 13, 2018. Accessed May 23, 2018. http://whatson.ae/ dubai/2018/02/75-per-cent-power-generated-solar-energy-2050/.

Honwana, Alcinda. *Youth and Revolution in Tunisia*. New York: Zed Books, 2013.

Horkheimer, Max. "Authority and the Family." In *Critical Theory: Selected Essays*, edited by Matthew J. O'Connell, 47–128. New York: Continuum, 1982.

Hourani, Albert. *Arabic Thought in the Liberal Age, 1798–1939*. New York: Cambridge University Press, 1983.

Hroub, Khaled. "Hamas after Shaykh Yasin and Rantisi." *Journal of Palestine Studies* 33, no. 4 (2004): 21–38.

Huebler, Friedrich, and Lu Weixin. *Adult and Youth Literacy: National, Regional and Global Trends, 1985–2015.* Montreal: United Nations Educational, Scientific, and Cultural Organization, 2013.

Hugo, Victor. *Les Misérables,* vol. 5. Translated by Lascelles Wraxall. Boston: Little, Brown, 1887.

Hulse, J. F. *Railroads and Revolutions: The Story of Roy Hoard.* El Paso: Mangan Books, 1986.

Human Rights First. *Islam and Equality: Debating the Future of Women's and Minority Rights in the Middle East and North Africa.* New York: Lawyers Committee for Human Rights, 1999.

Human Rights Watch. *Boxed In: Women and Saudi Arabia's Male Guardianship System.* New York: Human Rights Watch, July 16, 2016. Accessed May 21, 2017. https://www.hrw.org/report/2016/07/16/boxed/women-and-saudi-arabias-male-guardianship-system#page.

———. *"I Already Bought You": Abuse and Exploitation of Female Migrant Domestic Workers in the United Arab Emirates.* New York: Human Rights Watch, October 22, 2014. Accessed November 21, 2017. https://www.hrw.org/report/2014/10/22/i-already-bought-you/abuse-and-exploitation-female-migrant-domestic-workers-united.

———. *Internal Fight: Palestinian Abuses in Gaza and the West Bank.* New York: Human Rights Watch, 2008. Accessed July 12, 2018. https://www.hrw.org/reports/2008/iopt0708/iopt0708web.pdf.

———. "Iraq: ISIS Escapees Describe Systematic Rape." Human Rights Watch, April 4, 2014. Accessed March 16, 2016. https://www.hrw.org/news/2015/04/14/iraq-isis-escapees-describe-systematic-rape.

———. "Oman: Events of 2015." In *World Report 2016.* New York: Human Rights Watch, 2016. Accessed November 21, 2017. https://www.hrw.org/world-report/2016/country-chapters/oman.

———. "Palestine: Crackdown on Journalists, Activists Chilling Effect on Free Expression." Human Rights Watch, August 29, 2016. Accessed February 22, 2017. https://www.hrw.org/news/2016/08/29/palestine-crackdown-journalists-activists.

———. "Qatar: Events of 2015." In *World Report 2016.* New York: Human Rights Watch, 2016. Accessed November 20, 2016. https://www.hrw.org/world-report/2016/country-chapters/qatar.

———. "Saudi Arabia: 'Unofficial' Guardianship Rules Banned: Authorities Should Abolish the Entire System." Human Rights Watch, May 9, 2017. Accessed May 21, 2017. https://www.hrw.org/news/2017/05/09/saudi-arabia-unofficial-guardianship-rules-banned.

———. "Tunisia: Events of 2015." In *World Report 2016.* New York: Human Rights Watch, 2016. Accessed November 20, 2016. https://www.hrw.org/world-report/2016/country-chapters/tunisia.

Ibrahim, Raymond. *The Al Qaeda Reader.* New York: Doubleday, 2007.

Immerzeel, Walter, Peter Droogers, Wilco Terink, Jippe Hoogeveen, Petra Hellegers, Mark Bierkens, and Van Rens Beek. *Middle-East and Northern*

Africa Water Outlook. FutureWater Report 98. Wageningen, The Netherlands: FutureWater, 2011.

Inanc, Yusef. "Salafis and the Muslim Brotherhood: Egypt's Rival Islamist Groups." *Daily Sabah,* May 7, 2014. Accessed August 23, 2017. https://www. dailysabah.com/feature/2014/05/07/salafis-and-the-muslim-brotherhood-egypts-rival-islamist-groups.

Independent Commission on International Humanitarian Issues. *Winning the Human Race? The Report of the Independent Commission on International Humanitarian Issues.* London: Zed Books, 1998.

Inhorn, Marcia. *The New Arab Man: Emergent Masculinities, Technologies, and Islam in the Middle East.* Princeton: Princeton University Press, 2012.

International Covenant on Civil and Political Rights, 14668 U.N.T.S. 999, United Nations General Assembly (March 23, 1976).

International Covenant on Economic, Social and Cultural Rights, 14531 U.N.T.S. 993, United Nations General Assembly (January 3, 1976).

International Crisis Group. "Radical Islam in Gaza." Middle East Report 104, March 29, 2011. Accessed November 22, 2017. https://www.crisisgroup.org/ middle-east-north-africa/eastern-mediterranean/israelpalestine/radical-islam-gaza.

International Monetary Fund. "IMF Executive Board Approves US$12 Billion Extended under the Extended Fund Facility for Egypt." International Monetary Fund, November 11, 2016. Accessed September 1, 2017. https:// www.imf.org/en/News/Articles/2016/11/11/PR16501-Egypt-Executive-Board-Approves-12-billion-Extended-Arrangement.

———. "Qatar: Staff Concluding Statement." International Monetary Fund, March 5, 2018. Accessed December 11, 2018. https://www.imf.org/en/News/ Articles/2018/03/05/ms030518-qatar-staff-concluding-statement-for-the-2018-article-iv-mission.

———. *West Bank and Gaza: Report to the Ad Hoc Liaison Committee.* Jerusalem and Ramallah: International Monetary Fund, 2014.

International Renewable Energy Agency (IRENA). *Renewable Capacity Statistics 2018.* Abu Dhabi: IRENA, 2018. Accessed December 5, 2018. https://www. irena.org/-/media/Files/IRENA/Agency/Publication/2018/Mar/IRENA_RE_Capacity_Statistics_2018.pdf.

International Trade Center News. "What Did the Middle East and North Africa Trade in 2017?" International Trade Center, July 6, 2018. Accessed December 9, 2018. http://www.intracen.org/news/What-did-the-Middle-East-and-North-Africa-trade-in-2017/.

Internet Social Forum. "About Us." Internet Social Forum, 2018. Accessed July 12, 2018. http://internetsocialforum.net/isf/?page_id=927.

———. "Tunis Resolution." Internet Social Forum, 2015. Accessed August 23, 2017. http://internetsocialforum.net/isf/?page_id=832.

Ioanid, Radu. "The Sacralised Politics of the Romanian Iron Guard." In *Fascism, Totalitarianism, and Political Religion,* edited by Roger Griffin, 125–189. New York: Routledge, 2005.

Isaac, Jeffrey C. *Democracy in Dark Times*. Ithaca: Cornell University Press, 1998.

Isaacman, Allen. "Peasants and Rural Social Protest in Africa." *African Studies Review* 33, no. 2 (1990): 1–120.

Ishay, Micheline. "Globalization, Religion, and Nationalism in Israel and Palestine." In *Between Terror and Tolerance: Religious Leaders, Conflict, and Peacemaking*, edited by Timothy Sisk, 69–84. Washington, DC: Georgetown University Press, 2011.

———. *The History of Human Rights: From Ancient Times to the Globalization Era*. Berkeley: University of California Press, 2008.

———, ed. *The Human Rights Reader: Major Political Essays, Speeches, and Documents from Ancient Times to the Present*, 2nd ed. New York: Routledge, 2007.

———. *Internationalism and Its Betrayal*. Minneapolis: University of Minneapolis Press, 1995.

———. "The Spring of Arab Nations? Paths toward Democratic Transition." *Philosophy and Social Criticism* 39, no. 4–5 (2013): 373–383.

———. "Violent Islamism beyond Borders: Can Human Rights Prevail?" *Philosophy and Social Criticism* 42, no. 4–5 (2016): 363–374.

Ishay, Micheline, and David Kretzmer. "Reclaiming Human Rights: Alternative Approach to the Israeli-Palestinian Conflict." In *Israel and Palestine: Alternative Perspectives on Statehood*, edited by John Ehrenberg and Yoav Peled, 77–94. Lanham, MD: Rowman and Littlefield, 2016.

Islamic Resistance Movement, The (Hamas). "A Document of General Principles and Policies," May 1, 2017. Accessed September 11, 2017. http://hamas.ps/en/post/678/a-document-of-general-principles-and-policies.

Islamopedia. "Personal Status Code." Islamopedia. Accessed October 31, 2017. http://www.islamopediaonline.org/country-profile/tunisia/islam-and-legal-system/personal-status-code.

Israeli, Raphael. "State and Religion in the Emerging Palestinian Entity." *Journal of Church and State* 44, no. 2 (2002): 229–248.

Israel Population and Immigration Authority. "Labor Migration to Israel." 2016. Accessed November 22, 2017. https://www.gov.il/BlobFolder/reports/foreign_workers_in_israel_2016_report/he/foreign_workers_israel_review_0916.pdf.

Israeli Knesset. The Wye River Memorandum (October 23, 1998). Accessed October 31, 2017. http://www.mfa.gov.il/mfa/foreignpolicy/peace/guide/pages/the%20wye%20river%20memorandum.aspx

Isseroff, Amy. "Biography of Hassan Nasrallah." MidEast Web. Accessed October 16, 2007. http://www.mideastweb.org/bio-nasrallah.htm.

Jacobson, Thomas. *Ambassador Charles Malik and the Universal Declaration of Human Rights*. Colorado Springs: Focus on the Family, International Government Affairs Department, August 28, 2008. Accessed December 10, 2018. http://www.idppcenter.com/UDHR-Dr_Malik_book_summary.pdf.

Jahal, Entsar Abu. "New Initiative Aims to Protect Palestinian Working Women." *Al-Monitor*, October 18, 2016. Accessed January 8, 2017. https://www.

al-monitor.com/pulse/originals/2016/10/palestine-labor-employed-woman-rights-guideline.html.

Jamal, Amal. "Beyond Traditional Sovereignty Theory in Conflict Resolution: Lessons from Israel/Palestine." In *Israel and Palestine: Alternative Perspectives on Statehood*, edited by John Ehrenberg and Yoav Peled, 337–364. Lanham, MD: Rowman and Littlefield, 2016.

Jamali, Mohammed Fadhel. *Inside the Arab Nationalist Struggle: Memoirs of an Iraqi Statesman.* London: I. B. Tauris, 2012.

Jankowicz, Mia. "Jailed for Using Grindr: Homosexuality in Egypt." *The Guardian*, April 3, 2017. Accessed May 29, 2017. https://www.theguardian.com/global-development-professionals-network/2017/apr/03/jailed-for-using-grindr-homosexuality-in-egypt.

Jankowski, James, and Israel Gershoni, eds. *Rethinking Nationalism in the Arab Middle East.* New York: Columbia University Press, 1997.

Jefferis, Jennifer. *Religion and Political Violence: Sacred Protest in the Modern World.* New York: Routledge, 2010.

Jewish People's Council. The Declaration of the Establishment of the State of Israel. May 14, 1948. Accessed October 31, 2017. http://www.mfa.gov.il/mfa/foreignpolicy/peace/guide/pages/declaration%20of%20establishment%20of%20state%20of%20israel.aspx.

Jewish Telegraphic Agency. "General Assembly Places Resolution on Religious Persecution on Agenda." *JTA Daily News Bulletin*, November 11, 1946. Accessed July 12, 2018. http://pdfs.jta.org/1946/1946-11-11_257.pdf?_ga=2.259389578.1038213711.1531388889-1518379262.1531388889.

Jewish Virtual Library. "Fact Sheet: Jewish Refugees from Arab Countries." December 2015. Accessed December 14, 2016. http://www.jewishvirtuallibrary.org/jewish-refugees-from-arab-countries.

———. "Israeli Settlements: Jewish Settlements Established in Palestine/Israel." 2008. Accessed November 3, 2017. http://www.jewishvirtuallibrary.org/jewish-settlements-established-in-palestine-israel-1870-1997.

Jibril, Mahmoud. "Making Sense of Libya." Presentation at Josef Korbel School of International Studies, University of Denver. Denver, CO, September 26, 2016.

Kamrava, Mehran. *The Modern Middle East: A Political History Since the First World War*, 2nd ed. Berkeley: University of California Press, 2011.

Kant, Immanuel. *An Answer to the Question: "What Is Enlightenment?"* Translated by H. B. Nisbet. London: Penguin Books, 2009.

———. *Religion within the Limits of Reason Alone.* Translated by Theodore Greene and Hoyt Hudson. New York: Harper and Row, 1960.

———. "To Perpetual Peace: A Philosophical Sketch." In *Perpetual Peace and Other Essays*, translated by Ted Humphrey, 107–144. Indianapolis: Hackett, 1983.

Kanter, James, and Andrew Higgins. "E.U. Offers Turkey 3 Billion Euros to Stem Migrant Flow." *New York Times*, November 29, 2015. Accessed October 31, 2017. https://www.nytimes.com/2015/11/30/world/europe/eu-offers-turkey-3-billion-euros-to-stem-migrant-flow.html.

Kav LaOved. "The Population of Labor Migrants in Israel." *Annual Report*, 2006. Accessed December 10, 2018. https://hotline.org.il/wp-content/uploads /2006_Annual_Activities_Report.pdf.

Kawczynski, Daniel. *Seeking Gaddafi: Libya, the West, and the Arab Spring*. London: Biteback Publishing, 2010.

Kchaou, Mounir. *Le juste et ses normes: John Rawls et le concept du politique*. Tunis: Publications de la Faculté des Sciences Humaines et Sociales, 2007.

Keck, Margaret E., and Kathryn Sikkink. *Activists beyond Borders: Advocacy Networks in International Politics*. New York: Cornell University Press, 1998.

Keddie, Nikkie. *Women in the Middle East: Past and Present*. Princeton: Princeton University Press, 2007.

Kelly, Sanja, and Julia Breslin, eds. *Women's Rights in the Middle East and North Africa*. Plymouth, UK: Rowman and Littlefield, 2010.

Kenez, Peter. *The Birth of the Propaganda State: Soviet Methods of Mass Mobilization, 1917–1929*. Cambridge: Cambridge University Press, 1985.

Kennedy, Hugh. *The Great Arab Conquests*. Philadelphia: Da Capo Press, 2007.

Kershner, Isabel. "Support for Palestinian Authority Erodes as Prices and Taxes Rise." *New York Times*, February 1, 2012. Accessed July 10, 2016. http://www. nytimes.com/2012/02/01/world/middleeast/palestinian-authority-faces-protests-as-prices-rise.html.

Khader, Naser. "We Need a Muslim Reformation." *Newsweek*, March 26, 2015. Accessed August 23, 2017. http://www.newsweek.com/we-need-muslim-reformation-316906.

Khalaf, Roula. "The Search for a Muslim Martin Luther." *Financial Times*, January 14, 2015. Accessed August 16, 2016. https://www.ft.com/content/56682e1e-9bd7-11e4-b6cc-00144feabdc0.

Khaldûn, Ibn. *The Muqaddimah*. Edited by N. J. Dawood, translated by Franz Rosenthal. Princeton: Princeton University Press, 2015.

Khaleej Times. "Shops Sacked, Train Station Burned in Tunisia." *Khaleej Times*, January 15, 2011. Accessed September 24, 2015. https://www.khaleejtimes. com/article/20110115/ARTICLE/301159867/1016.

Khalidi, Rashid. *Brokers of Deceit: How the US Has Undermined Peace in the Middle East*. Boston: Beacon Press, 2013.

———. *Resurrecting Empire: Western Footprints and America's Perilous Path in the Middle East*. Boston: Beacon Press, 2004.

Khalidi, Rashid, Lisa Anderson, Muhammad Muslih, and Reeva Simon, eds. *The Origins of Arab Nationalism*. New York: Columbia University Press, 1991.

Khamis, S. "The Role of New Arab Satellite Channels in Fostering Intercultural Dialogue: Can Al Jazeera English Bridge the Gap?" In *New Media and the New Middle East*, edited by P. Seib, 39–52. New York: Palgrave Macmillan, Series in International Political Communication (2007): 39–51.

Khan, Tahira S. *Beyond Honour: A Historical Materialist Explanation of Honour Related Violence*. Oxford: Oxford University Press, 2006.

Khanna, Parag. *Connectography: Mapping the Future of Global Civilization*. New York: Random House, 2016.

Kimmel, Michael. *Revolution: A Sociological Interpretation.* Philadelphia: Temple University Press, 1990.

Kingdom of Saudi Arabia. *Vision 2030,* April 25, 2016. Accessed December 10, 2018. https://vision2030.gov.sa/download/file/fid/417.

Kingsley, Patrick. "80 Sexual Assaults in One Day—The Other Story of Tahrir Square." *The Guardian,* July 5, 2013. Accessed September 2, 2017. https:// www.theguardian.com/world/2013/jul/05/egypt-women-rape-sexual-assault-tahrir-square.

Kipling, Rudyard. "The White Man's Burden." *Modern History Sourcebook: Rudyard Kipling, The White Man's Burden,* 1899. Fordham University. Accessed August 18, 2008. http://legacy.fordham.edu/halsall/mod/kipling.asp.

Kirchgaessner, Stephanie, and Julian Borger. "Trump Aide Drew Plan on Napkin to Partition Libya into Three." *The Guardian,* April 10, 2017. Accessed September 2, 2017. https://www.theguardian.com/world/2017/apr/10/libya-partition-trump-administration-sebastian-gorka.

Kirkpatrick, David, and Alan Cowell. "Egyptian Government Figures Join Protesters." *Truthout,* February 4, 2011. Accessed August 1, 2017. http:// truth-out.org/archive/component/k2/item/94321-egyptian-government-figures-join-protesters?Itemid=228article.

Kleiman, Ephraim. "The Conditions of Economic Viability." *Palestine-Israel Journal* 14, no. 3 (2007): 15–21.

Kraft, Joseph. "Letter from Iran." *New Yorker,* December 18, 1978. Accessed November 18, 2017. https://www.newyorker.com/magazine/1978/12/18/letter-from-iran.

Kretzmer, David. "The Law of Belligerent Occupation as a System of Control: Dressing up Exploitation in Respectable Garb." In *Impacts of Lasting Occupation: Lessons from Israeli Society,* edited by Daniel Bar-Tal and Izhak Schnell, 31–61. New York: Oxford University Press, 2013.

Kumar, Isabelle. "David Grossman: Israelis 'More Prone to Fanaticism and Fundamentalism.'" *EuroNews,* March 3, 2016. Accessed August 10, 2017. http://www.euronews.com/2016/03/17/david-grossman-israelis-more-prone-to-fanaticism-and-fundamentalism.

Kurzman, Charles. "Death Tolls of the Iran-Iraq War." *Charles Kurzman,* October 21, 2016. Accessed December 21, 2016. http://kurzman.unc.edu/death-tolls-of-the-iran-iraq-war/.

Kuttab, Daoud. "Confidence-Building Measures Needed for Israel-Palestine Talks." *Al-Monitor,* August 7, 2013. Accessed February 15, 2017. https://www.al-monitor.com/pulse/originals/2013/08/confidence-building-measures-israel-palestine.html.

———. "Palestinian Journalists Facing Dual Restrictions." *Huffington Post,* May 9, 2016. Accessed February 22, 2017. https://www.huffingtonpost.com/daoud-kuttab/palestinian-journalists-f_b_9861126.html.

———. "Why Israel Is Suddenly Owning Up to Its Terrorism." *Washington Report on Middle East Affairs,* September 2015. Accessed June 12, 2016. https://

www.washingtonreport.me/2015-september/why-israel-is-suddenly-owning-up-to-its-terrorism.html.

Lacey, Robert. *Inside the Kingdom: Kings, Clerics, Modernists, Terrorists, and the Struggle for Saudi Arabia.* New York: Viking, 2009.

Lake, David. "Confederation in Israel-Palestine? Principles for Effective Design and the Continuing Challenges." *Lawfare*, August 26, 2015. Accessed January 10, 2017. https://www.lawfareblog.com/confederation-israel-palestine-principles-effective-design-and-continuing-challenges.

Langohr, Vickie. "Labor Movement and Organization." In *The Arab Uprising Explained*, edited by Marc Lynch, 180–200. New York: Columbia University Press, 2014.

Laqueur, Walter. *Fascism.* New York: Oxford University Press, 1996.

Law, Bill. "Bahrain Protests Prompt Global Concerns." BBC News, February 15, 2011. Accessed March 8, 2011. http://www.bbc.com/news/world-middle-east-12471243.

Lazaroff, Tovah. "Abbas at UNHRC Support Two-State Solution by Recognizing Palestine." *Jerusalem Post*, February 27, 2017. Accessed November 16, 2015. http://www.jpost.com/Arab-Israeli-Conflict/Abbas-at-UNHRC-Support-two-state-solution-by-recognizing-Palestine-482722.

Leggett, Jeremy. "Solar Energy in Saudi Arabia: Opportunity Became Inevitable." *Jeremy Leggett Blog*, April 2016. Accessed September 20, 2016. http://www.jeremyleggett.net/2016/04/the-opportunity-and-imperative-for-saudi-arabia-to-be-a-global-solar-hub/?utm_source—ena+Solar+Brief+-+April+2016&utm_campaign=April++2016+Mena+Solar+Brief&utm_medium=email.

Lenin, Vladimir. "The Right of Nations to Self-Determination." In *Collected Works*, vol. 20. Moscow: Progress Publishers, 1972.

Leveille, Dan. *Equaldex: The Collaborative LGBT Rights Knowledge Base.* February 25, 2014. Distributed by Equaldex Data. Accessed December 9, 2018. http://www.equaldex.com/.

Levy, Yagil. "Militarizing Peace: Why Did the Israeli Military Spearhead the Oslo Accords?" *Contemporary Politics* 14, no. 2 (2008): 145–159.

Lewis, Aidan. "Why Has Morocco's King Survived the Arab Spring?" BBC News, November 24, 2011. Accessed September 25, 2015. http://www.bbc.com/news/world-middle-east-15856989.

Lewis, Bernard. *The Assassins: A Radical Sect in Islam.* New York: Basic Books, 2003.

———. *The Crisis of Islam: Holy War and Unholy Terror.* New York: Random House, 2003.

———. *The Political Language of Islam.* Chicago: University of Chicago Press, 1991.

———. *What Went Wrong? Western Impact and Middle Eastern Response.* New York: Oxford University Press, 2002.

Libya Business News. "NOC Chairman Explains Unity Agreement." *Libya Business News*, July 5, 2016. Accessed September 4, 2017. https://www.libya-businessnews.com/2016/07/05/noc-chairman-explains-unity-agreement/2/.

Lieber, Dov. "Hamas Said to Accept Egyptian Plan for Palestinian Unity, Fatah Holding Out." *Times of Israel*, August 6, 2017. Accessed August 10, 2017. http://www.timesofisrael.com/hamas-said-to-accept-egyptian-plan-for-palestinian-unity-fatah-holding-out/.

Linehan, Thomas. "The British Union of Fascists as a Totalitarian Movement and Political Religion." In *Fascism, Totalitarianism, and Political Religion*, edited by Roger Griffin, 103–124. New York: Routledge, 2005.

Lustick, Ian S., ed. "Making Sense of the Nakba: Ari Shavit, Baruch Marzel, and Zionist Claims to Territory." *Journal of Palestine Studies* 44, no. 2 (2015): 7.

Luxemburg, Rosa. *The National Question: Self-Determination*. New York: Monthly Review Press, 1976.

Lynch, Marc., ed. *The Arab Uprisings Explained: New Contentious Politics in the Middle East*. New York: Columbia University Press, 2014.

———. "Assessing the Democratizing Power of Satellite TV." *Transnational Broadcast Studies* 14 (2005).

———. "Why Saudi Arabia Escalated the Middle East's Sectarian Conflict." *Washington Post*, January 1, 2016. Accessed September 4, 2016. https://www.washingtonpost.com/news/monkey-cage/wp/2016/01/04/why-saudi-arabia-escalated-the-middle-easts-sectarian-conflict/?utm_term=.5655b0464a2c.

Lynfield, Ben. "New Textbook Bodes Well for Egypt-Israeli Relations." *Jerusalem Post*, May 19, 2016. Accessed November 17, 2017. http://www.jpost.com/Israel-News/New-Textbook-Bodes-Well-for-Egypt-Israeli-Relations-454413.

Ma'an News Agency. "Report: Palestinian Female Labor Participation among World's Lowest." *Ma'an News Agency*, July 22, 2015. Accessed October 31, 2017. https://www.maannews.com/Content.aspx?id=766601.

MacFarquhar, Neil. "Economic Frustration Simmers Again in Tunisia." *New York Times*, December 1, 2012. Accessed August 4, 2017. http://www.nytimes.com/2012/12/02/world/africa/economic-frustration-simmers-again-in-tunisia.html.

Machiavelli, Niccoló. *The Prince*. New York: Dover, 1992.

Mahdavi, Pardis. *Passionate Uprisings: Iran's Sexual Revolution*. Palo Alto: Stanford University Press, 2009.

Maistre, Joseph de. "Études sur la Souveraineté." In *Oeuvre Complètes*. 2 vols. Geneva: Slatkine Reprints, 1979.

Malik, Charles. "Proposing Ground Rules for Committee Debates on Human Rights." United Nations Commission on Human Rights, February 4, 1947. Accessed December 10, 2018. https://www2.gwu.edu/~erpapers/humanrights/casestudies/ERandHR%20case%20study%20PDF.pdf.

Malka, Haim. "Maghreb Rising: Competition and Realignment." Center for Strategic and International Studies, April 3, 2015. Accessed September 2, 2017. https://www.csis.org/analysis/maghreb-rising-competition-and-realignment.

Manji, Ishad. *The Trouble with Islam: A Muslim's Call for Reform in Her Faith*. New York: St. Martin's Press, 2003.

Manna, Haytham. *Human Rights in the Arab-Islamic Culture*. Cairo: Cairo Institute for Human Rights Studies, 1996.

Marie-Prudhomme, Louis. "On the Influence of the Revolution on Women."
    Revolutions of Paris editorial, February 12, 1791. Accessed November 22, 2017.
    http://chnm.gmu.edu/revolution/d/483/.

Martin, Richard, and Abbas Barzegar, eds. *Islamism: Contested Perspectives on
    Political Islam*. Palo Alto: Stanford University Press, 2010.

Marx, Karl. "The Defeat of June, 1848." In *The Class Struggles in France, 1848 to
    1850*. New York: International Publishers, 1964.

———. *The Eighteenth Brumaire of Louis Bonaparte* (1852), chapter 1. Accessed
    August 28, 2016. https://www.marxists.org/archive/marx/works/1852/18th-
    brumaire/cho1.htm.

———. *Philosophy of World Revolution*. New York: International Publishers,
    1969.

Marx, Karl, and Friedrich Engels. "The Holy Family." In *Selected Works*. Moscow:
    Foreign Languages Publishing House, 1956.

Masters, Jonathan, and Mohammed A. Sergie. "The Arab League: Backgrounder."
    Council on Foreign Relations. Updated October 21, 2014. Accessed August 8,
    2016. https://www.cfr.org/backgrounder/arab-league.

Maududi, Syed Abul Ala. *Human Rights in Islam*. Leicester: Islamic Foundation,
    1976.

Mayer, Ann Elizabeth. *Islam and Human Rights: Tradition and Politics*, 5th ed.
    Boulder, CO: Westview Press, 2013.

McCarthy, Andrew. *Spring Fever: The Illusion of Islamic Democracy*. New York:
    Encounter Digital, 2013.

McCormick-Cavanagh, Conor. "Is Homophobia at All-Time High in Tunisia?"
    Al-Monitor, March 4, 2016. Accessed May 29, 2017. https://www.al-monitor.
    com/pulse/ru/contents/articles/originals/2016/05/tunisia-lgbt-homophobic-
    attacks.html.

———. "New Tunisian Law Takes Long Stride toward Gender Equality."
    Al-Monitor, July 28, 2017. Accessed October 31, 2017. https://www.al-
    monitor.com/pulse/originals/2017/07/tunisia-new-law-women-protection-
    violence-rape-2018.html.

McElroy, Damien. "Rome Will Be Conquered Next, Says Leader of 'Islamic
    State.'" *The Telegraph*, July 1, 2014. Accessed August 4, 2017. http://www.
    telegraph.co.uk/news/worldnews/middleeast/syria/10939235/Rome-will-be-
    conquered-next-says-leader-of-Islamic-State.html.

Menas Associates. "Hopes for Re-Opening of Algeria-Morocco Border." February
    22, 2016. Accessed August 21, 2017. https://www.menas.co.uk/blog/
    hopes-for-borders-re-opening-as-algeria-calls-for-better-ties-with-morocco/.

Mernissi, Fatima. "The Meaning of Spatial Boundaries." In *Feminist Postcolonial
    Theory*, edited by Reina Lewis and Sara Mills, 489–501. New York: Routledge,
    2003.

Michaelson, Ruth. "LGBT People in Egypt Targeted in Wave of Arrests and
    Violence." *The Guardian*, October 8, 2017. Accessed December 10, 2018.
    https://www.theguardian.com/world/2017/oct/08/lgbt-people-egypt-
    targeted-wave-arrests-violence.

Middle East Media Research Institute. "New Message Following Being Declared a 'Caliph,' Islamic State Leader Abu Bakr Al-Baghdadi Promises Support to Oppressed Muslims Everywhere, Tells His Soldiers: 'You Will Conquer Rome.'" *MEMRI Jihad and Terrorism Threat Monitor*, June 30, 2014. Accessed July 21, 2017. https://www.memri.org/jttm/new-message-following-being-declared-caliph-islamic-state-leader-abu-bakr-al-baghdadi-promises.

Middle East Monitor, The. "Israel's Rivlin Proposes 'Confederation' with Palestinians." *Middle East Monitor*, August 9, 2015. Accessed January 10, 2017. https://www.middleeastmonitor.com/20150809-israels-rivlin-proposes-confederation-with-palestinians/.

Middle East Quarterly, The. "Shimon Peres: Unplugged." *Middle East Quarterly* 2, no. 1 (1995): 75–78.

Miles, Tom. "U.N. Aided 38,000 Victims of Syrian Gender-Based Violence in 2013." Reuters, January 8, 2014. Accessed December 9, 2016. https://www.reuters.com/article/us-syria-crisis-rape/u-n-aided-38000-victims-of-syrian-gender-based-violence-in-2013-idUSBREA0711R20140108.

Mill, John Stewart. *J. S. Mill: 'On Liberty' and Other Writings*. Edited by Stefan Collini. Cambridge: Cambridge University Press, 1989.

Milton-Edwards, Beverly. *Contemporary Politics in the Middle East*, 2nd ed. Cambridge: Polity Press, 2006.

Minh, Ho Chi. *Declaration of Independence, Democratic Republic of Vietnam*. Hanoi, 1945.

Mir-Hosseini, Ziba. "Beyond 'Islam' vs. 'Feminism.'" *IDS Bulletin* 42, no. 1 (2011): 67–77.

Moghadam, Valentine, ed. *From Patriarchy to Empowerment: Women's Participation, Movements, and Rights in the Middle East, North Africa, and South Asia*. Syracuse: Syracuse University Press, 2007.

———. "Islamic Feminism and Its Discontents: Toward a Resolution of the Debate." *Signs: Journal of Women in Culture and Society* 27, no. 4 (2002): 1135–1171.

———. *Modernizing Women: Gender and Social Change in the Middle East*. Boulder, CO: Lynne Rienner Publishers, 2001.

———. "Women, Citizenship and Civil Society in the Arab World." In *Human Rights in the Arab World: Independent Voices*, edited by Anthony Tirado Chase and Amr Hamzawy, 89–106. Philadelphia: University of Pennsylvania Press, 2006.

Moghissi, Haideh. "Islamic Feminism Revisited." *Comparative Studies of South Asia, Africa and the Middle East* 31, no. 1 (2011): 76–84.

Mojab, Shahrzad. "Theorizing the Politics of 'Islamic Feminism.'" *Feminist Review* 69 (2001): 124–146.

Momani, Bessma. "Egypt's IMF Program: Assessing the Political Economy Challenges." *Brookings*, January 30, 2018. Accessed May 23, 2018. https://www.brookings.edu/research/egypts-imf-program-assessing-the-political-economy-challenges/.

Monshipouri, Mahmood. *Democratic Uprisings in the New Middle East: Youth, Technology, Human Rights, and U.S. Foreign Policy.* Boulder, CO: Paradigm Publishers, 2014.

Montell, Jessica. "Palestine and Human Rights Treaties: A Political Tool and a Boomerang." Foundation for Middle East Peace, February 5, 2015. Accessed February 20, 2017. https://fmep.org/blog/2015/02/palestine-human-rights-treaties-political-tool-boomerang/.

Monterescu, Daniel, and Noa Shaindlinger. "Situational Radicalism: The Israeli 'Arab Spring' and the (Un)Making of the Rebel City." *Constellations* 20, no. 2 (2013): 229–253.

Morgan, David. "Sunday Times Reporter Interview with President Gamal Abdel Nasser." *Bibliotheca Alexandria*, June 18, 1962. Accessed November 3, 2017. http://nasser.bibalex.org/Common/pictures01-%20sira3_en.htm.

Morocco World News. "NATO Determined to Reinforce Security Cooperation with Morocco, White House," *Morocco World News*, July 10, 2016. Accessed August 4, 2016. http://www.moroccoworldnews.com/2016/07/191037/nato-determined-to-reinforce-security-cooperation-with-morocco-white-house/.

Moscow Times. "Calculating the Cost of Russia's War in Syria." *Moscow Times,* October 20, 2015. Accessed December 5, 2018. https://themoscowtimes.com/articles/calculating-the-cost-of-russias-war-in-syria-50382.

Mosse, George. *Nationalism and Sexuality.* New York: Howard Fertig, 1997.

Mroue, Bassem. "Islamic State Publicly Kills Gays to Show 'Ideological Purity.'" *The Star*, December 2, 2015. Accessed February 29, 2016. https://www.thestar.com/news/world/2015/12/02/islamic-state-publicly-kills-gays-to-show-ideological-purity.html.

Mualem, Mazal. "How Politics Is Redefining 'Left' and 'Right' in Israel." *Al-Monitor*, May 13, 2016. Accessed November 3, 2017. https://www.al-monitor.com/pulse/tr/contents/articles/originals/2016/05/israel-right-left-camps-rule-of-law-minorities-rights-arabs.html.

Mussolini, Benito. "Fascism." In *The Nationalism Reader*, edited by Omar Dahbour and Micheline Ishay, 222–229. Amherst, NY: Humanities Press, 1995.

Musyimi-Ogana, Litha. *True Story of Women Peace Train: From Kampala to Johannesburg.* Bloomington, IN: Authorhouse, 2015.

Naji, Abu Bakr. *The Management of Savagery: The Most Critical Stage through Which the Umma Will Pass.* Translated by William McCants. Boston: John M. Olin Institute for Strategic Studies, 2006.

Najmabadi, Afsaneh. "(Un)Veiling Feminism." *Social Text* 18, no. 3 (2000): 29–45.

Naor, Arye. "The Security Argument in the Territorial Debate in Israel: Rhetoric and Policy." *Israel Studies* 2, no. 2 (1999): 150–177.

Naqib, Fadle. "Economic Aspects of the Palestinian-Israeli Conflict: The Collapse of the Oslo Accord." *Journal of International Development* 15, no. 4 (2003): 499–512.

Nasser, Afrah. "Yemen: Women Must Be in the Peace Talks." *Afrah Nasser Blog.* Accessed May 29, 2017. http://afrahnasser.blogspot.com/.

National, The. "UAE Is World's Top Donor of Development Aid in 2017." *The National*, April 9, 2018. Accessed May 23, 2018. https://www.thenational.ae/ uae/government/uae-is-world-s-top-donor-of-development-aid-in-2017-report-shows-1.720143.

Navrátil, Jaromír, ed. *The Prague Spring 1968: A National Security Archive Document Reader*. Translated by Mark Kramer, Joy Moss, and Ruth Tosek, edited by Antonín Bencík, Václav Kural, Marie Michálková, and Jitka Vondrová. Budapest: Central European University Press, 2006.

New York Times. "Amin Praises Hitler for Killing of Jews." *New York Times*, September 13, 1972, sec. Archives. Accessed July 1, 2015. http://www.nytimes. com/1972/09/13/archives/amin-praises-hitler-for-killing-of-jews.html.

———. "Disguised Fascism Seen as a Menace; Professor Luccock Warns That It Will Bear the Misleading Label 'Americanism.'" *New York Times*, September 12, 1938. Accessed December 9, 2018. https://www.nytimes. com/1938/09/12/archives/disguised-fascism-seen-as-a-menace-prof-luccock-warns-that-it-will.html.

———. "F.D.R.'s Old Pullman Is Back on the Tracks." *New York Times*, September 10, 1984. Accessed August 31, 2016. http://www.nytimes. com/1984/09/10/us/fdr-s-old-pullman-is-back-on-the-tracks.html.

Niebuhr, Gustav. *Beyond Tolerance: Searching for Interfaith Understanding in America*. New York: Viking, 2008.

Nikbakht, Daniel, and Sheena McKenzie. "The Yemen War Is the World's Worst Humanitarian Crisis, UN Says." CNN, April 3, 2018. Accessed May 23, 2018. https://www.cnn.com/2018/04/03/middleeast/yemen-worlds-worst-humanitarian-crisis-un-intl/index.html.

Noland, Marcus, and Howard Pack. *The Arab Economies in a Changing World*, 2nd ed. Washington, DC: Peterson Institute for International Economics, 2011.

North American Congress on Latin America. "Former Dictator Arrested for Stealing Children during Dirty War." NACLA, September 25, 2007. https:// nacla.org/article/former-dictator-arrested-stealing-children-during-dirty-war.

North Atlantic Treaty Organization (NATO). "The Arab Maghreb Union: The Forgotten Dream." Naples: NATO Strategic Direction South, May 12, 2018. Accessed December 5, 2018. https://www.thesouthernhub.org/systems/ file_download.ashx?pg=1108&ver=1.

Nosset, James Michael. "Free Exercise after the Arab Spring: Protecting Egyptian Minorities under the Country's New Constitution." *Indiana Law Journal* 89, no. 4 (2014): 1653–1689.

Noueihed, Lin, and Alex Warren. *The Battle for the Arab Spring: Revolution, Counter-Revolution and the Making of a New Era*. New Haven: Yale University Press, 2013.

NPR. "Transcript: Obama Seeks 'New Beginning' in Cairo." NPR, June 4, 2009. Accessed August 23, 2017. http://www.npr.org/templates/story/story.php? storyId=104923292.

Obama, Barack. *Words That Changed a Nation: The Most Celebrated and Influential Speeches of Barack Obama*. Seattle: Pacific Publishing Studio, 2009.

O'Donnell, Guillermo. *Modernization and Bureaucratic-Authoritarianism: Studies in South American Politics*. Berkeley: University of California, Institute of International Studies, 1979.

Ofek, Hillel. "Why the Arabic World Turned Away from Science." *New Atlantis: A Journal of Technology and Society* 30 (2011): 3–23. Accessed July 26, 2016. http://www.thenewatlantis.com/publications/why-the-arabic-world-turned-away-from-science.

Offe, Claus. *Europe Entrapped*. Cambridge: Polity Books, 2015.

———. "Referendum vs. Institutionalized Deliberation: What Democratic Theorists Can Learn from the 2016 Brexit Decision." *Dædalus: Journal of American Academy of Arts and Sciences* 146, no. 3 (2017): 14–27.

Oman Daily Observer. "GCC Has $240 Bln Worth Rail Projects in the Pipeline." *Oman Daily Observer* in Thomson Reuters Zawya, February 6, 2018. Accessed December 10, 2018. https://www.zawya.com/uae/en/story/ GCC_has_240_bln_worth_rail_projects_in_the_pipeline-ZAWYA20170 206043637/.

Omar, Manal. "The Women in the Middle of the War." *Foreign Policy*, March 18, 2015. Accessed December 11, 2016. http://foreignpolicy.com/2015/03/18/ the-women-in-the-middle-of-the-war/.

Oosterhuis, Harry. "Medicine, Male Bonding and Homosexuality in Nazi Germany." *Journal of Contemporary History* 32, no. 2 (1997): 187–205.

Ophir, Adi, Michal Givoni, and Sari Hanafi, eds. *The Power of Inclusive Exclusion: Anatomy of Israeli Rule in the Occupied Palestinian Territories*. Cambridge, MA: MIT Press, 2009.

O'Reilly, Marc J. "Oil Monarchies without Oil: Omani and Bharani Security in a Post-Oil Era." *Middle East Policy* 6, no. 3 (1999): 78–92.

Organisation for Economic Co-Operation and Development (OECD). *Development Aid Stable in 2017 with More Sent to Poorest Countries*. Paris: OECD, April 9, 2018. Accessed December 9, 2018. http://www.oecd.org/development/ financing-sustainable-development/development-finance-data/ODA-2017-detailed-summary.pdf.

———. *OECD Economic Surveys: Tunisia*. Tunisia: OECD, March 2018. Accessed December 9, 2018. https://www.oecd.org/eco/surveys/Tunisia-2018-OECD-economic-survey-overview.pdf.

———. *The Pursuit of Gender Equality: An Uphill Battle*. Paris: OECD, October 4, 2017. Accessed December 9, 2018. https://read.oecd-ilibrary.org/social-issues-migration-health/the-pursuit-of-gender-equality_9789264281318-en#page1.

———. *Women's Economic Empowerment in Selected MENA Countries*. Paris: OECD, October 7, 2017. Accessed December 9, 2018. https://read.oecd-ilibrary.org/development/women-s-economic-empowerment-in-selected-mena-countries_9789264279322-en#page1.

Osman, Tarek. *Egypt on the Brink: From the Rise of Nasser to the Fall of Mubarak.* New Haven: Yale University Press, 2011.

———. *Islamism: What It Means for the Middle East and the World.* New Haven: Yale University Press, 2016.

O'Sullivan, Arieh. "Praying Hard to Make the Rain Fall." *Jerusalem Post,* November 14, 2010. Accessed August 5, 2016. http://www.jpost.com/Video-Articles/ Praying-hard-to-make-the-rain-fall.

Owen, Roger, and Sevket Pamuk. *A History of Middle East Economies in the Twentieth Century.* London: I. B. Tauris, 1998.

Oxfam America. *Missiles and Food: Yemen's Man-Made Food Security Crisis.* Boston: Oxfam America, December 2017. Accessed December 5, 2018. https://www. oxfam.org/sites/www.oxfam.org/files/file_attachments/bn- missiles-food-security-yemen-041217-en.pdf.

Oz, Amos. "For Its Survival, Israel Must Abandon the One-State Option." *Los Angeles Times,* March 7, 2015. Accessed November 16, 2015. http:// beta.latimes.com/opinion/op-ed/la-oe-oz-two-state-solution-peace-israel- palestinians-20150308-story.html.

Paciello, Maria. "Tunisia: Changes and Challenges of Political Transition." MEDPRO Technical Report no. 3. *Mediterranean Prospects Project,* May 3, 2011. Accessed June 23, 2015. https://www.ceps.eu/publications/tunisia- changes-and-challenges-political-transition.

Palestinian Declaration of Independence (November 15, 1988). MidEast Web, 2002. Accessed October 31, 2017. http://www.mideastweb.org/plc1988.htm.

Parke, Phoebe, and Chris Giles. "Morocco's Megawat Solar Plant Powers Up." CNN News, May 17, 2018. Accessed December 9, 2018. https://www-m. cnn.com/2016/02/08/africa/ouarzazate-morocco-solar-plant/index. html?r=https%3A%2F%2Fwww.google.com%2F.

Patel, Eboo. *Sacred Ground: Pluralism, Prejudice and the Promise of America.* Boston: Beacon Press, 2012.

Pedahzur, Ami. *The Triumph of Israel's Radical Right.* Cambridge: Oxford University Press, 2012.

Peled, Yoav, and Nadim Rouhana. "Transitional Justice and the Right of Return of the Palestinian Refugees." *Theoretical Inquiries in Law* 5, no. 2 (2004): 317–332.

Peres, Chemi. "What My Dad Shimon Peres Taught Me about Israel—and the World." *New York Post,* September 9, 2017. Accessed June 5, 2018. https:// nypost.com/2017/09/09/what-my-dad-shimon-peres-taught-me-about- israel-and-the-world/.

Peres, Shimon. "Full Text of Peres Speech to European Parliament." *Haaretz,* May 12, 2013. Accessed August 10, 2017. http://www.haaretz.com/israel- news/full-text-of-peres-speech-to-european-parliament-1.508915.

———. "Shimon Peres's Plan for Peace and Development in the Middle East." *Acque e Terre* 20, no. 43 (April 1993): 15–20.

Peres, Shimon, and Arye Naor. *The New Middle East.* New York: Henry Holt, 1993.

Peri, Yoram. "The Political-Military Complex: The IDF's Influence over Policy towards Palestinians since 1987." In *Israeli Institutions at the Crossroads*, edited by Raphael Cohen-Almagor, 50–70. London: Routledge, 2005.

Perkins, Kenneth. *A History of Modern Tunisia*, 2nd ed. New York: Cambridge University Press, 2014.

―――. *Tunisia: Crossroads of the Islamic and European Worlds*. Boulder, CO: Westview Press, 1986.

Pew Research Center. *The World's Muslims: Religion, Politics and Society*. Washington, DC: Pew Forum on Religion and Public Life, April 30, 2013. Accessed July 20, 2015. http://assets.pewresearch.org/wp-content/uploads/sites/11/2013/04/worlds-muslims-religion-politics-society-full-report.pdf.

Pfeffer, Anshel. "Israel Is More Focused on 'Hasbara' Than It Is on Policy." *Haaretz*, May 2, 2012. Accessed December 10, 2018. https://www.haaretz.com/1.5200348.

Phillips, Sarah. *Carnegie Papers: Middle East Series: Evaluating Political Reform in Yemen*. Washington, DC: Carnegie Endowment for International Peace, Democracy and Rule of Law Program, 2007.

Pogash, Carol. "At Berkeley, Free (though Subdued) Speech, 50 Years Later." *New York Times*, October 1, 2014. Accessed April 6, 2017. https://www.nytimes.com/2014/10/02/us/free-though-subdued-speech-50-years-later.html?_r=0.

Polk, William. *Understanding Iraq*. New York: HarperCollins, 2005.

Pollack, Kenneth M. "Fear and Loathing in Saudi Arabia." *Foreign Policy*, January 1, 2016. Accessed September 2, 2017. http://foreignpolicy.com/2016/01/07/fear-and-loathing-in-saudi-arabia/.

―――. *The Persian Puzzle: The Conflict between Iran and America*. New York: Random House, 2004.

Pollack, Kenneth, Daniel Byman, Akram Al-Turk, Pavel Baev, Michael Doran, Khaled Elgindy, Stephen Grand, Shadi Hamid, Bruce Jones, Suzanne Maloney, Bruce Riedel, Ruth Santini, Salman Shaikh, Ibrahim Sharqieh, Ömer Taspinar, Shibley Telhami, and Sarah Yerkes. *The Arab Awakenings: America and the Transformation of the Middle East*. Washington, DC: Brookings Institution Press, 2011.

Pomerleau, Wayne. "Immanuel Kant: Philosophy of Religion." *Internet Encyclopedia of Philosophy*. Accessed August 23, 2017. http://www.iep.utm.edu/kant-rel/.

Prasad, Leela. "Railways to Start Trial Runs of Solar Train in Sunny Jodhpur." *Indian Express*. Accessed August 8, 2016. http://indianexpress.com/article/india/india-news-india/railways-to-start-trial-runs-of-solar-train-in-sunny-jodhpur-2798717/.

Prashad, Vijay. *Arab Spring, Libyan Winter*. Oakland, CA: AK Press, 2012.

Prince-Gibson, Eetta. " 'We Cannot Count on Men to Create Peace. We Have to Do It Ourselves.' " *Haaretz*, October 20, 2016. Accessed December 10, 2018. https://www.haaretz.com/israel-news/.premium-we-cannot-count-on-men-to-create-peace-1.5451575.

Promundo-US and UN Women. *Understanding Masculinities: Results from the International Men and Gender Equality Survey (IMAGES)—Middle East and North Africa.* Cairo and Washington, DC: Promundo-US and UN Women, 2017. Accessed December 9, 2018. https://imagesmena.org/wp-content/uploads/sites/5/2017/05/IMAGES-MENA-Multi-Country-Report-EN-16May2017-web.pdf.

Qutb, Sayyid. *Milestones.* Lexington, KY: SIME Journal (http://majalla.org), 2005.

Rabushka, Alvin, and Kenneth A. Shepsle. *Politics in Plural Societies: A Theory of Democratic Instability.* Columbus, OH: Charles E. Merrill, 1972.

Rafiq, AyeshaAayesh. "Child Custody in Classical Islamic Law and Laws of Contemporary Muslim World (An Analysis)." *International Journal of Humanities and Social Sciences* 4, no. 5 (March 2014): 267–277.

Ragson, Adam. "Leaked: The Six Clauses of the Fatah-Hamas Deal." *Jerusalem Post,* October 14, 2017. Accessed October 31, 2017. http://www.jpost.com/Arab-Israeli-Conflict/Leaked-the-six-clauses-of-the-Fatah-Hamas-rapprochement-deal-507401.

Rais, Faiza. "Syria under Bashar Al Assad: A Profile of Power." *Strategic Studies,* no. 3 (2004): 144–168.

Ram, Uri. "The Promised Land of Business Opportunities." In *The New Israel: Peacemaking and Liberalization,* edited by Gershon Shafir and Yoav Peled, 217–240. Boulder, CO: Westview Press, 2000.

Rankin, Jennifer. "Refugee Crisis: EU Allocates #eu700m in Extra Aid to Cope with Influx." *The Guardian,* March 2, 2016. Accessed September 2, 2017. https://www.theguardian.com/world/2016/mar/02/refugee-crisis-europe-eu-countries-greece-receive-700m-extra-aid-funds.

Rauf, Feisal Abdul. *What's Right with Islam Is What's Right with America.* New York: HarperCollins, 2004.

Ravitzky, Aviezer. *Messianism, Zionism, and Jewish Religious Radicalism.* Translated by Michael Swirsky and Jonathan Chipman. Chicago: University of Chicago Press, 1993.

Rediker, Ezekiel. "The Incitement of Terrorism on the Internet: Legal Standards, Enforcement, and the Role of the European Union." *Michigan Journal of International Law* 36, no. 2 (2015): 321–351.

Reel, Monte. "Djibouti Is Hot: How a Forgotten Sandlot of a Country Became a Hub of International Power Games." *Bloomberg Businessweek,* March 23, 2016. Accessed August 7, 2016. https://www.bloomberg.com/features/2016-djibouti/.

Reticker, Gini, dir. *The Trials of Spring.* Los Angeles: Thomas Cobb Group, 2015.

Reuters. "Four Algerians Set Selves on Fire, Echoing Tunisia." Reuters, January 17, 2011. Accessed July 4, 2018. https://uk.reuters.com/article/us-algeria-unrest/four-algerians-set-selves-on-fire-echoing-tunisia-idUKTRE70G1VC20110117.

———. "Yemen's Cholera Epidemic Likely to Intensify in Coming Months: WHO." Reuters, February 26, 2018. Accessed May 23, 2018. https://www.reuters.com/article/us-yemen-security-cholera/

yemens-cholera-epidemic-likely-to-intensify-in-coming-months-who-
idUSKCN1GA225.

Riedel, Bruce. "In Yemen, Iran Outsmarts Saudi Arabia Again." Brookings Institute,
December 6, 2017. Accessed December 5, 2018. https://www.brookings.edu/
blog/markaz/2017/12/06/in-yemen-iran-outsmarts-saudi-arabia-again/.

Rizvi, Anam. "UAE Bucks Global Trend as Women Lead the Way in Science
Studies." *The National*, June 28, 2018. Accessed December 9, 2018. https://
www.thenational.ae/uae/uae-bucks-global-trend-as-women-lead-the-way-
in-science-studies-1.745043.

Robins, Philip. *The Middle East.* Oxford: Oneworld Publications, 2009.

Robinson, Thomas W. "The Sino-Soviet Border Dispute: Background,
Development, and the March 1969 Clashes." *American Political Science
Review* 66, no. 4 (1972): 1175–1202.

Rock, Ahmed. "Down with Military Rule." Mp3 recording. Cairo: Revolution
Records, 2011. YouTube. Accessed November 21, 2017. http://www.youtube.
com/watch?v=OfGz3DR7ChU. Translation by Fouad Alkhouri.

Rogan, Eugene. *The Arabs: A History.* New York: Basic Books, 2009.

Rome Statute of the International Criminal Court, A/CONF.183/9, International
Criminal Court (July 17, 1998). Accessed December 10, 2018. https://www.
icc-cpi.int/nr/rdonlyres/ea9aeff7-5752-4f84-be94-0a655eb30e16/0/rome_
statute_english.pdf.

Roosevelt, Eleanor. "U.N. Deliberations on Draft Convention on the Political
Rights of Women" (December 31, 1951). In *Courage in a Dangerous World: The
Political Writings of Eleanor Roosevelt*, edited by Allida M. Black. New York:
Columbia University Press, 1999.

———. "Where Do Human Rights Begin?" (March 27, 1953). In *Courage in a
Dangerous World: The Political Writings of Eleanor Roosevelt*, edited by Allida
M. Black. New York: Columbia University Press, 1999.

———. *You Learn by Living.* New York: HarperCollins, 1960.

———. *You Learn by Living: Eleven Keys for a More Fulfilling Life.* New York:
Harper Perennial, 2011.

Roosevelt, Franklin. "The Four Freedoms." Franklin D. Roosevelt Presidential
Library and Museum. Accessed December 10, 2018. http://www.fdrlibrary.
marist.edu/_resources/images/msf/msf01407.

Ross, Dennis. *The Missing Peace: The Inside Story of the Fight for Middle East Peace.*
New York: Farrar, Straus and Giroux, 2004.

Ross, Michael. *The Oil Curse: How Petroleum Wealth Shapes the Development of
Nations.* Princeton: Princeton University Press, 2013.

Rouzi, A. A. "Facts and Controversies on Female Genital Mutilation and Islam."
European Journal of Contraception and Reproductive Health Care 18, no. 1 (2013):
10–14.

Roy, Olivier. *The Failure of Political Islam.* Translated by Carol Volk. Cambridge,
MA: Harvard University Press, 2001.

Royal Institute for Inter-Faith Studies. *Bulletin of the Royal Institute for Inter-Faith
Studies.* Vol. 13. Amman: Royal Institute for Inter-Faith Studies, 2011.

———. *Muslims and Human Communities: A Relationship of Harmony or Fear? In the Light of the Amman Message.* Amman: Royal Institute for Inter-Faith Studies, 2014.

Rubin, Barry, and Wolfgang Schwanitz. *Nazis, Islamists, and the Making of the Modern Middle East.* New Haven: Yale University Press, 2014.

Ruddle, Kenneth, and Mukhtar Hamour. "Statistical Abstract of Latin America for 1970." Los Angeles: UCLA Latin American Center, 1970.

Rumi, Raza. "Islam Needs Reformation from Within." *Huffington Post,* January 16, 2015. Accessed August 13, 2016. http://www.huffingtonpost.com/raza-rumi/islam-needs-reformation-f_b_6484118.html.

Rutherford, Paul. *Weapons of Mass Persuasion: Marketing the War against Iraq.* Buffalo, NY: University of Toronto Press, 2004.

Ryan, Yasmine. "Tunisian Blogger Becomes Nobel Prize Nominee." Al Jazeera, October 21, 2011. Accessed May 29, 2017. http://www.aljazeera.com/indepth/features/2011/10/2011106222117687872.html.

Sa'ar, Amalya. "Palestinian Women in the Israeli Workforce and the Idea of Economic Citizenship." *Economic Sociology: The European Electronic Newsletter* 16, no. 2 (2015): 14–20.

Sadiki, Larbi. *The Search for Arab Democracy: Discourses and Counter-Discourses.* New York: Columbia University Press, 2004.

Said, Edward. "The Morning After." *London Review of Books* 15, no. 20 (October 1993): 3–5.

———. *The Pen and the Sword: Conversations with David Barsamian.* Monroe, ME: Common Courage Press, 1994.

Saikal, Amin, and Albrecht Schnabel, eds. *Democratization in the Middle East.* New York: United Nations University Press, 2003.

Salama, Samir. "UAE Government Offices Need Childcare Facilities." *Gulf News,* March 24, 2010. Accessed December 11, 2016. http://gulfnews.com/news/uae/government/uae-government-offices-need-childcare-facilities-1.602029.

Salem, Maryam Ben, and Soumaya Cheikh. *Politique et jeunes femmes vulnérables en Tunisie.* Tunis: CAWTAR, 2013.

Salhab, Rana, Cynthia Corby, Farah Foustok, and Nour Khoury. *View from the Top: What Business Executives Really Think about Women Leaders in the GCC.* Deloitte and Touche, 2016. Accessed November 22, 2017. https://30percentclub.org/assets/uploads/Deloitte_and_30__Club_Study_-_View_from_the_top_(2).pdf.

Samaan, Magdy, and Declan Walsh. "Egypt Declares State of Emergency, as Attacks Undercut Promise of Security." *New York Times,* April 9, 2017. Accessed August 23, 2017. https://www.nytimes.com/2017/04/09/world/middleeast/explosion-egypt-coptic-christian-church.html?_r=0.

Samara, Adel. "Globalization, the Palestinian Economy, and the 'Peace Process.'" *Journal of Palestine Studies* 29, no. 2 (2000): 20–34.

Sanger, David. "Iran Complies with Nuclear Deal; Sanctions Are Lifted." *New York Times,* January 16, 2016. Accessed December 5, 2018. https://www.nytimes.com/2016/01/17/world/middleeast/iran-sanctions-lifted-nuclear-deal.html.

Sapir, Gideon, and Daniel Statman. "Minority Religions in Israel." *Journal of Law and Religion* 30, no. 1 (February 2015): 65–79.

Saudi Arabia: Permanent Delegation of Saudi Arabia to UNESCO. "Hejaz Railway." United Nations Educational, Scientific and Cultural Organization, August 4, 2015. Accessed August 21, 2017. http://whc.unesco.org/en/tentativelists/6026/.

Save the Children. *Too Young to Wed: The Growing Problem of Child Marriage among Syrian Girls in Jordan.* London: Save the Children, 2014. Accessed December 10, 2018. https://resourcecentre.savethechildren.net/node/8315/pdf/too_young_to_wed.pdf.

Sawyer, Tom. "The Cairo Railroad Museum." *Tom's Travel Blog*, March 10, 2015. Accessed November 3, 2017. http://sawyertravel.blogspot.com/2015/03/the-cairo-railroad-museum.html.

Schamis, Hector E. "Reconceptualizing Latin American Authoritarianism in the 1970s: From Bureaucratic Authoritarianism to Neoconservatism." *Comparative Politics* 23, no. 2 (1991): 201–220.

Scheer, Sander. "Bashar al-Assad and the 'Damascus Spring.'" *Zeytun*, March 24, 2010. Accessed May 3, 2012. http://www.archive-org-2013.com/org/z/2013-04-25_1930412_13/Security-arrangements-in-the-Gulf-Zeytun/.

Scheinfeld, Amram. "A Social Scientist's Evaluation of Kinsey's Study of Female Sex Behavior." *Cosmopolitan*, September 1953. Accessed December 3, 2016. http://blog.modernmechanix.com/kinseys-study-of-female-sex-behavior/.

Schlup, Leonard, and Donald Whisenhunt, eds. *It Seems to Me: Selected Letters of Eleanor Roosevelt.* Lexington: University Press of Kentucky, 2001.

Schor, Sophie R. "Hope Keeps Us Warm." *Jerusalem Post*, November 3, 2016. Accessed December 10, 2018. https://www.jpost.com/Opinion/Hope-keeps-us-warm-471614.

Schroeder, Christopher. *Startup Rising: The Entrepreneurial Revolution Remaking the Middle East.* New York: Palgrave MacMillan, 2013.

Segal, Jerome. "The Case for Binationalism." *Boston Review*, December 1, 2001. Accessed October 31, 2017. http://bostonreview.net/forum/case-binationalism/jerome-m-segal-binational-confederation.

Segran, Elizabeth. "The Rise of the Islamic Feminists: Muslim Women Are Fighting for Their Rights from within Islamic Tradition, Rather than against It." *The Nation*, December 4, 2013. Accessed November 1, 2017. https://www.thenation.com/article/rise-islamic-feminists/.

Seib, Philip, ed. *New Media and Prospects for Democratization.* New York: Palgrave Macmillan, 2007.

——. *New Media and the New Middle East.* New York: Palgrave Macmillan, 2007.

Shafir, Gershon, and Yoav Peled. "Peace and Profits: The Globalization of Israeli Business and the Peace Process." In *The New Israel: Peacemaking and Liberalization*, edited by Gershon Shafir and Yoav Peled, 243–264. Boulder, CO: Westview Press, 2000.

Shahidian, Hammed. "Saving the Savior." *Sociological Inquiry* 69, no. 2 (1999): 303–327.

Shaibany, Saleh. "Women in Oman Whose Husbands Marry Again Refuse to Be Second-Best." *The National*, April 1, 2011. Accessed November 10, 2015. https://www.thenational.ae/world/mena/women-in-oman-whose-husbands-marry-again-refuse-to-be-second-best-1.605269.

Sharon, Assaf. "Half a Loaf: In Israel and Palestine, Two States Are Still Better Than One." *Boston Review*, October 12, 2015. Accessed February 20, 2017. http://bostonreview.net/books-ideas/assaf-sharon-israel-palestine-two-state.

———. "The One State Delusion." In *Israel and Palestine: Alternative Perspectives on Statehood*, edited by John Ehrenberg and Yoav Peled, 115–132. Lanham, MD: Rowman and Littlefield, 2016.

Sherwood, Harriet. "Tunisian Coalition Party Fights for Women's Rights with Gender Violence Bill." *The Guardian*, October 24, 2016. Accessed December 30, 2016. https://www.theguardian.com/global-development/2016/oct/24/tunisia-gender-violence-bill-substance-progressive-image.

Siegel, Robert. "Journalist: Egypt's Anti-Terror Law Restricts Freedom of Expression." NPR, September 4, 2015. Accessed December 8, 2018. https://www.npr.org/2015/09/04/437597052/journalist-egypts-anti-terror-law-restricts-freedom-of-expression.

Siegel-Itzkovich, Judy. "BGU and Partners to Create Israeli, Palestinian and Jordanian Community Response Teams." *Jerusalem Post*, April 2, 2014. Accessed February 22, 2017. http://www.jpost.com/Health-and-Science/BGU-and-partners-to-create-Israeli-Palestinian-and-Jordanian-community-emergency-response-teams-347310.

Sikkink, Kathryn. *Evidence for Hope: Making Human Rights Work in the 21st Century*. Princeton: Princeton University Press, 2017.

Sinai, Ruth. "Poverty Level Holds Steady, but Income Gaps Continue to Widen." *Haaretz*, May 9, 2007. Accessed April 15, 2008. http://www.haaretz.com/print-edition/news/poverty-level-holds-steady-but-income-gaps-continue-to-widen-1.228866.

Sinha, Amitabh. "Catching the Sun at Bhadla Solar Park." *Indian Express,* June 26, 2018. Accessed December 5, 2018. https://indianexpress.com/article/india/bhadla-solar-park-rajasthan-catching-the-sun-india-biggest-solar-energy-park-jodhpur-power-plant-hot-winds-sand-storms-4709314/.

Smith, Denis Mack, ed. *Mussolini's Roman Empire*. London: Longman, 1976.

Smooha, Sammy. "The Model of Ethnic Democracy: Israel as a Jewish and Democratic State." *Nations and Nationalism* 8, no. 4 (October 2002): 473–503.

Snitkoff, Ed. "Gush Emunim." My Jewish Learning. Accessed August 10, 2017. http://www.myjewishlearning.com/article/gush-emunim/.

Solomon, Martha M., ed. *A Voice of Their Own: The Woman Suffrage Press, 1840–1910*. Tuscaloosa: University of Alabama Press, 2004.

Sotloff, Steven. "Bahrain's Shia Crackdown." *Foreign Policy*, September 10, 2010. Accessed November 11, 2017. http://foreignpolicy.com/2010/09/10/bahrains-shia-crackdown/.

Souaiaia, Ahmed. *Contesting Justice: Women, Islam, Law, and Society.* Albany: State University of New York Press, 2008.

Spectorsky, Susan A. *Women in Classical Islamic Law: A Survey of the Sources.* Leiden: Koninklijke Brill, 2010.

Sprinzak, Ehud. "The Israeli Radical Right: History, Culture and Politics." *Comparative Politics* 29 (January 1989): 1–29.

Sreberny, Annabelle. "Women's Digital Activism in a Changing Middle East." *International Journal of Middle East Studies* 47, no. 2 (2015): 357–361.

St. John, Ronald Bruce. *Libya: From Colony to Revolution.* Oxford: Oneworld Publications, 2012.

Staff, Toi. "Restored Northern Railway Sees Historic Maiden Voyage." *Times of Israel*, August 29, 2016. Accessed October 28, 2016. http://www.timesofisrael.com/restored-northern-railway-sees-historic-maiden-voyage/.

Stanley, Bruce. "How the Sun Might Help Solve a Looming Water Crisis in the Arab Gulf." *Bloomberg*, January 8, 2018. Accessed December 10, 2018. https://www.bloomberg.com/news/articles/2018-01-08/how-the-sun-might-help-quench-gulf-arabs-thirst-quicktake-q-a.

Statista. "Tunisia: Unemployment Rate from 2007 to 2017." Accessed December 9, 2018. https://www.statista.com/statistics/524516/unemployment-rate-in-tunisia/.

Steigmann-Gall, Richard. "Nazism and the Revival of Political Religion Theory." In *Fascism, Totalitarianism, and Political Religion*, edited by Roger Griffin, 82–102. New York: Routledge, 2005.

Sternhell, Zeev. "Fascist Ideology." In *Fascism: A Reader's Guide*, edited by Walter Laqueur, 315–378. Berkeley: University of California Press, 1976.

Stillman, Norman. *The Jews of Arab Lands: A History and Source Book.* Philadelphia: Jewish Publication Society of America, 1979.

Svec, Milan. "The Prague Spring: 20 Years Later." *Foreign Affairs* no. 66 (1988): 981–1001.

Tashkandi, A., and F. P. Rasheed. "Wife Abuse: A Hidden Problem. A Study among Saudi Women Attending PHC Centres." *East Mediterranean Health Journal* 15, no. 5 (2009): 1242–1253.

Tastekin, Fehim. "Davutoglu Proposes Refugee 'Container City.'" *Al-Monitor*, September 2015. Accessed August 5, 2016. http://www.al-monitor.com/pulse/originals/2015/09/turkey-syria-assad-boutique-state-refugees-container-state.html.

Tayler, Jeffrey. "Tunisian Woman Sent to a Psychiatric Hospital for Posting Topless Photos on Facebook." *The Atlantic*, March 22, 2013. Accessed May 20, 2017. https://www.theatlantic.com/international/archive/2013/03/tunisian-woman-sent-to-a-psychiatric-hospital-for-posting-topless-photos-on-facebook/274298/.

Telhami, Shibley. *The Stakes: America in the Middle East: The Consequences of Power and the Choice for Peace.* Boulder, CO: Westview Press, 2004.

Tétreault, Mary Ann, Gwenn Okruhlik, and Andrzej Andrezej Kapiszewski. *Political Change in the Arab Gulf States: Stuck in Transition.* Boulder, CO: Lynne Rienner Publishers, 2011.

Thabit, Ibn. "Al-Soo-al" [The Question]. Mp4 Recording. January 27, 2011. YouTube. Accessed November 22, 2017. http://www.youtube.com/watch?v=c_9pBiwS2lI. Translated by Sean O'Keefe. *Revolutionary Arab Rap: The Index.* August 28, 2011. Accessed November 22, 2017. http://revolutionaryarabraptheindex. blogspot.com/2011/08/ibn-thabit-question.html.

Thrope, Samuel. "The War on Women in Israel." *The Nation,* August 19, 2015. Accessed December 11, 2016. https://www.thenation.com/article/the-war-on-women-in-israel/.

Tibi, Bassam. *Arab Nationalism: Between Islam and the Nation-State.* New York: St. Martin's Press, 1997.

———. *The Challenge of Fundamentalism: Political Islam and the New World Disorder.* London: University of California Press, 2002.

———. *The Crisis of Modern Islam: A Preindustrial Culture in the Scientific-Technological Age.* Translated by Judith von Sivers. Boulder, CO: Westview Press, 1988.

———. *Islam in Global Politics: Conflict and Cross-Civilizational Bridging.* New York: Routledge, 2012.

———. *Islamism and Islam.* New Haven: Yale University Press, 2012.

Tilley, Virginia. *The One-State Solution.* Manchester: Manchester University Press, 2005.

Tilly, Charles. *European Revolutions, 1492–1992.* Cambridge: Blackwell Publishers, 1993.

———. *From Mobilization to Revolution.* Boston: Addison-Wesley, 1978.

Times of Oman. "300 Masterpieces Set for Louvre Abu Dhabi." *Times of Oman,* October 12, 2014. Accessed November 3, 2017. http://timesofoman.com/article/41634/World/300-masterpieces-set-for-Louvre-Abu-Dhabi.

Tismaneanu, Vladimir. "The Revolutions of 1989: Causes, Meanings, Consequences." *Contemporary European History* 18, no. 3 (2009): 271–278.

Tohidi, Nayereh. "'Islamic Feminism': Perils and Promises." In *Middle Eastern Women on the Move: Openings for and the Constraints on Women's Political Participation in the Middle East,* 135–146. Washington, DC: Woodrow Wilson International Center for Scholars, 2003.

Tomasevic, Goran, and Yeganeh Torbati. "U.S. Warplanes Launch Bombing Campaign on Islamic State in Libya," Reuters, August 1, 2016. Accessed August 7, 2016. https://www.reuters.com/article/us-libya-security/u-s-warplanes-launch-bombing-campaign-on-islamic-state-in-libya-idUSKCN10C2NF.

Torchia, Andrew. "IMF Endorses Saudi Plan for $500-Billion Business Zone." Reuters, October 31, 2017. Accessed November 17, 2017. https://www.reuters.com/article/us-saudi-imf/imf-endorses-saudi-plan-for-500-billion-business-zone-idUSKBN1D00HE.

Totten, Michael J. "Let Iraq Die: A Case for Partition." *World Affairs*. Accessed August 7, 2016. http://www.worldaffairsjournal.org/article/let-iraq-die-case-partition.

Trading Economics. "Egypt Unemployment Rate." Trading Economics. Accessed September 1, 2017. https://tradingeconomics.com/egypt/unemployment-rate.

———. "Tunisia Unemployment Rate." Trading Economics. Accessed September 1, 2017. https://tradingeconomics.com/tunisia/unemployment-rate?embed.

Trevelyan, George Macaulay. *British History in the Nineteenth Century, 1782–1901*. New York: Longmans, Green, 1922.

Tripp, Charles. *Islam and the Moral Economy: The Challenge of Capitalism*. Cambridge: Cambridge University Press, 2007.

Tunisia: Withdrawal of the Declaration with Regard to Article 15(4) and of the Reservations to Articles 9(2), 16(C), (D), (F), (G), (H) and 29(1) Made Upon Ratification, C.N.220.2014.TREATIES-IV.8, United Nations Depositary (April 23, 2014).

Tunisian National Institute of Statistics (INS). "Economic Growth of Third Quarter 2018 (La croissance économique au troisième trimestre 2018)." Tunis: 2018. Accessed December 10, 2018. http://www.ins.tn/sites/default/files/publication/pdf/PIB_2018-T3.pdf.

———. *Monthly Report (Bulletin Mensuel de Statistique)*. Tunis: INS, July 2018. Accessed December 10, 2018. http://www.ins.tn/sites/default/files/publication/pdf/bms%20juillet%20pour%20site_1.pdf.

Two States One Homeland, Together and Separate. Accessed November 25, 2015. http://2states1homeland.org/en.

Ulrichsen, Kristian. "Pushing the Limits: The Changing Rules of Kuwait's Politics." Rice University's Baker Institute for Public Policy, March 16, 2016. Accessed November 21, 2017. https://www.bakerinstitute.org/research/pushing-limits-changing-rules-kuwaits-politics/.

United Kingdom Science Museum. "Women and Psychiatry." Brought to Life: Exploring the History of Medicine. Accessed May 29, 2017. http://broughttolife.sciencemuseum.org.uk/broughttolife/themes/menalhealthandillness/womanandpsychiatry.

United Nations. "A Performance-Based Roadmap to a Permanent Two-State Solution to the Israeli-Palestinian Conflict." New York: United Nations, April 30, 2003. Accessed November 2, 2015. http://www.un.org/News/dh/mideast/roadmap122002.pdf.

———. Principles Relating to the Status of National Institutions (The Paris Principles), G.A. Res. 48/134, United Nations General Assembly (December 20, 1993). Accessed December 10, 2018. http://www.un.org/documents/ga/res/48/a48r134.htm.

———. Resolution 103(1): Persecution and Discrimination, November 19, 1946. Accessed July 12, 2018. http://www.un.org/en/ga/search/view_doc.asp?symbol=A/RES/103(I).

————. Universal Declaration of Human Rights G.A. Res. 217A, United Nations General Assembly (December 10, 1948). Accessed December 10, 2018. http://www.un.org/en/universal-declaration-human-rights/.

————. *Violence against Women: Assessing the Situation in Jordan.* United Nations. Accessed October 31, 2017. http://www.un.org/womenwatch/ianwge/taskforces/vaw/VAW_Jordan_baseline_assessment_final.pdf.

United Nations Department of Economic and Social Affairs. *The World's Women 2015: Trends and Statistics.* New York: United Nations Department of Economic and Social Affairs, 2015. Accessed October 10, 2017. https://unstats.un.org/unsd/gender/downloads/worldswomen2015_report.pdf.

United Nations Development Program. *Arab Human Development Report 2009: Challenges to Human Security in the Arab Countries.* New York: United Nations Development Program, 2009. Accessed November 3, 2015. http://www.arab-hdr.org/publications/other/ahdr/ahdr2009e.pdf.

United Nations Economic Commission for Africa. "AMU-Trade and Marketing Integration." United Nations Economic Commission for Africa. Accessed September 18, 2016. https://www.uneca.org/oria/pages/amu-trade-and-market-integration.

United Nations High Commissioner for Refugees (UNHCR) and United Nations Development Fund (UNDP). "Contributions to UNHCR, 2016." UNHCR, 2017. Accessed May 23, 2018. http://reporting.unhcr.org/sites/default/files/donor_ranking/2016%20-%20UNHCR%20Donor%20Ranking%20by%20Country.pdf.

————. "EUR 25 Million to Support Turkey in Providing Protection to Refugees and Asylum-Seekers." UNHCR, January 11, 2018. Accessed December 5, 2018. https://www.unhcr.org/tr/en/18513-multeciler-ve-siginmacilara-koruma-saglamak-uzere-turkiyenin-desteklenmesi-icin-25-milyon-avro-destek.html.

————. *Global Trends: Forced Displacement in 2017.* Geneva: UNHCR, June 25, 2018. Accessed December 5, 2018. https://www.unhcr.org/en-us/statistics/unhcrstats/5b27be547/unhcr-global-trends-2017.html.

————. "Operational Portal: Refugee Situations." UNHCR, 2018. Accessed December 11, 2018. https://data2.unhcr.org/en/situations.

————. *Registered Persons of Concern Refugees and Asylum Seekers in Jordan,* October 31, 2018. Accessed December 5, 2018. https://data2.unhcr.org/en/documents/download/66586.

————. "Syria Regional Refugee Response, Information Sharing Portal." UNHCR, November 1, 2017. Accessed November 3, 2017. http://data.unhcr.org/syrianrefugees/regional.php.

————. *3RP: Regional Refugee and Resilience Plan, 2017–2018.* Geneva: UNHCR, 2017. Accessed November 22, 2017. http://www.3rpsyriacrisis.org/wp-content/uploads/2017/02/3RP-Regional-Strategic-Overview-2017-2018.pdf.

————. *3RP: Regional Refugee and Resilience Plan 2018 Progress Report.* Geneva: UNHCR, 2018. Accessed December 5, 2018. https://reliefweb.int/sites/reliefweb.int/files/resources/3RP-2018-Progress-Report-Jan-June-2018.pdf.

———. *Turkey: Operational Update.* Geneva: UNHCR, August 31, 2018. Accessed December 5, 2018. https://data2.unhcr.org/en/documents/download/67065.

———. *Voluntary Contributions to UNHCR in 2017.* Geneva: UNHCR, October 31, 2017. Accessed December 5, 2018. http://reporting.unhcr.org/sites/default/files/donor_ranking/2017%20-%20UNHCR%20Donor%20Ranking%20by%20Country.pdf.

———. *"We Keep It in Our Heart": Sexual Violence against Men and Boys in the Syria Crisis.* Geneva: UNCHR, October 2017. Accessed December 10, 2018. https://data2.unhcr.org/en/documents/download/60864.

United Nations Human Rights Council (UNHRC). *"I Lost My Dignity": Sexual and Gender-Based Violence in the Syrian Arab Republic.* A/HRC/37/72/CRP.3, March 8, 2018. Accessed December 10, 2018. https://www.ohchr.org/Documents/HRBodies/HRCouncil/CoISyria/A-HRC-37-CRP-3.pdf.

United Nations International Children's Emergency Fund (UNICEF). "Child Marriage in Middle East and North Africa." Girlsnotbrides.org, 2016. Accessed October 31, 2017. https://www.girlsnotbrides.org/region/middle-east-and-north-africa/.

———. "Female Genital Mutilation." UNICEF, February 2018. Accessed December 9, 2018. https://data.unicef.org/topic/child-protection/female-genital-mutilation/.

United Nations Office of the High Commissioner for Human Rights (OHCHR). "Report: No One Unaffected by Sexual and Gender-Based Violence in Syrian Conflict." March 28, 2018. Accessed December 9, 2018. https://www.ohchr.org/EN/NewsEvents/Pages/SyriaReport.aspx.

United States, Department of State. *Egypt 2014 International Religious Freedom Report.* New York: United States Department of State, Bureau of Democracy, Human Rights, and Labor, 2014.

———. *Egypt 2017 International Religious Freedom Report.* Washington, DC: United States Department of State, Bureau of Democracy, Human Rights, and Labor, December 31, 2017. Accessed December 9, 2018. https://www.state.gov/documents/organization/281224.pdf.

———. *Tunisia 2014 International Religious Freedom Report.* New York: United States Department of State, Bureau of Democracy, Human Rights, and Labor, 2014. Accessed December 9, 2018. https://www.state.gov/documents/organization/238692.pdf.

United States, Office of the Press Secretary. "United States-Gulf Cooperation Council Second Summit Leaders Communique." April 21, 2016. Accessed September 29, 2016. https://obamawhitehouse.archives.gov/the-press-office/2016/04/21/united-states-gulf-cooperation-council-second-summit-leaders-communique.

United States Holocaust Memorial Museum. "German Jews during the Holocaust, 1939–1945." Accessed February 22, 2016. https://www.ushmm.org/wlc/en/article.php?ModuleId=10005357.

———. "Persecution of Homosexuals in the Third Reich." 2016. Accessed February 22, 2016. https://www.ushmm.org/wlc/en/article.php?ModuleId=10005261.

United States Institute of Peace. "Report: GCC Cooperation and Iran." *Iran Primer*, July 28, 2016. Accessed September 28, 2016. http://iranprimer.usip.org/blog/2016/jul/28/report-gcc-cooperation-and-iran.

UN Women. "Facts and Figures: Economic Empowerment." 2013. Accessed December 11, 2016. http://palestine.unwomen.org/en/what-we-do/economic-empowerment/facts-and-figures.

———. "Facts and Figures: Ending Violence against Women and Girls." August 2017. Accessed October 31, 2017. http://www.unwomen.org/en/what-we-do/ending-violence-against-women/facts-and-figures.

———. "A Snapshot of UN Women's Work in Response to the Crisis in Syria." May 3, 2016. Accessed October 31, 2017. http://www.unwomen.org/en/news/stories/2016/2/a-snapshot-of-un-womens-work-in-response-to-the-crisis-in-syria.

———. "Spring Forward for Women Program: Egypt." 2014. Accessed October 31, 2017. http://spring-forward.unwomen.org/en/countries/egypt.

Ventures Onsite. "GCC Railway Network to Not Halt Domestic Rail Development in Oman." Ventures Onsite, March 10, 2016. Accessed September 15, 2016. https://www.venturesonsite.com/news/gcc-railway-network-to-not-halt-domestic-rail-development-in-oman/.

Volpi, Frédéric. *Political Islam: A Critical Reader*. New York: Routledge, 2011.

Wadud, Amina. *Qur'an and Woman: Rereading the Sacred Text from a Woman's Perspective*. New York: Oxford University Press, 1999.

Wafi, Ali Abdel-Wahid. *Human Rights in Islam*. Translated by Derar Saleh Derar. Riyadh: Naif Arab Academy for Security Sciences, 1998.

Waghid, Yusef, and Nuraan Davids. "On the (Im)possibility of Democratic Citizenship Education in the Arab and Muslim World." *Studies in Philosophy and Education* 33, no. 3 (2014): 343–351.

Wagner, Roy. "Migrant Workers in Israel, and Rights." *Sh'ma Now*, March–April 2007. Accessed October 20, 2016. http://www2.mta.ac.il/~rwagner/publications/shma%20paper.pdf.

Wagtendonk, Anya. "Female Kurdish Fighters Take Arms against Islamic State Extremists." *PBS NewsHour*, August 21, 2014. Accessed December 11, 2016. https://www.pbs.org/newshour/world/female-kurdish-fighters-take-arms-islamic-state-extremists.

Waheesh, Niveen. "Half Way There: Egypt's Economic Reform Program and the IMF Loan." *Ahram Online*, May 11, 2018. Accessed May 23, 2018. http://english.ahram.org.eg/NewsContent/3/0/299267/Business/0/Half-way-there-Egypts-economic-reform-program-and-.aspx.

Walton, John. "Debt, Protest, and the State in Latin America." In *Power and Popular Protest: Latin American Social Movements*, edited by Susan Eckstein, 299–328. Berkeley: University of California Press, 1989.

Walzer, Michael. *A Foreign Policy for the Left*. New Haven: Yale University Press, 2018.

Wasik, Emily. "Inside the Forgotten Ghost Stations of a Once-Divided Berlin." Atlas Obscura, March 10, 2014. Accessed April 1, 2017. http://www.atlasobscura.com/articles/inside-the-forgotten-ghost-stations-of-a-once-divided-berlin.

Weber, Max. *Economy and Society*. Berkeley: University of California Press, 1978.

———. *The Sociology of Religion*. Boston: Beacon Press, 1991.

Weingast, Barry R. "The Economic Role of Political Institutions: Market-Preserving Federalism and Economic Development." *Journal of Law, Economics, and Organization* 11, no. 1 (1995): 1–31.

Weisberg, Hila. "31% of Israel's Top 100 Company Directors Are Women." *Haaretz*, March 6, 2014. Accessed May 29, 2017. https://www.haaretz.com/israel-news/business/.premium-1.578203.

Wells, Nick. "Saudi Arabia Struggles to Cope with Cheap Oil." CNBC, January 31, 2016. Accessed October 31, 2017. https://www.cnbc.com/2016/01/31/saudi-arabia-struggles-to-cope-with-cheap-oil.html.

West, Matthew. "Just How Low Can Oil Prices Go and Who Is Hardest Hit?" BBC News, January 18, 2016. Accessed November 3, 2017. http://www.bbc.com/news/business-35245133.

Wickham-Crowley, Timothy P. *Guerrillas and Revolution in Latin America: A Comparative Study of Insurgents and Regimes Since 1956*. Princeton: Princeton University Press, 1992.

Wieland, Carsten. *Syria, A Decade of Lost Chances: Repression and Revolution from Damascus Spring to Arab Spring*. Seattle: Cune Press, 2012.

Wiener, Jon. "Bridging the Divide: An Interview with Sari Nusseibeh." *Dissent Magazine*, April 8, 2007. Accessed August 10, 2017. https://www.dissentmagazine.org/online_articles/bridging-the-divide.

Willen, Bob, Ada Perniceni, Rudolph Lohmeyer, and Isabel Neiva. *Power Women in Arabia: Shaping the Path for Regional Gender Equality*. Istanbul: A. T. Kearney, 2016.

Willis, Michael J. "Lessons from Algeria's 'Dark Decade.'" *Foreign Policy*, January 31, 2014. Accessed November 6, 2015. http://foreignpolicy.com/2014/01/31/lessons-from-algerias-dark-decade/.

Wilson, Willow G. "From Virginity Test to Power." *The Guardian*, September 3, 2012. Accessed December 30, 2016. https://www.theguardian.com/lifeandstyle/2012/sep/03/virginity-test-to-power.

Wistrich, Robert. *Muslim Anti-Semitism: Clear and Present Danger*. New York: American Jewish Committee, 2002.

Women's Centre for Legal Aid and Counseling. *Palestinian Women and Penal Law: Policy Brief*. Ramallah and Geneva: Geneva Centre for the Democratic Control of Armed Forces (DCAF), May 2012.

Woodhouse, Murphy. "Feds Pick Preferred Route for Possible Tucson-Phoenix Passenger Railway." *Arizona Daily Star*, January 10, 2017. Accessed September 2, 2017. https://tucson.com/news/local/govt-and-politics/feds-pick-preferred-route-for-possible-tucson-phoenix-passenger-railway/article_05433289-614f-5df2-9a14-6742f5ac95a1.html.

World Bank, The. "By the Numbers: The Cost of War and Peace in the Middle East." February 4, 2016. Accessed September 1, 2017. http://www.worldbank.org/en/news/feature/2016/02/03/by-the-numbers-the-cost-of-war-and-peace-in-mena.

————. "Facing the Hard Facts in Yemen." September 25, 2012. Accessed December 9, 2018. http://www.worldbank.org/en/news/feature/2012/09/26/yemen-talking-points.

————. "GDP Per Capita (Current US$)." 2016. Accessed November 3, 2017. https://data.worldbank.org/indicator/NY.GDP.PCAP.CD.

————. "Labor Force Participation Rate: MENA." Accessed December 9, 2018. https://data.worldbank.org/indicator/SL.TLF.CACT.FE.ZS?locations=ZQ&name_desc=false.

————. "Labor Force Participation Rate: World." Accessed December 9, 2018. https://data.worldbank.org/indicator/SL.TLF.CACT.FE.ZS?name_desc=false.

————. "Life Expectancy at Birth, Female: MENA." Accessed December 9, 2018. https://data.worldbank.org/indicator/SP.DYN.LE00.FE.IN?locations=ZQ.

————. "Literacy Rate, Adult Female: MENA." Accessed December 9, 2018. https://data.worldbank.org/indicator/SE.ADT.LITR.FE.ZS?locations=ZQ.

————. "Mortality Rate, Infant: MENA." Accessed December 9, 2018. https://data.worldbank.org/indicator/SP.DYN.IMRT.IN?locations=ZQ.

————. *Poverty in the West Bank and Gaza after Three Years of Economic Crisis.* New York: World Bank Group, 2003.

————. *Progress Towards Gender Equality in the Middle East and North Africa Region.* Washington, DC: World Bank, September 2017. Accessed December 9, 2018. http://documents.worldbank.org/curated/en/801561511848725797/pdf/121679-WP-27-11-2017-15-23-11-MNAProgressTowardsGenderEqualityFINALSept.pdf.

————. *Renewable Energy Desalination: An Emerging Solution to the Water Gap in the Middle East and North Africa (MENA).* Washington, DC: World Bank, 2012.

————. "Trade Offers Path to Growth and Integration: Maghreb Countries Committed to Increasing Regional Trade." June 14, 2012. Accessed September 2, 2017. http://www.worldbank.org/en/news/press-release/2012/06/14/trade-offers-path-to-growth-and-integration.

————. "Tunisia: Data." 2018. Accessed December 9, 2018. https://data.worldbank.org/country/tunisia.

————. "Unemployment, Youth Total (% of Total Labor Force Ages 15–24) (Modeled ILO Estimate)." International Labor Organization. Accessed July 21, 2017. https://data.worldbank.org/indicator/SL.UEM.1524.ZS.

————. *West Bank and Gaza—Medium-Term Development Strategy for the Health Sector.* Washington, DC: World Bank, 1998.

————. "Women in Jordan—Limited Economic Participation and Continued Inequality." April 17, 2014. Accessed December 28, 2016. http://www.worldbank.org/en/news/feature/2014/04/17/women-in-jordan—limited-economic-participation-and-continued-inequality.

World Economic Forum. *The Global Gender Gap Report 2016.* Geneva: World Economic Forum, 2016.

World Trade Organization. *International Trade Statistics 2015.* Geneva: World Trade Organization, 2015.

Worth, Robert F. *A Rage for Order: The Middle East in Turmoil, from Tahrir Square to ISIS*. New York: Farrar, Straus and Giroux, 2016.

Wright, John. *A History of Libya*. New York: Columbia University Press, 2010.

Wright, Laurence. *The Looming Tower: Al-Qaeda and the Road to 9/11*. New York: Alfred A. Knopf, 2006.

Wright, Robin. "How the Curse of Sykes-Picot Still Haunts the Middle East." *New Yorker*, April 30, 2016. Accessed August 5, 2016. http://www.newyorker.com/news/news-desk/how-the-curse-of-sykes-picot-still-haunts-the-middle-east.

———. "Imagining a Remapped Middle East." *New York Times*, September 29, 2013. Accessed August 7, 2016. http://www.nytimes.com/2013/09/29/opinion/sunday/imagining-a-remapped-middle-east.html?pagewanted=all.

———. *Rock the Casbah: Rage and Revolution Across the Islamic World*. New York: Simon and Schuster, 2011.

Wright, Steve. "Five Benefits of Solar Energy." Energy Collective, July 27, 2013. Accessed August 8, 2016. http://www.theenergycollective.com/whirlwindsteel/247416/how-solar-power-benefits-society.

Yaros, Bernard. "Is Tunisia Ready for a Green Economy?" *TunisiaLive*, April 24, 2012. Accessed September 1, 2017. http://tn-news.com/v4_portal/article/view/1845239.

Yassin-Kassab, Robin. "The Sound and the Fury: How Syria's Rappers, Rockers and Writers Fought Back." *The Guardian*, November 26, 2015. Accessed November 26, 2015. https://www.theguardian.com/music/2015/nov/26/how-hip-hop-and-heavy-metal-are-waging-war-in-syria.

Yefet, Bosmat. *The Politics of Human Rights in Egypt and Jordan*. Boulder, CO: Lynne Rienner Publishers, 2015.

Ye'or, Bat. *The Dhimmi: Jews and Christians under Islam*. Cranbury, NJ: Associated University Presses, 1985.

Yiftachel, Oren. "Colonial Deadlock or Confederation for Israel/Palestine?" *Middle East Insights* 87 (2013): 1–11.

Yoh, John Gay. *Christianity in Ethiopia and Eritrea*. Amman: Royal Institute for Inter-Faith Studies, 1998.

———. *Christianity in the Sudan: An Annotated Bibliography*. Amman: Royal Institute for Inter-Faith Studies, 1999.

———. *Christianity in Uganda, Tanzania, Rwanda and Burundi*. Amman: Royal Institute for Inter-Faith Studies, 2000.

Young, Karen. "Small Victories for GCC Women: More Educated, More Unemployed." Arab Gulf States Institute in Washington, December 15, 2015. Accessed December 11, 2016. http://www.agsiw.org/small-victories-for-gcc-women-more-educated-more-unemployed/.

Zaki, Hind Ahmed. "Tunisia Uncovered a History of State Sexual Violence. Can It Do Anything?" *Washington Post*, April 11, 2016. Accessed December 30, 2016. https://www.washingtonpost.com/news/monkey-cage/wp/2016/04/11/tunisia-uncovered-a-history-of-state-sexual-violence-can-it-do-anything/?utm_term=.21829c9ff739.

ACKNOWLEDGMENTS

Between the time I first conceived this project to its final completion, I have accumulated many debts of gratitude. Writing the book has been quite a journey, with many stops along the way, and many fellow travelers with whom I shared the turmoil of 2011 and its aftermath helped me to process my experience in light of my previous scholarship.

Starting in Abu Dhabi, I want to thank numerous people who made my stay at Khalifa University possible: Hassan Barada, Richard Clarke, Arif Sultan Al-Hammadi, Hussein Al-Hamadi, Todd Laursen, Mohammed Al-Muallah. The wonderfully supportive colleagues and staff on campus included Luc Blais, Lorraine Charles, Stephen P. DeWeerth, Hanno Hildman, Abdel Isakovic, Adrienne Isakovic, Kinda Khalef, Mariette Leroux, Greg Moser, Beth Margolis, Regina Nockerts, Mohamed Olimat, Jean-Marc Rickli, Fabrice Safran, Leah Sherwood, and Miroslaw Skibniewski, all of whom made me feel welcome and provided stimulating conversations. I am also thankful to the many Emirati students whom I had the privilege of teaching at Khalifa University for helping me understand their lives and providing a conduit to deepen my exploration in the region.

Not far from the university, other engaging people nourished my intellectual life: Ivan Szeleny invited me to participate in many interesting seminars at the NYU campus of Abu Dhabi; Tzipi Aynot and Joel

Bernstein provided unique and salutary conversations from day one. I had the privilege of interacting regularly with journalists, diplomats, teachers, students, artists, investors, governmental officials, and other professionals who gave texture to my worldview, including April Longley Alley, David Alley, Paloma Berenguer, Margaret Coker, Philip Dufty, Talal Faris, Mishaal Al Gargawi, Benedicte Gimonnet, Greg Harris, Rehab Al-Khateeb, Brigitte Khair Mountain, Lucy Meta Cressida, Waleed Al-Muhari, Craig Nelson, and Kevin Simon, to mention only a few.

I am especially grateful for the trust and hospitality of Emirati leaders who invited me to teach political theory classes in royal palaces, at a time when the uprisings called for in-depth reflections about the future of their country and the region. My two years of teaching these classes and the high-level conversations that unfolded through them helped me acquire new layers of understanding, experiencing this small, rich, yet vulnerable country from the perspectives of its well-intentioned leaders. In a similar way, HRH El Hassan bin Talal of Jordan provided me with unique opportunities to discuss the Middle East, from conversations on international justice in Syracuse, Italy, to interviews at the Majlis in Amman.

During the uprising, I was in regular dialogue with a number of people by Skype or in person. I owe a special thanks to Claus Offe, who remains a faithful interlocutor on the MENA. We coauthored a conference paper on the Arab Spring, which we presented in Istanbul, providing a good entry point for my writing on this project. Claus has since read a few of these chapters and has been generous, as usual, with methodical and pertinent comments. I was further privileged to have him join me in interviewing political personalities, scholars, and activists in Tunisia and in Egypt. I greatly appreciate my long collaboration with David Kretzmer, who pushed me toward greater legal precision when considering the question of international law and human rights in Israel and Palestine. In the US, I could always count on my friend and teacher Stephen Bronner for encouragement and the most honest suggestions and criticisms. The passing of Benjamin Barber left a big void, as we conversed over decades about the Middle East and other relevant political theory issues. Jeffrey Isaac was always ready to offer his support; I benefited from his fiery intellect and his consistently sharp and reliable suggestions on various chapters. I owe a special thanks to Ahmed Abdel-Rabou, who offered many insightful comments on the chapters of this book and assisted me in my interview of relevant people when I traveled in Egypt. I remain greatly indebted to Mary Caponegro, Eliot Katz, and Robert Pyne for encouraging me to integrate art and poetry in my writing. This book was improved thanks to Robert Pyne's acute and probing editing, animated by his remarkable synthetic and imaginative mind and his uncanny optimism in the face of adversity. I am also thankful to William Frucht, Karen Olson, and Margaret Otzel from Yale University Press, and Eliza Childs, my copy editor, for their insightful comments, rigorous editing and most of all for believing in this project.

At the Korbel School for International Studies, I am thankful to both Danny Postel (who left us for new pastures) and Nader Hashemi of the Center for Middle East Studies for the many conversations with them and their Middle Eastern guests. Their work continues to sharpen my thinking on the MENA. I am thankful to my former dean, Chris Hill, who honored my request to stay in the region for several years. I also benefited from many conversations and comments with a great many colleagues and students in the US and abroad, notably Shlomo Avineri, Henri Barkey, Lisa Burke, George DeMartino, Jack Donnelly, Gidi Elazar, Eric Fattor, Alan Gilbert, Raslan Ibrahim, Terry Karl, Tom Farer, Stephen Holmes, Ilene Grable, Haider Khan, Alfredo Morabia, Carlangelo Liverani, Joel Pruce, Aaron Schneider, Philippe Schmitter and Zeev Sternhell.

My research assistants were diligent, patient, and helpful in the research, editing, and formatting of this book. I want to thank Keith Gehring, for shedding statistical knowledge into the political economy of chapter 2, and Adam Jepsen and Gina Jannone, who helped significantly with the heavy lifting on the research side. Finally, I want to thank Jacob McGuire, who was in the project from the beginning and jumped back in at the end with similar enthusiasm, insight, and attention to detail, and Abbey Vogel, Sophie Schor, and Robert Osborne, whose enthusiasm, focus, and intellect made a real difference at critical stages. I am also thankful to Brooke Vandevelder, the talented illustrator who worked with me on the main posters for the Levant Express, and also to Douglas Winter, Sydney Gauthier, Sarah Chasin, Elise Ishay, and Adam Ishay for their assistance with the maps and other illustrations.

I remember fondly my academic writing residency at the Bellagio Center in Italy, and I greatly appreciate the Rockefeller Foundation for providing me the opportunity to write the early chapters of this book in the company of such creative people as Larry Brilliant, Stephen Binder, Rogers Brubaker, Milumbe Haimbe, Ray Jayawardhana, Paul Kos, Patricia Mechael, Rosalyne Swig, John Skrentny, and Njeri Kinyanjui. There could not be a better place than Lake Como to start such an endeavor. I am also thankful for the University of Denver, which provided the research grants and sabbatical that made this writing possible.

I continue to enjoy vibrant intellectual conversations with David Goldfischer regarding the Middle East, and this book benefits from his encyclopedic knowledge, his fearless criticisms, and his careful editing. For this and other unique experiences we shared while in the Middle East, he deserves my special gratitude.

Last but not least, I am grateful for Adam Ishay and Elise Ishay, who resiliently accepted an overworked mother. They are my fountain of love, my source of pride, and my reliable compass throughout this project and beyond. This book is for them, my parents, my former teacher, and my students, who will continue to carry the human rights aspirations of the people from the Levant.

INDEX

Surnames starting with "al-" and "el-" are alphabetized by the following portion of the name.

Abbas, Mahmoud, 220
abortion, 188, 191
Abu Dhabi: American Community
    School of Abu Dhabi, 2; author in,
    1–3, 144; Louvre in, 125, 138; sexu-
    ality and homosexuality in, 197;
    water scarcity in, 149
Achcar, Gilbert, 44
Adams, John and Abigail, 185
Afghanistan: Iran-Saudi Arabia proxy war
    in, 98; ISIS in, 82; Soviet invasion
    of, 76, 159
Africa: anticolonialism in, 19, 21–22,
    101; and globalization, 62; security
    frameworks in, 171; socialist
    movements in, 65; US-Soviet
    proxy wars in, 25. *See also* Middle
    East-North Africa (MENA); *specific
    countries*
African Union, 170
Ahmed, Hamid, 213
Ahmed Rock (rapper), 46
Al Ahram (newspaper), 49, 123
Akbar (emperor), 134
Al Akhbar (newspaper), 49

al-Aqsa Martyr's Brigades, 100
Al-Azhar University, 132
Al Eqtisadiah (magazine), 47
Algeria: Arab Spring protests in, 41–42,
    57–58; education gender gap in, 45;
    freedom from fear in, 160, 171–173;
    women in, 62, 200
Al Gomhoria (newspaper), 49
Ali, Sharif Hussein bin, 59
Al Jazeera, 3, 49, 124
Allende, Salvadore, 31
Allon, Yigal, 95
al-Nusra (organization), 124
al-Qaeda, 76, 80–81, 85, 124, 159, 170
al-Qaeda in the Arabian Peninsula
    (AQAP), 80
Alt-Right (US), 241
"America First" movement, 145
American Community School of Abu
    Dhabi, 2
American University of Sharjah, 138
Amnesty International, 32, 209
AMU (Arab Mahgreb Union),
    172–173
Ansar al-Shari'a (organization), 79

323